I0030120

The Statutes of Wales (1908)

Collected, Edited and Arranged by

Ivor Bowen

Reprinted from the original with a new preface by
Richard W Ireland

Gwasg y Gors
Taliesin

www.gwasg-y-gors.com

on behalf of

Canolfan Materion Cyfreithiol Cymreig

Centre For Welsh Legal Affairs

2014

Published in Wales by Gwasg y Gors, Taliesin, SY20 8JH on behalf of the Centre for Welsh Legal Affairs.

For more information on the work of CWLA, news of its events and activities and contact details please visit http://www.aber.ac.uk/en/law-criminology/research/cwla/

ISBN 978-0-9927346-2-6

Printed by Amazon Createspace in the USA.

PREFACE TO THIS REPRINT

This is an opportune time to present Ivor Bowen's classic *The Statutes of Wales* to a new readership. The Law Commission has announced its intention to look into the state of current legislation affecting Wales with a view to improve its accessibility. Such a move has been prompted by the history of devolution in Wales and is to be warmly welcomed. Aberystwyth's Centre for Welsh Legal Affairs/Canolfan Materion Cyfreithiol Cymraeg has since its inception in 1999 taken a particular interest in the devolution process and has explored the possibility of producing its own guides to legislation in particular areas. Bowen's work, the precursor to any such enterprise, seemed to be an ideal starting point. What follows is a facsimile reproduction of the 1908 text, but the comments in this preface may help to give some background to the text and its author, as well as pointing out its utility to lawyers and historians today.

Ivor Bowen and the Statutes of Wales

Ivor Bowen Jones (he dropped the last name in 1883) was born in Bridgend in 1862, the son of an independent minister and his wife. Called to the Bar in July 1889 he took silk in 1913 and , following his involvement in raising the London Welsh Battalions in the First World War, held a succession of legal offices becoming a County Court Judge in 1918 and treasurer of Gray's Inn in 1923. His interest in Welsh history was evident from an early age, winning a prize for an essay at the Brecon eisteddfod of 1889 whilst he was still a student. Yet as his friend Thomas Artemus Jones (for this surely is the "T.A.J." who penned Bowen's obituary in *The Times* in 1934) observed "To future generations of his countrymen his Honour Ivor Bowen will be known by 'The Statutes of

Wales"'. It was not his only excursus into research on legal history, inter alia a piece on "Grand Juries, Justices of the Peace and Quarter Sessions in Wales" was published posthumously, but his death came too soon for completion of a volume on the Great Sessions.[1]

The volume is a collection of the statutes, and extracts from statutes, relating to Wales. It begins with Magna Carta 1215 and ends with the Education Act 1902 (though the partisan amongst us might have preferred him to have stopped at the previous statute, which confers privileges on graduates of the University of Wales). Bowen rather modestly described the work as "somewhat laborious" but a memorialist, Sir Robert Armstrong-Jones, hailed it more generously as "a colossal task…which must have involved great strain and much mental pressure". Undifferentiated historical legislation concerning the whole of England and Wales had been printed before, of course, in the shape of *Statutes of the Realm* (publication of which had begun in 1810) and *Statutes at Large* (the first ten "historical" volumes of which had been published in 1811). But Bowen's focus on Wales required vision and editorial commitment. The *Introduction* provides a commentary which, in its way, comprises a legal history of Wales, an enterprise not undertaken again, and not surpassed, until the admirable work of Thomas Glyn Watkin a century later.[2] Nothing similar had been done before and the aim was stated in Bowen's Preface, to place the legislation "within the reach of those who are interested in the constitutional development and history of the Welsh nation". Bowen's prose is functional and apparently

---

[1] Biographical details may be found in the entry for Bowen in the Welsh Biography Online website, the *Times* obituary of January 8th 1934 and the tributes which accompany Bowen's posthumously published article in (1933-4) *Transactions of the Honourable Society of Cymmrodorion.*

[2] The first edition of The Legal History of Wales was published in 2007, by University of Wales Press, the second in 2012.

objective, yet there is no doubt as to where his sympathies lay in this national history. Occasionally there are elegant observations, as where, in describing the disputes concerning the jurisdictional boundaries of the Council of the Marches and therefore, indirectly, the limits of discretionary government, in the seventeenth century, Bowen observes "In this, as in so many other cases, broad constitutional issues were argued on the narrowest legal grounds" (p.lxxii) In his Preface Bowen acknowledges the assistance of two barristers from the South Wales Circuit, C. H. Glascodine and H.S. Stowe, and a young man, John Jermine, who was to enter upon a legal career himself.

Bowen's text established itself as a piece of work significant, I venture to suggest, for its symbolic as well as its practical utility. As to the latter the great Lord Atkin referred to it in 1934 as "a volume that was absolutely essential to every student of their [the statutes'] past history inasmuch as it would be very difficult to get the information from any other source". Another great Welsh judge, Lord Thomas of Cwmgiedd LCJ, spoke in a lecture at Aberystwyth in 2014 of his affection for his own copy of *The Statutes of Wales*. But the second edition, which Thomas Artemus Jones called for in his tribute to Bowen, was never forthcoming. There is an argument to suggest that the work of the Law Commission in practical terms, and that of the scholars who have done so much work on Welsh legal history (Watkin's monograph perhaps in particular) in academic ones, means that Bowen's volume should perhaps stand like an Easter Island head: magnificent, but no longer useful.

I do not think that that is the case. Writing my recent book on the history of crime and punishment in Wales I often had Bowen open beside me, and a recent reading of the text before writing this present Preface suggested at times that I might have had it open more often still. It's a lawyer's text, interested primarily in what the legal provisions say rather than where they came from and where they went to. Were the early – modern statutes about disorder in Wales evidence of that disorder or of English propaganda? How much were statutes actually enforced after promulgation? For these and other issues the reader must look beyond the work which follows. Bowen himself was aware that more research was needed in particular areas; the use of Welsh in Great Sessions proceedings (p.xcviii) or the resort to courts outside Wales in civil jurisdiction (p.c). The Great Sessions records are now better known and utilised, particularly for information about crime, than they were in 1908, but there is still much work to be done.[3] *The Statutes of Wales* is still a decent starting point for those interested in Welsh legal history even when its approach, as well as its antiquity, means that it is no longer the finishing point. Its other virtues are more subtle than its potential continuing utility, but no less important. It marks the prodigious labour of a passionate man, written not for fame or profit or career, but in the leisure time and retirement of a busy public figure. Many of us could learn from that example.

The Text

The text which has been used for this reprint is one of the copies held in the Thomas Parry Library at Aberystwyth University. It has been scanned without editorial intervention, annotation or amendment. So, for example, the original typographical error at p.xxix which attributes a piece of legislation of Edward I to 1820 rather than 1280 remains unaltered, though I suspect that few will be misled by it. We have removed through the mysteries of computer technology

[3] Glyn Parry's A Guide to the Records of Great Sessions in Wales (1995) and the National Library of Wales database of the criminal records from the court from 1730-1830 are notable here , as is the work of inter alia Murray Chapman and Richard Suggett, which latter has addressed the issue of language use in the court.

the library stamps and marginal sidelining. This has been done only after a little hesitation, for one of the joys of a book is its status as a historical object in itself, quite apart from its contents. Such marks, however, tell us little of importance about the volume itself. Paradoxically I have decided to retain the manuscript inscription at the opening of the volume, thereby rendering that most personal of authorial interventions into a universal feature. Yet the recipient of the book, Alfred Mond, at the time of publication the Liberal M.P. for Chester but soon to represent seats in Swansea, is an interesting figure in his own right, and the inscription also gives us a glimpse of Bowen's own handwriting.

A number of people have contributed to this present reprint of Bowen's text. The work is, of course, out of copyright and many would have been content simply to reproduce it without more. However in accordance with Sir Thomas Browne's injunction "Let not the Law of thy Country be the *non ultra* of thy Honesty, nor think that always good that the Law will make good" I contacted the successors in title of the original publisher T. Fisher Unwin. Bloomsbury were happy for me to continue with the project and I thank them. Ceredigion's County Archivist, Helen Palmer, supplied biographical information with her invariable speed, efficiency and good humour. The greatest thanks are due to the two people who did the hardest work. Nigel Callaghan of Technoleg Taliesin, himself a dedicated pursuer of Welsh history, freely provided his equipment, expertise and support in the preparation of the text for production. It was a generous gesture, the most recent of many, and is much appreciated. Hannah Baumeister took time from other, more academic, pursuits to scan Bowen's original and arrange the resulting pages. I could not have wished for a more efficient or a more congenial member of the team.

Read Bowen's text and benefit from his labours. The man and his dedication deserve no less.

Richard W. Ireland

Centre for Welsh Legal Affairs/Canolfan Materion Cyfreithiol Cymraeg

Aberystwyth

August 2014

To

Sir Alfred Mond M. P.

with the best wishes of

the Author

10. May. 1912

THE STATUTES OF WALES

THE STATUTES OF WALES

Collected, Edited, and Arranged by

IVOR BOWEN

BARRISTER-AT-LAW, OF THE SOUTH WALES CIRCUIT

WITH AN INTRODUCTION

T. FISHER UNWIN

LONDON
ADELPHI TERRACE

LEIPSIC
INSELSTRASSE 20

1908

PREFACE

The parliamentary enactments relating to Wales have not been, and are not now, easily accessible. There are very few libraries which contain a complete collection of the statutes at large. I have collected in this volume all the Acts of Parliament and parts thereof which refer to Wales, in order that they may be placed, for the first time, within the reach of those who are interested in the constitutional development and history of the Welsh nation. I commenced this somewhat laborious work many years ago, but professional duties delayed its completion.

I have received much assistance from Mr. John Ballinger, the learned librarian of the Welsh Reference Library belonging to the City of Cardiff, and desire to acknowledge the many facilities granted to me by him for making use of that splendid collection.

I wish to thank my two learned friends, Mr. Charles Henry Glascodine and Mr. Harold S. Stowe, of the South Wales Circuit, and also Mr. John Henry Jermine, for their valuable aid in preparing this work for the press.

IVOR BOWEN.

Goldsmith Buildings, Temple.
April 10, 1908.

CONTENTS

CHRONOLOGICAL TABLE

OF THE

STATUTES RELATING

TO THE

DOMINION, PRINCIPALITY, AND COUNTRY

OF

WALES.

(NOTE.—Rep. = repealed. S.L.R. = Statute Law Revision Act.)

PAGE.	YEAR.	STATUTE AND CHAPTER.	TITLE.	HOW REPEALED OR OTHERWISE AFFECTED.
1	1215	17 JOHN, Clauses 56, 57, 58	Magna Charta	
2	1275	3 EDWARD 1, c. 17	Statute of Westminster 1. The King's Writ to run in the Marches of WALES	Rep. S.L.R. 1863
2	1284	12 EDWARD 1, c. 1 (Statutum Walliae)	The Statute of WALES. WALES annexed to the Crown of England	Rep. S.L.R. 1887
27	1315-1316	9 EDWARD 2	An ordinance concerning customs of WEST WALES and SOUTH WALES	
29	1315-1316	9 EDWARD 2	An ordinance concerning customs of NORTH WALES	
30	1353	27 EDWARD 3, Stat. 2, c. 18	Merchants of WALES may bring their wools to the Staples of England	Rep. 3 George 4, c. 41, s. 5

PAGE.	YEAR.	STATUTE AND CHAPTER.	TITLE.	HOW REPEALED OR OTHERWISE AFFECTED.
30	1354	28 EDWARD 3, c. 2	Lords of Marches of WALES shall be attendant and annexed to the Crown of England, and not to the Principality of WALES	Rep. S.L.R. 1887
31	1400–1	2 HENRY 4, c. 12	Certain restraints laid on Welshmen	Rep. 21 James 1, c. 28, s. 11
31	1400–1	2 HENRY 4, c. 16	Excesses committed by Welshmen on English neighbours by distressing of cattle, etc.	Rep. 21 James 1, c. 28, s. 11
32	1400–1	2 HENRY 4, c. 17	Welshman committing Felony in England and thereof attainted, and flieth to WALES, shall be executed	Rep. 21 James 1, c. 28, s. 11
33	1400–1	2 HENRY 4, c. 18	The Lords Marchers to keep ward in their Castles	Rep. 21 James 1, c. 28, s. 11
33	1400–1	2 HENRY 4, c. 19	Of suits against Englishmen in WALES	Rep. S.L.R. 1863
33	1400–1	2 HENRY 4, c. 20	Welshmen shall not purchase lands in England	Rep. 21 James 1, c. 28, s. 11
34	1402	4 HENRY 4, c. 26	Englishmen shall not be convict in WALES	Rep. S.L.R. 1863
34	1402	4 HENRY 4, c. 27	As to minstrels and vagabonds in WALES	Rep. 19–20 Vict. c. 64
34	1402	4 HENRY 4, c. 28	As to congregations in WALES	Rep. 21 James 1, c. 28, s. 11
35	1402	4 HENRY 4, c. 29	Welshmen not to carry Arms	Rep. 19–20 Vict. c. 64
35	1402	4 HENRY 4, c. 30	No armour or victuals to be carried into WALES	Rep. S.L.R. 1863
35	1402	4 HENRY 4, c. 31	Welshmen not to have castles	Rep. 21 James 1, c. 28, s. 11
36	1402	4 HENRY 4, c. 32	No Welshman shall bear office in WALES	Rep. 21 James 1, c. 28, s. 11

PAGE.	YEAR.	STATUTE AND CHAPTER.	TITLE.	HOW REPEALED OR OTHERWISE AFFECTED.
36	1402	4 HENRY 4, c. 33	Castles and walled towns in WALES to be kept by Englishmen	Rep. 21 James 1, c. 28, s. 11
36	1402	4 HENRY 4, c. 34	Englishmen married to Welsh women not to have office in WALES	Rep. 21 James 1, c. 28, s. 11
37	1407	9 HENRY 4, c. 3	Felons in SOUTH WALES	Rep. S.L.R 1863
37	1407	9 HENRY 4, c. 4	Concerning Felonies and Robberies in WALES	Rep. S.L.R. 1863
37	1413	1 HENRY 5, c. 6	Concerning rebellion in WALES	Rep. S.L.R. 1863
38	1414	2 HENRY 5, Stat. 2, c. 5	Outrages committed by the Welsh	Rep. S.L.R. 1863
39	1425-6	4 HENRY 6, c. 3, s. 5	Justices may amend Records, WALES excepted	Rep. 46-47 Vict. c. 49, s. 4
40	1429	8 HENRY 6, c. 15	Justices may amend Records, WALES excepted	Rep. 46-47 Vict. c. 49, s. 4
40	1430	9 HENRY 6, c. 3	Confirming Statute against Owen Glyndwr	
41	1441-2	20 HENRY 6, c. 3	Concerning outrages by Welshmen	Rep. S.L.R. 1863
43	1441-2	20 HENRY 6, c. 7	Foreign merchandise passing through or exported from WALES to be forfeited	Rep. S.L.R. 1863
44	1444-5	23 HENRY 6, c. 4	Concerning Welshmen outlawed	Rep. 19-20 Vict. c. 64
45	1446-7	25 HENRY 6	All statutes against Welshmen confirmed	Rep. 21 James 1, c. 28, s. 11
45	1448-9	27 HENRY 6, c. 4	Concerning Welshmen who take away Englishmen (Extending 20 HENRY 6, c. 3)	Rep. S.L.R. 1863
46	1449	28 HENRY 6, c. 4	To prevent undue distresses in WALES	Rep. S.L.R. 1863

PAGE.	YEAR.	STATUTE AND CHAPTER	TITLE.	HOW REPEALED OR OTHERWISE AFFECTED.
47	1495	11 HENRY 7, c. 33	To make void divers leases and offices within the Principality of WALES	
50	1529	21 HENRY 8, c. 6, ss. 6, 7	Concerning the taking of Mortuary fees in WALES	S. 6, rep. 13, Anne, c. 6, s. 1
51	1534	26 HENRY 8, c. 4	For punishment of perjury of jurors in the Lordships Marchers of WALES	Rep. S.L.R. 1863
52	1534	26 HENRY 8, c. 5	Ferries on the Severn	Rep. 19–20, Vict. c. 64
54	1534	26 HENRY 8, c. 6	Concerning Councils in WALES. Murders and Felonies committed within any Lordship Marcher in WALES to be tried in the next adjoining county, &c.	Rep. 19–20 Vict. c. 64
63	1534	26 HENRY 8, c. 11	For punishing Welshmen attempting any assaults or affrays upon the inhabitants of Hereford, Gloucester and Shropshire	Rep. S.L.R. 1863
64	1534	26 HENRY 8, c. 12	For purgation of convicts in WALES	Rep. S.L.R. 1863
67	1535	27 HENRY 8, c. 5	For the making of Justices of Peace in WALES	Rep. S.L.R. 1887
69	1535	27 HENRY 8, c. 7	For the abuses in the Forests of WALES	
72	1535	27 HENRY 8, c. 10, s. 16	The Statute of Uses	
73	1535	27 HENRY 8, c. 14, s. 7	Untanned hides of beasts killed within WALES to be exported freely	Rep. 3 Geo. 4, c. 41, ss. 2, 4
73	1535	27 HENRY 8, c. 24, ss. 1, 2, 3, 18	An Act for re-continuing the Liberties of the Crown	

PAGE.	YEAR.	STATUTE AND CHAPTER.	TITLE.	HOW REPEALED OR OTHERWISE AFFECTED.
75	1535	27 HENRY 8, c. 26	For Laws and Justice to be ministered in WALES in like form as it is in this Realm	Ss. 2–8, 17, 18 rep. in part, by 50–51 Vict. c. 55, s. 39; ss. 2, 3, 8, 22 rep. in part; ss. 18–21, 23–32 rep. S.L.R. 1887
93	1536	28 HENRY 8, c. 3	Giving the King authority to allot the Townships, Shire Divisions and Shire Towns within the Dominion and Principality of WALES during the three next ensuing years	Rep. S.L.R. 1863
94	1536	28 HENRY 8, c. 6	To continue Stat. 26 HENRY 8, c. 11 against Welshmen	Rep. S.L.R. 1863
95	1539	31 HENRY 8, c. 11	An Act for the allotting of certain Townships in WALES	Rep. S.L.R. 1863
96	1540	32 HENRY 8, c. 4	For trial of Treasons in WALES	Rep. S.L.R. 1863
96	1540	32 HENRY 8, c. 27	For the resumption at Calais, Berwick, and WALES	
97	1540	32 HENRY 8, c. 37, s. 2	Act for recovering arrears of rent by Executors not to apply to WALES	
97	1541	33 HENRY 8, c. 3	For folding of cloths in NORTH WALES	Rep. 49 Geo. 3, c. 109, s. 1
98	1541	33 HENRY 8, c. 13, ss. 3, 4	Concerning certain Lordships translated from the County of Denbigh to the County of Flint	Preamble, ss. 1–2, rep. S.L.R. 1887. Repealed as to coroners for Cheshire 23–24 Vict. c. 116, s. 7

PAGE.	YEAR.	STATUTE AND CHAPTER.	TITLE.	HOW REPEALED OR OTHERWISE AFFECTED.
99	1542–3	34–35 HENRY 8, c. 11	For the true making of Frizes and Cottons in WALES	Rep. S.L.R. 1863
101	1542–3	34–35 HENRY 8, c. 26	For certain ordinances in the King's Majesty's Dominions and Principality of WALES	Ss. 10, 22, 27–31 rep. 50–1, Vict. c. 55, s. 39; ss. 3–8, 11–20, 23, 24, 26–32, 34, 35, 40–46, 48, 49, 51, 53–55, 59, 60, 62–65, and in part, ss. 21–61, rep. S.L.R. 1887; s. 25 rep. 50–1 Vict. c. 71, s. 45.
133	1543	35 HENRY 8, c. 11	For the due payment of the Fees and Wages of Knights and Burgesses for the Parliament in WALES	Rep. 19–20 Vict. 6. 64
135	1547	1 EDWARD 6, c. 10	An act for exigents and proclamations in WALES	Rep. except in part ss. 1, 3–50–1 Vict. c. 55, s. 39. Rep. as to outlawry except in criminal proceedings, S.L.R. 1887
139	1548	2–3 EDWARD 6, c. 13, s. 16	Tithes of Marriage Goods in WALES abolished	
139	1554	1 MARY, Session 3, c. 11	An Act touching the Sea Sands in Glamorganshire	
141	1554	1–2 PHILIP and MARY, c. 15	To confirm the Liberties of the Lords Marchers in WALES	Rep. S.L.R. 1887
143	1557	4–5 PHILIP and MARY, c. 2, ss. 18, 19	For the having of Horse, Armour, and Weapon in WALES	Rep. 1 James 1, c. 25, s. 7

PAGE.	YEAR.	STATUTE AND CHAPTER.	TITLE.	HOW REPEALED OR OTHERWISE AFFECTED
143	1558	1 ELIZABETH, c. 11, s. 11	An Act limiting the time for laying on land Merchandise from beyond the seas	Rep. 6 Geo. 4, c. 105
144	1562	5 ELIZABETH, c. 5, s. 31	An Act for the maintenance of the Navy	Rep. 31–2 Vict. c. 45, s. 71
144	1562	5 ELIZABETH, c. 23, s. 6	An Act for the execution of the Writ de Excommunicato Capiendo.	
145	1562	5 ELIZABETH, c. 25	To fill up Juries "de circumstantibus" in WALES.	Rep. 6 Geo. 4, c. 50, s. 62
149	1562	5 ELIZABETH, c. 28	For the translating of the Bible and the Divine Service into the Welsh Tongue	Sect. 2, rep. S.L.R. 1863
151	1565	8 ELIZABETH, c. 20	To repeal ss. 6–10 of 26 HENRY 8, c. 6, and s. 33 of 34–35 HENRY 8, c. 26, as to trial of offences in the County of Merioneth	Rep. S.L.R. 1863
152	1575	18 ELIZABETH, c. 8	For the appointing and authorising of Justices of Assize in the Shires of WALES	Rep. S.L.R. 1863
156	1584	27 ELIZABETH, c. 6, s. 6	Proviso for Jurors in WALES	Rep. 6 Geo. 4, c. 50, s. 62
156	1584	27 ELIZABETH, c. 9	An Act for the amendment of errors in fines and recoveries in the twelve Shires of WALES and Town and County of Haverfordwest	Rep. S.L.R. 1887
162	1605	3 JAMES 1, c. 17	Welsh Cottons not to be sealed	Rep. 19–20 Vict. c. 64
163	1623–4	21 JAMES 1, c. 9	An Act for the Free Trade of Welsh Cloths	Rep. S.L.R. 1863

PAGE.	YEAR.	STATUTE AND CHAPTER	TITLE.	HOW REPEALED OR OTHERWISE AFFECTED.
165	1623-4	21 JAMES 1, c 10	Repealing s. 59 of 34-35 HENRY 8, c. 26, giving the King power to alter the laws of WALES	Rep. S.L.R. 1887
167	1623-4	21 JAMES 1, c. 28, s. 5	Concerning Welsh Cottons	Rep. S.L.R. 1863
167	1623-4	21 JAMES 1, c. 28, s. 11	Repealing laws of HENRY 4 and HENRY 6 against Welshmen	Rep. S.L.R. 1863
168	1640-1	16 CHARLES 1, c. 10, ss. 4, 9	For taking away the Star Chamber jurisdiction exercised before the Council of WALES	
169	1648	Commonwealth Statute	An Act concerning the sequestration of SOUTH WALES and County of Monmouth	
172	1649	Commonwealth Statute	An Act for the better propagation and preaching of the Gospel in WALES, and redress of some grievances	
179	1649	Commonwealth Statute	An Act for the admitting of the six Counties of NORTH WALES to a general composition for delinquency	
185	1659	Commonwealth Statute	An Act for taking the Accompts, and redressing of grievances concerning the Tithes and Church livings in WALES; and for advancement of Religion and learning there	
188	1662	13-14 CHARLES 2, c. 4, s. 27	Book of Common Prayer to be translated into the Welsh Tongue. Act of Uniformity	S. 27 rep. S.L.R. 1863
189	1667	19 CHARLES 2, c. 5	Extending Act concerning replevins and avowries to WALES	Rep. 42-3 Vict. c. 59

PAGE.	YEAR.	STATUTE AND CHAPTER.	TITLE.	HOW REPEALED OR OTHERWISE AFFECTED.
190	1670	22 CHARLES 2, c. 6, s. 8	An Act for sale of fee farm rents, proviso excluding WALES	Rep. S.L.R. 1863
190	1688	1 WILLIAM and MARY, c. 27	For taking away the Court holden before the President and Council of the Marches of WALES	Rep. S.L.R. 1867
191	1692	4-5 WILLIAM and MARY, c. 24, ss. 15, 19	As to the qualification of a juror in WALES	Rep. S.L.R. 1867
192	1693	5-6 WILLIAM and MARY, c. 4	To repeal 34-35 HENRY 8, c. 26, s. 55, limiting Justices of the Peace to each County	Rep. to "purposes and that," S.L.R. 1887
193	1695	7-8 WILLIAM 3, c. 38	For taking away the custom of WALES which hinders persons from disposing their personal estates by will	Rep. S.L.R. 1867
195	1697-8	9-10 WILLIAM 3, c. 16	For executing Judgments and Decrees saved in a clause or statute 1 WILLIAM and MARY, c. 27, made for taking away the court holden before the President and Council of WALES	Rep. S.L.R. 1867
196	1698-9	11-12 WILLIAM 3, c. 9	For preventing of frivolous and vexatious suits in the Principality of WALES and the Counties Palatine	Rep. 42-43 Vict. c. 59
197	1705	4 ANNE, c. 16, s. 24	An Act for the better advancement of justice, extending to WALES	Rep. S.L.R. 1867
197	1713	13 ANNE, c. 6	An Act for taking away mortuaries within the dioceses of Bangor, Llandaff, St. Davids, and St. Asaph, and giving a recompense therefor to the Bishops of the respective dioceses	Part of s. 1, from "the said proviso" to "repealed, annulled and made void," repealed S.L.R. 1887

PAGE.	YEAR.	STATUTE AND CHAPTER.	TITLE.	HOW REPEALED OR OTHERWISE AFFECTED.
202	1715	1 GEORGE 1, stat. 2, c. 37	An Act to grant the regalities and lands to the Prince of WALES	
202	1716	3 GEORGE 1, c, 15, s. 20, s. 22	Sheriff's oath. Sheriffs in WALES to account before Auditors in WALES	Rep. by the Sheriff's Act, 1887, 50–1, Vict. c. 55, s. 39
203	1721	8 GEORGE 1, c. 25, s. 6	An Act for setting down the time of signing Judgments in the Principality of WALES and the Counties Palatine.	Rep. 42–43 Vict. c. 59
204	1730	3 GEORGE 2, c. 25, s. 9	An Act for the better regulation of juries	
204	1732–3	6 GEORGE 2, c. 14, ss. 1, 3	An Act for preventing frivolous arrests, and for the use of the English language in the Courts of Great Sessions	Rep. 42–43 Vict. c. 59
206	1746	20 GEORGE 2, c. 42, s. 3	"WALES" to be included in England	
207	1758–9	32 GEORGE 2, c. 28, s. 11	Relief of imprisoned debtors in WALES	Rep. 50–1 Vict. c. 55, s. 39 as relating to sheriffs
207	1767–8	8 GEORGE 3, c. 14	An Act for providing proper accommodation for Judges in WALES	Rep. S.L..R 1867
209	1772	12 GEORGE 3, c. 30	Salaries of Welsh Judges	Rep. S.L..R 1861
210	1773	13 GEORGE 3, c. 51	An act to regulate proceedings in Courts of Great Sessions in WALES	Rep. S.L.R. 1861, see also sections 19–20 of 5 Geo. 4, c. 106
220	1793	33 GEORGE 3, c. 68	An Act remedying inconveniences in Courts of Great Sessions and in the County Courts of WALES	Rep. S.L.R. 1887

PAGE.	YEAR.	STATUTE AND CHAPTER.	TITLE.	HOW REPEALED OR OTHERWISE AFFECTED.
222	1809	49 GEORGE 3, c. 127, s. 5	An Act augmenting the salaries of the Justices of Great Sessions in WALES	Rep. S.L.R. 1861
223	1812	52 GEORGE 3, c. 155, s. 10	An Act to repeal Acts relating to religious worship and assemblies	Rep. S.L.R. 1873
223	1824	5 GEORGE 4, c. 106	An Act to enlarge and extend the power of the Welsh Judges	Rep. S.L.R. 1861
239	1827	7-8 GEORGE 4, c. 53, s. 3	An Act relating to the Excise	Rep. but re-enacted by 53-54 Vict. c. 21, s. 38, ss. 1.
239	1830	11 GEORGE 4, and 1 WILLIAM 4, c. 70, ss. 1, 13-20, 22-34, 39	An Act to abolish the separate jurisdiction for the Principality of WALES	S. 1, 13, 19, 20, 27 rep. by 42-43 Vict. c. 59; s. 22 rep. 32-33 Vict. c. 83, s. 20; s. 14, 16, 18, 23-26, 28-30, 34, 39, rep. by S.L.R. 1873; s. 31 Rep. S.L.R. 1890
248	1832	2-3 WILLIAM 4, c. 45, ss. 4, 8, 9, 10, 15, 32	Representation of the People Act	
251	1836	6-7 WILLIAM 4, c. 77, ss. 11, 19	An Act for carrying into effect the reports of the Commissioners appointed to consider the state of the Established Church in England and WALES	S. 11, Rep. 1-2, Vict. c. 106, s. 103
252	1837	7 WILLIAM 4, and 1 VICTORIA, c. 22, s. 23	Provision for Marriages in the Welsh Tongue	

PAGE.	YEAR.	STATUTE AND CHAPTER.	TITLE.	HOW REPEALED OR OTHERWISE AFFECTED
252	1838	1–2 VICTORIA, c. 106, ss. 103, 104, 105	Provision for benefices in WALES	S. 103 rep. S.L.R. (No. 2) 1874
254	1840	3–4 VICTORIA, c. 113, ss. 1, 2, 19, 22, 38, 39, 40, 51, 62, 66	To carry into effect the reports of the Commissioners of Ecclesiastical duties and revenues	S. 39 rep. 4–5 Vict. c. 39; s. 62 rep. 6–7 Vict. c. 77; s. 51 rep. in part, 36–37 Vict. c. 64, s. 3; ss. 2, 19,38,40 rep. by S.L.R. (No. 2) 1874
256	1841	4–5 VICTORIA, c. 39, ss. 14, 28	An Act relating to Ecclesiastical Commissioners Repealing ss. 38, 39, 40 of 3–4 VICTORIA, c. 113 (1840)	Rep. S.L.R. (No. 2) 1874
257	1842	5–6 VICTORIA, c. 112	An Act suspending preferments in the dioceses of St. Asaph and Bangor	Rep. S.L.R. (No. 2) 1874
258	1843	6–7 VICTORIA, c. 77	An Act for regulating the Cathedral Churches of WALES	S. 9, 10, 15, 16 repealed; s. 5 to "repealed; and that"; s. 8 to "Bishop of Bangor, and," and also from "provided" to end of that section; s. 13, from "that" to "repealed; and." Repealed by S.L.R. (No. 2) 1874
263	1844	7–8 VICTORIA, c. 91	An Act to Consolidate and amend the laws relating to Turnpike Trusts in SOUTH WALES	See 51–2 Vict. c. 42, s. 13
263	1845	8–9 VICTORIA, c. 11	An Act for assigning Sheriffs in WALES	Rep. 50–1 Vict. c. 55, s. 39

PAGE.	YEAR.	STATUTE AND CHAPTER.	TITLE.	HOW REPEALED OR OTHERWISE AFFECTED.
263	1845	8-9 VICTORIA, c. 61	An Act to make certain further provisions for the consolidation of Turnpike Trusts in SOUTH WALES.	See 51-2 Vict. c. 41, s. 13
264	1847	10-11 VICTORIA, c. 72	An Act for the further amendment of the laws relating to Turnpike roads in SOUTH WALES	See 51-2 Vict. c. 41, s. 13
264	1847	10-11 VICTORIA, c. 108	An Act for establishing the Bishopric of Manchester and amending certain Acts relating to the Ecclesiastical Commissioners for England	S. 1, in part, and s. 3 repealed S.L.R. 1875; s. 2, from "and whenever," rep. S.L.R. 1891
266	1860	23-24 VICTORIA, c. 68	An Act for the better management and control of the highways in SOUTH WALES	See 51-52 Vict. c. 41, s. 13
267	1863	26-27 VICTORIA, c. 82	To empower Bishops of Welsh dioceses to facilitate the making provision for English services in WALES	
268	1878	41-42 VICTORIA, c. 34	An Act to amend the laws relating to Highways in SOUTH WALES	See 51-52 Vict. c. 41, s. 13
269	1881	44-45 VICTORIA, c. 14	Repair of Highway roads in SOUTH WALES	See 51-52 Vict. c. 41, s. 13
269	1881	44-45 VICTORIA, c. 61	To prohibit sale of intoxicating liquors on Sunday in WALES	S. 3. rep. S.L.R. 1894
270	1882	45-46 VICTORIA, c. 67	South Wales Turnpike Roads Amendment Act	See 51-52 Vict. c. 41, s. 13
270	1885	48-49 VICTORIA, c. 54, s. 2	Pluralities Acts Amendment Act, 1885	
270	1887	50-51 VICTORIA, c. 55, s. 31	Extension to WALES of law relating to Sheriffs	

PAGE.	YEAR.	STATUTE AND CHAPTER.	TITLE.	HOW REPEALED OR OTHERWISE AFFECTED.
271	1887	50–51 VICTORIA, c. 58, s. 39 (1)	Mines, Inspectors of, to know Welsh	
271	1888	51–52 VICTORIA, c. 41, s. 13	An Act to amend the Laws relating to Local Government in England and WALES (1) Cesser of Tolls and application of Highways Act, 1878 (2) Transfer to County Council of property and liabilities of District Roads Boards	
272	1889	52–53 VICTORIA, c. 40	An Act to promote Intermediate Education in WALES	
280	1890	53–54 VICTORIA, c. 21, s. 38 (1)	WALES included under "England" in Inland Revenue Statutes	
280	1890	53–54 VICTORIA, c. 60, s. 1 (4)	An Act for the distribution of Duties on Customs and Excise	
280	1894	57–58 VICTORIA, c. 42, s. 2 (3).	Quarry inspectors to speak Welsh	
280	1898	61–62 VICTORIA, c. 58, s. 14	Marriages in Welsh tongue	
281	1901	1 EDWARD 7, c. 22, s. 118 (2)	Factory inspectors to know Welsh	
281	1902	2 EDWARD 7, c. 14	The University of WALES Act	
281	1902	2 EDWARD 7, c. 42, s. 17 (8)	An Act making further provision with respect to Education in England and WALES	

INTRODUCTION

THAT portion of the Dominions of the British Empire which retains, in modern language, the name of WALES, preserved a separate political existence for over a thousand years, until in the reign of HENRY the Eighth it became a part of the Realm of England, and the statutory incorporation which then took place has not altogether destroyed its separate character even until this day.

The three names "ENGLAND," "WALES," and "SCOTLAND" may be classed as geographical expressions. They are political names of parts of Britain, which have had varying meanings at different times, as the parts of the island to which they were applied have changed in area. The name "England," first used about the end of the tenth century, was applied to those parts which on the consolidation of the Heptarchy came and remained under the direct rule of the King of the English. The distinction between the English and the WELSH was not only to be found then, as now, in their language, race, and ancestry, but also in the political independence maintained by the smaller country long after the Anglo-Saxon states became consolidated in the Kingdom of England.

The time had been when a natural boundary between the two countries and peoples was approximately marked by the courses of the rivers Severn and Dee, but, owing to the superiority in military skill of the Anglo-Saxon races, the WELSH people were gradually driven back. The earthwork known as Offa's Dyke, constructed in order to keep the

WELSH out of the land acquired by the invaders, clearly indicates that the WELSH, though beaten, were not subdued. This entrenchment was an artificial boundary made by Offa in 779 A.D., which extended from the estuary of the Dee to the mouth of the river Wye. The debatable and fiercely contested land on both sides of this boundary was then, and subsequently, designated the "Marches of Mercia (England and WALES)"; it was a large district, difficult of access, subject to little control, the dwelling-place of lawless and predatory bands, who plundered, disturbed, and ravaged the adjoining territories.

A.D. 940.—The laws and customs which were observed by the WELSH, until the time of EDWARD the First, are to be found in the ancient Laws and Institutes collected, codified, and promulgated by Howel the Good in A.D. 940. Caradog of Llancarvan states that "Howel Dda constituted and gave lawes to be kept through his dominions which were used in WALES till such time as the inhabitants received the lawes of England in the time of Edward the first, and in some places long after." A remarkable gathering of WELSH representatives, consisting of clergy, chieftains, and delegates from every commote in WALES, was convened by Howel at Ty Gwyn (Whitland in Caermarthenshire), to examine the customs and ancient institutions of WALES. The duty imposed upon these representatives was that of framing wholesome laws on the basis of the ancient national laws, and of promulgating a code which bears witness to the care and perspicuity of its framers and to the nature of the national customs of the WELSH people. From this code, we find existing at that period three great divisions of WALES, namely, (1) *Gwynedd*, including the greater part of what is now known as NORTH WALES, with its capital at Aberffraw; (2) *Powys*, roughly speaking MID WALES, with its capital at Shrewsbury (Pengwern); and (3) *Deheubarth*, or SOUTHERN WALES, with its capital at Dynevor (near Llandilo). For our purpose, it is unnecessary to examine this collection of WELSH laws, or to determine whether this definite organisation of WALES was permanent or not. The authoritative edition is that published by the Record Commissioners in 1841, edited by Aneurin Owen, and intituled "Ancient Laws and Institutes of WALES: comprising laws supposed to be enacted by Howel the Good, modified by subsequent regulations under the native princes prior to the conquest by EDWARD the First; and anomalous laws consisting principally of institutions which by the Statute of Rhuddlan were admitted to continue in force." This collection clearly shows that the WELSH people held most tenaciously to their own laws and customs and to their national independence. They would submit neither to the arms nor to the laws of their persistent invaders, and this spirit continued to distinguish the nation for centuries afterwards. The laws and customs collected and promulgated by Howel Dda denote a high standard of legal proficiency, containing, it is true, many barbarisms, but comparing not unfavourably with the contemporary laws of the English; and it is remarkable that there were few alterations to be made when English statesmen began to devise amendments to them.

The systematic subjugation of WALES was attempted by William the Conqueror, when he organized a chain of great Earldoms settled along the border lands and in SOUTH WALES. This territory was divided into Lordships Marchers, some of them having originated in the submission of their WELSH owners, who had anticipated the success of the Norman power, but the greater part of these Baronies Marchers was acquired by conquest. Royal licences to make war upon the WELSH were granted by the Norman Kings to their vassals for services rendered, upon the usual conditions of feudal tenure, and in the Lordships so acquired the system of jurisprudence was dependent upon the will of the Lords, who exercised supreme power. Through these districts, during the Norman period, castles of great strength were built and garrisoned for military purposes and for offensive and defensive operations of war. Towns grew up around these strongholds, English settlement was encouraged, and municipal charters were granted with distinctive provisions marking the different laws and privileges applicable to the new settlers and the WELSH inhabitants. Within these districts, the Norman-English laws were, for the most part, administered, but in many of the territories the WELSH were allowed to enjoy their ancient customs when the same did not conflict with the interests of their invaders.

The following charter, granted by King JOHN, shows the policy pursued by the English Kings :—

CHARTER OF WILLIAM DE BRAOSE.

"John, by the Grace of God, etc. to William de Braose, and his heirs all lands etc. which he hath acquired, and which hereafter he shall be able to acquire over our enemies the WELSH to hold of us and our heirs save Kardigan and its dependencies which we retain. Dated at Caen 3rd June, 2 JOHN A.D. 1200 (Rot. Chart.)."

And we find that HENRY the First gave permission to Gilbert Fitzrichard de Clare to enter into Cardigan and Pembrokeshire in the following terms, "Thou wert continually seeking for a portion of the lands of the Britons from me, I will now give thee the land of Cadwgan son of Bleddyn: go and now possess it."

This system of legalised pillage and authorized plunder ceased when EDWARD the First obtained the submission of WALES to the English power, for after the Statute of Rhuddlan no new Lordships Marchers were, or could be, created.

The Lords Marchers had greater power in the Marches of WALES than the feudal lords possessed in England, for the control of the English Monarchs was not so strongly maintained over them. The result was that the "custom of the march" developed, and they became semi-independent magnates who were allowed to raise and maintain armies of their own and to make private war at will.

But throughout the Norman period the greater part of the Principality remained in the hands of WELSH princes, who ruled, according to their own customs and laws, over the territories which had not been seized by the marauding Barons of the Marches. Within these lands, the nominal political superiority of England was fitfully accepted, but practical independence was enjoyed by the WELSH chieftains in the internal government of their own provinces, and there the old national laws and customs were of full force and effect.

MAGNA CHARTA AND WALES.

A.D. 1215.—In the great Charter of Liberties, sealed by King JOHN on June 15, 1215, we find the first mention of WALES in the constitutional documents of our Realm. Although not a parliamentary statute, it has been printed at the commencement of the English Statutes, and requires notice inasmuch as the whole of the constitutional history of England has been described as being a commentary on this Charter. This Great Charter is the commencement of the formal history of English constitutional liberty. It secured from the astute sovereign who was forced to submit to it, a definite recognition of the old constitutional rights which he had constantly violated, and a pledge that he would not further evade them. In three of the clauses of this Charter, we find the evidence of the power and influence of Llywelyn the Great, who reigned in WALES from 1194 to 1240, the most important figure in WELSH mediæval history. He seized his opportunity when England was divided and weakened, and stemmed the English tide of conquest by destroying some of the most important of the Norman-English castles in WALES. He was, although married to King JOHN'S daughter, allied to the English Barons in their struggle with that sovereign, with the result that three clauses, numbered 56, 57, and 58 of the Great Charter, describe, protect, and preserve the privileges of the WELSH King, and restored to him the hostages and charters which had been obtained by the English sovereign as security for peace.

THE LEGISLATION OF EDWARD THE FIRST. THE STATUTUM WALLIÆ.

In 1255, the sole ruler of WALES was Llywelyn ap Gruffydd, and from this year until 1282 a bitter and prolonged struggle took place between him and the English as to the retention of sovereignty in WALES. EDWARD (afterwards EDWARD the First) in 1254, had been granted by his father, HENRY the Third, the Earldom of Chester, and came to Gwynedd to view his lands and castles. By the Treaty of Shrewsbury made on September 25, 1267, Llywelyn was recognized Prince of WALES, and overlord of all the WELSH magnates, excepting Meredith ap Rees, the representative of the old line of princes of SOUTH WALES. The *Perfeddwlad* or Middle Country, comprising the four cantrevs of Rhos, Dyffryn Clwyd, Tegeingl and Rhuvoniog, forming the district lying between Chester and the Conway, Edward's old patrimony, were ceded to Llywelyn, and although the latter promised to surrender many of his conquests, he was allowed to remain in possession of great tracts of land in MID and SOUTH WALES. This treaty did not bring lasting peace to WALES and the Marches. In 1276, Eleanor de Montfort, betrothed to Llywelyn, while on her way from France to be married to him, was captured and detained as a prisoner by EDWARD the First. Llywelyn could only obtain her liberation by signing articles in which he agreed to do homage to EDWARD and to cede to him the *Perfeddwlad*. By these articles, the ancient rights of the WELSH people in this district were preserved, but when EDWARD took possession of it, he began by converting it into shire-ground and introducing Norman-English laws instead of the WELSH laws and customs. EDWARD at the same time re-established the shire organizations of Caermarthen and Cardigan. The WELSH people under Llywelyn broke out again into rebellion, and Llywelyn died in battle on December 11, 1282, at Pont Orewyn, near Builth. On Llywelyn's death, his possessions passed to the English King, and two years afterwards, the important *Statutum Walliæ*—the Statute of WALES—was enacted at Rhuddlan by EDWARD the First, on Sunday in Mid-Lent,[1] 1284. It is the first great Act for the Principality, settling the civil and legal administration of WALES for nearly three hundred years.

A.D. 1275.—In the year 1275, the Statute of Westminster the First (3 EDWARD I, c. 17) was significant of the growing power of the central administration, and the new policy to be pursued towards the Lordship Marchers. Theretofore there was no jurisdiction in the English Courts over WALES. The maxim was, *Breve regis non currit in Walliam:* "the King's Writ runneth not into WALES"; and the Lords Marchers had regal powers within their Lordships; but, by the Statute of Westminster the First, it was provided that English law should be of effect within the courts and lands of the Marches of WALES.

A.D. 1284.—The Statute of WALES (12 EDWARD I, c. 1), was drafted upon the report of a Commission appointed by EDWARD before Llywelyn was finally subdued. The Commission (dated at Westminster, December 4, 1820) was issued to Thomas (Becke) Bishop of St. Davids, Reginald de Grey, and Walter de Hopton, appointing them to examine upon oath "unsuspected persons both WELSH and English," in order to obtain information respecting the laws and usages by which the Kings, his predecessors, had been accustomed to govern and order the Prince of WALES and the WELSH Barons of WALES and their peers and others their inferiors, and all particulars connected with such laws and usages. These Commissioners were commanded to appoint certain

[1] See "Political History of England," by Professor Tout, vol. iii. p. 133.

days and places for carrying on this inquiry, and to return and account to the King within three weeks of Easter. An order was also issued to all Justices, Sheriffs, Bailiffs, and other officers of the King in WALES, requiring them to cause to appear on the days appointed, all such witnesses as might be able to give information on the subject; and also requiring that they should attend upon, and render every assistance and advice to the said Commissioners, in order that all needful information might be obtained. This inquiry comprised fourteen interrogatories to be put to each of the witnesses. The Commissioners examined in all, 172 witnesses—that is, 19 in Chester; 53 in Rhuddlan; 36 in the White Monastery (probably Oswestry); 22 in Montgomery, and 42 in Llanbadarn Vawr. The interrogatories and the answers of the witnesses may be found in the appendix to *Wotton's Leges Wallicæ*. A translation is given in the paper on the "Historical Account of the Statute of Rhuddlan," by the Rev. Thomas Price (*Carnhuanauc*). The majority of the witnesses undoubtedly furnished evidence showing, that within the area of the Commissioners' jurisdiction, the English judicial system was replacing WELSH usages and laws. The evidence is, however, neither convincing nor satisfactory. Many of the witnesses, like William Launtelyn, Knight, on being sworn and diligently examined, said that they knew nothing. "The frequent profession of absolute ignorance and some rather evasive replies suggest that the witnesses were either carefully selected, or else under the influence of fear or motives of self-interest gave replies which they thought would be satisfactory to the English authorities. The survival of WELSH Customs, as to which there is ample testimony even as late as Tudor times, tends to confirm one's suspicions, but on the other hand the commission's questions dealt chiefly with procedure and the rights of barons and landed proprietors; and it may be urged that the supersession of WELSH law in regard to that part of the *corpus juris* was not inconsistent with the retention of WELSH usages in regard to other parts, or as to the holdings of land by inferior tenants in particular lordships."[1] The Commission extended only to a limited portion of WALES, viz., to the four Cantreds of Perfeddwlad, Iâl or Yale, Ystrad Alun (Mold), Montgomeryshire, Cardiganshire, part of Caermarthenshire and the WELSH Border from Chester to Bishop's Castle.

The *Statutum Walliæ* was not a parliamentary statute. It was the King's Charter "to all his subjects of his land of Snowdon, and of other his lands in WALES." It emanated throughout from his sole authority, and his own seal was affixed thereto. The absolute power of legislation which was assumed by EDWARD was that which belongs to the Crown after the conquest of an insurgent and independent country, but, although not the result of parliamentary deliberation, it was drawn up by the advice of the nobles of the Kingdom, and is included in the recognized Statutes of the Realm. It remained on the Statute book until it was repealed by the Statute Law Revision Act, 1887. It was "the most comprehensive code that any English legislator issued during the Middle Ages."[2]

The Statute of WALES is frequently referred to as the Statute of Rhuddlan, although there was another legislative Act, issued at the same time, by EDWARD, which is distinguished by the name of the Statute of Rothelan (12 EDWARD I). This was a royal ordinance, regulating the Exchequer, not requiring parliamentary authority.

The Statute of WALES commences with a preamble reciting what was conceived to be the political condition of the country at that time. It states that WALES, with its inhabitants, had hitherto been subject to the King by feudal right, but that Divine Providence, amongst other gifts, had "wholly and entirely transferred the land of WALES with its

[1] See Brynmor Jones and Rhys, "The Welsh People," chap. viii.
[2] "History of English Law," by Pollock and Maitland, vol. i. p. 220.

inhabitants" to the King's dominion. It was desired that the country should be governed with due order to the "honour and praise of God and of Holy Church and the advancement of justice." It was stated that the King having diligently heard, and fully understood "the laws and customs of those parts hitherto in use, had abolished some of them, allowed some, corrected some, and commanded certain others to be added thereto," and that the country was annexed and united unto the Crown of the Realm of England as a member of the same body.

The Statute provided that the Justice of Snowdon was to have the custody and government of the peace of the King in Snowdon, and the lands adjoining, and that he was to administer justice according to original writs of the King "and the laws and customs underwritten." Gwynedd and its appurtenances were divided into the three shires of Anglesey, Carnarvon, and Merioneth, and were collectively put under the Justice of Snowdon, whose seat was to be at Carnarvon, where Courts of Chancery and Exchequer for NORTH WALES were to be established. The district forming the County of Flint was to be obedient likewise to the Justice of Chester. In SOUTH WALES the shires of Cardigan and Caermarthen were reorganized, and put under the jurisdiction of the Justice of WEST WALES, whose Chancery and Exchequer Courts were appointed to be at Caermarthen.

The officers under the existing English shire system, such as Sheriffs, Coroners, and Bailiffs, were introduced into WALES. County Courts summoned by the Sheriff, who was the special representative of the King, were to be held monthly in the newly formed counties to deal with criminal cases and civil causes. Felons and criminals were to be indicted at these courts by the four adjacent townships, whilst the kindred of a dead man (termed "the Welsherie"), and accused persons were to be detained until the next coming on circuit of the King's Justice.

Twice in the year, once after the Feast of St. Michael, and

once after Easter, the Sheriff was to make his "*tourn*" in the several *commotes*, at which all freeholders, and all others holding lands and dwelling in that commote (except men of religion, clerks, and women) were to attend. The "commote" or "cymwd" was selected because it was the most ancient division of Cymric land. The "cantref" was a collection of "cymwds." The "cymwds" varied in size. There are several comparatively modern lists of these ancient divisions in existence, which show that they were well recognized in later times: they are mentioned in the laws of Howel Dda for administrative and legal purposes, and were doubtless in existence during all the mediæval history of the Country.[1] At his "tourn" the Sheriff, by the oath of twelve of the most discreet and lawful freeholders, or more at his discretion, made inquiry as to certain matters duly specified in section 4 of the statute, principally offences of a criminal character.

The Sheriff was to inquire, *inter alia* "of *Mascherers*, that sell and buy stolen meat knowingly; of *Whittawers*, that is, those that whiten hides of oxen and horses, knowing the same to have been stolen, that they may not be known again; of *Redubbers* of stolen cloths, that turn them into a new shape and change the old one, as making a coat or surcoat of a cloak and the like; of them that shear sheep by night in the folds, and that slay them and any other beasts; of them that take and collect by night the ears of corn in autumn and carry them away; and of them that give lodgings to persons unknown for more than two nights, etc., etc."

All the men of the whole "commote" were sworn and required to make due presentment as to the capital and lesser offences arising within their district. In capital offences they were to inform the Sheriff secretly of the names of the offenders to prevent their escape, but this secrecy was not required in the lesser offences. This grand jury brought

[1] See Brynmor-Jones and Rhys, "The Welsh People," Appendix A.

in their verdict or presentment, and the Sheriff proceeded, if necessary, to arrest the persons implicated.

The bailiffs of the "commotes" administered justice to parties in suits. One Coroner at least was elected in every commote. He was chosen in the full County Court, by royal writ, and took the oath of office before the Sheriff. In cases of dangerous wounding and homicide the Coroner required the Sheriff or Bailiff of the Commote to summon all persons of twelve years and upwards of the town wherein the casualty happened, and of the four adjoining townships. The Coroners were to make inquiry as to all the facts surrounding the crime, secretly giving up the names of the accused in writing to the Sheriff or Bailiff of the Commote, who committed the alleged offenders to prison until the King's Court was held. The goods of the accused were seized and valued, and a record of the facts of the case was enrolled, after the inquest, to be placed before the Justice.

It was provided that when a thief, manslayer, or other malefactor, availed himself of the very ancient custom of privilege of sanctuary, that is, fled to obtain the protection afforded by the Church, the Coroner was to summon all the good and lawful men of his neighbourhood, and to cause the abjuration of the realm by the fugitive in the following manner. The felon was to be brought to the church door, a seaport was assigned for him by the Coroner, and then the felon abjured the realm. A time-allowance was given to him to reach the seaport, and he was to be set on his journey on the King's highway bearing in his hand a cross, being commanded to depart the realm as speedily as possible, turning neither to the right hand nor upon the left. This privilege entailed perpetual banishment into a foreign Christian country. His lands escheated; his chattels were forfeited; and if he came back he was outlawed.

Forms and precedents in full of the original writs to be

used in actions at law, together with the letters patent to the King's Justices, are prescribed by the fifth section of the Statute; such as the writ of *Novel disseisin* (issued to the Sheriff at the request of the person disseised or dispossessed of land, commanding the Sheriff to summon a jury of twelve free and lawful men to decide whether the dispossession had been lawful and then to report to the Justice of Assize); also the writ of *Mort d'ancester* (giving authority to the Sheriff to summon a jury to determine whether the plaintiff's ancestor was seized or possessed of the lands in question at the day of his death, and if the plaintiff was the lawful heir). There are other writs set forth in the same section, after the model of the same writs in English Jurisprudence.

Actions for personal trespasses wherein the damages did not exceed forty shillings were pleaded before the Sheriff in the County Court; above that sum, before the Justice of WALES. Pleas of lands were not to be determined by wager of battle nor by the grand assize. The procedure is fully set out in the Statute. In trials of assize of *Mort d'ancester*, the claimant of the property could be resisted, if illegitimate, on the ground of bastardy, a fact which was inquired into by the Bishop of the place, who certified the result of his inquiry to the Chief Justice of WALES.

The Assizes were to be taken in the respective counties before the Justice twice, thrice, or four times yearly. Causes in actions relating to land, immovables, and movable property were to be tried before juries. There were to be formal pleadings before the case was tried, viz., documents in which the grounds of action and issues were clearly expressed. It was, however, specially enacted that any formal defect in these pleadings was not to fall within that hard rule which was the reproach of the Roman law at one time, and of the English law at a later period, viz., that a technical mistake vitiated the whole proceedings. He who failed in a syllable was not to fail in his cause.

Trespasses were punishable by fines, payment of damage, imprisonment, the trespasser being tried by his "country," that is, by his neighbours.

A woman's right to dowry had not been recognized in WALES until this Statute. It was then introduced, and a woman's dower was said to be twofold,—(*a*) where there was an assignment of the third part of the whole land belonging to the husband which was his during her coverture, and (*b*) when a son with his father's assent endowed his wife. The writ of reasonable dower was provided for cases under (*a*).

Trials relating to real property were always to be before a jury of good and lawful men of the neighbourhood, chosen by consent of the parties, and those relating to personal actions were to be according to the WELSH laws, as the people of WALES had been accustomed. Under the WELSH laws, in personal actions the evidence of witnesses was relied upon, but if no such evidence was procurable, then testimony by "purgation" was resorted to.

But it was expressly enacted that in criminal cases the English laws were to be followed and used.

The 13th section of the Statute of WALES regulates the very important question of the division of landed property at death. Herein EDWARD'S policy of recognizing and perpetuating the ancient laws and customs of the WELSH is shown. The WELSH rule of law was that the inheritance, at the death of the head of the family, became equally divided among the male children—a custom which is termed "gavel-kind" in English law. It therefore differed from the general English custom of primogeniture. The Statute enacted that in WALES the inheritance was to be divided equally among the heirs male, as it was wont to be "from the time whereof the memory of man is not to the contrary." Two alterations in the WELSH law were made for (*a*) bastards were not to share with the lawful heirs or inherit, and (*b*) upon the failure of male heirs the inheritance, was to descend to females, "although this be contrary to the custom of WALES."

The Statute of WALES closed the purely WELSH period, and heralded the introduction of English institutions into the Principality. Although the new political organization came into effect at once, the new legal provisions of the Statute of WALES took a considerable time in ousting and superseding the ancient WELSH laws.

In the Peniarth MSS. there is a copy of the Statute in WELSH, from which it appears that EDWARD ordered that two copies in Latin and one copy in WELSH should be kept in every commote for reference.

It will be seen that this Statute, based upon an extensive inquiry into WELSH laws and customs, laid down definite, well-considered, and effective procedure. It is striking evidence of a desire to adapt the procedure of the English legal system—modified by pre-existing national customs—to the wants of the WELSH people as understood by EDWARD and his advisers. The minute directions given in this enactment for the holding of the county courts, are the best evidence of the powers of the English shire moots existing at the end of the thirteenth century,[1] and they show clearly the defining and organizing process which was so remarkably developed by lawyers who advised EDWARD the First in the government of England. "The England that saw the birth of English law, the England of Magna Charta, and the first parliaments, was a much governed and little England."[2] A great part of the statute was highly technical, but the main purport of it shows the King's attempt to introduce into WALES a system that would, and did in fact, only require expansion to bring it into harmony with the necessities of a separate nationality. For more than two centuries after this Statute came into force the Principality of WALES remained isolated from the operation of general

[1] Stubbs's "Constitutional History," vol. ii. p. 117.

[2] Pollock and Maitland's "History of English Law."

political and legal reforms, being specially legislated for, separately administered, and except upon two occasions as is pointed out hereafter, unrepresented in the English Parliament.

In September, 1284, EDWARD commenced a royal progress through WALES to complete the administrative changes which he had instituted. Starting from Flint, with his principal officials, he passed through several districts, settling disputes, and establishing peace throughout the Principality. Finally he arrived in the lordship of Glamorgan, belonging to the Earl of Gloucester, who received the King as if he were a brother potentate. EDWARD did not again visit WALES until 1291, when he came to put an end to the overreaching pretensions of the Lords Marchers.

At the end of the thirteenth century WALES comprised a territory which was divided as follows:—

(1) Into Lordship Marchers, numbering about 140, held of the English Crown according to feudal right, by WELSH chiefs or Norman Lords. These Lordship Marchers existed not only on the borderland between WALES and England, but also in the interior parts of what is now the country of WALES.

(2) The "Principality," which consisted of the territories held by Llywelyn ab Gruffydd when conquered by EDWARD. The legal term for this land was *Parcella Principalitatis Walliæ.* It included the commotes organized under the Statute of WALES into the counties of Anglesea, Carnarvon, Merioneth, parts of Flintshire, Caermarthenshire, and Cardiganshire. EDWARD in 1280 had established a County Court at Caermarthen, and entered into possession of the counties of Cardigan and Caermarthen.

(3) The lordship of Glamorgan and the County palatine of Pembroke. The lowland portions of Glamorganshire constituted the Lordship of Glamorgan, the uplands being retained by WELSH chieftains, but the Lordship did not extend to the modern limits of the County. Pembrokeshire

had been granted in 1138 to Gilbert de Clare and was "in ancient tyme a County Palatyne and noe part of the Principalitie of WALES,"[1] and these lordships "of which that of Glamorgan was the most complete, were something very like States, and the skill and strength of that mighty monarch, EDWARD the First, was called in to undermine the too great independence of lords of his own race."[2]

An excellent map of WALES and the March at this period is published with volume iii. of the "Political History of England," by Professor Tout. "The Lordships of the March were not directly influenced by EDWARD'S legislation. They continued to hold their position as franchises until the reign of HENRY the Eighth, and under EDWARD the Third were declared by statute to be no part of the principality, but directly subject to the English Crown. Yet the removal of the pressure of a Native principality profoundly affected these districts. The policy of definition made its mark even here. The liberties of such Marches were defined and circumscribed, and whilst scrupulously respected, were incapable of further extension. The vague jurisdictions of the Sheriffs of the border shires were cleared up. Gradually the Marcher lordships passed by lapse into the royal hands, and even from the beginning there were regions, such as Montgomery and Builth, which knew no Lord but the King. All this was, however, an indirect result of the Edwardian conquest. Strictly speaking, it was no conquest of WALES, but merely of the Principality, the ancient dominions of Llywelyn, to which most of the Crown lands in WALES were joined."[3]

As the Statute of WALES did not apply to the Lordship Marchers, law and justice was administered therein according to the laws and customs of each particular lordship by officers appointed by the lord. After that statute, the legal position of the Lords Marchers and their rights became a matter

[1] Owen's "Pembrokeshire," p. 190.

[2] Marquis of Bute's address at Rhyl National Eisteddfod, 1892.

[3] "Political History of England," vol. iii. p. 167.

of grave import. The powers of the WELSH Princes had been abolished, and the custom of the March had to be settled. Between 1284 and 1291 many private wars occurred in WALES and the Marches, arising out of the conduct of the Lords Marchers. EDWARD the First returned to suppress this lawlessness, and the matter was brought to a head by the remarkable dispute between Gilbert, Earl of Gloucester, who was the ruler of the Lordship of Glamorgan, and the Earl of Hereford, in whose private jurisdiction the lands now forming the County of Brecknock were situate. EDWARD interfered, and in 1290 formally called on the Earls by proclamation to put an end to their hostilities. He summoned the Lords Marchers in order to determine the question whether they were to be obedient to the Crown or not. A court was convened at Llanthew, near Brecon, in 1291, at which Hereford appeared, but Gloucester did not. The King was at Amesbury in Wiltshire at this time, and hearing of Gloucester's action, he summoned a fresh court at Abergavenny for Michaelmas, 1291, at which both nobles appeared. There EDWARD presided, and the "scene when the day came, must have been impressive; one of our strongest and most law loving Kings was in full court, sitting in Judgment on the proudest of the old Norman aristocracy, on the deep and difficult question of the royal prerogative to override custom." Both Earls were imprisoned, their estates were confiscated, and by this trial EDWARD the First crushed the privileges of the Lords Marchers, and curbed their independent and tyrannical jurisdictions during his time. In the reign of EDWARD the Second, when the Crown was in the hands of a weaker King, the Lords Marchers resumed their old privileges, which were asserted and continued until the Tudor period. For a detailed and valuable account of WALES and the private wars in the Marcher Lordships, the work of Mr. J. E. Morris on the "WELSH Wars of King EDWARD the First" should be consulted.

The Ordinances of Edward the Second. 1315–6.

A.D. 1315–6.—After the *Statutum Walliæ* there is no legislation relating to WALES until the reign of EDWARD the Second (who was the first Prince of WALES), when two Ordinances were promulgated by that King which are of importance and are printed with the statutes hereafter. They were Ordinances concerning the customs of WEST WALES, SOUTH WALES, and NORTH WALES, and are to be found in Rymer's Fœdera.

An Ordinance differed from a Statute. A Statute was enacted by the King in Parliament and became a permanent addition to the law. An Ordinance was an executive act issued by the King in council, usually of a tentative and temporary nature; it could be recalled by the King; it was not enrolled in the statute book, although it might be converted into a statute. These Ordinances of EDWARD the Second altered and amended certain provisions of the *Statutum Walliæ*, and dealt with various grievances of the different parts of WALES. It will be noticed that EDWARD the Second declares therein that he was born in WALES, a statement of value in considering the disputed question as to the place of his birth. On reading these Ordinances carefully it will be seen that there are points of difference between them. Both deal with the custom of *Amobragium*, but nothing is said in the NORTH WALES Ordinance of *Westva*, *Blodwyte*, complaints of felonies and torts, and the superabundance of bailiffs.

In dealing with *Amobragium*, or "*Amobr*" (the fee payable to the Lord by his tenant on the marriage of the latter's daughter), the Ordinances set up a limit of time (within a year) when the fine could be enacted, and declared also that it should be levied only in those cases in which under the Princes of WALES it could be levied. These fines were farmed out to "*amoberers*," who greatly oppressed and impoverished the people. *Westva* was the "*gwestva*" of the WELSH laws, a fixed payment of food in lieu of the entertainment with which in earlier times the free tenants were obliged to supply their lord. *Blodwyte* was the fine inflicted for causing wounds or bloodshed. Under the Statute of WALES the Sheriff was obliged to diligently inquire concerning bloodshed by the oath of a jury, but by the Ordinance of WEST WALES and SOUTH WALES the jurisdiction of the King's Bailiffs was enlarged and they were directed to ascertain "by view" as to this. In the WEST WALES and SOUTH WALES Ordinance we find that where complaints concerning contracts and trespasses between Englishmen and WELSHMEN were to be decided by inquest, one half of the inquest was to be composed of Englishmen and the other half of WELSHMEN worthy of trust. The NORTH WALES Ordinance had no provision to this effect, but it is probable that this was also the general practice throughout NORTH WALES and required no such provision. Judge David Lewis in dealing with these Ordinances says[1] "that an exhaustive legal commentary on the Ordinances is impossible with the materials available at present. The period between the *Statutum Walliæ* and the incorporation Statute of HENRY the Eighth is a dark period in WELSH history, awaiting the examination of much material lying in the Records of the time. It may be possible after such an examination to answer the questions how the mixed Jury of WELSHMEN and Englishmen worked in practice. Did the English judges who came round take to it kindly? Were the juries addressed in both WELSH and English? How was this managed when the Judge knew no WELSH, and what part did the Latimer (Lladmerydd = Interpreter) play?"

The NORTH WALES Ordinance related to freemen and religious persons and removed the burdens which were placed on the former. The customary taxes due from villeins and strangers were to be taken as they were levied

[1] "Wales," vol. ii. p. 443.

by the former Princes of WALES, and freemen were not to be taxed unless the ordinary revenue was insufficient. The sons of freemen who wished to take holy orders had not been allowed to do so without obtaining a licence. Under this Ordinance of NORTH WALES, where a freeman had two sons, one of them was allowed to take orders without a licence from the King or Justiciar. Freemen were allowed to sell and give lands to other free WELSHMEN, but not to prelates, religious persons, secular officers, who, under pretence of their office, had been able to coerce the people to make such sales or gifts.

A.D. 1353–4.—In the reign of EDWARD the Third the Ordinances of the Staple (27 EDWARD 3, stat. 2, c. 18), prohibiting English merchants from exporting wool under pain of death, were promulgated (1353), and provision was made therein that the men of Ireland and WALES might take their wools and leathers for sale to the staple markets of England.

In 1353, certain statutes were made at Westminster, the first of which confirmed Magna Charta and all statutes before made and used. The second (28 EDWARD 3, c. 2) enacted that all the Lords Marchers of WALES should be perpetually attending and annexed to the Crown of England and not to the Principality of WALES, "in whose hands soever the same principality be or hereafter should come." EDWARD the Third had two objects in securing this measure—firstly, to convince his arrogant nobles that he was entitled to their complete allegiance, and, secondly, to limit the power or possible pretensions of any Prince of WALES who might be heir to the throne.

THE COERCION PERIOD.

During the fourteenth century the WELSH people lived under wretched political conditions. The policy of English statesmen aimed at the extirpation of every vestige of WELSH patriotism and nationality. English officials, traders, and settlers came to the country under the protection of the powerful castles, which, originally established by the Norman Kings, were rebuilt and strengthened to keep down the native WELSH. Oppression, violence, and tyranny followed in the train of these settlers. There are abundant signs during this period that the WELSH people resented the new officials and English ways, and that they struggled desperately and continuously against the dominant race. In the Lordships Marchers the stern, ruthless, and unjust rule of the over-lords provoked the WELSH to several abortive insurrections. Great abuses existed owing to the harsh and severe measures adopted by the new officials, and keen and bitter struggles ensued.

In 1400, the seething discontent of the WELSH broke forth under Owen Glyndwr's leadership. He was the last great WELSH military leader. His mysterious personality and soldierlike qualities produced a stimulating effect upon his despondent fellow-countrymen. At first an ubiquitous guerilla leader, he became subsequently the head of the most important revolt of the WELSH against the harsh rule of their conquerors. WELSH students from the universities of England, WELSH labourers working in England, WELSH soldiers who had served in France as mercenaries, flocked to his standard, and for fifteen years Glyndwr defied and successfully resisted the English power. He attacked the fortified castles of the rulers, and the greater part at one time or another fell into his hands. His daring, his magnetic and mysterious personality, and his rapid and deadly strokes at the official rulers made him feared. In 1404, he summoned WELSH parliaments to Dolgelly and Machynlleth. His aim was the independence of the WELSH Church and the freedom of his country. The establishment of two universities, one in NORTH WALES, the other in SOUTH WALES, was projected by him.[1] He became an ally of the King of France and of Hotspur, and generally instilled dread into the English authorities. Under these circumstances it is not

[1] Wylie's "History of the Reign of Henry the Fourth," vol. ii. pp. 313-4.

surprising to find legislative measures of a repressive character passed by the English Parliament.

A.D. 1400–1401.—The general character of the Acts relating to WALES and WELSHMEN, from 1400 until the accession of the Tudor dynasty, is that they were coercion measures, designed for the purpose of crushing the national spirit of the WELSH people. Six coercion Acts were passed in 1400–1401. They laid down that no WELSHMAN, "wholly born in WALES" could purchase lands or tenements within England nor within the Boroughs or English towns of WALES. A WELSHMAN could not obtain the privileges of a citizen or burgess in any city or borough or merchant town; could not become a municipal officer, and was forbidden to carry armour in any city or town on pain of imprisonment. Exemption from these statutes was often granted to certain WELSHMEN as a special favour. In consequence of the complaint that "the people of WALES—sometime by day, and sometime by night"—distrained and seized upon the cattle and goods of their English neighbours in counties adjoining the Marches of WALES, it was enacted that upon failure of redress the English were permitted to arrest all persons with their goods and chattels coming out of WALES and to retain them until full satisfaction was made to the complaining parties. If a WELSHMAN committed a felony in England, and repaired to WALES, the English officials in WALES were directed to execute him, upon a certificate given by the King's Justice. The Lords Marchers were to keep "sufficient stuffing and ward" in their castles in WALES in case of riots. No Englishman could be convicted at the suit of any WELSHMAN in WALES, except by the judgment of English justices, or by the judgment of Englishmen resident in the Principality.

A.D. 1402.—In 1402, nine further coercion Acts were passed. One established that Englishmen were not to be convicted by WELSHMEN in WALES. Another, in order "to eschew many diseases and mischiefs which have happened before this time in the Land of WALES," ordained that "no waster, rhymer, minstrel nor vagabond be in any wise sustained in the land of WALES to make *commorthies* or gathering upon the people there." This was probably directed against the bards who were engaged by Owen Glyndwr in rousing the martial spirit of the WELSH, and against the "*gwestwyr*," or purveyancers employed also by him to collect money and provisions (*cymortha*) for the insurrection. Another Act forbade "congregations and councils," unless they were for an evident and necessary cause, or were held by licence of the chief officials of the Lordships. WELSHMEN were not to carry arms without special licence; no food or armour was to be sent into WALES and an English Constable was appointed to prevent and seize such supplies; no WELSHMAN, unless he were a Bishop or a Temporal Lord, could possess a castle or defend his house. No WELSHMAN could be made Justice, Chamberlain, Chancellor, Treasurer, Sheriff, Steward, Constable of Castle, Escheator, Coroner, Chief Forester, Keeper of the Records, or Lieutenant in any part of WALES or of the Council of any English Lord, except Bishops in WALES. For the more sufficient custody of the "Land of WALES" all castles and walled towns were to be kept by Englishmen, and it was ordained that an Englishman married to any WELSHWOMAN of the amity or alliance of "Owain ab Glyndwr, traitor to our Sovereign Lord"—or to any other WELSHWOMAN—could not be put into office in WALES or its Marches.

A.D. 1407.—In 1407, two statutes were passed concerning felonies and robberies in WALES, after complaints had been made to the King by the Commons, at a parliament held at Gloucester, on October 20th of that year.

George Owen of Henllys says that: "By this it may be seen that those cruel Laws of *Henry the fourth* proceeded of malice against the whole Nation, for he made no such Laws against the rest of His Subjects of *France who Revolted and Rebelled against him* neither did he ever attempt to establish any Law for the good and quiet government of *WALES* or for the Abolishing any Cruel or Inconvenience which he found Grievous. But all his Laws were general Scourges and punishments against the whole People of the Country of WALES being then his Subjects and his Son *Prince of WALES*. We in England to this Day have not made the like against the *Spaniards* or any other Capital Enemies to this Realm." [1]

A.D. 1413–4.—In the reign of HENRY the Fifth two repressive statutes became law: the first, in 1413 (1 HENRY 5, c. 6), provided that no actions should be brought by WELSHMEN in respect of injuries sustained by them during the rebellion, except upon pain of paying treble damages, suffering imprisonment for two years, and making fine and ransom before being delivered out of prison; the second, in 1414 (2 HENRY 5, c. 5), gave power to Justices of Peace within certain Counties of England to inquire into and determine charges against WELSHMEN who had committed offences "with force and arms in the manner of war, sometimes by day and sometimes by night," in the bordering English counties.

A.D. 1425–1429.—In 1425 and 1429 two Acts were passed giving powers of amendment in records of the Courts to Justices in certain cases, but it provided in both Acts that they were not to extend to records and processes in WALES.

A.D. 1430.—In 1430, a personal statute confirmed all the previous judgments and processes against Owen Glyndwr (or Glendwrdy) and those who were his heirs or of his blood, on account of the "horribility of his so many treasons."

A.D. 1441–2.—Under HENRY the Sixth (by 20 HENRY 6, c. 3) WELSHMEN were to be adjudged guilty of high treason for committing offences that had not been effectually prevented by the preceding penal acts; and (by 20 HENRY 6, c. 7) foreign merchandise, coming to England through WALES without paying customs duty, was to be forfeited and the

[1] Owen's "Pembrokeshire," Part 3, p. 123.

offending party was to be tried in the county next adjoining in England.

A.D. 1444–5.—In 1444, an Act (23 HENRY 6, c. 4) against WELSHMEN, who were indicted for treasons and felonies, was passed, alleging that outlawed persons of WALES and the Marches came to slay, burn, rob, and do other offences in the County of Hereford; and directing that a *hue and cry* was to be raised against them by the officers of that County. In this Act it is also alleged that persons living in WALES and the Marches, so indicted and outlawed, came into the said County, to cities and burghs, to fairs and markets, sometimes by night, to there sell and buy merchandize and "tarry 2, 3, 4 days or more at their will and after return into their countries without execution of the law made upon them by the Sheriff of the said County." Fines were to be inflicted upon persons conversant with the *hue and cry* who did not assist in the arrest of such outlaws.

In the same year we find (see Rot. Parl., vol. v. pp. 104, 155) the English living in the English towns in WALES earnestly petitioning that the previous legislation, excluding WELSHMEN from bearing office in WALES, should be kept strictly in force.

A.D. 1446.—In 1446, all statutes against WELSHMEN were confirmed, and grants of privileges to WELSHMEN in NORTH WALES were made void.

A.D. 1448–9.—In 1448 (by 27 HENRY 6, c. 4), the legislation of 1441 concerning "WELSHMEN who take away Englishmen" was extended until the next Parliament, and in 1449, by 28 HENRY 6, c. 4, it was made a felony for persons in WALES and certain other districts to take away men and goods under colour of distress. This was to prevent the great assemblies of persons, riots, mayhems, and murders which were occasioned by such actions, and was not to prevent distresses which were lawful by the common law of England.

Towards the end of the fifteenth century, WALES and the

Marches could not accurately be described as a peaceful country, for according to Sir John Wynn in his history of the Gwydr family, "in those dayes in that wide worlde every man stood upon his guard and went not abroad but in sort and soe armed, as if he went to the field to encountre with his enemies." Hallam says that the WELSH frontier was constantly almost in a state of war, which a very little good sense and benevolence would have easily prevented, by admitting the WELSH people to partake in equal privileges with their fellow subjects. Instead of this, the mischief was aggravated by granting legal reprisals upon WELSHMEN.[1]

The internecine strife between the various Lordship Marchers, the privileges of the Marcher Lords, their oppression of the WELSH people, their tyrannical administration of justice in their Courts, and the hostility of the WELSH people to English official rule, were the chief causes of this deplorable state of affairs. A strong central government was required, and this became possible in the reign of HENRY the Seventh, to whom the powers of the Marcher Lordships had passed through the death of Richard the Third. All the estates of the Earldom of March had become forfeited to the Crown, and in 1488, an Act relating to the Crown Lands provided that in future all grants in the Marches were to be made under the great seal of England.

With the accession of the Tudor dynasty the coercion period passed away. HENRY the Seventh (Harry ap Tudor) was a WELSHMAN. Sir Rhys ap Thomas, a WELSHMAN, was largely instrumental in placing him on the throne. Henceforth, flattered by the knowledge that a King, proud of his WELSH ancestry, was ruler of Great Britain; treated with a sympathy they had never previously experienced; and judiciously managed by statesmanlike legislation based upon the concession of equal rights and full privileges, the people of the Principality and Dominion of WALES entered upon a more peaceful era.

[1] Hallam's "Middle Ages," vol. iii. p. 169.

THE TUDOR PERIOD.

A.D. 1495.—During the twenty-four years of the reign of HENRY the Seventh, the only Act that had special reference to WALES was passed in 1495. It is a private Act (11 HENRY 7, c. 33). It made void divers leases and offices "within the Principality of SOUTH WALES, NORTH WALES, and in the County Palatine of Chester and Flint and in divers other Castles, Manors, Lordships, Lands and Tenements in the Marches of WALES, and in the Counties of Hereford, and Salop, parcels of the Earldom of March." This was done because "much less rent was reserved to the King and Prince of WALES than might be reasonably required." In this Act, there are many provisions made in favour of certain officials such as the "Porter of Beeston Castle; the Master Forester of Snowdon Forest; Sir Rhys ap Thomas, the Chamberlain of SOUTH WALES and Captain of the Castle of Aberystwyth," &c., &c.

It was during the reign of the great Tudor monarch, HENRY the Eighth, that the most important statutes relating to WALES were passed. The strong personal character of that King, the importance of his initiative, his extraordinary power of carrying the nation with him, and his paternal but despotic policy, thinly disguised under constitutional reforms, are seen throughout the provisions of the many Acts relating to WALES passed by his subservient Parliaments.

In this reign, the abuses of clerical privileges were vigorously attacked by Parliament. In 1515, a Bill was introduced to limit "benefit of clergy." In the same year a petition was presented to the Crown, complaining that clergymen declined to bury their parishioners unless they were rewarded by the most precious jewel, suit of clothes, or other possession of the deceased person; and praying that every incumbent should be compelled to bury the dead or to administer the sacrament to the sick upon penalty of

£40.[1] Nothing was done in answer to the petition until 1529, when a Committee was appointed to draft a Bill dealing with these mortuary fees.

Mortuary fees were one of the "enormities of the clergy" which were highly oppressive and irritating. The clergy exacted mortuary dues not only from the fathers of families, but from widows, children, and servants. Poor men were driven by the curates to sell their goods in time of sickness "if there were such goods as were like to be their mortuaries." If a man died in one parish and had a household in another, mortuary fees would be claimed by the clergy in both places, and no religious burial would take place until they were paid. Mortuaries were demanded in many places where they had been previously unknown, and were "taken in such a manner that it made the people to think that the curates loved their mortuaries better than their lives."

A.D. 1529.—The Bill went through the House of Commons; but met with great opposition in the House of Lords from the Bishops. "My lords," said the Bishop of Rochester, in the Upper House, "you see daily what Bills come hither from the common house and all is to the destruction of the Church." Serious differences arose between the Lords and Commons as to the passing of the Bill, and it was only after the interposition of the King that the Act (21 HENRY 8, c. 6) was reluctantly passed by the peers. Under its provisions, no mortuary was to be taken of any person who should have less than ten marks in effects, nor except where the payment had been usual, nor in more places than one. No mortuary fees were to be taken for children and femes covert. By the sections relating to WALES, no mortuaries were to be there demanded except where they had been accustomed, and in those parts they were to be taken as specified in the Act, but it was provided that the Bishops of Bangor, Llandaff, St. Asaph, and St. Davids were to take such mortuary fees of the

[1] Letters and Papers, Henry 8, 2, 1315.

priests within their dioceses and jurisdictions as heretofore they had been accustomed. "Mortuaries were thus shorn of their luxuriance; when effects were small, no mortuary should be required; when large, the clergy should content themselves with a modest share. No velvet cloaks should be stripped any more from a rector's grasp; no shameful battles with apparitors should disturb any more the recent rest of the dead. Such sums as the law would permit should be paid thenceforward in the form of decent burial fees for householders dying in their own parishes, and there the exactions should terminate."[1]

It was not until 1713 (by 13 ANNE, c 6) that these special privileges were taken away from the WELSH Bishops. They were then abolished because the demand for and payment of the same impoverished the clergy, and lessened the small provision which the WELSH clergy generally were able to make for the support of their families. This abolition was accompanied by compensation to the WELSH Bishops. The Bishops of St. Asaph and Bangor and their successors were respectively to be entitled to the profits and advantages of the first rectory which should become void after June 24, 1714. To the Bishopric of Llandaff, the Treasurership, with the prebend belonging thereto, was to be annexed and united for ever; and to the Bishopric of St. Davids, the prebend of Llangammarch, with all its profits and benefits, passed as compensation.

A.D. 1534.—In 1534, an Act (26 HENRY 8, c. 4) was passed designed to prevent the undue resort to "jurors in WALES, by the friends and kinsmen of offenders on trial for felonies and murders whereby the jurors were openly and notoriously suborned to acquit the accused." It was therein enacted that a bailiff should be sworn for the true and diligent keeping of the said jurors; and that he, under the Justiciar's direction, "should not give the jurors any bread, drink or meat, fire or light, and should not suffer them to speak

[1] Froude's "History of England," vol. i. p. 244.

to any person nor speak to them himself, except to demand of them their verdict." If the juries gave an untrue acquittal, "contrary to good and pregnant evidence," upon notice or complaint to the Lord President and others of the Council of the Marches, the jurors might be bound over, together with the Justiciar, Steward or other officer, before whom such untrue verdict was given, to appear and be examined before the Lord President and Council of the Marches as to whether they had so misbehaved, and if this were proved, the jurors were liable to fine and imprisonment.

In the same year, a measure (26 HENRY 8, c. 5) was passed to prevent the escape of felons from Gloucestershire and Somersetshire "over the water of Severn" into SOUTH WALES. The keepers of ferries over the Severn were forbidden to convey in their boats any manner of persons, goods, or chattels between sunset and sunrise, excepting passengers whom they knew and could answer for.

The next Act of 1534 (26 HENRY 8, c. 6) describes the turbulent state of the WELSH people, still full of discontent at the presence of the English garrison. Its preamble recites that the "people of WALES and the Marches of the same not dreading the good and wholesome statutes and laws of this realm, have of long time continued and persevered in the perpetration and commission of divers thefts, murders, rebellions, wilful burning of houses, and other scelerous deeds, to the high displeasure of God, disquiet of the King's well disposed subjects, and disturbing of the public weal, which deeds were so rooted and fixed in the same people, that they were not likely to cease unless some sharp correction and punishment was provided." All persons, when duly summoned, were to appear at the Sessions courts or the courts of the Marches. On account of the unlawful exactions by the officers in the Lordships Marchers in WALES, where they had rule and authority, and on account of their wrongful committals to prison of the King's subjects, the King's Commissioners or Council of the Marches were empowered to send for the said officers, and the persons whom they had illegally imprisoned. If the illegal imprisonment were proved, then the Commissioners had power to order the said officer to pay to the injured parties the sum of not less than 6s. 8d. for every day of the wrongful detention besides a fine to the King's use. No weapons were to be brought into any court holden in WALES or the Lordships Marchers, or to any place within a distance of two miles from the same courts, nor to any town, fair, church or other assembly (except upon a "hue and outcry" made of any felony or robbery), nor into the highways, except by the command and assent of the Justices or other officers. No persons, without leave of the said Commissioners, were to make collections or exactions of goods or money under colour of marrying their children, saying or singing their first masses or gospels of any priests, or for the redemption of murders or felonies or for any other cause. No games of running, wrestling, or leaping were allowed; the game of shooting with the bow only was permissible. The punishment prescribed was one year's imprisonment and fine. The Courts were to be held in the most peaceable places, and any person casting anything into any Court was punished by imprisonment "any custom before this time to the contrary notwithstanding." (This referred to the ancient custom of casting "*arthel.*" Exiles who to avoid punishment, fled from the jurisdiction where they had committed a crime and placed themselves under the protection of the Lord of the commote, who undertook to defend them, were called *gwyr arddelw* (men of avowal), *arthelmen*, or *advocarii.*) Felonies committed within the WELSH Marches were made triable in the adjoining English county, and an acquittal in the courts of the Lordships Marchers was to be no bar against indictment in the ordinary courts within two years after the commission of the offence. The Justices in England could issue process into the Marches against offenders, and were to certify outlawries and attainders to the officers of the Marches, who were to convey the offenders into England. The liberties, laws, and privileges of the Lords Marchers were to be preserved. Offences committed in Merionethshire were to be tried before the King's Justices of NORTH WALES in Carnarvonshire and Anglesey (repealed in 1566); and the officers of all the Lordships Marchers were required to assist in securing culprits who escaped from one Lordship to another. The Lords Marchers had pretended to use a custom and privilege that none of the King's ministers and subjects could enter to pursue and apprehend such offenders.

A later Act of 1534 (26 HENRY 8, c. 11) punished WELSHMEN attempting any assaults or affrays upon the inhabitants of Herefordshire, Gloucestershire, and Shropshire. The inhabitants of these counties had been beaten, maimed, grievously wounded, and sometimes murdered for attempting to pursue felons into WALES or the Marches, so a penalty was imposed of one year's imprisonment over and above the punishment inflicted in the ordinary course of law.

The last WELSH Act of 1534 (26 HENRY 8, c. 12) was "An Act for purgation of convicts in WALES" ordering that WELSH clerks convicted of petty treason, murder and other offences were to give surety before two Justices of the county where the ordinary's prison was situated, or else of the adjoining county. By a previous Act (23 HENRY 8, c. 1) the ancient privilege of "benefit of clergy" had been taken away in England from criminals and clerks convict, who were thereafter required to provide sureties for good behaviour before two Justices of the Peace. Inasmuch as there were no Justices of the Peace of the *quorum* at this time in WALES, clerks in holy orders who were convicted were required to give such sureties in WALES before two Justices of the Shire.

By the several statutes of 1534, the King aimed at removing the trials of serious crimes from the jurisdictions of the Lordships Marchers. These Acts paved the way to a more thorough organization. "Over and above the unwillingness of juries to convict, the chief source of disorder lay in the regalities of the Lord Marchers. Here were a number of little kingdoms to which criminals could resort without fear of punishment or extradition, where, if fines were levied, they were levied for private profit, and not in open court, and where magnates like Lord Worcester or Lord Ferrers derived a revenue out of "the manifold selling of thieves." In the lordship of Magor there were living in those times five malefactors guilty of wilful murder, eighteen guilty of homicide, and twenty thieves and outlaws. Such a situation was clearly intolerable, and HENRY'S government determined to put an end to it by converting the lordships into shire ground." [1]

A.D. 1535.—An Act of 1535 (27 HENRY 8, c. 5) provided for the appointment, under the Great Seal, of Justices of the peace, Justices of the *quorum*, and Justices of gaol delivery for certain counties in WALES. These Justices were to have and exercise the same powers as similar Justices had and exercised in England; and they were to administer the criminal laws observed in the English counties, in order to put an end to the offences committed in the WELSH counties. The various Sheriffs and other peace officers of the King were obliged to attend upon the said Justices for the purpose of executing their precepts and processes, as was done in the English shires. The Justices of the peace and the Clerks of the peace were to be entitled to the same fees and allowance as in England. The receipts of the several counties and the Sheriffs' accounts were to be made at the King's Exchequers at Carnarvon, Caermarthen, Pembroke, and Cardiff, as was done by English officials at the King's Exchequer in Westminster. Another statute of the same year (27 HENRY 8, c. 7) abolished certain unlawful and unreasonable customs then existing "contrary both to the

[1] "Pol. Hist. of England," vol. v. p. 377.

Law of God and man" in some of the forests of WALES, where payments had been exacted from those travellers who passed through, unless they carried "tokens" or were "yearly tributors or chensers." Travellers found or espied twenty-four feet out of the highway lost a joint of their hands and all their money, and were also liable to a fine to the foresters. Beasts straying were accustomed to be captured, confiscated and marked with the forest mark, and to repossess themselves the owners thereof had to buy them back. All the King's subjects were thenceforth to be permitted to pass through the forests without paying toll, and stray cattle were to be restored to their owners upon repayment for their keep when detained. The abuses of these WELSH forest customs have their parallel in the forest laws and customs of the early Norman Kings.

The "Statute of Uses" (27 HENRY 8, c. 10) was an important measure of reform, enacted in 1535. On two previous occasions the passing of this statute had been defeated in Parliament. According to the common law of England, land was not subject to testamentary disposition, but descended according to the ordinary feudal rules. A custom had grown up of leaving estates in "use" or upon trust, and the Court of Chancery in England recognised that the *cestui qui use* possessed an equitable estate in land devised for his benefit. The liberty of testators had thus developed, depriving the over-lords of many of the privileges incident to the feudal system. The passing of this measure was not favoured by the gentry, but it was procured by ingeniously setting forth the embarrassing evils arising from these fictitious conveyances. It was therefore declared that persons entitled to the use of lands were to be to all intents and purposes the lawful possessors, and consequently to be liable to all the incidents of feudal tenure, just as if the lands had been made over to them by formal grant or conveyance. The 16th section provided that the Act was not to be prejudicial to any persons born in WALES or its Marches, and that they should hold any lands, &c., according to the tenor and under the authority of the same.

In the same year, in order to prevent the exportation of leather, an Act (27 HENRY 8, c. 14) was passed forbidding tanners to export hides or leather, but by section 7 of the Act, untanned hides of beasts killed within WALES and its Marches were allowed to be sold and exported by any persons "except only by tanners and such as had tan houses." This was part of the paternal legislation frequently indulged in by the early Tudor Parliaments.

A later Statute (27 HENRY 8, c. 24) of the same year shows that HENRY secured all the executive and judicial power in the realm of England, WALES and the Marches, by uniting all authority under the "Imperial Crown of this Realm." He alone was to be Lord and Ruler. It was part of the plan for rendering the process of law more effectual by placing every judicature in the Kingdom in his hands.

The first of the important measures of HENRY the 8th, by which WALES was, in 1535, admitted into the English polity, is entitled "An Act for Laws and Justice to be administered in WALES in like form as it is in this Realm" (27 HENRY 8, c. 26).

Its preamble recites, in the imposing style of Tudor English, that the "Dominion, Principality and Country of WALES" was and ever had been incorporated, annexed, united, and subject to the "Imperial Crown of this Realm as a very member and joint of the same, whereof the King's most Royal Majesty of very right, is very Head *King* Lord and Ruler," yet because in that same Country Principality and Dominion divers rights, usages, laws and customs were far discrepant from the laws and customs of England, and also because that the "people of the same Dominion have and do daily use a speech nothing like nor consonant to the natural mother tongue used in England, *some rude and ignorant people* have made distinction and diversity between the King's subjects of this Realm, and his subjects of the said Dominion and Principality of WALES, whereby great discord, division and sedition had grown between his said subjects." In order to extirp all the "sinister usages and customs" and to bring the subjects of his Realm and of his said Dominion of WALES to an amicable concord and unity, it was ordained that WALES should be incorporated with England, and that "all persons born, or to be born" in WALES should have all the liberties, rights, privileges, and laws which were enjoyed in England. It is in this preamble that the first instance is to be found where the Sovereign of England is unequivocally styled "King" of WALES.

By section 2, the WELSH laws of inheritance appertaining to the descent of manors, lands, and other hereditaments were abolished, and the laws of inheritance and other laws of England were to be used and executed in WALES in lieu thereof, but it was also provided by the 35th section of this Act that "lands, tenements, and hereditaments lying in WALES," which have "been used time out of mind by the laudable customs of the said country should be departible among issues and heirs male as if this Act had never been had nor made." These two sections seem inconsistent. The intention evidently was that persons who relied upon any right under the ancient WELSH system of tenure were called upon to prove that it existed before the time of legal memory. The apparent variance was, however, remedied by the complete abolition of WELSH customs and rules of descent in 1542 (34-35 HENRY 8, c. 26, s. 91); although the WELSH system of gavelkind still prevails in respect of customary lands in some manors of the Vale of Glamorgan, the manor of Talley in Caermarthenshire, Bishopston in Gower, and Liswerry and Pencarn in Monmouthshire.

The disorderly and turbulent Lordships Marchers within the Dominion of WALES, lying between the shires of England and the existing WELSH shires were dealt with by uniting some to English counties, and leaving the others to WALES. The lordships apportioned to WALES were formed into five new counties : viz., the shires of

(1) BRECKNOCK, including 16 specified lordships, townships, &c.

(2) RADNOR, including 16 specified lordships, townships, &c.

(3) MONTGOMERY, including 12 specified lordships, townships, &c.

(4) DENBIGH, including 10 specified lordships, townships, &c.

(5) MONMOUTH, which included 24 specified lordships, townships, &c. (This county was specially annexed to England, and excluded from the WELSH system of administrative justice.)

The following old WELSH counties were enlarged by the addition of various lordships, viz.:—

Glamorgan received nine, Pembroke twelve, Cardigan three, and Merioneth one; and other lordships were annexed to three of the English border counties.

The boundaries of the new WELSH counties were expressly defined, and their head or shire towns selected. The shire court of Brecknockshire was to be holden at Brecknock; that of Radnorshire, at New Radnor alternately with Rothergowy (Rhaiadr Gwy), or Rhayader, subsequently altered to Presteign by s. 118 of 34-35 HENRY 8, c. 20, 1542; that of Montgomery, alternately at Machynlleth and Montgomery; that of Denbighshire, alternately at Denbigh and Wrexham. In Monmouthshire, Monmouth was selected as the head town, the shire court to be there and at Newport alternately, and all actions in Monmouthshire were to be heard and determined as in an English shire. The position of Monmouthshire is somewhat anomalous. Technically it has been an English county since this Act, but it is often for administrative purposes, and sometimes by legislation, treated as part of WALES, or grouped with some of the WELSH counties. A large proportion of its inhabitants are WELSH in origin, in language, and habits, and the industrial development of the county has been closely allied to that of its adjoining shire, the county of Glamorgan.[1]

It was declared, by section 9 of this Act, that as the new WELSH counties were far distant from London, and because their inhabitants were "not of substance power and ability to travel out of their country to seek the administration of justice" the King was to have his Chancery and Exchequer at the Castles of Brecknock and Denbigh. The sheriffs and shire officials were ordered to render yearly accounts to a Baron of the Exchequer appointed for the purpose.

In the new shires a separate judicial system was instituted. Justice was to be administered according to the laws of England, and according also to such other customs and laws used in WALES as the King in Council should allow and think expedient, requisite, and necessary, and after such form and fashion as justice was used and ministered within the three ancient shires of NORTH WALES. The WELSH language was abolished in all the courts. All proceedings were to be carried on in the English tongue; no person using the WELSH speech was to enjoy or hold any office within the English realm, WALES, or the King's Dominions unless "he used and exercised the English speech or language."

By this measure the right of parliamentary representation was conferred upon WALES. One knight was to be chosen and elected to the sitting and future Parliaments for each of the shires of WALES. For every borough being a shire town (excepting Merioneth) one Burgess was to be likewise chosen.

[1] See "The Welsh People," by Brynmor Jones and Rhys, p. 16.

Two knights of the shire were to be elected for the county of Monmouth, and one Burgess for the borough of Monmouth. Fees to these representatives—"such fees as other knights of the Parliament" had—were to be levied and paid.

On only two occasions before the passing of this Act is there any record of WALES being represented in the English Parliament. The first was in 1322, when twenty-four members were summoned as representatives from SOUTH WALES and the same number from NORTH WALES to appear in the famous Parliament of York which enunciated the great constitutional principle that all legislative changes required the assent of the three estates of the Realm. The second occasion was in 1326–7, when forty-eight representatives appeared at Westminster in the Parliament which deposed EDWARD the Second.[1] From the passing of this Act of 1535 to the great Reform Act of 1832 there was no further change in the number of parliamentary representatives for WALES.

Every lay and temporal Lord Marcher, by the 14th and 30th sections of this Act, was to retain all his privileges and hold his accustomed courts. This was extended to ecclesiastical Lords in the reign of PHILIP and MARY (1–2 PHILIP and MARY, c. 15).

The "laudable customs" in vogue in the three ancient shires of NORTH WALES were saved, together with the liberties of the Duchy of Lancaster within WALES. It was expressly provided that the vested interests of persons who had enjoyed fees or offices should not be disturbed during their lives. It was also enacted that HENRY'S Act of 1534 (26 HENRY 8, c. 6), which dealt with the trial of murders and felonies committed within any Lordship Marcher in WALES, and provided for the trial of those offences in the next adjoining shire of England, was not to be affected in any manner.

That this Act of 1535 was only meant to be an instalment

[1] Lingard's "Hist. of England," iii. p. 328; Stubbs's "Const. Hist.," ii. pp. 382–392; Rymer, ii. $\frac{484}{840}$.

of legislation is shown by sections 26 and 27. Section 26 provided that after the prorogation or dissolution of that Parliament, the Lord Chancellor was to appoint a Commission to inquire into and view the shires of Carmarthen, Pembroke, Cardigan, Monmouth, Brecknock, Montgomery, Radnor, Glamorgan, and Denbigh, for the purpose of dividing them into hundreds, as in the English shires. There appears to be no record of this commission or its report. Rowland, in his *Mona Antiqua*, states that copies of the proceedings of these Commissioners were deposited in the office of the Chamberlain and Auditors of NORTH WALES, and that Sir William Gryffydd caused them to be translated by one Jenkin Gwyr, and that they were entitled "the extent of NORTH WALES," and section 3 of the later Act of 1542 also indicates that the Commission did its work. Section 27 provided also for a Commission to inquire and search out by all ways and means all the laws, usages, and customs used within the Dominion and Country of WALES, and to report to and advise the King in Council within a specified time, so that all such laws, if considered expedient and necessary, should be preserved and observed. No record of this Commission is to be found.

The great power of HENRY, with the subservience of his Parliament to his strong will and capacity, is exhibited by the 36th section. This enacted that his Majesty could suspend or revoke any part of this Statute at any time within the next three years, provided that the suspension or revocation was made under the Great Seal and proclaimed in every shire of WALES. His Majesty was also empowered to erect courts in WALES within five years after the end of the Parliament then sitting.

A.D. 1536.—In 1536, the King received parliamentary authority (28 HENRY 8, c. 3) to allot the townships of WALES at any time within the next three years, and to name and assign the shire towns. In the same year a statute (28 HENRY 8, c. 6) was passed continuing the Act of 1534 (26 HENRY 8, c. 11), against WELSHMEN making affrays in the Counties of Hereford, Gloucester, and Salop, until the last day of the next Parliament. It may be here observed that, so far as lawlessness was concerned, WALES did not stand alone at this period, for HENRY also had occasion to deal with rebellion and disorder in almost every part of his realm.

A.D. 1539.—In 1539 it was stated, that owing to more pressing business, the King had not had time to proceed with the allotment of townships in WALES, so an Act (31 HENRY 8, c. 11) extended this power for a further period of three years.

A.D. 1540.—The Act "for the Trial of Treasons in WALES" (32 HENRY 8, c. 4) provided that treasons committed where the original writs in Chancery "commonly runneth not" should be tried by the oaths of twelve men of the shire before the King's appointed Commissioners. Persons accused of treason or misprision of treason within the Principality and Dominion of WALES and the Marches of the same might be tried wheresoever the King should appoint, and by Commissioners of *oyer* and *terminer*, provided always that peers of the realm were to retain their ancient privilege of trial by their peers.

In the same year, by the Act (32 HENRY 8, c. 27) for the resumption at Calais, Berwick, and WALES, reciting that "whereas divers subjects of the King had by sinister and subtle means obtained divers grants and letters patents of offices within the King's Dominion of WALES, contrary to the common wealth of the country there: and also to the great disquieting vexation and trouble of the King's loving and obedient subjects," it was ordained that, from September 1, 1540, all such grants should be made void and of no effect.

Another Act of 1540 (32 HENRY 8, c. 37) enabled executors to recover and maintain actions for arrears of rent due to the testator: but, by section 2, it was not to apply to the manors or lordships or dominions in WALES or in the Marches whereof the inhabitants had been accustomed time out of mind to pay certain sums of money to every lord or owner of such lordship, manor, or dominion as duties on forfeiture.

A.D. 1541-2.—It was ordained by 32–33 HENRY 8, c. 3, that WELSH cloths made in NORTH WALES should be folded in pleats and cuttles as was done in other parts of the realm, so that buyers might plainly see the breadth and goodness of their purchases. This was done to prevent the complaints against the makers for having craftily rolled these cloths in such manner as to prevent the buyers ascertaining the making and measurement of the same. In the next year (by 34–35 HENRY 8, c. 11) we find another Act for the true making of WELSH frises and cottons in the towns of Caermarthenshire, Pembrokeshire, and Cardiganshire. This states that the manufacture in these towns had decayed and that "foreigners husbandmen and graziers" living in the country outside these towns were making their own wool into frises and cottons "after the most false and deceitful manner that may be." So to remedy this, it was ordered that the said frises and cottons should be of proper weight and measured as specified therein.

A.D. 1542.—The second great measure of HENRY the Eighth's reign affecting WALES became law in 1542. It established a new but independent system of law courts in WALES, a system of judicature which lasted for nearly three centuries, and in efficiency and simplicity was in advance of the technical and more complex legal system obtaining in England.

It is intituled "An Act for certain Ordinances in the King's Majesty's Dominions and Principality of WALES" (34–35 HENRY 8, c. 26), and its object was, as is stated therein, for the "good rule and order of the Dominion Principality and Country of WALES." It recites that it was passed at the humble suit and petition of the King's subjects in WALES, so that his said subjects "may grow and rise to more wealth and prosperity."

The Dominion, Principality, and Country of WALES was henceforth to be divided into twelve shires, eight of which were shires of long and ancient time, viz.:

Glamorgan.	Caermarthen.
Pembroke.	Cardigan.
Flint.	Caernarvon.
Anglesey.	Merioneth.

the remaining four being the new shires of

Brecknock.	Radnor.
Montgomery.	Denbigh.

which had been constructed and defined by the Act of 1535. These new counties, having been divided into hundreds as was provided for by legislation, the division was confirmed by this Act.

The new system of courts called the "King's Great Sessions in WALES" were to be held twice in every year. The twelve shires were divided into four circuits, each comprising three counties, presided over by one Justice, learned in the laws, to keep the Great Sessions. Later, in 1575, another Justice was added to each circuit (18 ELIZABETH, c. 8).

The circuits were—

Chester	Denbighshire Flintshire Montgomery	under the Justice of Chester.
Caernarvon	Caernarvonshire Merionethshire Anglesey	under the Justice of NORTH WALES.
Caermarthen	Caermarthenshire Pembrokeshire Cardiganshire	under the Justice of Caermarthen, &c.
Brecknock	Radnorshire Brecknockshire Glamorganshire	under the Justice of Radnor, &c.

The Justices, appointed under the Great Seal, were to hear all manner of pleas, actions, and criminal matters according to the laws, statutes, and customs of England. They were given the same powers as the King's Chief Justice and other Justices in the English Courts.

The Great Sessions were to be held for six days in every shire, of which fifteen days' notice was required to be given by proclamation.

Official seals were prescribed. All writs and processes were to be sealed. There are still extant seals which, within the Principality of WALES, were the chief emblems of sovereignty in WALES. This important and striking series of seals were known as the Royal Judicial Seals of the King's Great Sessions in WALES, and cover a period of three hundred years.[1] Stewards of manors were to continue to hold their courts, but were expressly forbidden to inquire into felonies. Officers of incorporated towns, according to their lawful grants and laudable customs, were to continue to hold pleas and to determine actions, provided that they followed the English laws and customs, and not WELSH laws, and provided also that in personal actions the issues joined should be tried by a jury of six men, as had been the custom in divers places in WALES. Power was granted to the King to dissolve boroughs which had their grants from the Lords Marchers, and in their place to erect others, and the King "was pleased and contented of his most gracious goodness" to allow existing officials to enjoy their ordinary fees for life. Regulations for judicial seals, fines, and fees were minutely set forth. For making process and entering process an official called a "prenotary" was appointed for each circuit. "The Prothonotary, or chiefe registrar, draweth all the pleadings, entreth and engrosseth the Records and Judgments in civill causes and ingrossing Fynes."[2] A marshal and crier were to attend upon the Justices, as in the English Courts. They were paid by fees, and upon the acquittal of a felon the marshal received fourpence and the crier a penny.

[1] See *Brit. Arch. Ass. Journal*, March, 1893.

[2] Doddridge, "Principality of Wales."

In addition to the Justices of Great Sessions the Lord Chancellor appointed eight Justices of the Peace and one "custos rotulorum" for each shire. This provision was extended in 1693 (5 W. & M., c. 4) by allowing the King to appoint as many Justices as he pleased. These Justices of the Peace met quarterly, and for urgent matters at other times. The President of the Council of WALES, the Justices of the Great Sessions, the King's Attorney and Solicitor were put in every commission of the peace. The Justices of the peace were qualified to sit "if of good name and fame, even if they did not dispend £20, and even if not learned in the law." They appointed two substantial gentlemen or yeomen, in each hundred, to be chief constables for the conservation of the peace. Sheriffs, the chief executive officers of the county, were to be nominated yearly according to English fashion by the President of the Council and Justices of WALES to the Privy Council, on the Morrow of All Souls (*crastino animarum*), altered later (by 24 GEORGE 2, c. 48) to the Morrow of St. Martin. The WELSH Sheriffs formerly had been elected for life, and, it is said, "sought more to enrich themselves by the office than to see justice administered." Sheriffs rendered accounts to the auditor for WALES, each sheriff having a yearly fee of £5. An escheator, who attended to the King's revenues and seized all escheated goods and forfeited lands, was appointed for every county. The sheriffs were to hold their monthly county courts and their hundred courts for pleas under forty shillings, as was the custom in England. In these courts, and also before Stewards in courts Baron, the trials were to be decided by the verdict of six men or by wager of law (the latter being a proceeding which consisted in a defendant discharging himself on his own oath, bringing with him at the same time eleven of his neighbours as compurgators to swear that they believed his denial to be true). The sheriff was to provide gaols and to continue to hold his "tourn" once after Easter, and once after Michaelmas. Fines were not to be inflicted in murder cases or felonies and no agreement between prosecutors and felons was to be made without the consent of the Justices of Great Sessions. No sale of stolen property in any fair or market was to prevent the true owner from seizing or recovering the same. The WELSH custom of tracking stolen property was recognized as legal, and the sale of any manner of beasts out of market was forbidden except upon credible testimony. By the 68th section two coroners were to be elected in and for every shire, as was done in England. The appointment was made by the freeholders of the shire, but since 1888 it has passed into the hands of the County Councils.

Errors of judgment before the Great Sessions in real actions or mixed actions (*i.e.*, actions partaking of the nature of both real and personal actions) were to be redressed by writ of error in the English Chancery; errors in personal actions were to be redressed before the President and Council of WALES, and urgent or weighty causes were to be directed into WALES by special command of the Lord Chancellor or the King's Council in England. There are many matters of minor importance dealt with in this Act, such as scales of fees and charges, tallages (taxes), aulnages (customs duties on cloths), regulations as to sealing of cloths and forbidding cloths made at home from being put to sale, subsidies and charges for knights of the shire, and retention of franchises and customs.

The town of Haverfordwest was made a county, with the right of returning one burgess to Parliament, and was placed under the jurisdiction of the King's High Justice of Pembrokeshire.

By this statute the WELSH system of land tenure and partition on death was finally abolished, and the 91st, 92nd, 93rd, 101st, and 128th sections are worthy of attention. The leading principle contained in these sections was that all lands in WALES were to be held subject to English tenure and not to be partible among heirs male after the custom of gavelkind, but should descend to the heirs according to the course of the common laws of the Realm of England. Lands were to be sold and mortgaged also according to English law.

As we have already noticed, the privileges of the Lords Marchers had been preserved by the 30th section of the Act of 1535. By the 101st section of the Act of 1542 the liberties, franchises, and customs of the Lordships Marchers were to be maintained according to the Statute of 1535 in those Lordships which had come into the hands of King HENRY the Eighth after the suppression of the monasteries and by purchase or attainder. The private rights and private property of the Lords Marchers were not to be affected. In 1849, in the case of the Duke of Beaufort *v.* Smith (19 *Law Journal* Reports, Exch., p. 97), it was held that s. 101 of 34-35 HENRY 8, c. 26, did not interfere with the private rights claimed by the Lords Marchers of WALES as lords of manors or owners of the land. This was a case where the Duke of Beaufort, as lord of the manor of Kilvey in the county of Glamorgan, claimed certain tolls. This manor is referred to in the Statute 27 HENRY 8, c. 26, s. 14 (1535), and its liberties and customs were saved by the 30th section of the same Statute. The defendant relied on the 101st section of the Act of 1542, alleging that the tolls claimed in 1849, being levied irrespective of any tenure, were taken away by that section; but in giving the decision of the Court Baron Rolfe held that the section was only intended to destroy the rights and privileges of the Lords Marchers as *quasi* conquerors, and did not refer to their private rights.

By the 102nd section peaceable possession by any persons for the space of five years of any lands or tenements in WALES was protected. The King's power is shown further in the 119th and 120th sections, which gave him power to make laws for WALES and to alter those existing at his pleasure. Such alterations and laws were to be of the same strength and effect as if they were made directly by authority of Parliament.

The Court of the President and Council in WALES and the Marches was for the first time formally established by the 4th section of this Statute. The history of this Court demands attention, for it played a most important part in the constitutional history of WALES.

The "Court of the Council in the Dominion and Principality of WALES and the Marches of the same" was one of the extraordinary Courts of the Tudor and Stuart periods. It was not altogether a new body created by this Statute, but a development of an institution, the "Prince's Council," which had existed ever since the time of the first English Prince of WALES for the purpose of administering his estates The Long Parliament partially abolished it; the Restoration revived it; and the Revolution of 1688 finally abolished it. By its organization an important step was taken towards the union of England and WALES, for the Principality and the Marches were for the first time united under one rule.

This Court was created for the purpose of establishing and maintaining order in the borderland which had been the scene of so much disturbance and misrule for years. The most turbulent districts within its jurisdiction were those which subsequently formed the counties of Radnor, Montgomery, and Denbigh. The following lordships are repeatedly mentioned as the haunts of criminals, viz.: Elvael, Arwystli, Kerry, Caedewen, and Cyfeiliog; and, according to Bishop Lee, Presteign was the place "where the thieves were thickest." The lordships of Chepstow and Gower in SOUTH WALES, the lordships of Oswestry and Powys, the shires of Merioneth and Cardigan were noted for their disorder, but the Marcher Lordships of Northern and Central WALES appear to have been the worst.

Up to the middle of the sixteenth century the main work of the Council consisted in punishing this lawlessness with which the Common Law Courts were powerless to deal. During the succeeding half century it acted both as a judicial and also as an administrative body—the instrument of the Privy Council in WALES and the Marches. During this period the dignity of the Council increased, and its organization became fixed; but the cases with which it dealt were less serious than in earlier years, and by the end of the sixteenth century its decline had commenced. In the seventeenth century it was mainly a Court for the settlement of petty suits, and the elaborate establishment which had descended from the days when Princes had kept Court at Ludlow seemed unnecessary.

The Council sat permanently at Ludlow, but met also occasionally at other places. It held Sessions at Hereford, Bewdley, Shrewsbury, Worcester, Gloucester, Tewkesbury, Hartlebury, Bridgnorth, Oswestry, and Wrexham. Bishop Lee, that "stowte travellinge president," went further afield in his duty, for he scoured WALES as well as the Marches in his search for criminals. Lee was President of the Council from 1534 to 1543. In company with Sir Thomas Englefield, the Chief Justice of Chester, he travelled through the country, studied its men and manners, discerned the secret roots of disorder, and set himself to pluck them out. The power of inflicting the death sentence was so lavishly exercised under his rule that it was said that within the space of six years over five thousand men were hanged. It was on his advice that the penal acts of 1534, which have already been noticed, were passed.[1] Another great President was Sir Henry Sydney (1559–1586), famous for his justice and mercy.

The area of the Council's jurisdiction was a debatable point, constituting the historical legal controversy of the seventeenth century, which, although in form concerned with the jurisdiction over the four English border counties, really raised the question of discretionary governments in general. In this, as in so many other cases, broad constitutional issues were argued on the narrowest legal grounds.

[1] See Hist. MSS. Commission, 1898; Report on Welsh MSS. i. p. 10; and "Political History of England," vol. v. p. 376.

The matter came to a head on November 3, 1608, when the Privy Council, with the Judges of England, met to decide whether JAMES the First could by his own prerogative, and the statute of 34 HENRY 8, c. 26, give power to the Lord President and Council of the Marches to exercise jurisdiction within these counties. The case was argued for six days. Coke led for those who denied the King's prerogative, and Bacon appeared for the President and Council. The Judges refused to decide the questions submitted to them, stating that if the matter came before them judicially, they would determine it to the best of their ability. It was during this controversy that Coke upheld the reputation of the English Bar for independence. There was great wrangling between him and King JAMES. The Judges were consequently given time to reconsider the matter. Their written opinion was given on February 3, 1609, but it was never published.

The point of greatest interest in the history of the Council is its relation to the central and local authorities. It was subordinate to the Privy Council and closely connected with the Star Chamber. It exercised a considerable measure of control over local Courts and local officials, especially over sheriffs and justices of the peace, and was thus a link between the central and the local government, facilitating thereby the working of the new institutions created for WALES by the legislation of HENRY the Eighth.

The Council of the Marches was also useful in carrying out the administrative work of the Privy Council. The administrative duties of the Lord President and his colleagues were extremely varied. Besides its military and economic functions, the Council was utilized for many other purposes. Proclamations were sent down to the Lord President for publication in WALES and the Border; he was expected to suppress false and seditious rumours, and to strengthen the hands of the Government in every possible way. Among the miscellaneous duties devolving upon him may be mentioned the collection of money for the repair of St. Paul's Cathedral; the supervision of certain royal forests, the removal of weirs and stakings in the Severn, and the arrangements for an Eisteddfod. Just as the Privy Council deliberated on all affairs of State, so in his narrower sphere the Lord President of WALES was responsible for the good administration of the counties within his jurisdiction. Perhaps his position cannot better be summed up than in a letter to the Earl of Bridgewater from the Vice-Admiral of NORTH WALES. "Nothing within this yr jurisdiction of WALES cann be strange to your Lordship, for that your Lordship is the true Center wher all other lines meete, and what is within the knowledge of any man of qualitie and understanding will be sure to finde a way under you."

In their decline, as during the period of their activity, the Court of Star Chamber and the Council of the Marches were closely linked. Much of the unpopularity of the latter body arose from its resemblance to the Star Chamber which in the England of the seventeenth century was a hated instrument of the royal prerogative. In the many articles of complaint against the Court of the Marches its resemblance to the Star Chamber is nearly always mentioned, and it is not surprising that both Courts were overthrown together.

The Council of the Marches also supervised the working of the Courts of Great Sessions. Thus in 1573 they were ordered by the Privy Council to see that there were two justices attending in person on each circuit at the Great Sessions to try the criminal cases before civil causes were disposed of.

The best description of the working of the Great Sessions and their relations to the Council of the Marches in the sixteenth century is given in George Owen's Dialogue on the Government of WALES. He points out the inconvenience of holding the Great Sessions in Lent when oats are being sown, and in August and September during the corn harvest. He adds that the Justices do not give enough time in hearing equity cases, and that many suitors are compelled to come before the Council of the Marches, which gives judgment more speedily and at less expense. Appeals in personal actions lay from the Courts of Great Sessions to the Council. Instances of the conflict of jurisdiction between the two bodies were not common, although there were many complaints in general terms of persons being drawn from remote parts of WALES to attend the Council. But it is obvious that sessions held twice a year in each circuit for six days at a time were inadequate to deal with the mass of legal business arising out of the rapid economic changes which were taking place in WALES.

The Council also exercised authority over the courts of the various boroughs within its jurisdiction. The sheriffs in WALES were bound to execute all lawful commands of the Lord President and Council. Several letters referring to the nomination of sheriffs are extant in the Welsh Shrievalty Papers (Bundle 6) among the Bridgewater MSS. Some of these are lists of leading gentry, with notes as to their fitness for office, *e.g.*, "John Vaughan of Glan y Llyn, Esq., very fitt for estate, not for his discretion, but his wife discreete."

From George Owen's Dialogue we gather that supervision of the WELSH sheriffs was highly necessary, owing to their practice of erecting new Hundred Courts for purposes of extortion. The Council, he says, had grievously fined sheriffs for keeping such courts, and in Brecknockshire the practice had been stopped.

A close connection may be traced between the Council of the Marches and the characteristic local official of Tudor times, the Justice of the Peace. WELSH Justices of the Peace were appointed by the Chancellor of England on the advice of the President, Council, and Justice of WALES. The Lord President was expected to choose suitable persons, and to keep them up to their work. He and the chief members of his Council were usually on the Commissions of the Peace for WALES and the Border Counties.

The Lord President was, usually, Lord-Lieutenant of the Counties of WALES and the Border Counties. In this capacity he performed military duties. In the seventeenth century, especially after the Restoration, his duties were merely those of a modern Lord-Lieutenant on an extensive scale.

In 1640, the fifth Parliament of CHARLES the First (the Long Parliament) was elected. Oliver Cromwell, a Welshman by descent, was one of its members. By this victorious Parliament a sweeping measure of constitutional reforms was carried out. The principal supports of the government of the Stuart kings were attacked and destroyed. The Star Chamber and its kindred institutions, viz., the Court of High Commissions, the Council of the North, and the Council of the Marches were the first dealt with. They had all degenerated into submissive instruments of the royal prerogative and the Stuart pretensions to absolute power. A special committee was appointed to consider their extraordinary jurisdiction. The knights and burgesses of the Counties of WALES and of the four adjoining English shires, the Marches of WALES, together with all the lawyers in the House of Commons, formed part of this committee. With a promptitude and decision not generally found in modern parliamentary commissions relating to WALES, this committee resolved that—

"(1) The jurisdiction of the Courte of the President and Counsell of the Marches of WALES as it is now exercised is a grievance of the subjects of those partes."

"(2) That the Courte of ye President and Counsell of the Marches of WALES is useless to the subjects of the 13 Countyes and fitt to be taken away by bill."

Following this report the Act, 16 CHARLES I, c. 10, involving the suppression of the Star Chamber and the

Court of the President and Council in the Marches of WALES, received the royal assent.

The civil work of the Court of the Marches did not however cease; it continued until the outbreak of the rebellion, and was resumed at the Restoration in 1660. It was finally abolished by 1 WILLIAM and MARY, c. 27 (1688). The grounds of suppression in that year were summarized as follows:—

(1) That the Court had been found by experience an intolerable burthen to the subject, contrary to the Great Charter, the known laws of the land and the birthright of the subject, and the means of introducing an arbitrary power and government.

(2) That matters determinable there may be redressed in the ordinary course of justice within the shires of the Principality.

The Courts of Great Sessions occupied the place of the Court of the Marches in civil and criminal matters arising in WALES until their abolition in the nineteenth century.

Between the Court of the Council of the Marches and the Common Law Courts at Westminster there was always a deep-seated jealousy, derived from professional dislike and an objection by lawyers to special jurisdictions. The arbitrary and extortionate fines of the Court of the Council of the Marches; its encroachment on the Common Law Courts; its failure to adhere to the duties imposed upon it; and its punishment of offences which had been already dealt with by the Ecclesiastical Courts, hastened its end. Before the close of the seventeenth century it had become also the willing servant of the royal will and prerogative, and, when confronted with the growing political strength of the people, its fall was inevitable.

In George Owen's Dialogue we find, however, that like many another institution which has degenerated, it contained some good features. It was, he says, "the very place of refuge for the poore oppressed of this country of WALES to flie unto. And for this cause it is as greatly frequented with sutes as any one Court at Westminster whatsoever, the more for that it is the best cheape Court in England for ffees and there is great speed made in trial of all causes."

The Council lived too long. If it had ended with the sixteenth century its record would probably have been higher. Its work had been done long before 1641. WALES had ceased then to be lawless and turbulent, and the ordinary courts of the land would have been sufficient for the maintenance of order and the settlement of disputes.

A full and accurate account of the history of this Council is to be found in the remarkably interesting and learned thesis written by Miss Caroline A. J. Skeel, D.Lit., F.R.Hist.S.

A.D. 1543.—The final legislation relating to WALES in the reign of HENRY the Eighth occurred in 1543. It was (35 HENRY 8, c. 11) an "Act for the due payment of the fees and wages" of members of Parliament. Every knight of the shire was to receive four shillings per day for his attendance in Parliament, and for so many days as were reasonably spent in going to and returning from Parliament. Every citizen burgess (borough member) was to receive two shillings per day. The sheriffs of the counties of WALES and Monmouthshire were to have full power to levy and collect the same, and were liable to a fine of £20 if they did not accomplish their duties within two months. The principal officers of the boroughs were also deputed to perform similar duties in providing for the payment of their local parliamentary representatives. The burgesses were, under this Act, to have a voice in the election of their members. The assessment for these payments was to be made by two Justices of the peace.

This Act was rendered necessary because the fees payable under the Act of 1535 had been negligently levied. It remained in force until its repeal by the Statute Law Revision Act, 1856, but the rights under the Act of 1535 were not repealed until the Statute Law Revision Act of 1887.

The ancient right of English members of the House of Commons to receive "wages," though it has long fallen into desuetude, was not created by any statute, neither has it ever been repealed by statute. It was a right to receive 4s. a day, if a knight of the county, and 2s. a day if a citizen or burgess, "and so it hath been time out of mind, which is particularly expressed in many records." It is worthy of note that the Acts of Union relating to Scotland and Ireland do not contain any reference to or provision for the payment of members of Parliament.

Upon reviewing the main features of the Acts of Parliament bringing about the legal union of the Dominion of WALES with England, it will be useful to summarize briefly the most important points which appear in this period of transition from mediæval to modern times.

The policy of the Tudor monarchy—a WELSH dynasty—in ruling WALES was that of establishing, so far as laws could establish it, a complete equality between the two nations; in delegating local government and administration to the people of WALES themselves; in introducing the whole system of English local government by permanently setting up the shire system; in uniting WALES with England by means of wise and far-seeing legislation; in paying deference to the national characteristics and aspirations of the WELSH people; in breaking up the Lord Marcherships; in removing the oppressive rule of the English officials, and in putting an end to the policy of coercive and repressive government.

In giving to WALES a separate judicature peculiar to the Dominion, although it was a system mainly administered by English lawyers and English-speaking judges, justice was brought within the reach of WELSH litigants. The Courts of Great Sessions became, in a sense, a national institution.

The admittance of WALES to parliamentary representation; the distribution of offices and honours to the WELSH nobility and gentry; and the gradual restoration of local government in lieu of the tyrannical rule of strange lords, led to and resulted in a better understanding between the two nations.

Even the rigorous proscription of the Welsh language by HENRY the Eighth did not last long, for within twenty years a great change came over Parliament and the government of the country, which is evidenced by the statute passed in 1562 during the reign of ELIZABETH for the translation of the Bible and the Divine services into the WELSH language. In this recognition of the Cymric tongue there was contained the seed of a great movement which had far-reaching results.

The historical consequences of the introduction of English land laws, entailing the abolition of the system of WELSH land tenures, were important. WELSH tribal customs and tenure were ousted by a long and difficult process. Not even the vigour of Tudor administration could by statutory process alter the ancient national conditions. The result has generally been that the smaller holdings of the WELSH yeomen have gradually disappeared and following the legislation of HENRY the Eighth the modern landlord system, with its great estates, has been developed.

After the time of HENRY the Eighth WALES made rapid progress. There was a strong national revival. Professor Tout, in "Wales under the Tudors," says, that "Schools were set up; a WELSH college founded at Oxford; WELSH grammars, dictionaries, histories were written; many WELSHMEN rose to eminence in the service of their Church, both in WALES and England. Agriculture prospered now peace was secure and markets accessible. As Churchyard, the WELSH poet, sang in describing the Worthiness of WALES:—

> "Markets are good, and victuals nothing dear,
> Each place is filled with plenty all the year;
> The ground manured, the grain doth so increase
> That thousands live in wealth and blessed peace."

"The coal mines of Flintshire and Glamorganshire were developed. The Society for the Mines Royal, set up in 1567, opened up the lead mines of Cardiganshire. The extinction of piracy made the coasts safe for trade. Many WELSHMEN emigrated into England and won good positions in camp, court, and mart. Everywhere the policy of the WELSH line of English Kings had proved abundantly successful." [1]

Although the modern physical boundary of WALES was and is arbitrary, although it coincides neither with race, language, nor physical configuration, yet it was clearly defined by the Tudor legislation, and the fierce, debatable border-land, the scene of so much suffering and ruin, has since that period ceased to be the fruitful cause of national enmity.

A.D. 1547.—In the first year of the reign of EDWARD the Sixth (1 EDWARD 6, c. 10) a technical measure, designed to complete the efficiency of the judicial procedure in WALES, became law.

A *writ of exigent* was a writ issued by the King's Justices commanding the sheriff to summon a defendant to appear and deliver himself up upon pain of outlawry. Outlawry meant putting a person out of the law for contempt in wilfully avoiding the execution of the process of the King's Court. Although now abolished in civil proceedings, it is formally kept alive in criminal procedure by the Forfeiture Act, 1870 (33–34 VICT., c. 23). But in the old English laws relating to crime and wrong, it was the law's ultimate weapon, involving not merely escheat and forfeiture, but a sentence of death. Later it was extended to civil procedure, with lessened penalties. Ample opportunity was given to a defendant for appearing before he was treated as contumacious, and the sheriff demanded his appearance from county court to county court. The King's Justices could order a *writ of exigent* to issue, and thereupon a proclamation was made bidding the defendant come in to the King's peace, and in case of non-appearance, ordering that he should be outlawed, but no man could be outlawed until his appearance had been so demanded in five successive county courts.

[1] "Wales under the Tudors," by Professor Tout, p. 510.

Before the Act of 1535 founding the several shires of WALES, the King's writ did not run in WALES, and by an Act of 1514 (6 HENRY 8, c. 4) proclamations awarded upon *writs of exigent* could not be directed into WALES, but only to the sheriff of the county next adjoining. By this Act of 1547, such writs and proclamations were to be issued by the King's Justices at Westminster against any persons dwelling in the Dominion and Principality of WALES, and to carry out its provisions the sheriffs for the counties of WALES and Chester were to have deputies in the Courts at Westminster to receive all writs, so that persons resident in WALES were to be outlawed in the same manner as in England.

A.D. 1548.—It appears from a clause in an Act passed in 1548 (2-3 EDWARD 6, c. 13, s. 16) that the tithe question was one which even at that time commanded the notice of Parliament. A custom then existed in many parts of WALES that "the parsons and curates in those parts" levied tithes on "such cattle and goods as hath been given with the marriage of any person." This custom was expressly declared by Parliament to be "grievous and unreasonable especially where the benefices are else sufficient for the finding of the said ministers and curates." Tithes on marriage goods were therefore abolished, notwithstanding the existence of any such custom. No compensation for vested interests was furnished by this Act.

A.D. 1554.—In this year was passed an Act touching the sea sands of Glamorganshire. In order to prevent the damage caused in that county owing to sand being driven by the "outrageous course and rage of the sea" to land by storms and winds, authority was given to Commissioners of Sewers to take steps to save the good ground lying on the sea coasts from hurt and destruction. Leland, in his Itinerary of WALES, which he made in 1536-1539, describes the sea coast referred to in the following terms: "From Newton to Kenfike Ryver a 6 miles. Of these 6 miles 3 be high cliffes on the shore; the other low shore and sandy grounde. For the rages of Severn Se castith ther up much sand. From Kenfik to Aber-Avon a 2 miles by low shore, parte morisch and sandy with the rages of Severn."

In the same year (by 1–2 PHILIP and MARY, c. 15) the privileges of the Lords Marchers temporal were extended to spiritual Lords Marchers, whose interests had been forgotten in the previous Act of 1535.

A.D. 1557.—During the same reign an Act (4–5 PHILIP and MARY, c. 2) came into operation "for the having of horse armour and weapons in WALES." This was intended for the better defence of the realm, but in the 18th section a proviso was inserted whereby the Act was not to extend to persons dwelling within the counties of NORTH WALES and SOUTH WALES. These were required only to find one long-bow and one sheaf of arrows, over and besides such other armour as it was the custom to provide. This Statute repealed all other Acts respecting the keeping of armour and horses, and shows the quantity and kind of armour and weapons that were to be furnished and kept, at that time, by persons of different estates. It is possible to ascertain from its terms the proportion of the several kinds of troops maintained then for national defence. The military authorities of that period were not very solicitous to introduce the general use of firearms into the country, for they considered the WELSH long-bow equal in efficiency to the small firearm or arquebus (known also and referred to in this Act as the Haquebut or Hachbutt).[1] The skill and reputation of the WELSH archer with his long-bow had been firmly established for centuries. Giraldus Cambrensis describes the bows in his time as made of wild elm, unpolished, rude, and uncouth, not only calculated to shoot an arrow to a great distance, but also to inflict very severe wounds in close fight. The bow-armed WELSH from Gwent and Morganwg were the allies of EDWARD the First. HENRY the Seventh in 1508 by statute forbad the use of the cross-bow, in order to induce the more frequent practice of

[1] Meyrick's "Ancient Armour," vol. iii. p. 21.

archery. HENRY the Eighth encouraged and practised the use of the long-bow. It is uncertain when the long-bow of the WELSH ceased to be carried into battle, but it was not used after the early part of the seventeenth century.

A.D. 1558.—The ancient customs and liberties of the inhabitants of Anglesey, Flint and Carnarvon as to landing foreign merchandise and the payment of customs were preserved to them by 1 ELIZABETH, c. 11, s. 11.

A.D. 1562.—In 1562, by the 31st section of 5 ELIZABETH, c. 5, it was provided that the wines of France could be brought into the ports of Cardiff, Newport, Carnarvon, Beaumaris, and other ports in WALES in limited quantities. By the 6th section of 5 ELIZABETH, c. 23, passed in the same session for correcting the laxity that had crept into the practice in the ecclesiastical courts with reference to the process of excommunication, we find that *Writs de excommunicato capiendo* in WALES, where the Queen's writ did not then run, were directed to be sent to the Chief Justice or Justices there, and were not to be returnable to the Queen's Bench in England. In the same year an Act (5 ELIZABETH, c. 25) extended a previous measure made in 1542 as to the summoning of jurors. The latter was a "wholesome and profitable statute" concerning the appearance of Juries in Nisi Prius, which did not apply to the twelve shires of WALES in certain cases. It was deemed necessary to remedy the procedure in the Courts of Great Sessions of the Principality in this respect. In civil and criminal trials in the latter courts, where, by reason of the default of the jury or of challenges to the jury, there was not a sufficient number of the jurors empanelled to try the issues, the Judge was to direct the sheriff to add to the jury panel the names of a sufficient number of persons qualified to act as jurymen who might be present or could be found. These jurors were called *tales de circumstantibus.*

But the Act for the translation of the Bible and the Divine Service into the WELSH tongue (5 ELIZABETH, c. 28) was the most interesting and important result of the legislation of 1562 relating to WALES. It commences by stating that "the Queen, like a most godly and most virtuous Princess, having chief respect and regard to the honour and glory of God, and the soul's health of her good subjects," had, in the first year of her reign, ordered a Book of Common Prayer to be used throughout her Realm of England, WALES, and the Marches of the same, "that thereby Her Highness's most loving subjects, understanding in their own language the terrible and fearful threatenings rehearsed in the Book of God against the wicked and malefactors; the pleasant and infallible promises made to the elect and chosen flock; with a just order to rule and guide their lives according to the commandment of God might much better learn to love and fear God, to serve and obey their Prince and to know their duties towards their neighbours, which Book, being received as a most precious jewel, with an unspeakable joy of all such her subjects as did and do understand the English tongue, *the which tongue is not understanded of the most and greatest Number of all her Majesty's most loving and obedient subjects inhabiting this Her Highness's Dominion and Country of WALES—being no small part of this Realm:* who therefore are utterly destitute of God's Holy Word, and do remain in the like or rather more darkness and ignorance than they were in the time of Papistry." The evil condition of WALES in matters of religion at this period is described by Strype in his Life of Archbishop Parker, and is confirmed by this preamble.

The Bishops of Hereford, St. Davids, St. Asaph, Bangor, and Llandaff and their successors were therefore required to take order amongst themselves for the soul's health of the flocks committed to their charge within WALES, and were commanded to see that the whole Bible should be translated into the British or WELSH tongue.

The whole Divine Service was to be used and said in the British or WELSH tongue. The parishioners were to pay one-half of the cost of the books and the vicar or parson the remaining half. If the bishops or their successors neglected to carry out these provisions each one was to be fined £40, to be levied on their goods and chattels.

By the 2nd section of this Act (which section was repealed in 1863) it was also provided that the services were to be said in the WELSH tongue until the Bible was translated; and once every week at least the Articles of the Christian faith, the Ten Commandments, and the Litany, with such other part of the Common Prayer as was appointed, were to be read in the WELSH tongue.

The Bible and the Prayer Book in the English language were also to be bought and placed in every church throughout WALES, to remain in convenient places within the said churches, "that such as understand them may resort at all convenient times to read and peruse the same, and also such as do not understand the said language may, by comparing both tongues together the sooner attain to the knowledge of the English tongue."

The Reformation in England had not deeply affected WALES. The majority of the WELSH-speaking people had accepted the Tudor policy affecting the Church with equanimity. They continued in their old beliefs just as if no Parliamentary measures relating to ecclesiastical affairs had been passed. They returned under MARY without difficulty to their old faith, and under ELIZABETH Protestantism again secured their qualified approval. It was during the reign of "Good Queen Bess," owing to the efforts of able, zealous WELSHMEN, and the Act with which we are now dealing, that the real Reformation in WALES began. In 1567, the first WELSH New Testament and the WELSH version of the Prayer Book were published by William Salesbury and Richard Davies. But the translation into WELSH, as ordered by this Act, of the whole Bible did not occur until 1588, when Dr. William Morgan did the work. This translation vitally influenced the religious and literary life of the WELSH nation; it gave a new stimulus to the continuance of the WELSH language; it produced a demand for education; and laid the foundations of the modern national movement in WALES.

A.D. 1566.—In 1566, by 8 ELIZABETH, c. 20, the provisions of sections 6–10 of 26 HENRY 8, c. 6 (1534) as to the trial of felonies in the county of Merioneth were repealed. The Act of 1534 had directed that not only were such offences, when committed in the county of Merioneth (one of the three ancient shires of NORTH WALES), to be tried in the next English shire adjoining, but at the discretion of the Justices they might also be heard and determined in the counties of Anglesea and Caernarvon. This was a state of affairs declared to be "much to the discredit of the inhabitants of Merionethshire," so the jurisdiction in Anglesea and Caernarvon was taken away by Parliament, and Merionethshire ceased to be singled out for special legislative treatment.

A.D. 1575.—Additional Justices were appointed for WALES by 18 ELIZABETH, c. 8. This statute referred to the Great Sessions, and declared that by the good administration of justice "the same Principality and Dominion of WALES, and the said County Palatine of Chester, are reduced to great obedience to her Majesty's laws, and the same greatly inhabited, manured, and peopled," and that one Justice in each circuit was unable to deal with the many great and weighty cases which arose. It was therefore provided at the most humble petition and suit of Her Majesty's subjects of the said Principality and Dominion of WALES that there should be two justices learned in the laws in every of the said circuits who, with their associates, should hold the Courts of Great Sessions.

A.D. 1584.—By a statute promulgated in 1584 (27 ELIZABETH, c. 9) a system of registration of the transfer of real property was devised for WALES. The various writs of "fines and recoveries" were to be enrolled on parchment An office of enrolment was instituted in every WELSH shire and in the county of Haverfordwest, wherein all fines and recoveries were to be enrolled. These enrolments were to be examined and signed by the Justices of Great Sessions. A large number of these "*pedes Finium*" are preserved in His Majesty's Record Office, and it is said that they are almost, if not absolutely, complete for some of the counties of WALES.

A.D. 1605.—In 1605, it was provided (3 JAMES I, c. 17) that no persons were to incur any penalty for selling WELSH cottons which were not sealed as containing certain breadth, length, or weight. It was also provided that no WELSH cottons were to be searched or tried in the water by any one except the buyer.

A.D. 1623-4.—The benefits arising from the manufacture of cloth in WALES were referred to in the preamble of 21 JAMES I, c. 9. It was stated that in this manufacture many thousands of the poorer sort of the WELSH people had been set to work in preceding ages, whereby, having free liberty to sell to whom and where they would, they were not only relieved and maintained themselves and their families in good sort, but also grew to such wealth and means of living as they were thereby enabled to pay and discharge all taxes imposed upon them for the relief of the poor and for the service of the King and the Commonwealth. The drapers of Shrewsbury had obtained some orders of restraint whereby the inhabitants of WALES were much prejudiced in the freedom of the market for the buying and selling of their cloths "to their great damage, as was verified by the general voice of the Knights and Burgesses of the twelve shires of WALES and of the County of Monmouth." In 1622, the clothiers of NORTH WALES and Oswestry had complained that in spite of the order in Council for re-settling the market at Oswestry the Shrewsbury drapers still tried to draw all the trade thither, and the dissatisfied WELSHMEN requested the punishment of the chief offenders against their privileges.[1] It was enacted therefore that WELSH cloths should be freely

[1] See Dom. Papers, James I., p. 463 (1619-1623).

bought and sold; that they should be freely exported to foreign parts, paying customs; but that WELSH cloths should not be sold "by any foreigners" by retail within the town of Shrewsbury or any other corporate town or privileged place contrary to any lawful charter then in use.

Apart from the clear view presented in this Act of the social and industrial prosperity of a large class of the WELSH people at this time, it also shows that the general opinion of the Principality was formally deferred to and consulted upon a question materially affecting its inhabitants.

In consequence of the loyalty and dutiful subjection of the subjects of the Dominion of WALES, the section of the Act of WALES of 1542, giving King HENRY the Eighth power to alter any laws or make any new laws concerning the Dominion or Principality of WALES, was repealed by 21 JAMES I, c. 10. All distinction between the subjects of England and WALES was abolished, "His most excellent Majesty tendering the common and constant good of the said country and Dominion of WALES."

Section 5 of a further Act of the same session (21 JAMES I, c. 28) regulated the quantity and quality of WELSH cottons. By the 11th section of the same Act the cruel laws, which formed the coercion acts of HENRY the Fourth, together with the Act passed in 1446–1447 confirming all statutes against WELSHMEN, were formally repealed.

THE COMMONWEALTH PERIOD.

During the period of the Commonwealth there were four statutes directly relating to WALES which require notice. They are not to be found in the Statutes at Large, because for lack of any royal assent they were not Statutes in the legal acceptation of the term.

These Acts were not considered or passed by the House of Lords, for that legislative body was abolished on February 6, 1649, by a resolution, passed without a division, of the remnant of the House of Commons. The latter body then claimed for itself the name and authority of the Parliament of England, and resolved that the "House of Peers in Parliament is useless and dangerous and ought to be abolished."

A.D. 1648.—The first of these Statutes, passed in 1648, dealt with the sequestration of SOUTH WALES and the County of Monmouth. The House of Commons requiring revenue, inflicted severe penalties on those counties which had taken a prominent part in the Civil War, fines being imposed upon each county, accompanied by directions as to the manner of payment and how the compositions of these payments were to be made. The total sum of fines thus levied upon the several counties for their respective delinquencies was £20,500, made up as follows:—

		£
On the County of	Pembroke	3,500
,, ,,	Cardigan	3,000
,, ,,	Carmarthen	4,000
,, ,,	Glamorgan	3,500
,, ,,	Brecknock	2,000
,, ,,	Radnor	1,500
,, ,,	Monmouth	3,000
		£20,500

A number of persons were nominated in the Act to act as Commissioners to carry its provisions into effect.

A.D. 1649.—The second statute of this period, passed in 1649, is known as "the Act for the better propagation of the Gospel in WALES and redress of some grievances." It created a commission of seventy-one persons empowered to eject such clergy as they judged guilty of any delinquency, scandal, malignancy, or non-residence" and to supply their places with "godly and painful men." The Commissioners were to manage the profits of all sequestered livings, which they were to divide, as specified in the Act, between the wives and children of the ejected ministers, the approved preachers and schoolmasters, and the widows of godly ministers. For the maintenance of the new preachers the Commissioners could appropriate the revenues of all parochial benefices "which now or hereafter shall be in the disposing of Parliament or any other deriving authority from them." The funds obtained from these sources were to provide stipends not exceeding £100 per annum for the new ministers, and not exceeding £40 per annum for the new schoolmasters. Allowances not exceeding the yearly sum of £30 might be made to the widows and children of godly ministers. Pensions amounting to one-fifth of the value of the benefices were to be granted to the ejected ministers. The Commissioners obtained the control of large sums of money under this Act.

Full powers were granted to the Commissioners as a Committee of Indemnity to deal with all acts of high misdemeanour, oppression, and injury, the only appeal being to the Committee of Indemnity which sat in London. The provisions of this Act were strictly carried into effect. About 185 benefices passed into the hands of the Commissioners, and the vacant places were filled with vigorous substitutes. "The most conspicuous of the intrusive ministers was Vavasor Powell, a perfervid WELSHMAN, who was able to speak to his countrymen in their native tongue and who, by the sincerity of his own life, gained numerous converts even in that unpuritanical land."[1] Under this Act charges of malignancy, either alone or in conjunction with other offences, were preferred against about twenty clergymen. "Delinquency" was charged in a few cases, "insufficiency" in a dozen cases; "plurality" was complained of in some instances; and a number of incumbents were charged with unbecoming conduct, chiefly drunkenness. Two Cardiganshire incumbents were charged with keeping alehouses.

[1] Gardiner's "History of the Commonwealth," vol. ii. p. 249.

Itinerant preachers were appointed by the Commissioners rather than a settled ministry, and a great number of the parishes were provided with preachers selected from the humbler class of the population.

When the Act expired in 1653, Oliver Cromwell authorized the Commissioners to "go on cheerfully in the work as formerly, to promote these good things, and to protect men in the said work." This they did until the restoration of CHARLES the Second.

A.D. 1649.—Later, the third statute, "An Act for the admitting of the six Counties of NORTH WALES to a general composition for their delinquency," was passed in 1649 "at the humble and earnest request of divers of the inhabitants of the said Counties." The total sum inflicted as fines upon these Counties was £24,000, made up as follows:—

			£
On the County of		Denbigh	3,000
"	"	Flint	2,000
"	"	Carnarvon	4,000
"	"	Merioneth	3,000
"	"	Montgomery	3,000
"	"	Anglesey	9,000
			£24,000

to be paid to the Treasurers at War for the army. Commissioners were appointed in each county for the purposes of the Act, and there were provisions therein excepting certain classes of delinquents from any pardon or benefits. Compensation was also to be made to certain persons who had "done very good and faithful service to the Commonwealth, some of them having had their houses burnt, and their whole estates kept from them for divers years by the enemy (to their total ruin) for their affection to the Parliament."

A.D. 1659.—The fourth statute, passed in 1659, was "An Act for taking the accounts and redressing of grievances concerning the tithes and church livings in WALES, and for advancement of religion and learning there." Under the Commonwealth the executive power was vested in the Cromwellian "Council of State," which was empowered by this Act to appoint persons within the counties of WALES and Monmouthshire to take the accounts of the Act for the better propagation of the Gospel in WALES. The Commissioners were required to value the church livings, tithes, and ecclesiastical revenues; to inquire how many ministers and schoolmasters had been ejected since 1649, and how many were fit to be restored; to ascertain how many livings had become void since the said year; to whom the patronage belonged; how the respective churches and parishes had been supplied, and what were the qualifications of those who supplied the same, &c., &c. All grants or leases of any glebes or tithes belonging to any parsonage or vicarage with cure of souls, made by the patron and incumbent after February 22, 1649, were rendered absolutely void.

A.D. 1662.—Two years after the Restoration of CHARLES the Second, the famous Act for the Uniformity of public worship and for establishing the form of making, ordaining, and consecrating Bishops, priests, and deacons in the Church of England (13–14 CHARLES 2, c. 4) became law. It re-enacted the Uniformity Act of 1 ELIZABETH, c. 2 (1558–1559) and subsequent Acts of the same character. It aimed at obtaining universal agreement in public worship, and with this object the Book of Common Prayer was directed to be used in all parish churches and chapels within the Kingdom of England and the Dominion of WALES.

By section 27, the Bishops of Hereford, St. Davids, St. Asaph, Bangor, and Llandaff were to "take such order among themselves for the soul's health of the flocks committed to their charge within WALES," that the Book of Common Prayer should be translated into the WELSH tongue; that the whole Divine Service should be used in the WELSH language by the ministers and curates throughout WALES, where the WELSH tongue was commonly spoken; that printed WELSH and English copies of the Book of Common Prayer should be placed in the parish churches at the expense of the parish before May 1, 1664, so that "such as understand them may resort at all convenient times to read and peruse the same, and also such as do not understand the said language, may by conferring both tongues together, the sooner attain to the knowledge of the English tongue."

By this Act, which came into force on August 24, 1662 (and was not repealed until the reign of Queen Victoria) every minister, in order to be qualified to hold a living or to legally conduct any public religious service, was required, if not episcopally ordained before, to submit to be episcopally re-ordained; to declare his unfeigned assent and consent to everything contained in the Book of Common Prayer; to take the oath of canonical obedience; to engage not to endeavour to make any change or alteration of government either in Church or State; and to hold it unlawful, upon any pretence whatsoever, to take up arms against the King. The general provisions of this Act were to apply to the Dominion of WALES, as well as to the Kingdom of England. In answer to this Act, over two thousand ministers in England, and one hundred and six ministers in WALES, refused to subscribe to the required declarations, preferring ejectment from their livings, with imprisonment, poverty, and suffering. The Act of Uniformity of 1662 was followed by, and administered rigorously in conjunction with, the Conventicle Act of 1664 and the Five Mile Act of 1665. Legislation of this character had the effect which it generally produces. WALES remained for more than a century in a precarious condition in matters of religion (and adopting the words of the preamble to the Act of Uniformity) to the "great decay and scandal of the reformed religion and to the hazard of many souls."

A.D. 1692.—By section 15 of 4 WILLIAM and MARY, c. 24, jurors in every county of the Dominion of WALES were required to have a qualification of £6 per year in estate, provided that any person could serve upon the *Tales* in every county if he had an interest therein of three pounds by the year. In England the figures were respectively £10 and £5.

A.D. 1693.—In this year the 55th section of 34-35 HENRY 8, c. 26 (1542), which had limited the number of Justices of the Peace in any of the shires of WALES to eight, was repealed by 5-6 WILLIAM and MARY, c. 4. The Crown was to have power to nominate and appoint any number of Justices of the Peace in WALES as was fitting and convenient, according to the ways and methods followed in such appointments in England. Notwithstanding the terms of the repealed section, the number of Justices therein prescribed had been frequently exceeded.

A.D. 1695.—A statute (7-8 WILLIAM 3, c. 38) was passed in 1695 enabling the inhabitants of WALES to dispose of their property and personal effects by will. It abolished an ancient custom in WALES, whereby widows and children of persons dying there were entitled to a certain portion of the goods and chattels of their late husbands or fathers (called the "*reasonable part*"), notwithstanding any previous disposal thereof by will or deed, and notwithstanding also that a competent jointure had been made by settlement. By this custom, if a testator left neither wife nor child, the whole was at his disposal. If he left a wife without a child, or if he left a child or children only, his property was divided into two equal parts, one of which he could dispose of by will (called the "dead's part"), the other half belonged to the widow or to the child or children. If he left both wife and children, then the division was tripartite, the wife took one share (the "wife's part"); the child or children took another share (the "bairn's part"); while the remaining share could be disposed of by the testator in his last will and testament.

This custom was equivalent to the law which is still retained in Scotland. By this Act, the restricted powers of bequest in WALES were abolished, and widows, children, and other relations of testators were wholly barred from any claim on his personal estate otherwise than was provided for by his will.

A.D. 1697.—By 1 WILLIAM and MARY, c. 27 (1688) which abolished the Court of the Marches, it was directed that Judgments and Decrees passed before June 1, 1689, were not to be repealed. As that clause had become ineffectual, because no provision had been made authorising the Courts at Westminster and the Courts of the Great Sessions of WALES to execute or carry into effect any such judgments, an Act of 1697 (9–10 WILLIAM 3, c. 16) gave powers to the King's Chancery, the Court of Exchequer, and his Majesty's Court of Great Sessions, to issue execution upon every judgment so made, and to review, affirm, reverse, or rehear the same.

A.D. 1698.—In 1698, by 11–12 WILLIAM 3, c. 9, the provisions of two general Acts for the prevention of frivolous suits (namely, 22–23 CHARLES 2, c. 9, s. 9, and 43 ELIZABETH, c. 6) were extended to the Courts of Great Sessions for the Principality of WALES, so that in actions of trespass, theft, battery or other personal actions, where the damages were found to be under 40s., the plaintiff was not to recover more costs than the damages so found. Sheriffs in WALES were not to hold prisoners to special bail in small actions because it was oppressive and vexatious.

A.D. 1713.—In this year the Act for taking away mortuaries within the WELSH dioceses was passed (13 ANNE c. 6). Its provisions have already been noticed.[1]

A.D. 1715.—In the first year of GEORGE the First it was made lawful for his Majesty to grant the Crown regalities and lands in NORTH and SOUTH WALES and Cheshire to the Prince of WALES, in such manner and form as the

[1] P. li.

Principality of WALES and Earldom of Chester had formerly been granted to the Princes of WALES.

A.D. 1716.—An Act (3 GEORGE 1, c. 15) was passed in this year for the better regulating of the office of sheriffs. By section 20, sheriffs in WALES were directed to take the old form of oath on their accession to office, and not to adopt the new form of oath provided for sheriffs in English counties, and by section 22 they were directed to submit their accounts to the Auditor of WALES. These sections were repealed by the Sheriffs' Act of 1887. After the passing of 1 WILLIAM and MARY, c. 22 (1688), which took away the Court of the President and Council of the Marches of WALES, sheriffs were nominated yearly by the Justices of the Great Sessions of WALES in their respective circuits. After 1845, by the operation of 8 and 9 VICTORIA, c. 11, the WELSH sheriffs were nominated and appointed at the same time and place as the sheriffs for the English shires, and by the Sheriffs Act of 1887 (50–51 VICTORIA, c. 55, s. 31) the counties of WALES were placed on the same footing as the English counties in respect of the law relating to sheriffs and under-sheriffs.

A.D. 1721.—By 8 GEORGE 1, c. 25, s. 6, Judges and officers of the Courts of Great Sessions in WALES were required to enter their judgments in the Court records, stating the time when so entered.

A.D. 1730.—Owing to the evil practices and abuses which had arisen before 1730, in the summoning of jurors, an Act (3 GEORGE 2, c. 25) was passed for the better regulation of juries. Section 9 thereof regulated the practice of summoning jurors in WALES.

A.D. 1732-3.—It was directed by section 3 of 6 GEORGE 2, c. 14, that the proceedings in the Courts of Great Sessions were to be in the English language. This followed an Act (4 GEORGE 2, c. 26, 1730–1) establishing the use of the English language in courts of justice within England and Scotland, and remedying the mischiefs arising from the proceedings in those courts being carried on in an unknown language.

In England, for many centuries, Latin had been the language of voluminous official and judicial records, and it was not dislodged from this position until 1731. French slowly supplanted Latin as the literary language of the English law, and "legal proceedings were formerly all written in Norman or Law French, and even the arguments of counsel and decisions of the Court were in the same barbarous dialect, an evident and shameful badge, it must be owned, of tyranny and foreign servitude."[1] The Acts of Parliament were *written* in French until the fourth year of the reign of HENRY the Seventh, but they were exclusively *printed* in English after that date. The Act of 1730-1 enacted that the records of the Courts, as well as all other legal proceedings, were to be in the English tongue and language only, and not in Latin or French, or any other tongue or language whatsoever. In the Courts of WALES it had been previously ordained by 27 HENRY 8, c. 26, s. 20, that the English language was to be used, and not the WELSH language. There is very little evidence available at present to determine whether WELSH was used in the Courts of Great Sessions, either in the oral or written proceedings, to any extent whatsoever.

The statute of 1732-3 cleared up the doubts which had arisen upon the application of the Act of 1730-1, and English was to be used thenceforth in all the Courts in WALES.

A.D. 1746.—A very important clause affecting WALES was introduced in an Act (20 GEORGE 2, c. 42) passed in 1746 to enforce rates and duties upon houses, windows, and lights. It was declared by the 3rd section that where "England" only should be mentioned in any Act of Parliament it should be deemed to comprehend WALES and the town of Berwick-upon-Tweed, a town which was originally part of Scotland. Although the other portions of this Act have been repealed this clause still remains law. We find also in the 3rd section of 7-8 GEORGE 4, c. 53, passed in 1827, that in all Acts of

[1] "Blackstone's Commentaries," vol. iii. c. 21.

Parliament relating to the revenue or excise, WALES was to be included where "England" or "Great Britain" was mentioned. This was re-enacted in 1890 by 53–54 VICTORIA, c. 21, s. 38 (1).

A.D. 1758.—In an Act of 1758 for the relief of debtors (32 GEORGE 2, c. 28), the 11th section provided that the Justices of the Great Sessions in WALES were to hear and determine in a summary manner complaints as to any abuses arising where gaolers, bailiffs, and others employed in the execution of legal process had in their respective offices been guilty of misconduct towards prisoners under arrest.

A.D. 1767–1772.—By the Act (8 GEORGE 3, c. 14, 1767–8) Parliament directed that the sheriffs of the several counties in WALES were to provide necessary lodging and other accommodation for the Justices of Great Sessions when on circuit, and an allowance not exceeding ten pounds for each county and for each sessions, was to be made by the Auditor, out of the land revenues of the Crown derived from the Principality of WALES, to the sheriffs for the said expenses. By a further Act (12 GEORGE 3, c. 30, 1772), owing to the considerable surplus accruing from the stamp duties appropriated for the payment of the salaries of the WELSH Judges, it was ordered that increases of salary should be made from and after April 5, 1772, to the Judges, but subject to a reasonable abatement if the surpluses did not continue and were insufficient.

A.D. 1773.—An Act (13 GEORGE 3, c. 51) was passed to discourage the practice of commencing trifling and frivolous suits in the Courts at Westminster upon causes of action arising within WALES, and of trying the said actions in the nearest adjoining English county to that part of the Dominion of WALES in which they had arisen. The origin of the Courts at Westminster assuming this jurisdiction over causes in WALES, and directing the trial in the adjoining English county, does not distinctly appear. But undoubtedly this practice had existed for a considerable time, and was firmly established; in fact, it was said by Lord Ellenborough, C.J., in 1814 (see Goodright against Williams, 2 Maule and Selwyn's Reports, p. 274), to have been a practice which had originated in the common law, and to have been followed time out of mind. The practice was to try all issues arising in SOUTH WALES in Herefordshire, and actions from NORTH WALES in the county of Salop. It was a practice which was the subject of considerable controversy, and there is a very learned and elaborate argument on the point in Hargreave's Law Tracts. We have already pointed out that section 6 of 26 HENRY 8, c. 6, provided in 1534, that felonies and serious criminal offences arising within the Lordships Marchers of WALES were to be tried in the next adjoining English county, which provision was afterwards confirmed by the 85th section of 34-35 HENRY 8, c. 26, but the general practice in civil suits was said to have prevailed (see Ambrose against Rees, 11 East's Reports, p. 370) even before the time of HENRY the Eighth. How this practice was affected by the jurisdiction of the Courts of Great Sessions is a matter upon which at present, owing to the absence of material information, we are unable to throw much light. But the truth most probably is that the assumption of the English Courts to exercise this jurisdiction, and to continue this practice, was founded on mere usurpation, and, like many other usurpations of jurisdiction, was supported by legal fictions. This Statute of 1773 provided that, after January 1, 1774, when actions arising within WALES were brought in any of his Majesty's Courts of Record outside WALES, and the plaintiff recovered a debt or damages under £10, no costs were to be given to him, and the defendant was to be entitled to a non-suit unless the Judge certified that the cause was proper to be tried in England, or that a question of title was involved. (The limit of £10 was subsequently altered in 1824 to £50.) WELSH Judges were authorized to appoint a deputy in certain cases. Special juries were to be struck in the Courts of Great Sessions as in the Courts at Westminster, the party applying for a special jury being required to pay the fee for striking such jury, being not more than one guinea to each special juror for such service, except in causes where a view was had. WELSH Judges were empowered to appoint persons to take affidavits concerning proceedings in their circuit, but no Commissioner authorized to take affidavits could do so during the time for holding the Great Sessions. The Justices of Great Sessions might authorize any person to take recognizances of bail. Other matters relating to procedure are dealt with in this Act, which concluded by ordering that in all cases where penalties were fixed by any statutes, and which were directed to be recovered in the Courts at Westminster, they might be recovered in the Courts of Great Sessions.

A.D. 1793.—An Act in 1793 (33 GEORGE 3, c. 68) further dealt with and remedied certain inconveniences which were found to exist in proceedings in the Courts of Great Sessions and in the County Courts of WALES. In cases where judgments had been obtained in the Courts of Great Sessions, and the persons or effects could not be found within the jurisdiction of those Courts, any Court at Westminster might issue execution. Clauses in the Act of 1542 relating to the Sheriff's County or Hundred Courts were repealed.

A.D. 1809.—By 49 GEORGE 3, c. 127, s. 5, in 1809, a further augmentation of four hundred pounds as salary was made to the Chief Justice of Chester, to the Second Justice of Chester, and to each of the Justices of the Great Sessions for the Counties of WALES.

A.D. 1812.—By the Act (52 GEORGE 3, c. 155), in 1812, which applied to England and WALES, certain statutes relating to religious worship and assemblies and persons teaching or preaching therein were repealed, and persons affected thereby could claim exemption upon producing a certificate of having made and taken certain oaths and declarations required by this Act. By section 10, the penalty for producing any false certificate was fixed at

£50, which penalty could be recovered in WALES at the Courts of Great Sessions.

A.D. 1824.—The business of the Courts of Great Sessions had greatly increased before 1824, and it was found from experience that suitors experienced many inconveniences from the delays occasioned by the want of powers in the WELSH Judges to make alterations in the practice, in order to assimilate the procedure to the Courts in England. Therefore an Act (5 GEORGE 4, c. 106) was passed in that year enlarging and extending the powers of the Judges in the several Courts of Great Sessions in WALES and amending the laws relating to the same. Until the abolition of these Courts, the uniform course of practice which was followed was regulated mainly in accordance with this Act, and such of the preceding Acts as were applicable. It is not necessary to refer here to all its provisions, but some may be noticed. Before this Act, whenever a suit was commenced in any WELSH county every stage of the legal proceedings had to be followed in that county; and all further proceedings, whenever the Sessions for such county ended, were suspended until the ensuing Sessions. By the 11th section the WELSH Judges were empowered, when Courts were sitting in any county, to make rules and orders in suits depending in the other counties. By the 12th section, when the Courts were not sitting in WALES, the WELSH Judges were authorized, if necessary, to make orders in London or other places outside the jurisdiction. By the 13th section, writs could be issued from one WELSH county to another. By the 19th section, the Act of 1773 relating to the trial of WELSH causes at the Assizes in the next English county was repealed, and in lieu thereof it was provided that if an action were brought wherein the plaintiff did not recover £50 he was to be non-suited and the defendant was to recover costs against the plaintiff, unless the Judge certified that there was a title to the land in question, or that the case was proper to be tried in such English county. The intention of this clause was to prevent the parties from resorting to the English Courts in actions under £50, thereby materially increasing the business of the Great Sessions. By the 29th section, the qualifications of jurymen of the Courts of Great Sessions were fixed to be an estate of freehold or copyhold of £8 yearly value or upwards, or any life interest or estate for the term of ninety-nine years of the yearly value of £15.

THE WELSH JUDICATURE.

A.D. 1830.—On July 23, 1830, an Act (1 WILLIAM 4, c. 70) was passed to put an end to the separate jurisdiction for the Principality of WALES, and to make more effectual provision for the administration of Justice in England and WALES.

As this Act abolished the last vestiges of distinction in legal procedure between England and WALES, it is proposed to summarize the leading characteristics of a system of jurisprudence which had lasted in the Dominion of WALES for three centuries. It was in many respects superior to that prevailing in England, besides being familiar to the WELSH people, and adapted by long use to their habits and customs.

It was brought into permanent existence, as already stated, by the Act of HENRY the Eighth, in 1542, promulgated upon the basis of reports made by Commissioners after inquiries on the spot, and it was too favourably said by Barrington "to contain a most complete code of regulations for the administration of justice, framed with such precision and accuracy that no one clause of it hath ever yet occasioned a doubt or required an explanation." It received the approval of two of the greatest of English jurists, Lord Coke and Lord Bacon. Coke refers to the WELSH Courts as the "excellent, venerable variety of seats and courts of justice, with their proper jurisdictions, according to the laws of England—the golden metwand, whereby all men's causes are fully and evenly measured"; and it was observed by Lord Bacon that they were founded by an Act that had required no further explanation!

But in the early part of the nineteenth century, when public attention was given to the very necessary reforms that were demanded in the technical absurdities and vexatious requirements of the English laws, the special judicature of WALES was (probably quite unnecessarily) included in the scope of the proposed innovations.

In 1780, Burke had in his "plan for the better security of the Independence of Parliament, and the economical reformation of the civil and other establishments" included a Bill "for the more perfectly uniting to the Crown the Principality of WALES and the County Palatine of Chester and for the more commodious administration of justice within the same." He said, in the House of Commons, on December 18, 1780, that he thought that the addition of a judge to each of the English Courts at Westminster would be sufficient for WALES, but his original plan was to abolish five out of the eight WELSH judgeships which existed, and to throw the counties into districts. His opposition to the WELSH judicature was on account of expense, and not upon general grounds. In 1798, a Select Committee of the House of Commons on finance in Courts of Justice recommended that the four Circuits in WALES should be amalgamated.

Another Select Committee was appointed by the House of Commons to examine into the administration of Justice in WALES. This Committee made an interim report in 1817, and in 1820 further evidence was submitted by it, without any report being presented. In 1821 they made a final report. This was not adopted, but the Act of 1824 (which has already been noticed), without disturbing the Courts, established a uniform course of procedure. After a long and heated controversy and many debates in both Houses of Parliament, the statute of 1830 was passed, terminating the authority and jurisdiction of the Courts of Great Sessions.

WALES had enjoyed its own separate judicature, with its own technical machinery, for the most part independent of the London Courts. Writs were issued, actions commenced and decided without any reference to the Courts at Westminster.

The four WELSH circuits in 1817 contained altogether, exclusive of the County of Chester, a population of 611,788 persons. For these circuits, eight paid judges were required, but they had no right to any pension on retirement. The salary of the Chief Justice of Chester, at the end of the history of the Courts of Great Sessions, was £1,630 per annum; the second judge at Chester received £1,250 per annum, and the remaining WELSH Judges were paid £1,150 per annum respectively, and were entitled also to other fees. They were eligible to sit in the House of Commons, and to hold office under Government during the pleasure of the Crown. Lord John Russell complained in the House of Commons in 1820 that, as the WELSH Judges were permitted to sit in that assembly, their posts were looked upon as retainers or rewards for their party support. It was objected against them that they used their abundant leisure to practise at the English Bar, and that as twelve judges were enough for England, eight were too many for WALES. Between 1542 and 1830, 217 Judges of the WELSH Circuits had been appointed, out of which number only thirty were natives of WALES and Monmouthshire. It was also alleged that sometimes hypothetical cases from WALES, stated under feigned names, were submitted for opinion to the WELSH Judges when acting as counsel in England, but the answer made to this allegation was that they refused to give their opinion unless they received an absolute assurance that the case did not arise within their jurisdiction. It was also complained that the WELSH Judges were sometimes oddly selected, and that it did not add to the legal business to have the same Judge sitting for a great number of years in the same courts. Burke was very severe in his criticism of the

WELSH Judges, and nicknamed them the "yellow admirals of the law." Lord Brougham, in his "Recollections of a WELSH Judge," says that "there was a great charm about the old WELSH Circuits. The whole appearance of the Court was different from an English Court; the habits of the people, and even their dress, was distinct; and then, as in most cases the witnesses could not speak English, and had to be examined through an interpreter, you might well fancy yourself in a foreign country. Indeed, in addresses to the jury, whether by the Bar or from the Bench, it was but too obvious that the majority frequently understood but little of what was said to them."

The Courts sat only in spring and autumn, the circuits lasting about six weeks. Each circuit court was supreme within its own jurisdiction, resulting in the establishment of a peculiar standard of practice which alone was acknowledged as having authority within its own district. The Judges had not the power to compel the attendance of witnesses residing out of the counties within their immediate jurisdiction, and they were compelled by statute to sit six days in each circuit town. The course of business on each circuit was that on the Monday, the first day, the Court was opened after the Judges came into the circuit town. On Tuesday the Judges went to church at twelve, and afterwards charged the grand jury. On Wednesday, the "do nothing at all day," any adjourned cases were disposed of. On Thursday Crown cases and trials of prisoners were proceeded with. On Friday new issues were tried; and on Saturday morning a Court was held for any other business, and in the evening the Judges left for the next circuit town. When the two Judges differed in their opinions, no judgment was pronounced, and there was no appeal in equity matters except to the House of Lords, or by writ of error in matters of law to the King's Bench. Applications for a new trial had to be made immediately (to the same Judges who had tried the cause) at the close of the first trial. All barristers of the English Inns of Court were entitled to practise in these Courts, but no attorneys except those admitted by the Court for each circuit. The Northern and Oxford Circuits of the English Bar supplied the Chester and SOUTH WALES Circuits with counsel. It was not the professional usage or etiquette for King's Counsel to practise in WALES. Junior counsel practised in every branch—civil, criminal, and equitable. There were eighty attorneys in the Carmarthen district.

In the Courts of Great Sessions both law and equity cases were heard and determined. It was stated that proceedings in a suit at equity were, in consequence of the shortness of the circuit, more dilatory and prolix even than in the Court of Chancery of England. It is difficult to say how equity came to be administered in these WELSH Courts. The statute of HENRY the Eighth does not specifically confer any equitable jurisdiction on the Justices of Great Sessions. The Court of Chancery in England was open to WELSH suitors. Still, there was in the WELSH Courts a concurrent jurisdiction between these two branches of jurisprudence that was not brought about in England until the Judicature Act of 1875.

Criminal business was also dealt with by the WELSH Judges on circuit, but it frequently happened that the WELSH Judges had not the same opportunities for acquiring and preserving that experience of criminal law which the English Judges enjoyed in so eminent a degree, and the constitution of the WELSH Courts did not afford to the accused persons or suitors the advantages which arise out of a varied succession of Judges. If a difficulty arose in a criminal trial, the WELSH Judges drew up a case, signed it, and sent it for the opinion of twelve of the Judges of England, who always attended to it, but under protest that they were not bound to take it into consideration.

During the years 1812 to 1823 the average number of criminal cases tried yearly before the Courts of Great Sessions was one hundred. The average, in the same period, of Bills of Chancery and decrees was eighty-five per annum; and of common law causes, one hundred and nineteen per annum.

There was a Chamberlain holding the Circuit Seal in each circuit, and an Auditor of WALES who audited and received the fines and revenues, paying the same into the Exchequer at Westminster. It was the Auditor's duty to superintend and collect the land revenues, to audit the accounts, the land taxes, assessed taxes and property taxes, and to pass the Sheriffs' Accounts. The audits were held for the respective circuits at St. Asaph, Conway, Carmarthen, and Brecknock. An Attorney-General and Solicitor-General, possessing the same privileges as the holders of the similar offices in England (although no mention is made of them in the Act of HENRY the Eighth), were appointed on each circuit. No indictment in a criminal matter could be presented until the Attorney-General affixed his signature thereto.

The Court officials were reported to have been generally conversant with the WELSH language.

The bulk of the evidence given by lawyers who were acquainted with the WELSH circuits was in favour of the retention of the system, subject to certain reforms. Lord Mansfield (who was at one time Chief Justice of Chester) said that it seemed to him to be a great advantage to the WELSH people that they should have the opportunity of trying their disputes at home at very little expense. Mr. Oldnall Russell, practising on the Carmarthen Circuit, maintained that a Judge, who knew something of the manners and customs of the WELSH people and their peculiar habits and dispositions, would certainly have an advantage over Judges who were not so informed.

Mr. Sergeant Heywood, another practising counsel, said that there were in WALES certain peculiar circumstances of a local nature which supported the necessity of a separate jurisdiction. There were little shades of difference between the English and WELSH character, and Judges who went the circuit once only, could not find themselves perfectly conversant with WELSH manners and feelings, and it was therefore better for the WELSH people to have Judges who came often amongst them. Further, he maintained that although in many instances the proceedings had to be held in the native language of the country, the business was conducted with such regularity and regard to justice that the country was satisfied with the system.

The Commissioners summed up their report in favour of the abolition of the WELSH system by stating "that they could not but think that, however well adapted those Courts might have been in their origin to the circumstances of a country newly subdued and in which the English language was at that time almost unknown, having little or no means of communication with the seats of justice in England, and liable to all the jealousies inspired by recent enmity, yet the lapse of years and the great changes that had taken place in the condition of WALES had removed most, if not all, the reasons on account of which the institution of local jurisdictions was resorted to in preference to the established tribunals of the Country."

It must be noted here that the abolition of the WELSH Courts of Great Session was not brought about at the instance of the main body of the WELSH people, or of WELSH suitors, but at the instance of the landed gentry of WALES. The wishes of the humble WELSH suitors were not so much regarded as the ambition of the nobility and landed proprietors of that time to make WALES a part of the judicial system of England.

There was considerable danger in the alteration, for it was a change, from a fairly efficient method of judicature which had grown after three centuries of useful working into a national institution easily capable of being reformed, to the acknowledged defects and notorious costliness of the English system. For sixteen years, that is, until the introduction of the modern County Court system in 1846, there were no common law Courts in Wales for deciding cases of small amounts, and equitable matters had to be dealt with in the tortuous maze of the English Chancery Court as then existing. It is true that the old system of County Courts established during the reign of EDWARD the First, remained in WALES, but the jurisdiction of these ancient County Courts did not exceed 40s., and they were presided over by the under-sheriff, who was a judge for one year, and an advocate, when his yearly term of office expired. In these County Courts there were considerable grievances, so great, for instance, that in 1818 a meeting of the people of the county of Pembroke was held to discuss them, and it was then resolved thereat that the increase of litigation was destructive of public tranquillity and highly injurious to their county, and that the law of the land was made the instrument of the greatest oppression on the lowest orders. In the Carmarthen County Courts during nine years there were 10,912 pleas, and in the baronial courts of the same county, 3,024 pleas, giving plenty of work to the attorneys.

The long establishment of this separate jurisdiction shows that WALES had until 1830, as Scotland still has, a provincial judicature which distinguished it from any other part of the United Kingdom ; a law system adapted to its special needs and circumstances, expeditious, cheap, and in several marked features excelling the English system.

The Act of 1830, which put an end to the WELSH system, provided for an additional Justice for each of the three English Common Law Courts, viz., the King's Bench, the Common Pleas, and the Exchequer of Pleas. The jurisdiction of the English superior Courts at Westminster was made to extend over WALES and Chester, and the Courts of Great Sessions were abolished. The Act came into effect on October 12, 1830. All suits in the WELSH Courts, both in law and equity, were transferred to the Courts of Chancery or Exchequer in London. Welsh attorneys were to be admitted as attorneys of the Courts at Westminster. Assizes for the trial of criminal and civil matters were henceforth to be held in the WELSH counties and the county of Chester as in the Counties of England. Out of the consolidated funds compensation was given to the WELSH Judges and persons affected by the abolition of their Courts. The records of the Courts were to be transferred to the Clerks of the Peace of the several Counties. The existing salaries and pensions of the English Judges were fixed by this measure.

Thus the present system of holding Assizes in WALES and Chester was inaugurated. In establishing the new WELSH Circuit two Judges were appointed under the King's Commission to hold the Assizes in WALES, one taking the six counties of SOUTH WALES, the other going to the NORTH WALES counties both meeting at Chester for the purpose of holding the Assizes there. There are now two divisions of the WELSH Circuit, forming the "SOUTH WALES and Chester Circuit," and the "NORTH WALES and Chester Circuit." Since 1872, owing to the great increase of legal business in Glamorganshire, it has been necessary for both Judges to meet in SOUTH WALES as well as at Chester, so both divisions of the WELSH Circuit now meet at the latter city and in Glamorganshire for the holding of the Assizes.

A.D. 1832.—In 1832, an Act to amend the representation of the people in England and WALES (2–3 William 4 c. 45), better known as "the Reform Act," was passed to correct divers abuses that had long prevailed in the choice of members to serve in the House of Commons; to grant electoral privileges to large, populous, and wealthy towns and to deprive many inconsiderable places of the right to return members; to increase the number of Knights of the shire and to extend the elective franchise.

WALES was at that period chiefly an agricultural country, but in Glamorganshire and Monmouthshire the great industries which now exist were beginning to develop, bringing about great increases in the population. Under the Reform Act WALES obtained five new members, making thirty-two members instead of the twenty-seven members provided for by the Act of 1535. By section 4, Merthyr Tydfil was created a new borough with the right of returning one member; by section 8, certain places as scheduled in the Act were to have a share in the elections for shire towns and certain boroughs; one additional county member was given to Glamorganshire, one member was given to Swansea and its contributory boroughs, one additional county member was given to Carmarthenshire and Denbighshire, and one additional county member to the county of Monmouth. By subsequent general Acts relating to the Parliamentary franchise, these electoral arrangements have been completely altered. In 1867, Merthyr Tydfil received an additional representative. In 1885, Beaumaris, Brecknock, Haverfordwest, Cardigan and Radnor Boroughs were disfranchised; Glamorganshire obtained the right of sending five members to the House of Commons, and an additional representative was given to Monmouthshire and Swansea.

Legislation for the Established Church in Wales.

One of the results of the vigorous efforts for the improvement of public institutions which followed the Reform Act of 1832 was the appointment of a standing body now known as the "Ecclesiastical Commission," invested with very important powers. Under the operation of the Ecclesiastical Commission extensive changes were made in the distribution of the revenues of the Church of England in WALES.

A.D. 1836.—In 1836, an Act of great consequence became law. It recognized the special needs of the WELSH people as to the performance of ecclesiastical duties in the WELSH language, and is also highly important because it was the first instance of separate legislation in Church matters for WALES during the nineteenth century. The Act (6–7 William 4, c. 77) recites that, in 1835, two separate commissions were issued, to consider the state of the several dioceses in England and WALES, and that the Commissioners had made four several reports bearing date respectively the 17th of March, 1835, the 4th of March, the 20th of May, and the 24th of June, 1836. The Commissioners had recommended in these reports (*inter alia*), that upon the first avoidance of the sees either of Saint Asaph or Bangor, the Bishop of the other see should become the bishop of the two sees, which were to be united, and that thereupon he was to become seized and possessed of all the property, advowsons, and patronage belonging to the see so avoided.

The Act of 1836 first established the permanent body now known as the "Ecclesiastical Commissioners of England," having the control of considerable funds derived from a rearrangement and suspension of ecclesiastical revenues. One central corporation was thus substituted for the many local and independent corporations of the Church, so far as the management of property was concerned a constitutional change of great importance, regarded as having made a serious breach in the legal theory of ecclesiastical property. The Commissioners were directed to prepare a scheme best adapted to prevent the appointment of any clergyman not fully conversant with the WELSH language to any benefice with cure of souls, in any parish in WALES, the majority of the inhabitants of which did not understand the WELSH language.

A.D. 1838.—The Pluralities Act of 1838 (1 and 2 Victoria, c. 106) repealed that part of the Act of 1836 relating to the scheme propounded by the Ecclesiastical Commissioners as to preventing the appointment of any clergyman not fully conversant with the WELSH language to certain benefices in WALES, and in lieu thereof provided that the Bishops of the WELSH dioceses could refuse institution or licence to any spiritual person who, upon due examination and inquiry, should be found unable to preach, administer the sacraments, perform other pastoral duties, and converse in the WELSH language. A right of appeal to the Archbishop of Canterbury was preserved to such spiritual person against the decision of the Bishop, and by section 105 the provisions of the Act were made to apply to the appointment of curates within the several Welsh dioceses in cases where the ecclesiastical duties were not satisfactorily performed by reason of insufficient instruction in the WELSH language. In 1885, by the Act amending the Law relating to Pluralities (48–49 VICTORIA, c. 54) (which was to be construed as one with the Act of 1838), the term "ecclesiastical duties" in the case of benefices in WALES and the county of Monmouth was defined to include such ministrations in the WELSH language as the Bishop should direct to be performed, but so that not more than one WELSH service on every Sunday should be required, and provision made for the English-speaking portion of the population. In 1886, the Marquis of Abergavenny presented a clergyman, who could not speak WELSH, to a rectory in the county of Monmouth, within the diocese of Llandaff. The Bishop of Llandaff (Dr. Richard Lewis) thereupon commissioned certain persons to hold an inquiry as to whether the parish required a pastor with a knowledge of WELSH. The report was in the affirmative, and the Bishop refused to admit or institute the nominated clergyman. Thereupon the patron brought an action in the nature of a "*quare impedit*" against the Bishop for such refusal. It was held by Baron Huddleston (*Law Reports*, 20 Q.B.D., p. 460) that the "due examination and inquiry" required by the 104th section of the Pluralities Act, 1838, meant examination and inquiry as to the clergyman's knowledge of the Welsh language, and that the Bishop was justified in his refusal. In this case a very interesting reference was made to the case of Albany *v.* The Bishop of St. Asaph, decided in the time of Queen ELIZABETH, (*Leonard's Reports*, p. 31), to the effect that it was a good ground of refusal by a Bishop to institute a clergyman, if he could not speak WELSH, in a parish where the parishioners did not understand English, for he could not instruct his flock according to his duty and charge.

A.D. 1840.—In 1840, an Act (3–4 VICTORIA, c. 113) was passed to carry into effect the fourth report of the Commissioners of Ecclesiastical Duties made on June 24, 1836. It enacted that all the members of chapter (except the dean) in the cathedral churches of Saint Davids and Llandaff should be styled canon, and that there should be two canons in each. After the passing of this Act no appointment in these cathedral churches or to the collegiate church of Brecon should convey any right of title whatsoever to any endowments then belonging to such office. The canonries of Saint Davids were to be in the direct patronage of the Bishop, and the whole revenues divided into parts, between the dean, the canons, and the archdeacon of Cardigan; due provision was to be made out of the endowments of the collegiate church of Brecon for the archdeaconries of Carmarthen and Brecon. The archdeacon of Llandaff was to be dean of the cathedral church, and the corporate revenues of Llandaff were to be divided between the Bishop, the dean, and canons. All lands and endowments belonging to Saint Davids, Llandaff, and the collegiate church of Brecon vested absolutely in the Ecclesiastical Commissioners for England, who were entitled to make therefrom provision for the College at Lampeter, and to provide incomes for the various dignitaries.

A.D. 1841.—In 1841, the provisions of the Act of 1840 relating to the division and application of the revenues of the chapters of St. David's and Llandaff and the collegiate church of Brecon were repealed by 4–5 VICTORIA, c. 39, s. 14. By the 28th section thereof nothing in the Act was to apply to the dioceses of St. Asaph and Bangor, which remained in a state of suspended animation under the temporary provisions of previous Acts of Parliament (5–6 WILLIAM 4, c. 30;

6–7 WILLIAM 4, c. 67; and parts of 2–3 VICTORIA, c. 55). These temporary provisions suspending appointments in the latter dioceses were extended until August 1, 1842, but the Bishop of Bangor was to be permitted to make certain appointments and perform his ordinary episcopal duties in the meantime.

A.D. 1842.—A measure (5–6 VICTORIA, c. 112) followed in 1842 suspending any appointments to ecclesiastical preferments in the dioceses of St. Asaph and Bangor until October 1, 1843. It recited and continued the two Acts passed in 1835 (5–6 WILLIAM 4, c. 30) and 1836 (6–7 WILLIAM 4, c. 67), which had suspended appointments generally until Parliament should have had time to consider the reports of the Commissioners appointed as to ecclesiastical duties.

A.D. 1843.—In 1843, by 6–7 VICTORIA, c. 77, the suspensory measures relating to the dioceses of St. Asaph and Bangor were repealed, and the general Acts establishing the Ecclesiastical Commission were extended to these sees. Four resident canons were to be appointed in each of the WELSH dioceses of St. Asaph, Bangor, St. Davids, and Llandaff. These canonries were to be in the direct patronage of the Bishops. Two of them were to be permanently annexed to the archdeaconries in the respective dioceses. Houses of residence were to be provided for the canons of St. Asaph, Bangor, and Llandaff, and also for the Dean of Llandaff. The archdeaconry of St. Asaph was no longer to be held by the Bishop of St. Asaph, and the archdeaconries of Bangor and Anglesea were to be dissevered from the bishopric of Bangor. The archdeaconry of Llandaff was to be separated from the deanery of Llandaff. Out of the proceeds of the revenues of ecclesiastical estates in the Principality of WALES, vested in the Ecclesiastical Commissioners, provision was to be made for the maintenance of a clergyman, being a native of the Principality, to officiate in WELSH in a church or chapel within London or Westminster or the suburbs for the performance of divine service according to the Church of England. More favourable provisions were made for St. David's College at Lampeter.

A.D. 1847.—On February 10, 1847, a Commission was appointed to consider the state of the bishoprics in England and WALES. This Commission reported, and some of its recommendations became law in the same year (10–11 VICTORIA, c. 108). The dioceses of St. Asaph and Bangor were continued as separate bishoprics, and the bishopric of Manchester was founded. The Commission had recommended taking away one bishop from NORTH WALES and joining the sees of St. Asaph and Bangor, and had recommended also that one bishop should be taken away from SOUTH WALES, and that Llandaff should be united with the see of Bristol. There was a strong feeling displayed in WALES against these proposals, with the result that these particular recommendations were omitted from the Act. Under section 2, a very important provision relating to the constitution of our country became law, viz., that the number of Lords Spiritual then sitting and voting as Lords of Parliament was not to be increased by the creation of the new bishopric of Manchester. A protest was also entered in the House of Lords against the procedure established by this section for filling up vacancies among the Lords Spiritual. This protest was made by a few of the lay and spiritual lords, because "it constituted a dangerous precedent, and was at variance with the principle of an hereditary peerage, and contrary to the privileges of the Lords Spiritual and Temporal."

A.D. 1863.—By an Act (26–27 VICTORIA, c. 82) the WELSH Bishops were empowered to make provision for English services in certain parishes of WALES. As the law stood, in all parishes in WALES in which WELSH was the tongue commonly spoken by the people the whole Divine Service was required to be used and said in the British or WELSH tongue. It was provided that wherever any ten or more inhabitants in any parish, district, or place in WALES should certify in writing to the Bishop that they were desirous of having Divine Service performed and the Sacraments administered in English, and undertook to provide a building to be used as a chapel for the same and a spiritual person to officiate therein, then the Bishop was to be entitled to license such chapels and ministers when nominated by the incumbent of the parish. If the incumbent refused or failed to nominate the minister, the Bishop could do so. The licensed building was not to be a parochial chapel, except with the consent of the incumbent, whose rights as to fees and emoluments were not to be affected by the passing of this Act.

A.D. 1837.—By section 23 of 7 WILLIAM 4 and 1 VICTORIA, c. 22 (1837), regulating the registration of marriages, it is provided that in all places where the WELSH tongue is commonly spoken the solemn declaration to be used in the celebration of marriages before the Registrars is to be truly translated into the WELSH tongue and furnished to every Registrar throughout WALES, and that it is lawful to use that translation in all places where the WELSH tongue is commonly spoken.

THE TURNPIKE ROAD ACTS IN SOUTH WALES.

A.D. 1844.—An Act (7–8 VICTORIA, c. 91) to "consolidate and amend the laws relating to Turnpike Trusts in SOUTH WALES" became law in 1844. Its title does not indicate the fact that stormy events led to its enactment. In 1789, the SOUTH WALES Association for the improvement of roads had been formed at Swansea, its principal object being to obtain a complete amendment of the highway road between the New Passage over the Severn at Newnham and Hubberston in Pembrokeshire, with an improvement of the road from Chepstow to Gloucester, in order to provide good communication between SOUTH WALES and London. During the reign of GEORGE the Third a number of private

Acts of Parliament were successfully promoted by persons who were interested in Turnpike Trusts, giving them statutory powers to make and regulate roads. The Trustees of these Turnpike Roads in SOUTH WALES were authorized to raise moneys by tolls sufficient to pay the interest upon the debts incurred in making the roads and keeping them in repair. In order to raise this money tolls had been largely increased; payments of these charges were frequently demanded; side-bars on the roadsides had been multiplied improperly, and every means adopted by the trustees to swell their revenues. Strangers to the localities, who were professional toll renters, became tenants of the gate houses, farming the tolls, and exacting the utmost from the discontented public. Many practices were followed by these persons which no law could justify. In Carmarthenshire alone there were twelve different Trusts, and although the amount of the tolls was limited by the statutory powers given, there was no such limit as to the number of gates at which they could be levied on the public. No reason existed why the Turnpike Trustees should not, if they so desired, have established a turnpike gate and demanded a toll at intervals of one hundred yards throughout the county of Carmarthen. They interpreted and administered the law as they thought fit, and there was no appeal from their decisions.

Resistance to the payment of such tolls broke out in Carmarthenshire in the spring of 1843 on the riotous demolition of some of the turnpike gates. The Trefechan gate in the Whitland Trust was first attacked. From this district the resistance spread to the other counties of SOUTH WALES. The leader of the movement concealed his identity under the name of "Rebecca"; his followers called themselves the "Children of Rebecca" in allusion to the Scriptural text, "Let thy seed possess the gates of those which hate them." Parties of five or six hundred men, mostly mounted, armed with pickaxes, sledges, hatchets, and guns, rioted through the counties of Carmarthen, Pembroke, Cardigan, and parts of Radnor, Brecon, and Glamorgan. They were headed by their leader, who was mounted; they were disguised in female attire, with blackened faces. So well did the rioters keep counsel and so secretly did they manage their forays that, in spite of the efforts of the local magistrates, assisted by large bodies of military sent into the district, no effectual check was put upon their proceedings for months.

Although the Rebecca riots are chiefly remembered in connection with WALES, it is extremely interesting to note that nearly one hundred years earlier similar disturbances took place in England, where turnpikes had been first established. In August, 1749, a great number of people in Somersetshire and Gloucestershire, some disguised in women's clothes, headed by leaders on horseback with blackened faces, had attacked the turnpike gates in those counties. They were called "Jack a Lents." The course of these disturbances was much like that of the later Rebecca riots of the nineteenth century in WALES.

But the turnpike gate extortions in SOUTH WALES were not the only cause of these riots. A Royal Commission was appointed on October 7, 1843, to make a full and diligent inquiry into the state of the laws, as administered in SOUTH WALES, which regulated the maintenance of turnpike roads and bridges. The Commission made their report on March 6, 1844, and from it we learn that there was deep-seated agrarian discontent in SOUTH WALES, not only at the exactions of the Turnpike Trusts, but also in connection with the costly administration of the poor law and the high salaries of poor law officers; the vexed question of tithes and the increased amounts payable for tithes under the Tithes Commutation Act of 1836; the permanent increase of county rates; the fees of Justices' clerks and the administration of justice by the magistrates; the cost of recovering small debts; and the position of the Established Church of England in the districts. The Commission, while calling attention to these matters, simply dealt with the task referred to them, and finally recommended that the debts chargeable upon the several Turnpike Trusts in SOUTH WALES should be ascertained and redeemed, and that they should be consolidated and placed under uniform management and control. In the Turnpike Act of 1844 Parliament adopted its recommendations. Commissioners were appointed for the six counties of SOUTH WALES to inquire into the Turnpike Trusts, to ascertain and estimate their debts, and to award to persons entitled moneys due therefrom. These sums were advanced by the Public Works Loan Commissioners, and charged on the Consolidated Fund. All local Acts for making, repairing, or regulating turnpike roads were repealed and a "County Roads Board" was established in each county to manage the turnpike roads under the provisions of the general Turnpike Acts. Equal tolls were to be taken at all gates in the same county, and a toll once paid cleared seven miles in the same or two miles in an adjacent county. Local boards, called "District Roads Boards," were authorized. Several amending Acts relating to these turnpike roads were passed in the years 1845, 1847, 1860, 1878, 1881, and 1882. The provisions of the principal and amending Acts cannot be of any particular value at the present time, and are not printed in this volume, for by the 13th section of the Local Government Act of 1888 the whole of the machinery of the County and District Roads Boards in SOUTH WALES was transferred to the County Councils then established.

A.D. 1881.—The sale of intoxicating liquors on Sunday in WALES was prohibited by the Sunday Closing Act (44-45 VICTORIA, c. 61). This was passed at the instance of the majority of the Parliamentary representatives for WALES. Monmouthshire was treated as a part of England, and not included within its provisions. A Royal Commission was appointed in 1889 to inquire into the working of this Act.

A.D. 1887.—In the Coal Mines Regulation Act (50-51

VICTORIA, c. 58), by the 39th section (sub-section 1), it was enacted by Parliament that, in the appointment of Inspectors of mines in WALES and Monmouthshire, among candidates, otherwise equally qualified, persons having a knowledge of WELSH were to be preferred. By the Quarries' Act, 1894 (57–58 VICTORIA, c. 42, s. 2, ss. 3) and by the Factory Act of 1901 (1 EDWARD 7, c. 22, s. 118, ss. 2) similar provisions were made for the appointment of WELSH-speaking Inspectors of quarries and factories.

A.D. 1889.—An Act (52–53 VICTORIA, c. 40) to promote intermediate Education in WALES was passed in 1889. It provided for the intermediate and technical education of the inhabitants of WALES and the county of Monmouth. Like most modern legislation, the Act itself refers to and incorporates many powers contained in other Acts of Parliament. It established joint education committees in every county. These were required to prepare schemes utilizing educational endowments and buildings and, where necessary, establishing new public schools, to be administered by county governing bodies constituted under each scheme. The funds made available for this work are derived from county rates, endowments, Government grants, school fees, and local subscriptions. The Act came into operation on November 1, 1889. It was a permissive Act, enabling the various County Councils to set its machinery in motion, and has since been generally adopted in WALES and Monmouthshire with most valuable results. It was the result of the WELSH national educational movement which owed its chief impetus to the late Sir Hugh Owen. In 1881, a committee had been appointed to inquire into the condition of intermediate and higher education in WALES. This committee reported on August 18, 1881, and since then its recommendations have been adopted in almost every particular both as to higher and intermediate education. In 1885, Mr. Mundella introduced a Bill for Intermediate Education for WALES, in which for the first time the principle of a

Treasury Grant in aid of intermediate education was embodied in a Government Bill, though this was not regarded as a satisfactory measure and did not become law. The Act of 1889 originally provided for a WELSH Board of Education, but the measure was accepted by the WELSH Parliamentary representatives without this provision as a large instalment of educational facilities.

A.D. 1890.—By 53–54 VICTORIA, c. 60, s. 1, ss. 4, passed in 1890, the Councils for the counties, where the WELSH Intermediate Education Act of 1889 applied, were given financial powers to apply certain customs and excise duties towards intermediate and technical education.

A.D. 1902.—The last Statute requiring notice is the University of WALES Act, 1902 (2 EDWARD 7, c. 14). On the 30th of November, 1893, her late Majesty Queen VICTORIA granted a charter constituting and founding a University in and for WALES with the name of the University of WALES. By this Act Parliament recognized the degrees of the new University and conferred upon graduates of the University of WALES (Prifysgol Cymru) the same privileges and exemptions given to the Universities of Oxford, Cambridge, London, and the Victoria University at Manchester. A supplemental charter was granted in 1906 to the University of WALES by his present Majesty King EDWARD the Seventh, who as Prince of WALES was its Chancellor, and as King is now its Protector.

We have now discussed the considerable number of public Statutes collected in this volume, and only a few general observations remain to be made. It has been thought unnecessary to reprint any of the marginal notes thereto, for they do not form any part of the Acts of Parliament. Where convenient, the older forms of spelling are left unaltered, and it has been found impracticable to include the long catalogue of private and local Acts promulgated by the Imperial Parliament in relation to WALES. Such private legislation will demand separate and prolonged consideration.

The chronological table printed in this volume is based upon the edition of the Statutes of the Realm, published by the Record Commissioners, which extended until the reign of Queen Anne. Subsequently we have to depend upon Ruffhead's edition and the ordinary editions of the Statutes at Large. The table explains how the various statutes have been respectively repealed or affected by subsequent legislation, and it will be perceived that the majority are not now in practical use. The long-contemplated revision of our Statute Law commenced in 1856, with the result that most of the spent and obsolete Acts, which were not applicable to modern circumstances, have been gradually expunged from the Statute Roll. But it is specially provided by the various Statute Law Revision Acts, that repeals thereby made shall not revive or restore any jurisdiction, office, custom, right, title, privilege, practice, or procedure not existing or in force at the time of the repeal. Notwithstanding this provision, the point was raised in 1862 in the Court of Exchequer, in the case of the Attorney-General *v.* Jones (see 33 *Law Journal* Reports, Exchequer, p. 249), whether the laws of Howel Dda were still applicable in WALES. The question was whether one of the laws of Howel Dda (viz., that "whosoever owneth the land on the side of the shore, he owneth the breadth of his land on the shore, and he may make a weir upon it if he will, but if the sea cast anything on the land or on the shore, the king owneth it, for the sea is a packhorse to the king") was still in force by virtue of the statutes 12 EDWARD I and 27 HENRY 8, c. 26, s. 31. The counsel for the Crown rested their case, in the first instance, on the *prima facie* title of the Crown to the seashore between high and low-water mark. On the part of the defendant it was contended that by the Venedotian Code of the laws of Howel Dda the seashore in Anglesea, Carnarvon, and Merioneth did not belong to the King, and that the laws of WALES were, under the statutes 12 EDWARD I (*Statutum Walliæ*) and 27 HENRY 8, c. 26, s. 31, still in force in that country. The jury returned a verdict for the Crown. A rule for a new trial was subsequently obtained by the defendant on the ground of misdirection by the Judge in directing the jury that the ancient laws of WALES did not apply to this case, but Bramwell, B., in making the rule absolute, left this point to be dealt with by the Judge at the new trial, without commenting thereon. The case came on for the new trial before Channell, B., at the Chester Summer Assizes in 1862. To prove the laws of Howel Dda, the defendant called Mr. Black, the former assistant-keeper of the Public Records, who produced an extract examined by him from the Cottonian Manuscript in the British Museum, containing the Venedotian Code, which in his opinion was of the date of the latter part of the twelfth century. He also produced a certified copy and translation of certain entries on the original roll, preserved among the Chancery Rolls, relating to WALES (9 EDWARD I, A.D. 1279 and 1280); the entries consisting of a certificate and apprise under a commission issued by EDWARD I, with instructions thereto annexed; a writ of aid for those Commissioners; and a writ addressed to Llywelyn Prince of WALES respecting the result of the inquiry instituted by the King.

On objection taken, Baron Channell was of opinion that the return to the Commission of EDWARD I, apart from the references to be found in text-writers, showed that there had been laws enacted, administered, or compiled by Howel Dda; but after consulting Crompton, J., he ruled (observing, however, that the point was not free from difficulty) that the Cottonian MSS. was not admissible in evidence as proof of what those laws were. The particular law of Howel Dda, relied upon in support of the defendant's case, not being proved, the question of its present existence and validity was not raised. The jury, upon the direction of the Judge, upon other grounds found a verdict for the defendant. The important point remained undecided, and is left open for further argument by some patriotic litigant.

In the case of Bunbury *v.* Hewson, decided in 1849 by the Court of Exchequer of Pleas (see 3 Exchequer Reports, p. 558), it was contended that the ecclesiastical laws and customs of England did not extend to Wales. The point raised was whether an action could be maintained by the executors of a deceased incumbent against the executors of his predecessor, for dilapidations which occurred during the incumbency of the predecessor. The plaintiff stated in his declaration that by the law and custom of England hitherto used and approved of such an action would lie at common law. The defendant replied that there was no precedent of such an action by the executor of a deceased incumbent, and further submitted that, the living in question being in Wales, the law and custom of England at the time stated in the declaration did not extend to Wales. (The defendant was the executor of the Vicar of the parish church of Swansea, who was seised in right of the said vicarage of and in certain glebe lands lying and being in the parish of Kenfig and Pyle in the county of Glamorgan.) Baron Parke, in giving judgment in favour of the plaintiff, held that the action was maintainable, and overruled the objection that the vicarage being in Wales prevented the application of the English law and customs, upon the ground that the laws of England were extended in 1535 to Wales by the statute 27 Henry 8, c. 26.

In this Introduction only a brief summary of the provisions and objects of the various statutes has been given, together with such explanatory matter considered necessary to assist the reader in understanding the scope of this legislation and making any further research. It does not profess to be a complete investigation of the historical circumstances connected with the legislative enactments concerning WALES. It is but a preliminary exploration made into the trackless desert of the library of the Statutes of the English Parliament, and it is solely intended as a guide to a closer and more efficient examination of the historical treasures which lie therein. The more detailed scrutiny of the history of the WELSH nation will, we trust, be rendered easier by the inclusion within this volume of the principal statutes relating to the Dominion, Principality, and Country of WALES.

THE STATUTES OF WALES

A.D. 1215] **Magna Charta. Clauses 56, 57, and 58, relating to Wales.**

"56. If we have dispossessed or removed any Welshmen from their lands, or franchises, or other things, without legal judgment of their peers, in England, or in Wales, they shall be immediately returned to them; and if a dispute shall have arisen over this, then it shall be settled in the borderland by judgment of their peers, concerning holdings of England according to the law of England, concerning holdings of Wales according to the law of Wales, and concerning holdings of the borderland according to the law of the borderland. The Welsh shall do the same to us and ours.

"57. Concerning all those things, however, from which any one of the Welsh shall have been removed or dispossessed without legal judgment, of his peers, by King Henry our father, or King Richard our brother, which we hold in our hands, or which others hold, and we are bound to warrant to them, we shall have respite till the usual period of crusaders, those being excepted about which suit was begun or inquisition made by our command before our assumption of the cross. When, however, we shall return or if by chance we shall desist from our journey, we will show full justice to them immediately, according to the laws of the Welsh and the aforesaid parts.

"58. We will give back the son of Llewellyn immediately, and all the hostages from Wales and the charters which had been liberated to us as a security for peace."

A.D. 1275]

3 Edward 1, c. 17.

STATUTE OF WESTMINSTER I.

THE KING'S SOVEREIGNTY OVER THE MARCHES OF WALES.

"And these to be intended in all places where the King's Writ lieth and if they be done in the Marches of WALES, or in any other place where the King's Writ be not current, the King, who is sovereign Lord over all, shall do right there unto such as will complain."

A.D. 1284]

12 Edward 1.

THE STATUTE OF WALES.

I. WALES ANNEXED TO CROWN OF ENGLAND.

EDWARD, by the Grace of God King of England, Lord of Ireland, and Duke of Aquitain, to all his Subjects of his Land of Snowdon, and of other his Lands in Wales, Greeting in the Lord. The Divine Providence, which is unerring in its own Government, among other gifts of its Dispensation, wherewith it hath vouchsafed to distinguish Us and our Realm of England, hath now of its favour, wholly and entirely transferred under our proper dominion, the Land of Wales with its Inhabitants, heretofore subject unto us, in Feudal Right, all obstacles whatsoever ceasing; and hath annexed and united the same unto the Crown of the aforesaid Realm, as a Member of the same Body. We therefore, under the Divine Will, being desirous that our aforesaid Land of Snowdon and our other Lands in those parts, like as all those which are subject unto our Power, should be governed with due Order to the Honour and Praise of God and of Holy Church, and the Advancement of Justice, and that the People or Inhabitants of those Lands who have submitted themselves absolutely unto our will, and whom We have thereunto so accepted, should be protected in security within our peace under fixed Laws and Customs, have caused to be rehearsed before Us and the Nobles of our Realm, the Laws and Customs of those parts hitherto in use: Which being diligently heard and fully understood, We have, by the advice of the aforesaid Nobles, abolished certain of them, some thereof We have allowed, and some We have corrected; and We have likewise commanded certain others to be ordained and added thereto; and these We Will shall be from henceforth for ever stedfastly kept and observed in our Lands in those parts according to the Form underwritten.

II. Regulations of the Jurisdiction, and its Division into Counties, and Appointment of Officers.

We have Provided and by our command ordained, That the Justices of Snowdon shall have the Custody and Government of the Peace of Us the King in Snowdon, and our Lands of Wales adjoining; and shall administer Justice to all Persons whatsoever, according to the original Writs of Us the King, and also the Laws and Customs underwritten. We likewise will and ordain that there be Sheriffs, Coroners, and Bailiffs of Commotes in Snowdon, and our Lands of those parts. A Sheriff of Anglesea, under whom shall be the whole Land of Anglesea, with its Cantreds, Metes, and Bounds. A Sheriff of Caernarvan, under whom shall be the Cantred of Arvan, the Cantred of Arthlencoyth, the Commote of Cruthin, the Cantred of Thleen, and the Commote of Yvionith. A Sheriff of Meirioneth, under whom shall be the Cantred of Meirioneth, the Commote of Ardovey, and the Commote of Penthlin, and the Commote of Deyrinoin, with their Metes and Bounds. A Sheriff of Flint, under whom shall be the Cantred of Englefeud, the Land of Maillor Sexeneyth, and the Land of Hope, and of the Land adjoining to our Castle and Town of Rothelan unto the Town of Chester, shall from henceforth be obedient under Us to our Justice of Chester, and shall answer for the Issues of the same Commote at our Exchequer of Chester. There shall be Coroners in the same Counties, to be chosen by the King's Writ, the tenor whereof is to be found among the original Writs of the Chancery. There shall likewise be Bailiffs of Commotes who shall faithfully do and discharge their Offices and diligently attend thereto, according to what shall be given them in charge by the Justices and Sheriffs. A Sheriff of Carmarthen, with its Cantreds and Commotes and antient Metes and Bounds. A Sheriff of Cardigan and Llanbadarn, with its Cantreds and Commotes, and Metes and Bounds. There shall be Coroners in these Counties, and Bailiffs of Commotes, as before.

III. Of the Office of Sheriff in Wales; and the Manner of holding Courts.

The Sheriff ought to execute his Office in this Form, to wit; When any one shall have complained to him of any Trespass done to him against the Peace of our Lord the King, or of the taking and wrongful detaining of Cattle, or of an unjust taking, or of Debt, or any other Contract not fulfilled and the like, either by Writ or without Writ, first let him take Pledges of prosecuting his Claim, or the party's Oath if he be a poor man, and afterwards make Execution as is more fully declared, in this manner, the Defendants in each case shall be summoned to be at the next County Court, to answer unto the Plaintiffs; at which Court, after Summons made and Proof thereof, if they come not, they shall be summoned again by Award of the Court, to be at another Court next ensuing, to answer as before; at which, if they come not, after Summons repeated and Proof thereof, they shall be summoned by Award of the Court a third time, to be at the next third County Court to answer as before; at which Court, if they come not, then the Plaintiffs by Judgment of the Court, as well in Pleas by Writ as Plaints without Writ, shall recover their Demands together with Damages or Amends, as well in movables as in immovables, according as the Actions require. And for such Defaults a Penalty shall be incurred to our Lord the King, according to the Law and Custom of Wales. And when the parties shall have appeared to plead, each shall be received without Fine to relate the Truth of his Case; and according to the Plaints Answers and Allegations on either side, shall be the Proceeding to Judgment for the Plaintiff or Defendant, by the Award of the County Court; and the Punishment shall be according to the Quality and Quantity of the Offence. And it is to be known that the County Court ought to be holden in this Manner, to wit, from Month to Month in such Place as our Lord and King shall ordain; and this upon Monday in one County, upon Tuesday in another, upon Wednesday in a third County, and upon Thursday in a fourth, and not upon any other days. And the Sheriff shall proceed thus in the holding of his County Court. First he shall hear and receive before himself and the Coroner and the Suitors of the County, the presentments of Felonies and of Casualties that shall have happened between two Counties, touching the death of a man, in this manner; That the four Townships next to the place where the fact of the Manslaughter or Misadventure shall have happened, shall come to the next County Court, together with him that found the dead man, and the Welshery, that is the Kindred of the Person slain, and there shall present the Fact of Felony, the Case of Misadventure, and the manner of either: Declaring thus, That on such a day, at such a place, it fell out that such an one, known or unknown, was found slain feloniously, or drowned, or otherwise dead by misadventure, and such an one found him, who is present, &c. And that Presentment shall be forthwith inrolled, as well in the Coroner's Roll as in the Sheriff's. And if there should be present man or woman that would sue by Appeal, there shall be Pledges to prosecute taken forthwith, and the Appeal shall be sued in that County Court. So that if the Appellees should appear, they shall straight be taken, and detained in the prison of our Lord the King until the coming of the Justice, and be safely kept; And if they should not appear, then upon the Prosecution of the Appellor they shall be exacted from one County Court to another; and if they come not at the fourth Court, or be not taken to pledge, they shall be outlawed, and Women shall be waived. And if they should not appear at the first County Court where they shall be exacted, their Lands and Chattels shall be forthwith taken and seized in the hand of our Lord the King, and shall be delivered into Ward of the Townships, as hereunder. In the same manner shall the proceeding be in an Appeal of Wounding, Maihem, Rape, Arson, and Robbery, against the Appellees, if they should not appear. And if they should appear, and find sufficient Pledges, six at the least, or more, to abide Judgement at the coming of the Justice, they shall straight be replevied. And it is to be known, that the Proceeding to Outlawry is not to have place against Appellees of Force, Command, Direction, or Receit, until some one be convicted of the Fact.

IV. The Turn.

The Sheriff shall make his Turn in his several Commotes twice in the year, in some place certain to be therefore assigned; that is to say, once after the Feast of Saint Michael, and once after Easter. At which Turn all Freeholders and others holding Lands and dwelling in that Commote, at the Time of the Summons for holding the Turn, except Men of Religion, Clerks, and Women, ought to come thither. And the Sheriff, by the Oath of twelve Freeholders, of the most discreet and lawful, or more at his discretion, shall diligently make Inquiry upon the Articles touching the Crown and Dignity of our Lord the King hereunder written:

Of Traitors to our Lord the King and the Realm, the Queen, and their Children, and their Abettors. Of Thieves, Manslayers, Robbers, Murderers, Burners that make felonious Burnings, and their Receivers and accessaries. Of Mascherers, that sell and buy stolen Meat knowingly. Of Whittawers, that is, those that whiten Hides of Oxen and Horses, knowing the same to have been stolen, that they may not be known again. Of Redubbers of stolen Cloths, that turn them into a new Shape, and change the old one, as making a Coat or Surcoat of a Cloak, and the like. Of Outlaws and Objurers of the Realm that have returned to it. Of such as have withdrawn themselves against the coming and Eyre of the Justice, and have returned after the Eyre. Of Ravishers of Maids, Nuns, and Matrons of good repute. Of Treasure trove. Of turning Water Courses. Of Hindrance, Restraint, and narrowing of the Highway. Of Walls, Houses, Gates, Ditches, and Marl-pits raised and made near unto the publick Way, to the Nuisance of the same Way, and to the Danger of Passengers; and of them that raise and make the same. Of Forgers of the Money and Seal of our Lord the King. Of Trespassers in Parks and Vivaries. Of Breakers of the Prison of our Lord the King. Of Takers of Pigeons flying from Dovecotes. Of those who make Pound-breach; that is, Breakers of the Inclosures wherein Beasts are impounded. Of Forstall, that is, of the Stopping of Cattle. Of Hamsoken, that is, of breaking into houses. Of Thefbote, that is, of taking Amends for Theft without leave of the King's Court. Of them that do imprison any Freeman whatsoever. Of Usurers. Of Removers and Falsifiers of Landmarks. Of non-observance of the Assize of Bread and Beer, and of Breakers thereof. Of unlawful Bushels Gallons and other Measures. Of unlawful Yards and Weights and them that sell therewith. Of them that give Lodgings to persons unknown for more than two nights. Of Blood spilt; of Hue and Cry levied. Of them that shear Sheep by Night in the Folds, and that flay them or any other Beasts. Of them that take and collect by Night the Ears of Corn in Autumn, and carry them away; and of all other the like Trespassers. Let Inquiry also be made of the Rights of our Lord the King withdrawn, as of Custodies, Wardships, Marriages; Reliefs, Fees, Advowsons of Churches, if any there be, Suits to the County and Commotes; who shall have withdrawn them, and from what time; and of them that shall have taken upon them to exercise Royalties without Warrant, as Gallows, Fines for Breach of the Assize of Bread and Beer; Plea of *Vetitum Namium;* and other the like Rights which specially and by Prerogative belong to the Crown of our Lord the King. The Sheriff in making his View and Turn, shall first cause to come together forthwith before him all the men of the whole Commote, and shall cause them to swear that they will true Presentment make to the twelve or more of the Jury chosen by the Sheriff; and that they will conceal nought that is true, nor say ought that is false, of those things that shall be given them in charge in behalf of our Lord the King; and the Oath being taken, the above written Articles shall be laid before them and they shall be charged to make diligent Inquiry upon each: and if they should find any who, for their Offence ought to lose Life or Limb, they shall intimate their Names to the Sheriff secretly; lest the Men so indicted should escape if they were present in the Turn and were indicted publicly. But of the rest of the Articles they may well declare their Answers openly and in publick, and return their Verdict; and then it shall be told them to go apart by themselves, and diligently to treat and inquire of those things that are given them in charge. And when they shall have been well informed, they shall return and render their Verdict and make their Presentment. But the Sheriff, in receiving the Verdicts and Recognitions shall not seek to trouble them that make Presentment; nor shall he take Fines of them for not being troubled. And when the Verdict or Presentment of the Jury is brought in, the Sheriff shall forthwith, or as soon as he may, take and keep in Prison, or discharge upon sufficient Bail, such as have been indicted of Offences whereof the Punishment is Death or Loss of Limb. And of the rest of the Articles there shall forthwith be Correction and due Execution made in all and every the Matters aforesaid, according to the Inquisitions. And the Bailiffs of Commotes shall from henceforth hold their Commotes and do and administer Justice to the Parties in Suit.

V. Of the Officer of Coroner: that is to say, of the Pleas of the Crown in Wales.

It is provided, That in every Commote in Wales there shall be one Coroner at the least who shall be chosen in the full County Court by the Writ of our Lord the King, according to the Form among other Royal Writs in the following Roll contained: and he shall there make Oath before the Sheriff, that he will be faithful to our Lord the King, and that he will faithfully do and execute all things belonging to the Office of Coroner. And his Office shall be this; that when he shall be required by any one to come to view a Man dead by Felony, or drowned, or in any other manner dead by Misadventure; and also to view a Man grievously wounded, so that his Life be despaired of, that he shall forthwith require the Sheriff or Bailiff of the Commote to cause to come before him at a certain Day and Place, all Persons of twelve years of age and upwards of that town wherein the casualty shall have happened, and of the four Townships next adjoining; and by their Oaths he shall faithfully, cautiously, and secretly and diligently make Enquiry of the Felony, the Felons and their Chattels; likewise of the Fact and the Manner thereof, that is to say, who hath been guilty of the Fact, who of Force, and what manner of Force, who of Command or Direction, and who of Receit after the Fact; and of the Chattels of all those who shall be found guilty thereof by the Inquest. He shall likewise make Inquiry who first found the Body, and his Name shall be enrolled, and he shall be attached by Pledges, whose Names shall be enrolled, to come to the next County Court, and also before the Justice in his Circuit. And, the Inquisition being made, he shall forthwith cause the same to be inrolled distinctly and openly, together with the Names of those who shall have been found guilty, and their Chattels; and he shall secretly deliver to the Sheriff, if he be present, or to the Bailiff of the Commotes, their Names in Writing; giving in Charge on the behalf of our Lord the King, that straight their Bodies be taken and safely kept in the Prison of our Lord the King until they stand upon their Acquittal in the Court of our Lord the King; and he shall cause their Chattels to be faithfully appraised, and shall set down in his Roll as well the particular Chattels, as the Value thereof; and shall cause the said Chattels, by the view of the Sheriff or Bailiff and of the other liege Subjects of our Lord the King who shall be there present, to be delivered to every of the Townships wherein the said Chattels shall severally be found; that they may duly answer for the same upon the coming of the Justice of our Lord the King. The Coroner, when he shall make Inquisition concerning the Dead shall inquire of the Welshery, that is to say, the Kindred of the dead Man: And if any one on the part of the Father, and another on the part of the Mother shall appear, and say that they are of his Kindred, and the same be testified by liege Subjects of the King, he shall straight cause their Names to be inrolled in this Roll. But if none of the Kindred should appear, it shall likewise be inrolled in his Roll that none doth appear; that the Justice at his coming may the more clearly proceed in what is fit to be done thereupon. The Coroner also shall diligently make Inquiry of the happening of the Accident, and the manner thereof; and according to what he shall find upon the Inquest, shall cause the same to be distinctly inrolled. He shall likewise inquire who found the body, and cause his Name to be inrolled, as above.

Sanctuary.

Moreover when a Thief, or a Manslayer, or other Malefactor shall fly to the Church, the Coroner, as soon as he shall be certified thereof, shall direct the Bailiff of our Lord the King for that Commote to cause to come before him at a certain day the good and lawful Men of the neighbourhood; and in their presence, after Recognition made of the Felony, shall cause the Abjuration to be made in this manner: That the Felon shall be brought out unto the Church Door, and a Sea Port shall be assigned him by the Coroner, and then he shall abjure the Realm; and, according as the Port assigned shall be far or near, the term shall be set for his going out of the Realm aforesaid: So that in journeying towards that Port, bearing in his Hand a Cross, he shall not in any manner turn out of the King's Highway, that is to say, neither upon the right hand nor upon the left, but shall always hold to the same until he shall depart the Realm.

VI. The Forms of the King's Original Writs to be pleaded in Wales.

The Writ of Novel Disseisin for a Freehold, whereof any Freeholder shall have been disseised unjustly and without Judgement.

The King to the Sheriff of Anglesey, Greeting. A. hath complained unto us that B. and C. unjustly, and without Judgement have disseised him of his Freehold in N. after the Proclamation of our Peace in Wales, in the eleventh year of our Reign. And therefore We command you, that if the aforesaid A. shall give you Security to prosecute his Claim, then you shall cause the said Tenement to be reseised of the Chattels that shall have been taken in the same; and the same Tenement with the Chattels to be in place until a certain day, whereof our Justice shall give you Notice. And in the mean time cause twelve free and lawful men of that neighbourhood to view that Tenement, and their names to be put in writing. And summon them by good Summoners that they be then before our Justice aforesaid, ready to make Recognition thereof: And put by Gage and Safe Pledges the aforesaid B. and C. or their Bailiffs, if they be not found, that they be then there to hear that Recognition. And have there the Summoners, the Names of the Pledges, and this Writ.

Dated at Carnarvon such a day and year (Or elsewhere).

For Novel Disseisin of Common of Pasture, thus:

A. hath complained unto Us that B. and C. unjustly, &c., have disseised him of his Common of Pasture in N. that is appurtenant to his Freehold in the same Town; or in another, if so be the case; after our Peace, &c. And therefore we command you that if the aforesaid A. shall give you Security, &c. then you shall cause twelve free, &c. to view that Pasture and the Tenement, and their names to be put in Writing; and summon them by good Summoners to come before the aforesaid Justice, &c. ready to make Recognition thereof; and put by Gage and Safe Pledges the aforesaid B. and C., or their Bailiffs, if they be not found, that they be then there to hear that Recognition. And have there, &c.

Dated &c.

Or thus:

A. hath complained unto Us that B. unjustly, &c. hath raised or pulled down, a certain Hedge, or a certain Fence, or hath obstructed or narrowed a certain Way, or hath turned aside the Course of a certain Water, or hath made or pulled down, or made higher, a certain Pond in N. to the Nuisance of his Freehold in the same Town; or in another, if so be the case; after our Peace, &c. And therefore we command you that if the aforesaid A. shall give you security, &c. then you shall cause twelve, &c. to view that Hedge or that Fence, or that Way, or that Watercourse, or that Pond, and the Tenement, and their Names to be put in Writing. And summon them, &c. to come before our Justice, &c. ready, &c. and put by Gage, &c. the aforesaid B. or his Bailiff, &c. that he be then, &c. and have, &c.

Dated &c.

And the Forms of the Writs shall be changed according to the Diversities of the Cases.

Writ of Mortdancester.

The King to the Sheriff, Greeting. If A. shall give you Security to prosecute his Claim then summon by good Summoners twelve free and lawful men of the Neighbourhood of N. to come before our Justice, ready upon their oath to make Recognition whether B. the Father of the aforesaid A. was seised in his Demesne as of Fee of such a Manor with the Appurtenances, or of so much Land with the appurtenances, in N. on the day when he died; and whether he died since the Proclamation of our Peace in Wales, in the eleventh year of our Reign. And whether the same A. be his next Heir. And in the mean time let them view that Manor or that Land, and cause their names to be put in writing. And summon by good Summoners C., who now holdeth that Manor, or that Land, that he be then there to hear that Recognition. And have there the Summoners and this Writ.

And Letters Patent shall be made in these words, until our Lord the King shall ordain otherwise:

The King, to His Justice, Greeting. Know Ye that We have constituted you our Justice, together with those whom Ye shall think fit to be associated unto you to take the Assize of Novel Disseisin and Mortdancester in the Parts of Wales. And therefore We command you that on certain days and places, which you shall therefore provide, you do take those Assizes; doing therein what appertaineth to Justice, according to the Law and Custom of our Realm. Saving unto us the Amercements and other things therefore due unto us: for We have given command to our Sheriffs, that they do cause these Assizes to come before you, at certain days and places which you shall for the same make known unto them. In witness thereof we have caused these our Letters Patent to be made unto you. Dated &c.

And there shall be a Writ Close, by the Command of the Justice, to be directed to the Sheriffs in this Form:

The King, to the Sheriff, Greeting. We command you that you cause to come before our Justice at certain days and places which he shall make known unto you, all the Assizes of Novel Disseisin and Mortdancester arraigned before the said Justice by our Writs, together with the original Writs, Attachments, and all other Proceedings concerning the said Assizes; and this Writ. Dated &c. And the Form of the Writ shall be changed according to the Diversities of the Cases; that is to wit; if the Mother or the Brother, or the Sister, or the Uncle, or the Aunt, were seised in Demesne as of Fee of the Thing demanded by Process of Mortdancester, on the Day when they died. And when many Coheirs and Parceners of any Inheritance demand that Inheritance, that is to say, when one of them demandeth on the Death of Father or Mother, Brother or Sister, Uncle or Aunt, and another or others of those demand on the Death of a Grandfather or Grandmother or Cousin, Male or Female, a Writ of Mortdancester shall be made to them upon their Case; because that part of the said Writ that toucheth the kind of Ancestor who is dead, according to the Clause thereof commonly used, draweth unto it the Nature of other Articles touching Coheirs in remoter degrees.

The General Writ; which in one Case concerneth the Right, and in another the Possession.

The King to the Sheriff, Greeting. Command A., that justly and without Delay he render to B. the Manor of N. with the Appurtenances, whereof the aforesaid A. deforceth him, as he saith; and unless he shall so do, and if the aforesaid B. shall give you Security to prosecute his Claim, then summon by good summoners the aforesaid A. that he be before our Justice, to show wherefore he hath not done it. And have there the Summoners and this Writ. Dated &c. Or this: Command A. that justly, &c. he render so much land, with the appurtenances in N. as before. And in like manner that Writ shall be granted before the Justices in the Bench, if the demandant chooseth.

The Writ of Dower in Wales.

The King to the Sheriff, Greeting. Command A. that justly and without delay, he render to B. who was the wife of C. her reasonable

Dower that to her belongeth of the Freehold that was the aforesaid C.'s, late her Husband, in N. whereof she hath nothing, as she saith, and whereof she complaineth that the aforesaid A. deforceth her; and unless he shall so do, and if the aforesaid B. shall give you Security to prosecute her Claim, then summon by good summoners the aforesaid A. that he be before our Justice, &c. to shew, &c. and have there the summoners and this Writ. Dated &c. And the Form of the Writ shall be changed according to the diversity of the Cases; to wit, if the woman should have been endowed at the Church door, by the Consent and Will of the Father, or other ancestor whose Heir he may be or ought to be.

The Writ of Debt.

The King to the Sheriff, Greeting. Command A. that justly and without delay, he render to B. One hundred Shillings, which he oweth to him and unjustly detaineth, as he saith; and unless he shall so do, and if the aforesaid B. shall give you security to prosecute his Claim, then summon by good summoners the aforesaid A. that he be before our Justice to shew wherefore he hath not done it; and have there the summoners and this Writ. Dated &c. And if Chattels or Sacks of Wool should be demanded, the Writ shall be as underwritten:

The King to the Sheriff, Greeting. Command A. that justly and without delay, he render to B. one Sack of Wool, of the Value of Ten Marks, which he unjustly withholdeth from him; or Chattels to the Value of Ten Marks, which he unjustly withholdeth from him, as he saith. And unless he shall so do, &c. as before. And the Forms of like Writs shall be made according to the Plaintiff's shewing, and to the diversities of the Cases. And such Writs of Debt, to be pleaded before the Justice, shall not be made of a less sum than Forty Shillings. But Pleas of Debt that amount not to the Sum of Forty Shillings, shall be pleaded in the County Court, and likewise in the Commote. And if it happen the Plaintiff should choose to plead of such in the County Court, then let there be made to him this Writ, which is called Justicies.

We command you, that you hold to Justice A. that justly and without delay he render to B. One Hundred Shillings which he oweth to him, as he saith, and he may reasonably prove that he ought to render the same; so that we may hear no more Complaint thereof for Failure of Justice, &c. Dated &c.; or thus, That he render to him a Sack of Wool, of the Value of Ten Marks, which he unjustly withholdeth; or Chattels to the Value of Ten marks, which he unjustly withholdeth from him, as he saith, as he may reasonably prove; So that, &c. Dated &c. And a Pone shall be thereupon made if demanded, in this Form: The King to the Sheriff, Greeting.

Put, at the request of the Plaintiff before our Justice, &c., at such a day, the Plaint that is in your County Court by our Writ, between A. and B. of a Debt of One hundred Shillings, which the same A. demandeth of the aforesaid B. and summon by good summoners the aforesaid B. that he be then there to answer thereof to the aforesaid A. and have there the summoners and this Writ; and the other Writ. Dated &c.

The Writ of Covenant.

The King to the Sheriff, Greeting. Command A. that justly and without delay he keep with B. the Covenant made between them of one messuage, ten acres of land and five acres of woodland, with the appurtenances in N. And unless he shall do so &c., then summon the aforesaid A. that he be, &c. to shew, &c. Dated &c.

And let Writs of Covenant be made according to the complaints of the contracting parties and the diversities of the cases, whether before the Justice, or in the County Court, at the will of the plaintiffs. And if they choose to plead in the County Court let them have the Writ called Justicies, and thereof a Pone shall be made if it be demanded.

The Form of the Writ of Attorney.

The King to the Sheriff, Greeting. Know ye that A. hath before us made his attornies B. and C. to win or lose in the plaint that is before you by our Writ between the said A. demandant, and D., tenant of one messuage, with the appurtenances in N. And therefore we command you that you do for this purpose receive the aforesaid B. and C. or either of them if both cannot be present, in the place of him the said A. Dated &c.

And in the same manner shall Writs of Attorneys be made in other cases, according to the diversities of the cases and the forms of the Writs.

The Form of Writ for Choosing the Coroner.

The King to the Sheriff, Greeting. We command you that in your full County Court, and by the assent of the same County you cause a Coroner to be chosen; who, having taken oath as the custom is, shall thereafter do and observe those things that belong to the office of Coroner in the aforesaid County; and that you cause to be chosen one who hath best knowledge and ability to execute that office; and that you make known unto us his name. Dated &c.

And if he should be sick, or should die, or for any other cause be unable to execute his office, then let another Writ be made, changing what ought to be changed.

VII. Of Pleas.

Some are to be determined by the Assize; some by Juries:

By the Assize are to be determined,—

When one who is seised of a freehold being afterwards disseised by force demandeth seisin to be restored to him in this case there is provided the Writ of Novel Disseisin in the form above written among the other original Writs of the Chancery: In like manner for common of pasture when one being disseised of his common of pasture appurtenant unto his freehold demandeth seisin to be restored to him; for this case also there is provided the same Writ of Novel Disseisin by the changing of certain words in the Form above written among the other original Writs of the Chancery; wherein the proceeding is to be thus: First the Sheriff, having taken from the plaintiff two pledges to prosecute shall cause to be chosen twelve free and lawful men &c. of the neighbourhood where the tenement or pasture lieth, and shall cause them to view the tenement and in like manner the pasture, and shall attach the Disseisors, as it is contained in the Writ: Afterwards, when the parties and the Assize shall come before the Justice the plaintiff shall be asked of what freehold or of what common or pasture he complaineth that he is disseised, and according to his complaint and the answer of the adverse party they shall proceed to the taking of the Assize, unless the Disseisor can say anything wherefore the Assize ought to tarry, and if the Assize do pass for the plaintiff he shall recover his seisin, together with the damages taxed by the Assize against the Disseisor; and the Disseisor shall abide in mercy of our Lord the King, or shall be committed to prison to be ransomed if the Disseisin were done outrageously and with an armed force.

There are certain other Writs which are to be determined by the Assize, to wit: of a pond made, pulled down or raised higher; of a fence raised or pulled down; of a hedge raised or pulled down; of a way obstructed or narrowed; of a watercourse turned aside; and according to the diversity of the cases the original Writ shall be changed: which Writs are contained above with the writs of Novel Disseisin; and the proceeding therein is after the same manner as is above said in the Writ of Freehold and of common of pasture. In the above-said Writs of Assize of Novel Disseisin no essoin or delay lieth; but the proceeding to do justice beginneth on the first day.

There is another Writ of Assize: When any one demandeth seisin of a tenement whereof his ancestor died seised, that is to say, the father, brother, uncle and grandfather; for which case there is provided the Writ of Mortdancester in the form contained in the aforesaid Roll among the other Writs. And it sometimes happeneth that seisin of an ancestor is demanded where the ancestor hath not died seised, but was seised on the day when he entered into religion, or began a pilgrimage in which journey he died; and then in place of the clause "on the day whereon he died" shall be put "on the day whereon he entered into religion," or "began his pilgrimage," &c., in which pilgrimage, &c., and if, &c.

In this Writ of Mortdancester the proceedings shall be after this manner: First pledges to prosecute being found, and the assize elected, and view made by the jurors the tenant shall be summoned by good and lawful summoners, that he be before the Justice at a certain day; and the summons shall contain warning of fifteen days at the least, at which day, if he come the Justice shall proceed in the execution of his office, and if he come not at that day, he shall be punished for his default according to the provision of the Welsh law, that is to say, by three cows or the value thereof; and he shall be summoned again by two other summoners by a summons containing the like warning of fifteen days as before is said; at which day, whether he come or not, the Justice shall proceed to do his office, unless he shall cause himself to be essoined for being beyond sea, and then there shall be given him the space of forty days, so that he have ebb and flood; and let him that shall so essoin himself beware; for if, being within the four seas he falsely essoin himself of being beyond sea, and be there convicted by good proof or by good inquest he shall be punished as for the default at the first by amerciament according to what is contained in the Welsh law; and also he shall be estopped from saying anything against the Assize unless he can vouch to warranty. And be it known that neither in the Writ of Mortdancester nor in any Writ of a plea of land doth any essoin lie, except only the essoin of being beyond sea, and this before the tenant or deforciant appeareth in Court; and the essoin of being in the King's service, which lieth in every stage of the plea when the King shall be pleased to warrant the same: But let him beware that he doth not falsely cause himself to be essoined of the King's service; for if he should fail of the King's Warrant he shall be punished for his default by amerciament to be made to our Lord the King according to the Welsh law, and by paying to the adverse party his expenses of that day, according to the Justice's discretion.

In these Writs of Mortdancester the proceedings shall be after this manner: First, the Writ being read, wherein is contained the claim of the demandant the deforciant shall be asked if he can say ought wherefore the Assize ought to tarry, which, if he cannot, the Justice shall take the assize by the jurors who may best know the truth, according to the form of the Writ. And if the assize pass for the demandant, seisin shall be adjudged to the demandant with damages taxed by the jurors, and the deforciant shall abide in the King's mercy. But the deforciant may allege many things against the assize; for he may vouch to warranty, and then the arrival of the warrantor is to be waited for; whom the Justice shall cause to come by one summons at the first, and if it be necessary by resummonses as hath been said in the case of the principal deforciant; and he shall be punished for a default, as is aforesaid. If after resummons he come not, nor shall essoin himself the assize shall proceed against him by default. And if the assize pass for the demandant seisin of the thing in question shall be adjudged to the demandant. And the deforciant shall have to the value of the land of the warrantor. But if the warrantor come, and require to have that shewn him whereby he ought to warrant, it behoveth the voucher to shew the Deed that maketh mention of the warranty, or of a gift made by the warrantor or his ancestor, whose heir he is, wherein it is declared that he ought to hold of the feoffor and his heirs; or to shew that the warrantor were seised of his homage for the tenement demanded, which is to be inquired of if it should be denied by those before whom he shall say he did the homage, together with other free and lawful men sworn; or that he holdeth that tenement in exchange for another tenement: If hereupon the deforciant can bring his warrantor to warrant he shall abide in the King's mercy because he hath denied the warranty, yet nevertheless it shall be considered that he may warrant and make answer to the assize if he choose. The deforciant may allege many other things against the assize, to wit; That the ancestor, of whose death &c. committed felony for which he was hanged, outlawed, or as a public thief, escaping and not obedient to the law, beheaded; or that he abjured Wales upon confession of the felony before the Coroner: The deforciant may also object bastardy to the demandant; and thereupon the Bishop of the place shall be directed to make inquiry of the truth of the fact; and thereof to certify the Chief Justice of Wales; and according to what the Bishop shall have certified they shall proceed to judgment without taking the assize. And if the Bishop return that he is a bastard he shall be estopped from making the demand and if he return that he is legitimate the Justice shall cause the deforciant to come by summons, and, if it be necessary, by resummons, reserving to the King as hath been often said the amerciaments for default; after the resummons, whether he come or not, the demandant shall recover his demand by the Bishop's testimony, whose testimony shall not be gainsaid, and he shall remain in the King's mercy. Many other things he may allege which it is hard to enumerate; as that the ancestor, on whose death the assize is arraigned, was a Villain, and held the land in villainage; or that he held it at will, or for term of life or years, in which cases the assize of Mortdancester lieth not, and the above said assize of Novel Disseisin and Mortdancester ought not to be taken but in their proper counties, lest the country should be overcharged with trouble and expense; but the assizes shall be taken by the Justice twice thrice or four times in the year.

VIII. Of Inquests, Juries, and Trials.

It hath been treated in part of Writs and Assizes, and of the proceeding therein: It behoveth now to speak of Pleas that are to be determined by inquests or by juries: Whereof some are of things immovable, as of tenements; or of movables, as of debts and chattels; some of both kinds; some of trespasses. But first something is to be said of tenements and immovable things, for which there is a Writ provided, the form whereof is contained among the other Writs of those parts; the process upon that Writ is such; first, there being found pledges to prosecute, the sheriff shall cause the tenant to be summoned by good summoners that he appear at a certain day, at which day, if he come not, he shall be summoned again for another day; and if he come not at the second day, he shall be summoned to appear at the third day; at which day, if he come not, nor cause himself to be essoined, seisin shall be awarded to the demandant by default and the deforciant shall abide in the King's mercy, reserving nevertheless unto the King the amerciaments for every default, as hath been said before.

Now when the deforciant shall appear by reason that the plaintiff's demand cannot be known from the words of the Writ, for that the causes of suing are many and almost infinite, it is necessary that the demandant should count against the deforciant, and express the cause of his demand; and this by words that contain the truth without exception to words; not following that hard rule, He who fails in a syllable fails in the whole cause.

Of the causes of suit, what they may be, and ought to be, it is fit that something should be briefly said. Oftentimes the demandant hath right by this; that his ancestor held the land in demand, and was thereof seised as of right and fee; and then the demandant must count of the descent of kin descending to himself. It happeneth also that a man demiseth land for term of life or years, after which term the land ought to revert to himself or his heirs; or likewise that it ought to revert to him after the death of a woman-tenant in dower; or as an escheat after the death of his tenant, being a bastard, because such an one cannot have other heir than one lawfully begotten of his own body; or after the death of his tenant, who hath committed felony: In any of the four cases aforesaid, or where, after the death of anyone the land ought to remain unto another by the form of the gift; in these cases and the like the demandant shall declare his demand according to his case, and in these cases and the like wherein the aforesaid Writ is to be used, that and none other shall be used.

And the demandant's count being heard the tenant shall have a view of the land, if he require it, and a day shall be given within which the view shall be had. And at the day given after the view, the deforciant shall make answer who may vouch to warranty by the aid of the Court, as it hath been said in the Writ of Mortdancester; and the Justice shall cause the warrantor to come, as he caused the principal, by one summons, and if it be necessary by a second and a third; at which, if he come not, he being punished upon every default, as is aforesaid, seisin of the thing in question shall be awarded to the demandant for the default of the warrantor; and the deforciant shall have to the value of the land of the warrantor; and the warrantor shall be in mercy. If the warrantor come and freely warrant, he shall be received to answer and defend the plea without having a view of the land; but if he shall deny the warranty, the plea of the warranty shall be carried on between them, after the manner above directed in the Writ of Mortdancester; but if the deforciant except against the demandant, that his ancestor, whose seisin he demandeth, or any one in the descent, were a bastard, so that nothing can descend from him or through him, he shall be heard; or he may shew a deed of feoffment of his ancestor, or of quit claim of any one in the descent: and upon the affirmation of the one party, and the denial of the other, the parties shall descend to the lawful inquest: and by the verdict of the inquest shall the plea be determined, because pleas of land in those parts are not to be determined by battle, nor by the Grand Assize. So if he should except that the ancestor or any one in the descent committed felony, whereby the action lieth not for him; in which case if he to whom this is opposed denieth it, the matter ought rather to be determined by the record of the Justices or of the inquest of the country of the hanging and beheading, and also by the record of the Coroner of the outlawry and abjuration. In like manner on the demand of a tenement that ought to revert after a term passed or by the condition of the gift, upon the affirmation of the one party, and the denial of the other, they shall descend to the inquest of the country, and according to their verdict shall the judgment be.

IX. Trial of Personal Actions.

Concerning the other article, to wit, of movables, debts and chattels it remaineth to speak; for which there is provided the Writ of debt in the form above written. In this Writ the proceedings shall be after this manner. First, there being found pledges to prosecute, the Debtor and defendant shall be summoned to be before the Justice at a certain day, at which, if he come not, he shall be summoned again, and if, at the second day he come not, nor essoin himself, the debt shall be adjudged to the plaintiff by default, together with damages at the discretion of the Justice, or by the inquest of the country at the will of the Justice; and the Debtor shall abide in the King's mercy, reserving always to the King the amerciaments for every default. But if the Debtor appear the plaintiff must then declare his demand, and the cause of his demand; that is to say, if he is indebted unto him in an hundred marks, which he lent him, the day of payment whereof is passed; or for land; or an horse; or for other goods or chattels whatsoever sold to him; or for the arrears of a rent in not going out of tenement; or upon other contracts; whereupon he must produce his suit, or shew the deed of obligation or tally: The demand being heard and understood, and also the declaration of the plaintiff, the Debtor shall answer thereto; and if he acknowledge the debt, judgment shall be given against him, and it shall be levied of his goods and chattels &c. If he deny the debt, and his bond be brought forth against him, the writing must be verified by the witnesses named in the bond, if they be living, together with the jury, and if there be no witnesses named, or if they should be dead, it shall be verified by the jury only; and according to their verdict shall judgment be awarded. But if the plaintiff have not a bond, but produce his suit only, or a tally, the adverse party may deny that he is indebted to him in anything, and make his defence by wager of law, that is, by his own oath, and eleven others swearing with him, or by the country, at his election. It happeneth sometimes that the Debtor confesseth that he did once owe the debt, and allegeth payment thereof. In this case he must shew a quittance of the payment; or else the plaintiff may deny by wager of law that he hath received aught, or likewise by the country &c. This Writ of Debt shall not be granted for a less sum than forty shillings; for of a less debt the plea shall be in the County Court, either with Writ or without.

X. Of Covenants and Mixed Actions.

Concerning the third article; in which there is provided the Writ of Covenant, whereby sometimes movables are demanded, and sometimes immovables, by force of a covenant entered into between the parties, which may differ from the law in the form described in the Place above named. The proceeding upon this Writ is thus: First, there being found pledges to prosecute, the defendant shall be summoned once, and if it be necessary, a second time; and if he come not upon the second summons nor essoin himself, the demand and declaration of the plaintiff shall be heard, and the thing demanded shall be taken into the King's hand, if it be a tenement; and if it be a chattel that or its value shall be taken into the King's hand; and another day shall be given him; and if, within fifteen days he shall replevy the thing so taken into the King's hand, and appear at the day given him, he shall be received to answer and defend; but if not, the plaintiff's demand shall be awarded to him by default, together with damages taxed as is said before in the Writ of Debt; and he shall remain in the King's mercy. Saving always to the King the amerciaments for the default as aforesaid. The plaintiff's complaint being heard, and the declaration of his demand, the defendant shall make answer; and upon the affirmation of the one party, and the denial of the other, they shall proceed to the inquest, and the business shall be determined by the inquest of the country. And it is to be known that sometimes a freehold is demanded by the Writ of Covenant, as where any man letteth land to another to farm, rendering therefor a certain rent under a condition added thereto in the writing of Covenant, that if he be not satisfied for the rent it shall be lawful for him to enter into the land that he hath demised, and to hold the same; if he to whom the land hath been demised do not pay the rent, and he who hath demised it hath not the means of entering into the land demised according to the tenor of his writing, by reason of the power of his adversary in this case he ought to recover the tenement by the Writ of Covenant, together with damages. Where sometimes a covenant is made between parties that the one shall infeoff the other of a certain tenement, and shall deliver seisin unto him at a certain day, if afterwards he should transfer that tenement by feoffment to a third person, since he cannot annul that feoffment by virtue of the first contract that was not carried into effect, in that case the injured party cannot have other redress by Writ of Covenant, but this only: that he have a satisfaction in money for his damages; and thus in one case there lieth an action to demand a tenement by Writ of Covenant, and in another case money or damages, or the tenement. And for that contracts in covenants are infinite it would be difficult to make mention of each particular; but according to the nature of each covenant by the affirmation of the one party and the denial of the other, it will either come to be tried by inquest upon the fact; or it will come to an acknowledgement of the writings brought unto judgment, and according to that acknowledgement judgment will be awarded; or the writings will be denied; and then it will come to an inquiry into the making of the writings by the witnesses named in the writing, if there be such, together with the jury: and if there should be no witnesses named, or they should be dead, then by the jury only.

XI. Concerning the Fourth Article, to wit, Personal Trespasses:

Whereof it is provided that all trespasses wherein the damages do not exceed forty shillings shall be pleaded before the Sheriff in the County Court without Writ by gages and pledges: trespasses that exceed the sum of forty shillings shall be pleaded before the Justice of Wales after this manner: The plaintiff, before he be heard by the Justice, shall swear that his demand exceedeth the sum of forty shillings; and this being done, and pledges to prosecute found, the Justice shall command the Sheriff or bailiff of the place that he cause to come before him within a short term, him of whom complaint is made; and the plaintiff's complaint being heard, the defendant shall make his answer: And since in a plea of trespass the defendant can hardly do otherwise than make his defence by the country, the Justice, by consent of parties, shall make inquiry of the truth by lawful inquest, and that inquiry made, if he find the defendant guilty, he shall punish him by imprisonment or by ransom or by amerciament, and payment of damages to the injured party, according to the quality and the quantity of the offence: So that this punishment be for example to others, and make them fear to offend, and whereas mention is made above of the consent of parties, it may happen that the defendant will refuse the trial by the country; in which case if the plaintiff offer to verify the trespass done unto him by the country, and the defendant refuse the same, he shall be taken for convict, and shall be punished as though he were convict by the country.

XII. Of Dower.

And whereas heretofore women have not been endowed in Wales, the King granteth that they shall be endowed. The dower of a woman is twofold: one is an assignment of the third part of the whole land that belongeth to her husband which were his during coverture, whereof there lieth the Writ of Reasonable Dower elsewhere described in its place, with the other Writs for Wales. The proceeding in this Writ is thus: There being found pledges to prosecute, the deforciant shall be summoned to appear at a certain day, at which, if he come not, he shall be summoned again; at which day, if he come not the woman shall have her dower awarded unto her; that is to say, the third part &c. together with damages, &c. But if the defendant appear he shall be received to answer without having a view of the land; and the woman's demand being made, the tenant shall be directed to answer if he can allege anything wherefore she ought not to have her dower; and if he can allege nothing, the woman shall recover, as above. If he should object that she ought not to have her dower because she was never espoused in lawful matrimony to him whom she calleth her husband, then the Bishop shall be charged to make inquiry of the truth thereof: and that inquiry made, he shall certify it to the Justice of Wales. And according to the Bishop's certificate shall the proceeding to judgment be, after this manner: If the Bishop certify that she was not the lawful wife she shall be foreclosed of her action of dower; if he certify that she was the lawful wife the tenant shall be summoned to appear at a certain day to hear his judgment; at which day if he come not, he shall be summoned unto another day, at which day, whether he come or not,—there being no essoin allowed, the woman shall recover her dower and damages, and the tenant in mercy. Saving always to the King the amerciaments for default. But if he object that she ought not to have her dower because her husband did not hold the tenement whereof she demandeth dower, either on the day when he married her or at any time after, in fee, so that he can thereof have endowed her, the truth of this fact is to be inquired of by the country only, and according to their verdict shall the judgment be awarded. If it be objected unto her that she ought not to have her dower because her husband committed felony, then if the felony be proved, she shall not recover dower. So if it be objected unto her that her husband lost the land whereof she demandeth dower, by judgment, as that whereunto he had not right; if this be denied, and be proved by the record of the Justices before whom that land was lost, or by the country if it were lost in the County, or inferior Court, she shall be precluded from having her action of dower.

The other dower is when a son endoweth his wife by the assent of his father; the form of the Writ whereof is to be found among the rest; wherein the proceeding is after this manner: The deforciant shall be summoned as in the other Writ of Dower, and in like manner his contumacy shall be punished as in the other Writ of Dower; but if he come at the day given him then the woman's demand being made he shall answer thereto; and if the endowment made in the said form and the consent of the dower be denied, and it be established by the country that the husband did endow her, at the Church door, of his father's tenement, and that the father in his own person or by a special messenger therefor sent did consent to that dower, the woman shall recover her dower and damages. It is also to be known that in either Writ the tenant may vouch to warranty, with the aid of the Court, and the proceeding in the plea of warranty shall be as is before directed; but there is a difference between this case of dower and that above, by *præcipe*, where the mode of proceeding endeth in the warranty; because there the demandant in that case always recovereth the thing demanded, and the tenant, out of the land of the warrantor to the value: In the case of dower it is otherwise, because the tenant will keep his land in peace, and the woman will have to the value of her dower demanded, out of the land of the warrantor. Provided that the tenant hath of the land of her husband to the value whereby this may be done, but if otherwise not. Concerning other assignment of dower there is nothing said for the present.

XIII. Inheritance by the Law of Wales.

Whereas the custom is otherwise in Wales than in England concerning succession to an inheritance inasmuch as the inheritance is partible among the heirs male, and from time whereof the memory of man is not to the contrary hath been partible, our Lord the King will not have that custom abrogated; but willeth that inheritances shall remain partible among like heirs as it was wont to be; and partition of the same inheritance shall be made as it was wont to be made; with this exception, that bastards from henceforth shall not inherit, and also shall not have portions with the lawful heirs nor without the lawful heirs; and if it happen that any inheritance should hereafter upon the failure of heir male descend unto females, the lawful heirs of their ancestor last seised thereof, We Will of our especial Grace that the same women shall have their portions thereof to be assigned them in our Court, although this be contrary to the custom of Wales before used.

XIV. Mode of Trials.

And whereas the people of Wales have besought us that we would grant unto them, that concerning their possessions immovable, as lands and tenements, the truth may be tried by good and lawful men of the neighbourhood, chosen by consent of parties; and concerning things movable, as of contracts, debts, sureties, covenants, trespasses, chattels, and all other movables of the same sort, they may use the Welsh Law whereto they have been accustomed; which was this: that, if a man complain of another upon contracts or things done in such a place that the plaintiff's case may be proved by those who saw and heard it, when the plaintiff shall establish his case by those witnesses whose testimony cannot be disproved, then he ought to recover the thing in demand, and the adverse party be condemned; and that in other cases which cannot be proved by persons who saw and heard, the defendant should be put to his purgation, sometimes with a greater number, sometimes with less, according to the quality and quantity of the matter or Deed: and that in theft, if one be taken with the mainour, he shall not be admitted to purgation, but be holden for convict: We, for the common peace and quiet of our aforesaid people of our land of Wales, do grant the premises unto them: yet so that they hold not place in thefts, larcenies, burnings, murders, manslaughters and manifest and notorious robberies, nor do by any means extend unto these; wherein we will that they shall use the Laws of England, as is before declared.

And therefore we command you that from henceforth you do steadfastly observe the premises in all things. So notwithstanding that whensoever and wheresoever, and as often as it shall be our pleasure, we may declare, interpret, enlarge, or diminish the aforesaid Statutes, and the several parts of them, according to our mere will, and as to us shall seem expedient for the security of us and of our land aforesaid. In witness whereof our seal hath been affixed to these presents. Given at Rothelan on Sunday in Mid Lent in the twelfth year of our Reign.

A.D. 1315-1316]

9 Edward 2.

An Ordinance concerning the Customs of West Wales and South Wales.

The King to all to whom these presents shall come, greeting. Know ye that, whereas in our present parliament, called together at Lincoln, on behalf of our beloved and faithful men of the parts of West Wales and South Wales certain petitions had been presented to us, concerning the removal of certain grievances heretofore brought upon them, as they represent, by our officers of those parts, beyond our knowledge, and concerning the granting of certain favours by us.

We, being minded to do away with undue grievances, and in the desire to confer more ample favour upon our aforesaid lieges, for that we were born in the country of Wales, also because those whom their place of birth especially associates with loyalty to their king will render themselves more inclined and more ready to obey us the larger the favours with which we shall have approached them, have thought proper of our special grace, for their greater tranquility and convenience, that what is written below shall be granted to them.

To wit, that the custom which is called *Amobragium* henceforth be not exacted except within a year from the time of the offence in respect of which the said custom ought to be paid becoming known, but so that if within the year so mentioned it is demanded, though it be permitted to remain unpaid during that year, yet after the completion of that year it be paid in full, and henceforth only be levied in those cases in which in the time of the princes of Wales it was wont to be levied. And that the goods of freemen of those parts be not taxed by our officers where the goods of our own villeins and the goods of *spadones* and men of the Avowry are sufficient; but we will in the first place that the goods of our villeins and next afterwards the goods of *spadones* and men of the Avowry, be taxed just as in the time of the princes of WALES as it is alleged was accustomed to be done. And that the custom which is called Blodwyte henceforth be not demanded or taxed, except the shedding of blood be lawfully ascertained by the view of our bailiffs or otherwise by inquisition. And that complaints concerning contracts between Welshmen and Welshmen, or concerning trespasses inflicted upon Welshmen by Welshmen brought or to be brought in the Welshery the proceedings to be carried on according to Welsh law; and that in these complaints which concern us or an Englishman or foreigner, whether they arise by virtue of our writs or in any other manner, let them proceed and be conducted as has hitherto been accustomed. And if, concerning these which shall have arisen between Englishmen and Welshmen an inquest has to be taken, then let one half of the inquest be of Englishmen, and the other half of Welshmen worthy of trust. And that in the custom which is called taking *Westva*, for which a cow or five shillings are paid, it be in the election of our bailiffs to receive the cow which the tenants offer or five shillings, and that our bailiffs shall not in any way extort any other cow than that tendered, so long as it is worth five shillings. And that as to felonies and those torts which they may have been accused of by our bailiffs officially, or even caught in committing, they may for the two years first following the next Easter put themselves upon a lawful inquest of twelve jurors of the parts where the felonies or trespasses were committed, and by their verdict submit to judgment as is meet. And that the superabundance of our bailiffs in those parts be removed and their number for the future measured out at the discretion of Our Justice for the time being, as, for our convenience, and the relief of the men of those parts, to our said Justice shall best appear expedient.

We desire and firmly ordain that all and singular the premises as are above set out be kept and inviolately observed, and that our bailiffs and officers acting in contravention be severely punished by our Justice, or, in default, by us.

A.D. 1315-1316]

9 Edward 2.

An Ordinance concerning the Customs of North Wales.

This ordinance, and the preceding ordinance for West Wales and South Wales are identical from " The King" down to the words " was accustomed to be done." After which it proceeds, but not treating of Blodwyte and the other customs referred to in the West Wales and South Wales ordinance printed above, as follows :—

And that a freeman having two or more sons may freely and without obtaining a license from us or our Justiciary, be able to prefer in the first tonsure one of them whichever he shall have chosen. And that the freemen of Wales may be able for three years immediately following to sell and give lands, tenements and their rents to other free Welshmen, so, however, that sales and gifts of this sort be not made to prelates, religious persons, or to our secular officers or those of others, or to ecclesiastics, who, under pretence of their office, shall be able to coerce others of the people to sell or give lands, tenements, or rents, while in their offices, and that our Justice of those parts for the time being . . . that sales or gifts of this kind shall not be brought about by the coercion of any secular or ecclesiastical persons against the will of the sellers or donors, and that all services and penny-moneys of lands, tenements, and rents, whether to be sold or given, be made to us by the buyers or givers of them as fully as they ought to be made to us by the hands of sellers or donors of such lands, and that our damage in sales and gifts of this kind be not involved, and that the ordinances lately made in the time of our father Edward of illustrious memory, formerly King of England, and in our time at Kenyngton (upon certain petitions then presented by the men of the community of North Wales), be sent to our Justice of those parts, and in all and singular their articles be kept and observed by the Justice aforesaid and that all persons wishing to have remedy from the said Justice shall pursue their remedy according to the said ordinances, and that in defect of the same our Chancellor for the time being shall make such remedy as is proper by our writ of Chancery according to the form of the ordinances aforesaid, which we will to be enrolled in our Chancery. We desire and firmly ordain (*conclusion as in previous ordinance*).

A.D. 1353] 27 Edward 3, Statute 2, c. 18.

FROM THE ORDINANCE OF THE STAPLES.

THAT MEN OF IRELAND AND WALES MAY BRING THEIR WOOLS AND LEATHER TO THE STAPLES OF ENGLAND.

Because we do well perceive that Merchants strangers do not come so commonly into Ireland nor into WALES for to merchandize as they do into England. We will of our special Grace that it shall be lawful to the people of Ireland and WALES which cannot utter their wools leather woolfels and lead in Ireland and WALES to merchants strangers to come with their said Merchandises that after they be customed and cocketted in Ireland and in WALES to any of our staples in England which them shall please bringing their cockets witnessing their merchandises, which they shall discharge at the Staples in England; so that they, when they shall come to the Staples in England, or they that bought their said merchandises of them shall not pay any time, custom nor subsidy for the said merchandises so customed in our said lands of Ireland or WALES, and our Treasury and the Barons of our Exchequer of England shall be certified two times by the year at the least, that is to say, at Easter and Michaelmas, how much wools, leather woolfels and lead shall pass out of the said Land of Ireland and of the custom thereof paid; and in case that the Merchants or other people of Ireland or of WALES, after that they be in the sea with their said merchandises do pass to any place other than to the Staples in England they shall incur the pains and forfeitures in the said Third Article.

A.D. 1354] 28 Edward 3, c. 2.

LORDS OF THE MARCHES OF WALES SHALL BE ATTENDANT TO THE CROWN OF ENGLAND, AND NOT TO THE PRINCIPALITY OF WALES.

Item, it is accorded and established, That all the Lords of the Marches of WALES shall be perpetually attending and annexed to the Crown of England, as they and their ancestors have been all times past, and not to the Principality of WALES, in whose hands soever the same Principality be, or hereafter shall come.

A.D. 1400–1]

2 Henry 4, c. 12.

Certain restraints laid on persons wholly born Welshmen.

It is ordained and established that from henceforth no Welshman wholly born in Wales, and having father and mother born in Wales, shall purchase lands and tenements within the Towns of Chester, Salop, Bridgenorth, Ludlow, Leominster, Hereford, Gloucester, Worcester, nor other Merchant towns joining to the Marches of Wales, nor in the suburbs of the same upon pain of forfeiture of the same lands and tenements to the Lords of whom such lands or tenements be holden in chief. And also that no such Welshman be from henceforth chosen or received to be citizen or burgess in any City Borough or Merchant Town; and that such Welshmen which now be in any such said City Borough or Franchise Town, being citizens or burgesses, shall find sufficient surety and put a good caution of their good bearing as well towards our Sovereign Lord the King and his Heirs of his Realm of England as for to hold their loyalty to the governance of such Cities Boroughs or towns for the time being in salvation of the same cities Boroughs or towns if the same Welshmen will dwell therein: So that none of them from henceforth be received or accepted to no Office of Mayor, Bailiff, Chamberlain, Constable, or Warden of the ports or of the Gaol, nor to the Common Council of such cities boroughs or towns, nor that he be in no wise made other Occupier or Officer in the same; nor that none of the said Welshmen from henceforth bear any manner armour within such City Borough or Merchant Town, upon pain of forfeiture of the same armour and imprisonment until they have made fine in his behalf.

A.D. 1400–1]

2 Henry 4, c. 16.

Excesses committed by the Welsh on their English neighbours by distressing of cattle, &c., amercing of people, &c.

Item, Whereas upon the grievous complaint made to our Sovereign Lord the King by the Commons in the Parliament, how the people of Wales, sometime by day and some time by night cometh within the counties joining upon the Marches of Wales and doth take divers distresses of horses, oxen, kine, sheep, swine, and other their goods to a great number, and the same doth lead, drive and carry away to the Seigniories where they be resiant, and there withholdeth them till *gree* be made at their will, and that as well of them that have not offended as of them that have offended. And also the said people of WALES doth daily arrest the people of the said Counties coming with their merchandises or other their goods and chattels, and affirmeth Plaints against them of debts covenants trespasses and other actions, whereof they be not parties nor pledges, to the intent to grieve them by divers and outrageous amerciaments and costs, to the great impoverishing and utter undoing of the people of the said Counties: Our Sovereign Lord the King, considering the mischiefs aforesaid, and willing thereupon to provide remedy, by the assent and advice of the said Lords, and at the request of the Commons, hath ordained and established, That if any people of the said Counties be arrested and grieved as afore is said forthwith Letters Testimonials shall be made reciting their grievance, directed to the Governors or Stewards where such offenders be resiant, with their goods or chattels received in WALES under the seals of the Sheriffs of the said Counties or of the Mayors and Bailiffs of the Cities and Boroughs or Stewards of Franchises where such people so grieved be dwelling; to the intent that the said Governors or Steward shall do to be delivered to them their distresses goods and chattels so taken or arrested; and if they make not delivery of such distresses goods or chattels so taken or arrested within seven days after request so to them made, then it shall be lawful to the English people so grieved to arrest all men that cometh with the goods and chattels of them of the Seigniories of WALES where such offenders be inhabiting or resiant, and the same to retain till that full satisfaction be made to the said parties grieved, with their myses, costs and expenses, together with their distresses goods and chattels aforesaid.

A.D. 1400-1]

2 Henry 4, c. 17.

IF A WELSHMAN COMMIT A FELONY IN ENGLAND, AND THEREOF IS ATTAINTED, AND AFTER FLIETH INTO WALES, UPON CERTIFICATE OF THE KING'S JUSTICES HE SHALL BE EXECUTED.

It is ordained and stablished that if any Welshman from henceforth do enter in the counties joining to the same in the Realm of

England, and in the same do burn, kill, ravish, or commit any other felony or trespass whereof he is attainted within the Realm of England by the laws of the same Realm by outlawry or abjuration, and repaireth into WALES and abideth there; that upon the certification and records to be made by the Justices of our Sovereign Lord the King in England before whom they shall be so convict under their seals to the Lords and Ministers where such Felons shall be found in WALES, final execution be made upon the same felons by the same Lords or Ministers, and that upon a grievous pain.

A.D. 1400–1]

2 Henry 4, c. 18.

THE LORDS MARCHERS IN WALES SHALL KEEP SUFFICIENT GUARDS IN THEIR CASTLES.

It is accorded and established that the Lords of the Marches of WALES shall ordain and set sufficient stuffing and ward in their Castles and Seigniories of WALES, to the intent that in time to come no loss riot nor damage come to our Sovereign Lord the King nor his Realm, nor to none of his liege people by their tenants resiants, nor none the other Welshmen in their default as they come and be done for default of good Governance in time past.

A.D. 1400–1]

2 Henry 4, c. 19.

OF SUITS AGAINST ENGLISHMEN IN WALES.

It is ordained that no whole Englishman by three years next following shall be convict at the suit of any Welshman within WALES, except it be by the judgment of English Justices or by the judgment of whole Englishmen Burgesses or by inquest of Boroughs Towns and Englishmen of the Seigniories where such Englishmen be arrested.

A.D. 1400–1]

2 Henry 4, c. 20.

WELSHMEN SHALL NOT PURCHASE LANDS IN ENGLAND NOR IN THE ENGLISH TOWNS OF WALES.

It is accorded and assented that from henceforth no Welshman be received to purchase lands nor tenements within England, nor within the Boroughs nor English Towns of WALES upon pain to forfeit the same purchases to the Lords of whom the same lands and tenements be holden as such estate which the said purchaser had in the same; nor that no Welshman shall be accepted Burgess, nor to have any other liberty within the Realm, nor within the Boroughs and Towns aforesaid.

A.D. 1402]

4 Henry 4, c. 26.

ENGLISHMEN SHALL NOT BE CONVICTED BY WELSHMEN IN WALES.

It is ordained and stablished that no Englishman lieged to our Sovereign Lord the King be convict by any Welshman within Franchises or without, in any County Hundred or Court within the lands of WALES, of whatsoever Estate, but by Englishmen, and of the next venue, and people of good fame and not procured, nor that the English Burgesses which have married Welsh women have franchises with the English Burgesses.

A.D. 1402]

4 Henry 4, c. 27.

AGAINST WASTERS, MINSTRELS, &c., IN WALES.

Item, to eschew many diseases and mischiefs which have happened before this time in the Land of WALES by many Wasters, Rhymers, Minstrels and other Vagabonds; It is ordained and stablished that no Waster, Rhymer, Minstrel nor Vagabond be in any wise sustained in the Land of WALES to make Commorthies or gathering upon the Common people there.

A.D. 1402]

4 Henry 4, c. 28.

AGAINST CONGREGATIONS IN WALES.

Item, it is ordained and stablished that no congregations be made nor suffered to be made by the Welshmen in any place of WALES, for to make or take any Council, unless it be for an evident and necessary cause, and by license of the chief officers and ministers of the same Seigniory where such thing shall be done and in the presence of the same officers and ministers, upon pain of imprisonment, and to make fine and ransom at the King's Will.

A.D. 1402]

4 Henry 4, c. 29.

WELSHMEN SHALL NOT BE ARMED.

It is ordained and established that from henceforth no Welshman be armed, nor bear defencible armour to Merchant Towns, Churches, nor Congregations in the same, nor in the highways, in a fray of the Peace, or of the King's liege people, upon pain of imprisonment, and to make fine and ransom at the King's Will; except those which be lawful liege people to our Sovereign Lord the King.

A.D. 1402]

4 Henry 4, c. 30.

NO VICTUAL OR ARMOUR SHALL BE CARRIED INTO WALES.

It is ordained and stablished that no Englishman nor Welshman of what Estate or condition that he be, send, or bring, by colour of merchandize or other way, any victual or armour to any parts of WALES without the special license of our Sovereign Lord the King or of his Council, unless it be for stuffing, or in storing of Castles and English Towns, upon pain of forfeiture of the same victuals or armour: And that in every part of the Marches of WALES, and towns in the Marches there be English Constables for to inquire search and arrest all such victuals and armour and the same Constables for their travel shall have the sixth part of such forfeitures so by them found.

A.D. 1402]

4 Henry 4, c. 31.

WELSHMEN SHALL NOT HAVE CASTLES.

It is ordained and established that no Welshman shall have Castle fortress nor house defensive of his own nor of other to keep, otherwise than was used in the time of King Edward, Conqueror of WALES, upon pain of forfeiture of the same, except Bishops and other Temporals Lords for their own bodies.

A.D. 1402]

4 Henry 4, c. 32.

NO WELSHMAN SAHLL BEAR OFFICE.

It is ordained and established that no Welshman be made Justice Chamberlain, Chancellor, Treasurer, Sheriff, Steward, Constable of Castle, Receiver, Escheatour, Coroner, nor Chief Foresters nor other officer, nor Keeper of the Records nor Lieutenant in any of the said offices in no part of WALES, nor of the Council of any English Lord, notwithstanding any patent made to the contrary with this clause (*non obstante quod sit Wallicus natus*) except Bishops in WALES; and of those and other whom the King our Sovereign Lord hath found his good and lawful liege people he will to be advised by his Council.

A.D. 1402]

4 Henry 4, c. 33.

CASTLES AND WALLED TOWNS OF WALES SHALL BE KEPT BY ENGLISHMEN.

For the more sufficient custody of the Land of WALES, and to the intent that a man may have the better knowledge of the condition of the people there; it is ordained and stablished that the Garrisons of the Castles and Walled Towns there be purveyed and stored sufficiently of valiant English persons, strangers to the Seigniories where the said Castles and Towns be set, and not of any man mixed of the said parties or Seigniories in WALES or the Marches of the same; until the said Land of WALES be otherwise justified and appeased for the time to come.

A.D. 1402]

4 Henry 4, c. 34.

ENGLISHMEN MARRIED TO WELSH WOMEN SHALL NOT BEAR OFFICE IN WALES.

It is ordained and stablished that no Englishman married to any Welsh woman of the amity or alliance of Owain ap Glendour, Traitor to our Sovereign Lord, or to any other Welsh woman, after the rebellion of the said Owain; or that in time to come marrieth himself to any Welsh woman, be put in any office in WALES, or in the Marches of the same.

A.D. 1407]

9 Henry 4, c. 3.

FELONS IN SOUTH WALES SHALL BE TAKEN OR THE COUNTRY SHALL SATISFY FOR THEIR OFFENCES.

Touching felonies and robberies within any Seigniory of South WALES: It is ordained and stablished that the people of the country where such felons be born received or dwell shall take the same felons, and bring them to the gaol of the same country where they shall be taken; or else they shall be charged, and make satisfaction of the felonies and robberies aforesaid after the performance, and that by the ordinance and award of the Lord of the same Seigniory.

A.D. 1407]

9 Henry 4, c. 4.

DISCLAIMER OF FELONY IN WALES ABOLISHED.

It is ordained and established that no thief nor felon in WALES, openly known, be suffered to disclaim out of the Seigniory where the felony was done; and that such manner of disclaiming be utterly put out; and that as well the said thieves openly known, as other thieves, be put to answer as privy to the indictments or accusement in the same Seigniories where the thieves be taken, without being delivered by disclaiming, or by Letters of Mark in any manner.

A.D. 1413]

1 Henry 5, c. 6.

NO ACTIONS SHALL BE BROUGHT BY WELSHMEN IN RESPECT OF INJURIES SUSTAINED IN THE LATE REBELLION.

Whereas in the time of this rebellion of WALES many of the King's lawful liege people as well Englishmen as Welshmen have been in divers parts of WALES upon the correction of rebels there by the commandant of the same our Sovereign Lord the King and his Council, at the which time some of the said rebels, as well on horseback as on foot, found armed in making of war against their faith and ligeance, were slain, and some maimed, beaten, wounded, taken and imprisoned, their goods and chattels carried away by the said liege people for the cause aforesaid as it was well lawfull, according as by our said Sovereign Lord the King and his Council afore this time hath been ordained in this behalf: And notwithstanding many of the said rebels being yet alive, and other next of blood to those rebels so dead with their friends, now daily make quarrels and great pursuit against the said faithful liege people dwelling or resiant in those parts and in the Shires being next to WALES surmising in them that they such things as is aforesaid to themselves or to their cousins or friends falsely have done by the which they demand of the said faithful liege people high amends, threatening that they otherwise would be thereupon avenged, whereby the said faithful liege people be many times sore and grievously vexed in many parts and Lordships of WALES some of them by indictments accusements or impeachments, and some by menaces distresses taken, and some by their body taken and imprisoned until that they have made *gree* to them in this behalf; or that they would them excuse of the death of such rebels so slain by one assache, after the custom of WALES, that is to say, by the oath of 300 men, and of all such other trespasses before specified acquit themselves; to the great damage and destruction of the said faithful liege people and evil example in time to come: It is ordained and stablished that such quarrel action or demand be not made from henceforth by art nor by engine to any of the faithful liege people by any of them which have been rebels nor by their adherents, be he cousin, ally or friend, nor by any other, upon pain to pay to the party grieved his treble damages, and to be imprisoned by two years after that he be convict, and moreover to make fine and ransom in this behalf before that he be delivered out of prison.

A.D. 1414] **2 Henry 5, Statute 2, c. 5.**

OUTRAGES COMMITTED BY THE WELSH.

Forasmuch as since the rebellion of the Welshmen now late reformed many of the rebels of WALES, with other their adherents with force and arms in the manner of war, sometimes by day and sometimes by night, have come into the Counties of Salop Hereford and Gloucester and in other places bordering upon the same countries and in divers woods and other places there hid and lodged have traitorously and feloniously taken many of the King's faithful liege people, some in riding about their merchandises and doing their own businesses, and some in their houses where they were abiding doing their works in their husbandry, in God's place and the King's and those the King's liege people so taken have carried out of their country to divers parts of WALES, and them have kept and withholden with them in the mountains of those parts of WALES by half a year, sometime more and sometime less until they have ransomed some of the said liege people at an C. li., and some more after their rate, in like manner as is used in time of war to the great damage and mischief of the people of the said counties and countries and to an evil example if it be not the sooner remedied as the King by the grievous complaint of the Commons hath perceived: Our Sovereign Lord the King, willing against all such offenders to ordain a due punishment hath ordained and stablished, that the Justices of Peace within the Counties of England assigned for the same, shall have power to inquire, hear and determine all manner of such treasons, and felonies as well at the King's Suit as at the party's; so that in case that such offenders will not appear before the said Justices to answer as the law requireth in this behalf until they be according to the custom of the Realm outlawed, then the same Justices shall certify by their letters under their seals the officers of the Seigniories in which such outlaws be withdrawn, abiding or resiant of the outlawry upon them so pronounced; and that the same officers upon that certification, take the bodies of those outlaws and do execution upon them in the same Seigniory as the law demandeth without fine or ransom in this behalf to be made.

A.D. 1425-6] **4 Henry 6, c. 3, s. 5.**

JUSTICES IN CERTAIN CASES MAY AMEND THEIR RECORDS ACCORDING TO FORMER STATUTES.

"5. Provided always, That this Statute do not extend to Records and Processes in the Parts of WALES, nor to Records and Processes whereby any Person is or shall be outlawed at any Man's Suit."

A.D. 1429]

8 Henry 6, c. 15.

JUSTICES MAY IN CERTAIN CASES AMEND DEFAULTS IN RECORDS, WALES EXCEPTED.

Item: It is ordained and established that the King's Justices, before whom any Misprision or Default is or shall be found, be it in any Records and Processes which now be, or shall be, depending before them, as well by way of Error as otherwise, or in the Returns of the same, made or to be made by Sheriffs, Coroners, Bailiffs of Franchises, or any other, by Misprision of the Clerks of any of the said Courts of the King, or by Misprision of the Sheriffs, Under-Sheriffs, Coroners, their Clerks, or other Officers, Clerks, or other Ministers whatsoever, in writing one Letter or one Syllable too much or too little, shall have power to amend such Defaults and Misprisions according to their Discretion, and by Examination thereof by the said Justices to be taken where they shall think needful. Provided that this Statute do not extend to Records and Processes in the Parts of WALES; nor to the Processes and Records of Outlawries of Felonies and Treasons, and the Dependencies thereof.

A.D. 1430]

9 Henry 6, c. 3.

CONFIRMING STATUTE AGAINST OWEN GLENDOWER.

Item, Considering the great Insurrections Rebellions and horrible Treasons imagined and committed by *Owen Glendwrdy* of WALES, against the Royal Majesty of King Henry, Grand-father of our Sovereign Lord the King that now is, whereof he was indicted, as it appeareth in an Indictment made before Thomas late Earl of Arundell, John Durley and Thomas Lee by the Commission of the said Grand-father to inquire, with other, of all manner of Treasons, Insurrections and Enemies of the same King the Grandfather, as in the said Commission is more fully contained: And thereupon the said Indictment of high and heinous Treasons brought into the King's Bench at Westminster, and Process thereof made till the same Owen after Proclamation made in Five Counties, was outlawed, and after in the full Parliament holden at Westminster, the Fourth Year of the same King the Grandfather, was called and named of Record Traitor to the said King the Grandfather, as well by Statute as by the Letters Patents of the said King the Grandfather; and for the horribility of his so many Treasons, it was ordained by Statute in the same Parliament that no English Man married to any WELSH Woman of the Amity and Alliance of the said Owen, Traitor to the King, should be put in Office in WALES, nor in the Marches; and also considering how the said Owen and his Adherents were excepted in many general Graces and Pardons granted by the said King the Grandfather to his liege People at divers Times, because of the Insurrections Rebellions and horrible Treasons aforesaid: For the Weal of all the Realm, and for the Repression of all such horrible Treasons from henceforth to be compassed of the Assent of the Lords and Commons aforesaid, It is ordained and established, by the Authority of this present Parliament, That all manner of Indictments, Inquisitions, Processes, Records, Judgements, Ordinances and Statutes made and expressed, taken, had, pursued or declared against the said Owen, be affirmed, authorised and stablished for Law by Authority of this present Parliament, and by the same Authority shall be effectual and sufficient in the Law for to bind and conclude for ever, all that be Heirs or of the Blood of the said Owen, notwithstanding any Default or Misprision had in this Party; or any Error in Writing or in leaving out of the Name or Place or the Indorsement of the said Commission, or of Negligence adding or leaving out more or less than behoveth, or any other Default in the said Indictments, Inquisitions, Records or Judgements notwithstanding: so that this present Ordinance be not prejudicial to any of the Heirs or of the Blood of the said Owen, as to any Lands in Tail.

A.D. 1441-2]

20 Henry 6, c. 3.

CONCERNING OUTRAGES BY WELSHMEN.

Item, forasmuch as at the grievous complaint made to the King by the Commons in the Counties of Hereford, Gloucester, and of Shropshire, which Counties be adjoining to the Marches of WALES, and in the Counties of Somerset Chester and Bristol, it was shewed to the same our Sovereign Lord the King, that whereas another time, in Time of the noble King Henry, Grandfather to our Sovereign

Lord the King that now is, the second year of his Reign, for the great oppressions and extortions, which they of WALES, and of the Marches of WALES daily made to people dwelling in the said Counties of Hereford, Gloucester and Shropshire, in taking, bringing, and bearing away of their horses, beasts and other goods and chattels, out of the same Counties into the said Marches, and such good horses and chattels there withholding till Gree be made at their Will; It was ordained and established That if any horses beasts goods or chattels, be taken within the same Counties, and driven or brought out of the said Counties into WALES or into the Marches of WALES, that then the Sheriffs of the same Counties, Mayors or Bailiffs of Cities and Boroughs or Bailiffs of Franchises where such takings be made, shall send their letters under their seals to the Governors, or to the Stewards of the Seigniories where such offenders be abiding, that they shall deliver such distresses so taken, within eight days of the receipt of the said letters; and if they do not, that the parties so grieved shall take any person goods or chattels coming out of the said Seigniories where such offenders be abiding, and them shall withhold, till that they be restored to their goods so taken, with their damages, costs, and expenses: Which Statute is not sufficient remedy, forasmuch as the said offenders be dwelling sometime in one Seigniory and sometime in another, and have no place certain to tarry; and also they take to the most number of people of the said Counties coming into WALES and into the Marches of WALES, and out of the said Counties, and them withhold, till Gree be to them made at their Will; and also oftentimes the parties grieved durst not make execution of the said Statute for doubt of death and many other mischiefs and inconveniences which thereof should ensue, so that the said offenders be the more bold to take, drive, bring and carry away the people of the said Counties, their horses beasts goods and chattels of the said Counties into WALES and into the Marches of WALES whither they fled before the said Statute, to the perpetual destruction and impoverishment of the said Commons, except that speedy remedy thereof be made: Our said Sovereign Lord the King, willing against such mischiefs and inconveniences to provide a remedy in this behalf, hath ordained by the Authority aforesaid, That if any people of the said Counties in WALES, or in the Marches of WALES, to drive, bring, carry away, or withhold, such takings and withholdings, their abbetments and receipts in WALES, they having knowledge of such offences, aforesaid, shall be judged high treason: And he that is thereof attainted it shall be done of him as of a traitor to our said Sovereign Lord the King; and that the Justices of Peace, in their Sessions in the said Counties, shall have power to inquire, hear and determine of all such offenders, their abbettors and receivers. And to make process against such persons indicted by two Capias and one Exigend, every capias containing the space of two months at the least betwixt the date of every capias, and the day of the return of the same; and that mention be made in the said Writs of Capias that the Sheriffs of the said Counties for the time being shall make proclamation in their Counties that all such persons indicted shall appear before the said Justices in their Sessions to answer of the matters contained in the said indictments. Provided also that the Lords Marchers, of whom such offenders, their abettors and Receivers hold lands and tenements, shall have the forfeit of them, and the Lords Marchers the forfeiture of their goods and chattels found within their Seigniories after that they shall be attainted of the offences aforesaid: And that this ordinance shall endure till the end of six years.

A.D. 1441-2] **20 Henry 6, c. 7.**

FOREIGN MERCHANDISE PASSING THROUGH OR EXPORTED FROM WALES WITHOUT CUSTOM PAID SHALL BE FORFEITED.

Item, it is accorded and ordained by the authority aforesaid, That if any hereafter bring any merchandises coming from any parts beyond the sea to any port or place within the land of WALES and after that send into England, and there discharge them out of any ship or vessel, the customs and subsidies thereof to the King not paid; or if any person in any of the said ports and places in WALES ship any wools, woolfels or other merchandise of the staple to be brought to the parts beyond the sea, not customed, nor the subsidy to the King not paid, shall forfeit the same goods and merchandises; and that the King shall have his suit in this behalf in a county next adjoining in England to the port in which such merchandises shall be shipped or brought into WALES: And that this ordinance shall endure till the next Parliament.

A.D. 1444-5]

23 Henry 6, c. 4.

Concerning Welshmen outlawed.

Item: Whereas divers Persons dwelling in Wales and in the Marches of Wales, indicted and outlawed of Treasons and Felonies, coming into the County of Hereford to Cities and Burghs, Towns, Fairs, and Markets, and to other Places within the said County sometime by Night, and there sell and buy Merchandize and tarry by 2, 3, 4 Days or more at their Will, and after return into their own Countries without grievance, Impeachment or Execution of the Law made upon them by the Sheriff of the said County, his Ministers, or by any other Person, by reason that the Sheriff and his Ministers oftentimes have no knowledge of their Persons, nor of their being within the said County, and other Persons, some for Favour and Amity, and some for Doubt of Hurt; by reason of which nondoing of due Execution of the Law, the said Persons indicted and outlawed, and other Offenders, of Wales and of the Marches aforesaid, doubt not to come, slay, burn, rob, and to do other Offences in the said County, to the perpetual Destruction and Impoverishment of the Commons of the said County: Our said Sovereign the King, considering the Premises, hath granted by Authority aforesaid, That if the Sheriff, Under-Sheriff, or any Sheriff's Minister, Mayor and Bailiffs of Towns and Boroughs, or any other Person conversant within the said County, know and see any such Person indicted or outlawed in any Place within the said County, that he shall arrest, take and bring him to the Gaol within the said County, and there shall deliver him to the Gaoler, after the Law of the Realm; and if any such Person indicted or outlawed will disobey the Arrest to be made in the Form aforesaid, that he against whom such Disobeisance is made, shall levy Hue and Cry: and that every Person that is conversant within the said County that heareth the Hue and Cry, shall come and aid him that levieth the said Hue and Cry, to take the said Offender, and shall do their Power that to do, and if they cannot take him, they shall follow and pursue him out of the said County with Hue and Cry: And that the Sheriff, Under-Sheriff and their Ministers, Mayor and Bailiffs, conversant and hearing of such Hue and Cries, shall make due Execution of the said Ordinance according to their Power, upon pain, that is to say, the said Sheriff, Under-Sheriff and their Ministers, Mayors and Bailiffs, to make fine and Ransom to the King; and the said Persons conversant and Hearers, that is to say, a Knight 100 shillings, an Esquire Forty Shillings, and all other Inhabitants Twenty Shillings: And that the Justices of Peace in the said County for the Time being, shall have Power to inquire, hear, and determine upon the Defaults and Negligences of the said Sheriff, Under-Sheriff, Ministers, Mayor and Bailiffs conversant and Hearers of the said Hues and Cries. And moreover the King will that the Statute of Westminster primer, touching like Matter, shall be put in Execution.

A.D. 1446-7]

25 Henry 6.

ALL STATUTES AGAINST WELSHMEN CONFIRMED.

Our Sovereign Lord the King, at his Parliament holden at Saint Edmundsbury, in the Feast of Saint Scolast; that is to say the tenth day of February, the twenty-fifth year of his reign, by the advice and assent of the Lords Spiritual and Temporal, and the Commons of his Realm in the said Parliament assembled, and by Authority of the same Parliament, hath approved, ratified and affirmed all manner of Statutes made in any Parliament against Welshmen before this time, not repealed: And morever hath ordained by the authority aforesaid, That all grants of franchises, markets, fairs and other liberties to buy or to sell (to bake, or to brew, and to sell,) within the towns of North WALES, made to any Welshman before this time shall be voided and of no value. And that all the villains of our Sovereign Lord the King within North WALES shall be bound and constrained to do such labour and services as they of right have used to do of old time, notwithstanding any grant made to them or any usage used by them of a later time to the contrary; and that such officers shall have power to compel them to do such labours and services as they have used to compel them before this time lawfully.

A.D. 1448-9]

27 Henry 6, c. 4.

CONCERNING WELSHMEN WHO TAKE AWAY ENGLISHMEN.

Whereas at the grievous Complaint of the Commons of the Counties of Hereford, Gloucester, and Shropshire which be adjoining to the Marches of WALES, and of the Commons of the Counties of Somerset,

Bristol, and Chester, at the Parliament holden at Westminster the 20 year of the Reign of our Sovereign Lord the King that now is, It was ordained by Authority of the said Parliament, that if any People of the said Counties, their Goods and Chattels were wrongfully taken in any of the said Counties by any men of WALES, and out of the said Counties into WALES, or into the Marches of WALES conveyed, carried, or brought or retained, that such Taking or Takings, Receipts, Abettments, or withholding of such Offences aforesaid, shall be judged High Treason, and whosoever thereof shall be attainted shall be taken and judged as Traitors to our Sovereign Lord the King; and that the Justices of Peace in their Sessions in the said Counties shall have Power to enquire, and there to determine of all such Offenders, their Abettors and Receivers, and to make Process against the Persons so indicted by 2 capias and an Exigent, every Capias containing the Space of two Months betwixt the date thereof and the Return of the same; and that Mention shall be made in the said Writs of Capias that the Sheriffs of the Counties for the Time being shall make Proclamation in their Counties, that they so indicted shall appear before the said Justices in their Sessions, to answer to the Matters contained in the said Indictments; Provided always, that the Lords Marchers, of whom such Offenders, their Abettors and Receivers shall hold their Lands and Tenements, shall have the forfeiture thereof, and also the Forfeiture of their Goods and Chattels found within their Seigniories, after that they shall be attainted of such Offences; which Ordinance should endure but for 6 years then next ensuing: Our said Sovereign Lord the King, at the Request of the Commons of the said Counties, by the Advice and Assent of the aforesaid, will, that the said Ordinance made in the said Parliament holden at Westminster the said Twentieth Year of his said Reign for such wrongful Taking shall endure for six years and shall take Effect and be in his Force till the next Parliament, and then to expire.

A.D. 1449]

28 Henry 6, c. 4.

OFFENCES IN WALES AND LANCASHIRE IN TAKING AWAY MEN AND THEIR GOODS UNDER COLOUR OF DISTRESS.

Item, whereas divers misruled persons of the Counties and Seigniories Royals in WALES and of the Duchy of Lancaster in the said parts, daily take and use to take divers persons goods and chattels in the said Counties, Duchy and Seigniories, by the name and under colour of distress, where they have no manner of fee, seigniory nor cause to take such distress, but feign some actions and quarrels to grieve and destroy the faithful people of the said Counties Duchy and Seigniories against law, reason and conscience; and the aforesaid persons, goods and chattels so taken, bring and carry out of the Counties Duchy and Seigniories aforesaid where they be taken, to divers other places in England and WALES; and many times, for taking of such distresses, and in resistance of them, great assemblies of people, riots, maims and murders be made and had, and if it be not hastily remedied other inconveniences be like thereof to follow, of which takings, bringings, and carryings in this behalf no due punishment is, wherefore the people of the said parts daily abound and increase in evil governance: Our said Sovereign Lord the King, willing to remedy the said premises, by advice assent and authority aforesaid, hath ordained and stablished, That if any person take any goods chattels or person in any of the said Counties, Duchy or Seigniory and them bring or carry to any places out of any of the said Counties, Duchy or Seigniories in which they be taken, to any other places, That all manner of such takings, bringings or carryings shall be had and judged felony; and if any person thereof be duly attainted in any manner, that he shall have execution as a felon should have, and that no manner of person in the said Counties, Duchy, or Seigniories, nor in none other places in WALES arrested accused or indicted of felony in any manner shall be admitted to disclaim out of the said County Duchy or Seigniory where he is so indicted accused or arrested. Provided always that no person shall be indamaged nor grieved by this ordinance for taking within his fee, or for any manner of cause wherefore distress or taking is lawful by the common law of England; This ordinance to endure for five years.

A.D. 1495] **11 Henry 7, c. 33.**

AN ACT FOR THE MAKING VOID OF DIVERS LEASES AND OFFICES WITHIN THE PRINCIPALITY OF WALES, &c.

To the discreet Commons in this present Parliament assembled. Where in divers Castles Manors Lordships Lands and Tenements with their appurtenances, as well in the Principality of South WALES North WALES and in the County Palatine of Chester and Flint and in divers other Castles Manors Lordships Lands and Tenements in the Marches of WALES and in the Counties of Hereford and Salop, parcels of the earldom of March, and now being in the Prince's hands by the King's grant during his pleasure, divers leases of Manors lands and tenements parcel of the premises hath he made for term of life lives or term of years underneath the seals in those parts of old time used and accustomed and upon the same leases much lease rent reserved unto the King and Prince, then the said Lordships Manors lands and tenements might reasonably be set for, to their great hurt and damage; Be it therefore ordained established and enacted by authority of this Parliament, that all such leases from the feast of Saint Michael the archangel next coming be utterly void and of none effect.

And also be it enacted by the same authority, that all leases hereafter to be made to any person or persons for term of life lives or term of years, by the Prince in or of any of the Lordships Manors lands and tenements parcels of the said Earldom of March, while they be in his hands as is abovesaid, be good and effectual to any such person or persons to whom they shall be so made.

And over that be it ordained and enacted by authority aforesaid that all grants of offices granted or made of or within any Castle Manor lands tenements and their appurtenances parcels of the Principality of WALES, Duchy of Cornwall, the earldom of Chester and Flint, or parcel of the earldom of March within the Marches or in the Counties of Hereford and Salop now being in the Prince's Hands, wherein due exercise is not necessary nor needful, And all grants of offices within any of the premises which were none offices the first year of King Edward the 4th. And also all grants of offices being of old time accomptants within the said Principality and County Palatine of Chester and Flint, be utterly void and of none effect: Provided alway that if any person or persons which now have to farm of the said Lordships Manors lands or tenements will give so much for them as any other person or persons will give for them, he or they shall have preferment in the taking of the same farm, which he or they now have and hold before any other, finding sufficient surety for the same.

Provided alway that this Act of resumption provision or ordinance made in this present Parliament, nor none other act nor acts made or to be made hereafter in the same, extend not nor in any wise be prejudicial or hurtful unto Thomas Salesbury of the Lordship of Denbigh Squire, of or to the farms of Kilford and Rigol granted to him by our letters patents with the two Cornemylles which he hath by proclamation and the Courtrolles within the Lordship of Denbigh, and also of the office of Sheriff of the County of Flint, to the said Thomas granted by my Lord Prince's letters patents during his gracious pleasure, but that all and every of the said letters patents and lease of the said Cornemylles and all things in them contained, stand and be effectual to the said Thomas, the said Act or Acts, provision ordinance or resumption notwithstanding.

5. Proviso for W. G. ap Robyn, Sheriff of Caernarvon.

6. Proviso for Richard Young, Woodward of Caernarvon.

7. Proviso for William Trefry, Comptroller of the Coinage.

8. Proviso for the Marquis of Dorset.

9. Proviso for John Edwards, Bailiff of Beardley.

10. Proviso for John Monkeley, Collector of Customs in Cornwall.

11. Proviso for Johnap Med ap Ieo Lloid, Sergeant of the Peace, &c., Denbigh.

12. Proviso for John Fowler, Constable of Ludlow Castle.

13. Proviso for Annuity to Ran: Brereton.

14. Proviso for lease to I. Hanley.

15. Proviso for Robert Henbury, Clerk of the Mills in Chester.

16. Proviso for T. Colbrond, Porter of Beeston Castle.

17. Proviso for R. Birkhened, Lessee of the Friths of Hanconway and Dynllane.

18. Proviso for John Lawton, Comptroller of Pleas &c. in North WALES.

19. Proviso for Thomas Heven, Keeper of Pembridge Park.

20. Proviso for the Woodwards of Merioneth and Parkkeepers of Malewyg.

21. Proviso for Hic: Manley, Parker of Denbigh Little Park.

22. Proviso for Earl of Derby and Lord Strange.

23. Proviso for Sir John Dawn, hereditary Master Forester of the Forests of Mare and Mondrem, in Cheshire.

24. Proviso for Res ap Lln ap Hulkyn, Sheriff of Anglesey.

25. Provided alway that this Act of Resumption or any other Act or Acts made or to be made in this present Parliament, extend not nor in any wise be prejudicial or hurtful unto Sir Rice ap Thomas,

Knight, of or for any of our grants and letters patents to him made of the Chamberlainship of South WALES and the Captainship of the Castle of Aberwstwyth.

26. Proviso for Henry Ley, Keeper of the Parks of Hellysbury and Lanteglis.

27. Proviso for Ralph Bryne, Porter of Rutland Castle, Flintshire.

28. Proviso for Thomas Ferrour, Master Forester of Snowdon Forest.

29. Proviso for Piers Stanley, Escheator and Sheriff of Merioneth.

30. Proviso for the Grantees of the Amobreship and Rectorships of Caernarvon, Anglesea and Merioneth.

31. Proviso for Edw: Courtenay, Earl of Devon, Constable of the Castle of Rastormell, &c.

A.D. 1529] **21 Henry 8, c. 6, ss. 6, 7.**

AN ACT CONCERNING THE TAKING OF MORTUARIES OR DEMANDING RECEIVING OR CLAIMING OF THE SAME.

6. And be it also enacted by the authority aforesaid that no Mortuaries nor Corse presents, nor any sum or sums of money or other thing for any Mortuary or Corse present shall be demanded taken received or had in the parts of WALES nor in the Marches of the same, nor in the Town of Calais or Berwick nor in the Marches of the same; but only in such parts and places of WALES Marches and Towns aforesaid where Mortuaries have been accustomed to be taken and paid; And in those parts and places no Mortuaries nor Corse presents nor any other thing for Mortuary or Corse present from henceforth be demanded taken received or had but only after the form order and manner above specified in this present Act and none otherwise nor of any other person or persons than is limited by this present Act upon the pain above contained in this present Act.

7. Provided also that it shall be lawful to the Bishops of Bangor, Llandaff, St. David's and St. Asaph, and likewise to the Archdeacon of Chester to take such Mortuaries of the Priests within their Dioceses and Jurisdictions as heretofore have been accustomed.

A.D. 1534]

26 Henry 8, c. 4.

An Act for Punishment of Perjury of Jurors in the Lordships Marches in Wales.

Where for lack of diligent and sure custody of Jurors sworn for trials of murderers felons and accessaries of felonies and murders in Wales and the Marches of the same, divers adherents friends and kinsfolks to such offenders have resorted to the same Jurors, and have suborned them to acquit divers murderers felons and accessaries openly and notoriously known contrary to equity and justice; It is therefore enacted by the King our Sovereign Lord and the Lords spiritual and temporal and the Commons in this present parliament assembled and by the authority of the same, that forthwith upon the charge given to any inquest hereafter to be taken and sworn before any Justiciar, Steward, Lieutenant or other Officer within Wales or the Marches of the same, of for and upon any traverse against the King or the trial or any recognizance broken or any other forfeiture, forfeited to the King, or of, for, and upon the trial of any murderer felon or accessary of felony or murder, One Officer or other person shall be deputed and sworn in the presence of the said Justiciar or other officer, for the true and diligent Keeping of the same Jurors; And that the same officer or other person so sworn, without the special commandment of the said Justiciar or other officer shall not do or suffer to be ministered to the same Jurors any bread drink meat fire or light, nor shall suffer the same Jurors to speak to any person or persons, nor the same Officer or other person sworn without commandment aforesaid shall not speak to the said Jurors but only to demand of them of their agreement, unto such time as the same Jurors shall have given their Verdict; any usage or custom heretofore used to the contrary notwithstanding: And if the same Officer or other person so sworn in form aforesaid do not execute and accomplish the premises in the oath before rehearsed in every point and article, then the same Officer or other person so sworn shall be punished and imprisoned, and make fine and ransom to the King's Highness by the discretion of the said Justiciar, Steward, Lieutenant or other Officer.

And also be it enacted by the authority aforesaid that if the same Jurors do acquit any such felon, murderer or accessary upon whose trial they shall be charged, or give any untrue Verdict against the King upon the trial of any traverse recognizance or other forfeiture, contrary to good and pregnant evidence ministered to them by persons sworn before the said Justiciar, Steward, Lieutenant or other Officer, or that the said Jurors or any of them do eat, drink, or speak to or with any other person or persons than to such as be sworn with them, or otherwise misdemean themselves, after they be sworn and before they have given their verdict, that then the Lord President and other of the Council of the Marches for the time being, upon notice or complaint thereof to them made, shall not only have power and authority by this present Act to call such Jurors before them, but also the same Justiciar, Steward, or other officer afore whom any such acquittal, untrue verdict, or misdemeanour shall happen to be made, shall have full power and authority to compel such Jurors and every of them upon pain of imprisonment to be bounden by recognizance in a certain sum of money by their discretion to be limited, that the same Jurors and every of them shall personally appear at a certain day, by the same Justiciar, Steward or other officer to be limited, before the Lord President and other of the Council aforesaid for the time being, then and there to abide and stand to such direction and order as the same Council shall make ordain and decree of in and upon the same: and that the same council shall thereupon have authority and power by examination or otherwise to hear and determine all and every such cause, and shall have like authority to commit every of the same Jurors to prison or other punishment as shall be thought most meet by the discretion of the said Council, or otherwise assess or tax every such Juror to his fine or ransom by the same discretion to be paid and levied of their lands goods and chattels to the use of the King's Highness.

A.D. 1534]

26 Henry 8, c. 5.

AN ACT THAT KEEPERS OF FERRIES ON THE WATER OF SEVERN SHALL NOT CONVEY IN THEIR FERRY-BOATS ANY MANNER OF PERSON GOODS OR CHATTELS AFTER THE SUN GOING DOWN TILL THE SUN BE UP.

Forasmuch as daily divers felonies robberies and murders be many times committed and done in the counties of Gloucester and

Somerset, in the parts near adjoining unto the Water called the Water of Severn between England and South WALES, and after such murders and felonies done the said robbers felons and murderers with the said goods so robbed and stolen make their conveyance with the said goods so stolen by night at divers passages or ferries over the said river or water, as the passages of Auste, Fremeland, Pyrton, Arlyngham, Nowenham, Portsedes Point, and all such other like passages over the said river in to South WALES, or into the forest called the Forest of Dean also adjoining to the same water, and when they be over the said water then the goods so stolen be by divers privileges there kept, albeit the Owner and Owners have true and perfect knowledge thereof yet they so robbed and spoiled be without remedy for to obtain their said goods so stolen, and so that the secret and sudden conveyance by night of the said goods over the said ferries and passages doth not only greatly encourage divers persons to come out of the parts of South WALES to steal rob and murder divers persons in their houses in the said counties joining upon the said borders of WALES, but also causeth many robberies and felonies in sundry ways to be committed and done upon the said border near adjoining to the same river, to the great damage and hurt of the King's Subjects inhabiting there unless some remedy therefore be provided : It may therefore please the King our Sovereign Lord and the Lords Spiritual and Temporal and the Commons in this present parliament assembled and by the authority of the same, to enact that every person or persons taking upon him or them to have and keep any of the said passages or any other passage upon Severn aforesaid, from henceforth do not convey neither carry with any manner barge boat or other vessel any person or persons with horses, mares, oxen, kine, or any other cattle, nor no other person or persons before the time of the sun rising in the morning, and after the time of the sun being gone down at night; upon pain of imprisonment and fine to be set on him that shall so convey or carry over any of the said passages over the said river of Severn out of England in to WALES or the Forest of Dean, or out of WALES or the said Forest of Dean into England unless the said passengers and every of them have good knowledge of such person and persons and of their dwelling places, and upon request to them made by any person or persons do disclose the name and the dwelling place of every such person or persons so by them conveyed over the said water, to any such person or persons requiring the same, If suit be made for or after them upon any outcry, hute, or fresh suit of or for any felony robbery, murder and manslaughter, committed and done from henceforth: And that the King's Justiciars of Peace within every the said Counties of Gloucester and Somerset at their Quarter Sessions shall have full power and authority to call before them all such persons which hereafter shall keep any of the said passages, or any other ferry or passage over the said water into WALES or the said forest, or out of WALES or the said forest into England, and to bind them with sufficient sureties with them in recognizance in such sums of money as it shall seem to the discretion of the said Justiciars of peace, that they and every of them being passengers and Keepers of ferries and passages as is aforesaid, from henceforth shall not after the said times before limited and appointed convey or carry, nor cause to be conveyed nor carried, any manner of person or persons or any kind of cattle, but such persons as they do know and will answer for, and know where their abidings, dwellings and habitations be, and upon request made to them or any of them as is above said shall from time to time disclose as well the same person or persons as the goods and cattles so passing the said passages upon fresh suit made or hereafter to be made upon any felony murder or robbery, committed and done in the borders of the Counties aforesaid, or in any other place within this realm or South WALES.

A.D. 1534]

26 Henry 8, c. 6.

THE BILL CONCERNING COUNCILS IN WALES.

"Forasmuch as the People of WALES and Marches of the same, not dreading the good and wholesome Laws and Statutes of this Realm, have of long Time continued and persevered in Perpetration and Commission of divers and manifold Thefts, Murthers, Rebellions, wilful Burnings of Houses and other scelerous Deeds and abominable Malefacts, to the high Displeasure of God, Inquietation of the King's well-disposed Subjects, and Disturbance of the Publick Weal, which Malefacts and scelerous Deeds be so rooted and fixed in the same People, that they be not like to cease, unless some sharp Correction and Punishment for Redress and Amputation of the Premisses be provided, according to the Demerits of the Offenders": Be it therefore enacted by the King our Sovereign

Lord, and the Lords Spiritual and Temporal, and the Commons, in this Parliament assembled, and by Authority of the same, that all and singular Person and Persons dwelling or resiant within WALES, or in the Lordships Marchers of the same, from Time to Time, and at all Times hereafter, upon such Monition or Warning given for the Court to be kept in WALES, or in any of the Lordships Marchers aforesaid, as before this time hath been used, shall personally repair, resort and appear before the Justice, Steward, Lieutenant or other Officer, at all and every Sessions, Court and Courts, to be holden before the same Justice, Steward or other Officer, in any whatsoever Castle, Fortress or other Place within WALES, or within the Precincts, Limits and Jurisdictions of every the Lordships Marchers or Seigniories aforesaid, or the Marchers of the same, as by the said Justice, Steward or other Officer shall be appointed; and then and there shall give his or their personal Attendance, to do, execute and accomplish all and every Thing and Things which to him or them shall affere and appertain, upon Pain of such Fines, Forfeitures and Amerciaments as shall be affered, assessed and taxed by the Justice, Steward or other Officer, to the King's Use, if it be within any of the King's Lordships Marchers; and if it be within any other Lordships Marchers, then to the Use of the Lord of the said Lordship Marcher for the Time being; the said Forfeitures and Amerciaments to be levied, perceived and taken by way of Distress of the Goods and Chattels of every Person not appearing at the said Court or Courts, or not doing, executing or accomplishing his Duty as is abovesaid.

"2. And forasmuch as the Officers in the Lordships Marchers in WALES have often and sundry Times heretofore unlawfully exacted of the King's Subjects within such Lordships where they have had Rule or Authority, by many and sundry Ways and Means, and also committed them to strait Duress and Imprisonment for small and light feigned Causes, and extortiously compelled them thereby to pay unto them Fines for their Redemptions, contrary to the Law": Therefore be it further enacted, That if any Steward, Lieutenant or any Officer of any Lordship Marcher, do feign, procure or imagine any untrue Surmise against any Person or Persons that shall so give their personal Attendance before them at such Court or Courts, and upon the same untrue Surmise commit them to any Duress or Imprisonment, contrary to the Law, or contrary to the true and laudable Custom of that Lordship, that then upon Suit made unto the King's Commissioners, or Council of the Marches for the Time being, by any such Person or Persons so imprisoned, or by any of their Friends, that then the same Commissioners or Council shall have full Power and Authority to send for such Steward, Lieutenant or Officer, and also for the Person or Persons so imprisoned; and if the same Person or Persons so imprisoned, can evidently prove before the said Council, by good and substantial Witness or otherwise, that his Imprisonment was upon any feigned Surmise, without Cause reasonable or lawful, that then the same Commissioners shall have full Power and Authority to assess the said Officer, to pay to the said Person or Persons wrongfully imprisoned, 6s. 8d. for every Day of their Imprisonment or more by the Discretions of the said Commissioners, according to the Hurts and Behaviour of the Person or Persons imprisoned.

3. And that the same Commissioners shall set further Fine upon the said Officers, to be paid to the King's Use, as by their Discretions shall be thought convenient; and in case the same Officer do refuse to appear before the same Commissioners incontinent after any Commandment to them directed and delivered after any such Complaint made to the same Commissioners, that then the same Commissioners shall have full Power and Authority, upon every Default made by any Officer or Officers, to assess and set upon every such Officer or Officers making Default, such Fine or Fines to be levied to the King's Use, as by their Discretions shall be thought convenient; and that the same Commissioners shall have full Power and Authority to compel the said Officer or Officers by way of Imprisonment, as well to pay such Fines as shall be set and taxed upon them to the King's Use, as to pay unto every Person or Persons so imprisoned, such Sums of Money as they shall be sessed to pay for their wrong Imprisonment.

4. And be it also enacted by Authority aforesaid, That no Person or Persons dwelling or resiant within WALES or the Lordships Marchers of the same, of what Estate, Degree or Condition soever he or they be of, coming, resorting or repairing unto any Sessions or Court to be holden within WALES, or any Lordships Marchers of the same, shall bring to bear, or cause to be brought or born to the same Sessions or Court, or to any Place within the Distance of two Miles from the same Sessions or Court, nor to any Town, Church, Fair, Market or other Congregation, except it be

upon a Hue or Outcry made of any Felony or Robbery done or perpetrated, nor in the Highways, in Affray of the King's Peace, or the King's liege People, any Bill, Long-bow, Cross-bow, Hand-gun, Sword, Staff, Dagger, Halbert, Morespike, Spear or any other manner of Weapon, Privy Coat or Armour defensive, upon Pain of Forfeiture of the same Weapon, Privy Coat or Armour, and to suffer Imprisonment and make Fine and Ransom to the King's Highness by the Discretion of the King's Commissioners of his Marches for the Time being, except it be by the Commandment, License or Assent of the said Justices, Steward or other Officer, or of the Commissioners or Council of the Marches for the Time being.

5. And That no Person or Persons from henceforth, without License of the said Commissioners in Writing, shall within WALES, or the Marches of the same, or in any Shires adjoining to the same, require, procure, gather, or levy any Commorth, Bydale, Tenant's Ale, or other Collection or Exaction of Goods, Chattels, Money, or any other Thing, under Colour of marrying, or suffering of their Children saying or singing their first Masses or Gospels, of any Priests or Clerks, or for Redemption of any Murther, or any other Felony, or for any other Manner of Cause, by what Name or Names soever they shall be called; nor shall make or procure to be made any Games of Running, Wrestling, Leaping, or any other Games (the Game of Shooting only excepted and foreprized) upon Pain of one whole Year's Imprisonment of every Person or Persons as shall gather or procure to be gathered, any such Collection or Exaction, or shall make or procure to be made any Games as is aforesaid; and further, they and every of them shall make such Fine as by the Discretion of the King's Commissioners of his Marcher shall be thought convenient: and further, the said Commissioners by this present Act shall have Power and Authority to hear and determine the said Offences by their Examination; and that no Person or Persons shall hereafter at any Time cast any Thing into any Court within WALES, or in the Lordships Marchers of the same, by the Mean or Name of an Arthel, by Reason whereof the Court may be letted, disturbed or discontinued for that Time, upon Pain of one whole Year's Imprisonment of any such Person or Persons as shall cast or cause to be cast any such Arthel into any Court or Courts hereafter to be holden within WALES or the Lordships Marchers of the

same; any Custom before this Time used to the contrary notwithstanding.

6. And that all Sessions and Courts hereafter to be holden within WALES, or the Lordships Marchers of the same, shall be kept within the most sure and peaceable Place within the same Lordship Marcher, where the said Justice, Steward or other Officer shall appoint; and for the Punishment and speedy Trials, as well of the Counterfeiters of any Coin current within this Realm, washing, clipping or minishing of the same, as of all and singular Felonies, Murthers, wilful burning of Houses, Manslaughters, Robberies, Burglaries, Rapes and Accessaries of the same, and other Offences feloniously done, perpetrated and committed, or hereafter to be done, perpetrated and committed, within any Lordship Marcher of WALES: Be it enacted by the Authority aforesaid, That the Justices of the Gaol-delivery and of the Peace, and every of them for the Time being, in the Shire or Shires of England where the King's Writ runneth, next adjoining to the same Lordship Marcher, or other Places in WALES, where such counterfeiting, washing, clipping or minishing of any Coin current within this Realm, or Murther, hath been or hereafter shall be committed or done, or where any other Felonies or Accessaries shall be hereafter committed, perpetrated or done, shall have from henceforth full Power and Authority at their Sessions and Gaol-delivery, to inquire by Verdict of twelve Men of the same Shire or Shires next adjoining within England where the King's Writ runneth, there to cause all such Counterfeiters, Washers, Clippers of Money, Felons, Murtherers and Accessaries to the same, to be indicted according to the Laws of this Land, in like Manner and Form as if the same Petit Treasons, Murthers, Felonies and Accessaries to the same had been done, committed or perpetrated within any of the said Shires within the said Realm, and also to hear, determine and judge the same according to the Laws of this Realm.

7. And that all foreign Pleas pleaded by any of the said Malefactors and Offenders, shall be tried and determined in the said Shire or Shires; and that the Acquittal or Fine making for any of the Causes aforesaid in any of the Lordships Marchers, shall be no Bar for any Person or Persons, being indicted in the said Shire or Shires, within two Years next after any such Murther or Felony done.

8. And further it is enacted, That the said Justices of Peace and

Gaol-delivery and every of them, shall have full Power and Authority, to award all Manner of Process, as well of Outlawry as otherwise, against all and every such Offender and Offenders so indicted in manner and Form and according to the Customs and Laws used and accustomed within this Realm of England; and that the said Justices or two of them, afore whom any such Offender shall happen to be outlawed, or attainted by Outlagary, shall immediately upon the same Outlagary or Attainder, direct and send unto the King's Officers of his Lordships Marchers or to their Deputies, or unto the Lord or Lords Marchers of the same Lordship Marcher, or to his or their Officer or Officers, or to their Deputies, wherein such Offence, Murther or Felony shall happen to be done, or where any such Offender, Murtherer or Felon shall happen to be resiant, a Certificate under the Seals of them or two of them, of any such Outlagary or Attainder; commanding them and every of them by the same, under Pain of Forfeiture of a hundred Pounds to the King, to be levied and perceived as well of the Goods, Chattels, Lands and Tenements of the same Lord or Lords Marchers, as of the Goods and Chattels, Lands and Tenements of the King's Officer there, to apprehend and attach, or cause to be apprehended and attached, the Body or Bodies of the same Offender or Offenders so outlawed or attainted, and safely to keep or cause to be kept, the same Offender or Offenders, till such convenient Time before the next Sessions of the King's Justices of the Gaol-delivery of the Shire where such Offender or Offenders shall happen to be outlawed or attainted, as to the King's Officers of his Lordships Marchers, or to their Deputies, or unto the Lord Marcher or Lords Marchers, of the same Lordship Marcher, or his or their Officer or Officers, or their Deputies, where such Offender and Offenders shall be apprehended, attached, detained and kept, shall be thought expedient for the Conveyance and conducting of the same Offender or Offenders, in Manner and Form following, to be delivered from the King's Officers or their Deputies, or the Lord Marcher or the Lords Marchers, or his or their Officer or Officers, to other Persons assigned by this Act to receive and convey such Offender or Offenders, by Indenture to be made between the Deliverer or Deliverers, and the Receiver or Receivers, that is to say, that the King's Officers of his Lordship Marcher, or their Deputies, or the Lord or Lords Marchers of the Lordship Marcher, or his or their Officer or Officers, or their Deputies, where such Offender or Offenders shall be apprehended, attached, detained and kept, shall safely and surely conduct and convey, or cause to be conducted and conveyed, the same Offender or Offenders, to the next Lordship Marcher toward the Shire where the same Offender or Offenders shall happen to be outlawed or attainted; and that the King's Officers of the same Lordship Marcher, or their Deputies, or the Lord or Lords Marchers of the same Lordship Marcher, or his or their Officer or Officers, or their Deputies, shall receive, and safely and surely conduct and convey the same Offender or Offenders to the next Lordship Marcher; and so the King's Officers of every Lordship Marcher, or their Deputies, or the Lord or Lords Marchers of the same Lordship, or his or their Officer or Officers, or their Deputies, to receive, conduct and convey safely and surely, every such Offender or Offenders, from one Lordship Marcher to another Lordship Marcher, by Indenture, as is aforesaid, unto the Time that such Offender or Offenders shall be safely delivered before the said Justices of the Gaol-delivery; upon Pain of Forfeiture by every of the King's Officer or Lord Marcher, by whose Default the same Offender or Offenders shall nor may not appear before the same Justices at their said Sessions, there to stand and abide the Order of the King's Laws, *C. li.* to be levied and perceived of the Goods and Chattels, Lands and Tenements of the same Officer or Lord, to the King's Use.

9, And that all and every Officer and Officers, Lord and Lords, or other Persons to whom any Certificate shall be directed as is abovesaid, shall at the next Sessions and Gaol-delivery to be holden after the Apprehension or Attachment of such Offender or Offenders, return the same Certificate in due Form, and what he or they have done in that Behalf, upon the Pain aforesaid; saving alway to all and every Offender and Offenders, all and singular Traverses, Challenges, Exceptions, Advantages, and all other Pleas to, of, and upon the Outlawry pronounced and promulged against the same Offender or Offenders, in Manner and Form as is and hath been used and accustomed by the Laws of this Realm for any the King's Subjects dwelling within the same Realm.

10. Provided always, and be it enacted by the Authority aforesaid, That if any Person or Persons which shall happen hereafter to be indicted, outlawed, arraigned, convicted or attainted by Force of this Act, do find such sufficient Sureties before the King's

Justices of the Gaol-delivery as by their Discretions shall be thought convenient, that the same Person or Persons shall not from thenceforth commit nor do any Felony, Murther or felonious Offence, nor be accessary to any Felony, Murther or felonious Offence, but at all Times from thenceforth shall be of good Behaviour against the King our Sovereign Lord, his Heirs and Successors, his and their Laws and Subjects, that then the same Justices of Gaol-delivery for the Time being, with and by the Assent, Consent and Agreement of the Lord President, and two of the King's Commissioners, or Council of the Marches for the Time being, or three of them at the least, whereof the Lord President, or one of the said Council, to be one, shall and may by their Discretions, for one Time only, admit any such Offender to a certain Fine or Sum of Money on him by them to be assessed and taxed, to be surely paid to the King's Use; and shall have full Power and Authority, by this present Act, to discharge any such Offender or Offenders, so arraigned, outlawed, convicted and attainted of all and every such Felony, Murther or felonious Offence, and Accessaries of the same, and of all Executions and Punishments of Death, which the same Offender or Offenders should suffer by the common Laws of this Realm, so that the same Offender or Offenders stand not appealed of the said Felony, Murther or felonious Offence, or as Accessaries of the same Offences, at the Time of his said Discharge; and that every such Offender so discharged, as is above said, shall be for the said Offence or Offences done within any of the King's Lordships Marchers, or any other Lordships Marchers, discharged as well against the King's Highness, his Heirs and Successors, as against all other Lord Marchers, for one Time only.

II. Provided alway, and be it enacted by the Authority aforesaid, That this present Act, or any Thing therein contained, shall not extend nor take place to abridge, deprive or minorate any Liberties, Privilege or Authority of any Lords Marchers, heretofore granted to the same Lord, or lawfully used or accustomed by the said Lord or any of his Ancestors, unless the foresaid Offenders happen to be indicted, outlawed, arraigned, convicted or attainted by Force of this Act, as is above said, within two Years next after such Murther or other felonious Offence perpetrated, done or committed, within the said Lordships Marchers, or any of them; any Thing in this present Act before rehearsed to the contrary notwithstanding.

12. And furthermore be it enacted by the Authority aforesaid, That all Murthers, Robberies, Felonies and Accessaries of the same, which shall happen hereafter to be done, perpetrated or committed within the Shire of Merioneth in WALES, shall and may be from henceforth enquired, heard and determined in the Counties of Carnarvon or Anglesea, before the King's Justice of NORTH WALES, or his Deputy, for the Time being, by Verdict or Inquest to be taken by the Inhabitants of the same Shires of Carnarvon or Anglesea, or otherwise, if by the Discretion of the Justice there, or his Deputy, it shall be thought convenient: And that the same Justice, or his Deputy, for the Time being, shall have full Power and Authority by his Discretion, by Force of this present Act, to hear and determine all and every the aforesaid Murthers, Felonies, Robberies and Accessaries, in Form aforesaid.

13. "And where heretofore upon divers Murthers, Robberies and Felonies perpetrated and done, as well within the Lordship Marchers of WALES, as in other Places of WALES without the same Lordships, the Offenders divers Times flee and escape from the same Lordship or other Place where such Offence was committed, and have repaired and resorted into another Lordship Marcher, and there by the Aid, Comfort and Favour of the said Lord of the same Lordship, or his Officer or Officers, have been abiding and resiant, into the which Lordships the same Lords Marchers have and do pretend a Custom and Privilege, that none of the King's Ministers or Subjects may enter, to pursue, apprehend and attach any such Offender thereunto repaired, as is aforesaid, by reason whereof the same Offenders went unpunished, to the Animation and Encouraging of other evil-disposed People": It is therefore enacted by the Authority above said, That every Officer and Officers, and their Deputies, upon Commandment given by the Commissioners or Council of the Marches for the Time being, shall bring, send or deliver every such Offender to the Officer of the Lordship Marcher, or other Place, where any such Offence is or shall be committed or done, upon the Metes and Bounds of the said Lordships, or to the said Commissioners or Council, according as to the said Officers by them shall be commanded, under Pain of xl. li. the said Commandment or Commission to be directed to any such Officer, to be sent, conveyed and delivered by a Serjeant at Arms, or a Pursevant, attendant on the said Council in the Marches for the Time being.

A.D. 1534]

26 Henry 8, c. 11.

An Act for punishment of Welshmen attempting any Assaults or Affrays upon any the inhabitants of Hereford Gloucester and Shropshire.

Forasmuch as in times past divers and sundry the King our Sovereign Lord's subjects, inhabited as well in Wales as in the Marches of the same, have heretofore used at sundry times, when awful process hath been attempted against them or against their kinsmen or friends for sundry robberies murders or felonies by them committed, or for any suits or processes of the Law pursued or sued against any person or persons inhabiting or dwelling within Wales or the Marches of the same, within the Counties of Gloucester Salop and Hereford have lain in a wait and suddenly of prepensid malice have not only met with the pursuers of the said suits in the said Counties and in places near adjoining to the same, but also have beaten mayhemed grievously wounded and some times murdered divers of the same pursuers, for the only attempting and pursuing of such felonies, whereby hath ensued no little violation and disturbance of the King's peace, to the great disquieting of all the said parts and to the right perilous example of all other like offenders; Be it therefore ordained established and enacted by the King's said Highness his Lords Spiritual and temporal and the Commons in this present parliament assembled and by the authority of the same that if any manner person or persons inhabited or dwelling in Wales or in the Marches of the same at any time hereafter upon any prepensid malice shall presume to assault beat hurt wound or mayhem any other the King's subjects of the said Counties, that then he or they so attempting, whatsoever they be, being indicted and convicted thereof shall suffer imprisonment without redemption for the space of one whole year, in such prison or prisons as unto the Justices before whom he or they shall be so convicted shall be thought convenient, with such further pain and punishment as he or they should have had if this Act had never been had or made; this Act to endure unto the last day of the next parliament.

A.D. 1534]

26 Henry 8, c. 12.

An Act for purgation of Convicts in WALES.

Where in the Parliament summoned and holden at London the 3rd. of November in the 21st year of the reign of our Sovereign Lord King Henry the eighth and from thence adjourned unto Westminster in the County of Middlesex, and after divers prorogations there also holden the 15th day of January in the 23rd. year of the reign of our said Sovereign Lord King Henry the eighth: It was enacted among other, that no person nor persons which from thenceforth should happen to be found guilty, after the laws of this Land, for any manner of petty treason, or for any wilful murder of malice prepensid, or for robbing of any Church Chapels or other holy places, or for robbing of any person or persons in their dwelling houses or dwelling place, the owner or dweller in the same house his wife his children or servants then being within and put in fear and dread by the same, or for robbing of any person or persons in or near about the Highways, or for wilful burning of any dwelling houses or barns wherein any grain of corns should happen to be, nor any person or persons being found guilty of any abettment, procurement helping, maintenance or counseling of or to any such petty treasons murders or felonies, should from thenceforth be admitted to the benefit of his or their clergy, but utterly be excluded thereof and suffer death, in such manner and form as they should have done for any the causes or offences abovesaid if they were no clerks; such as be within holy orders, that is to say of the orders of subdeacon or above, only excepted; And also it was then and there by authority aforesaid further enacted, that every such person and persons, within such orders of subdeacon or above which at any time from thenceforth should be found guilty of any petty treason, or of any murder of malice prepensid, or of any of the felonies above rehearsed, or of any accessary to petty treason wilful murder or to any other the felonies above specified, and admitted to his or their clergy and delivered to the Ordinance for the same, should not in any wise from thenceforth be suffered to any purgation, nor be set at liberty, but remain and abide in perpetual prison, under the Keeping of the Ordinary to whom he should be committed and his successors, without any manner of purgation, during the natural life of every such convict; except only such person or persons so being within such holy orders, and convict of or for any of the offences aforesaid, and delivered to the Ordinary for the same, do find two sufficient sureties by Recognizance before two of the King's Justices of his peace, within the same Shire where the petty treason, murder or felony whereof he was convicted was committed and done, whereof one of them to be of the Quorum, that such Convict shall be of good abearing against the King our Sovereign Lord his Laws and Subjects; every such convict to be bound in the sum of £40, and every his sureties in £20, and that no surety be taken unless such as may dispend in lands tenements or hereditaments yearly, above all charges, of estate of inheritance of chart hold 26s. 8d. or else be worth £20 in movable substance at the time of the taking of such recognizance; and that two Justices of Peace, whereof one to be of the Quorum, by authority aforesaid have power and authority to take such recognizance; And that the said Justices afore whom any such recognizance shall be taken shall certify the same into the King's Bench within four months next after the taking thereof upon pain to lose and forfeit 100s. for every default thereof. And forasmuch as there be no Justices of Peace nor of the Quorum within WALES, nor in divers other Places, Cities Honours Lordships and Manors within the King's Dominion, whereas a Lord Marcher Steward Lieutenant Deputy or other Officer of any such Place City Honour Lordship or Manor have authority and power, by custom or other wise, to arraign afore him or them any such person or persons being within such holy orders of Subdeacon or above, for committing or doing any of the said petty treasons murders felonies or any other of the said offences; And if it happen the same person so being thereof arraigned to be found guilty, for to admit him to his clergy if he pray the same before judgment, and further to do and execute against any such offender being so arraigned before them, in like manner and form as Justices of the Gaol delivery, within the Shire ground, have to do by virtue of the King's Commission unto them directed: By reason whereof every such person or persons within such orders of Subdeacon or above, being convict of any of the said petty treasons murders felonies or any other the said offences, before any Lord Marcher, Steward Lieutenant Deputy or other Officer within WALES, or within any other Place City Honour Lordship or Manor within the King's Dominion where no Justices of Peace be, and thereupon committed unto the Ordinary as clerk convict shall there remain during the natural life of any such convict, the said former Act and Statute notwithstanding; For that there be no Justices of the Peace nor of the Quorum there as the said petty treason murder or felony whereof he is so convicted was committed and done, to take surety by recognizance for the good abearing of every such convict, in manner and form as in the said former Act is rehearsed; Be it therefore enacted by the King our Sovereign Lord, and the Lords Spiritual and Temporal and the Commons in this present parliament assembled and by authority of the same, that every such parson and parsons within such orders of Subdeacon or above, being convict of any petty treason or of any murder of malice prepensid, or of any of the said felonies above rehearsed, or of any accessary to petty treason wilful murder or to any other the said felonies above specified, before any Lord Marcher Steward Lieutenant Deputy or other Justice or officer within WALES, or within any other Place City Town Honour Lordship or Manor within the King's Dominion where no Justice of the Peace and of the Quorum be, and thereupon the same convict admitted unto his Clergy, that the same person or persons, so being within such Holy orders and convict before any such Lord Marcher Steward Lieutenant Deputy or other Justice or officer in WALES, or within any such Place City Town Honour Lordship or Manor within any the King's Dominion where be no Justices of the Peace and of the Quorum, of or for any of the offences aforesaid, and delivered unto the Ordinary as Clerk convict for the same, shall or may find two sureties by recognizance for his good abearing before two of the King's Justices of the Peace, whereof the one to be of the Quorum, in the Shire where the same Convict is or shall be kept in the Ordinary's prison, if the same prison be within the Shire ground where Justices of Peace and of the Quorum be, or else before two of the King's Justices of the Peace, whereof the one to be of the Quorum, in the next Shire adjoining unto the same prison. And that the same two Justices of the Peace, whereof the one to be of the Quorum, to have Power and Authority to take such recognizance and to certify the same, in like manner and form and upon like pain as it should or ought to have been done by virtue of the said former Act, if the same petty treason murder felony or other offence, of or for which any such convict was or shall be so convict and admitted unto his clergy as is aforesaid, had been committed and done within the Shire ground where Justices of the Peace and of the Quorum be.

A.D. 1535]

27 Henry 8, c. 5.

An Act for making of Justices of peace in WALES.

The King's Highness considering the manifold robberies murders trespasses riots routs embraceries maintenances oppressions ruptures of his peace and many other malefacts which been daily practised perpetrated committed and done within his Counties and County Palatines of Chester and Flintshire in Wales adjoining to the said County of Chester, and also in his Counties of Anglece otherwise called Anglesey Kayernarvon and Merioneth within his Principality of North Wales, And also in his Counties of Cardigan, Carmarthen, Pembroke and Glamorgan in South Wales, by reason that common Justice hath not been indifferently ministered there like and in such form as it is in other places of this his Realm; By reason whereof the said murders robberies thefts trespasses and breaking of the peace have remained unpunished to the great animation of evil doers in the same Counties: For redress and amputation whereof and to the intent that one Order of ministering of his Laws should be had observed and used in the same as in other places of this Realm of England is had and used, It is ordained and enacted by the King our Sovereign Lord and the Lords Spiritual and Temporal and the Commons in this present parliament assembled and by the authority of the same, that the Lord Chancellor of England or the Lord Keeper of the Great Seal for the time being from time to time and at all times shall have full power and authority by his discretion to nominate and appoint Justicers of peace, Justicers of the Quorum and Justicers of Gaol delivery, in the said Counties of Chester Flint Anglesey Carnarvon Merioneth Cardigan Carmarthen Pembroke and Glamorgan by Commission under the King's great Seal; which shall have full power and authority to inquire hear and determine all manner of thing and things inquirable presentable or determinable before Justicers of Peace, Justicers of Quorum and Justicers of Gaol delivery in other Shires of this Realm of England, by force or virtue of any Statute or Statutes made and to be made or by the course of the common Laws of this Realm; and that the said Justicers of peace Justicers of Quorum and Justicers of Gaol delivery so to be named and appointed by the said Lord Chancellor or Lord Keeper of the great seal, and every of them shall have like power and authority within the said Counties of Chester Flint Anglesey

Carnarvon Merioneth Cardigan Carmarthen Pembroke and Glamorgan to do use and execute every thing and things as other Justices of peace Quorum and Gaol delivery have within any other of the Shires of this Realm of England, and also shall be sworn astricted and obliged to the Keeping of their Sessions of the peace, and to the due execution of all and singular Statutes and Ordinances made and to be made, in like manner and form and under like pains and penalties as Justicers of peace Justicers of Quorum and Gaol delivery in other Shires of this Realm of England been and shall be bounden and obliged; any Act statute prescription usage custom liberty or privilege had made accustomed or used to the contrary notwithstanding.

And it is further enacted by the authority aforesaid that the estreats of the issues fines and amerciaments taxed lost set or forfeited by or before such Justicers of peace Quorum and Gaol delivery in the said Counties of Chester and Flint shall be returned and certified into the Exchequer of Chester before the King's Chamberlain there, And that the estreats of the issues fines and amerciaments taxed set lost or forfeited by or before the Justicers of peace Quorum and Gaol delivery in the said Counties of Anglesey Carnarvon and Merioneth and every of them shall be returned and certified into the King's Exchequer at Carnarvon to and before the King's Chamberlain of North WALES; And that the estreats of the issues fines and amerciaments taxed set lost or forfeited by or before the Justicers of peace Quorum and Gaol delivery in the said Counties of Carmarthen and Cardigan and every of them shall be returned and certified into the King's Exchequer at Carmarthen to and before the King's Chamberlain of South WALES; And that the estreats of the issues fines and amerciaments taxed set lost or forfeited by or before the Justicers of Peace Quorum and Gaol delivery in the County of Pembroke shall be returned and certified into the King's Exchequer at Pembroke; And that the estreats of the issues fines and amerciaments taxed set lost or forfeited by or before the Justicers of Peace Quorum and Gaol delivery in the said County of Glamorgan shall be returned and certified into the King's Exchequer at Kayerdyff; And that the said estreats of the said issues fines and amerciaments certified and returned into every of the foresaid Exchequers shall be indented in such like manner and form as is used in the King's Exchequer at Westminster; And that the said Justicers of Peace and

Quorum or Gaol delivery in every of the said Shires shall direct such like process by estreats indented with the estreats certified into the said Exchequers to the Sheriffs of every of the said Counties for the levying and gathering of the said issues fines and amerciaments in such like manner and form as is used by the Justicers of Peace Quorum and Gaol delivery within this Realm of England; and that every Sheriff of the said Shires shall make their accompts in every of the said Exchequers of and for the said Issues fines and amerciaments upon the estreats to them directed in manner and form as is used in the King's Exchequer at Westminster.

And it is also enacted by the authority aforesaid that the said Justicers of Peace and Clerks of the Peace, within the said Counties of Chester Flint Anglesey Carnarvon Merioneth Cardigan Carmarthen Pembroke and Glamorgan and every of them, shall be paid and allowed of the said Issues fines and amerciaments such like fees profits and commodities as other Justicers of Peace and Clerks of the Peace in other Shires of this Realm have and ought to have.

And it is farther enacted by authority aforesaid that the Sheriff or his Deputy and all other his Ministers in all and every of the said Shires, and all Coroners, High Constables, Petty Constables and other Officers within every of the said Shires shall be obliged and bounden to be as well attendant unto the said Justicers of Peace Quorum and Gaol Delivery in all and everything and things concerning their authorities, as in executing and returning of all precepts and processes to them directed by any of the said Justicers, in like manner and form and under like pains and penalties as all and every Sheriffs Coroners and other Officers be and shall be bounden and obliged by any Statute or Common Law in other Shires of this Realm of England; any act statute prescription usage custom liberty or privilege had accustomed or used to the contrary notwithstanding.

A.D. 1535] **27 Henry 8, c. 7.**

An Act for the Abuses in the Forests of WALES.

"Where divers and many Forests be in Wales, and the Marches of the same, as well of the Inheritance and Possessions of our Sovereign Lord the King, as of divers others being Lords Marchers; within which Forests certain unreasonable Customs and Exactions have been of long Time unlawfully exacted and used, contrary both to the Law of God and Man, to the express Wrong and great impoverishing of divers of the King's true Subjects, the Effect of which said unlawful Exactions and Customs be hereafter declared; that is to wit, It hath been there unlawfully used, that if it fortuned any of the King's Subjects to pass go or ride through or in any Way or Path of any of the said Forests, not having upon him or them that so shall fortune to pass go or ride a Token delivered to him or them by the Chief Foresters Rulers Walkers or Farmers the which Token shall be well known amongst all them that are Walkers and Rulers under him or them; or that he or they that shall so fortune to pass go or ride in or through any of the said Forests, be not yearly Tributors or Chensers, then he or they so going riding or travelling in or through any of the said Forests, having no Token, or being yearly Tributors or Chensers, as is aforesaid, have used to pay by unlawful Exactions unto the said Foresters Rulers Walkers and Farmers of the said Forests a grievous Fine or Reward; And if any Person or Persons, not having such Token or Tokens, and not being a yearly Tributor or a Chenser, as is aforesaid, should happen to be taken found or espied by any of the said Foresters Rulers Walkers or Farmers, or their Assigns, by the Space of 24 Foot out of the Highway, then he or they so being taken found or espied out of the Highway, within any of the said Forests as is aforesaid, to forfeit and lose unto the said Foresters Rulers Walkers and Farmers, all such Money and Gold as should be then found upon him or them so being taken in any of the said Forests, out of the Highway, as is aforesaid.

2. "And also the same Person or Persons so being taken or found out of the Highway, to forfeit and lose a Joint of one of his or their Hands, or else to make Fine therefore with the said Foresters Rulers Walkers and Farmers, at the Will and Pleasure of the said Rulers Walkers or Farmers:

3. "And if also that it happen any Beast or quick Cattle to come go or escape into any of the said Forests by Stray or Thiefstolen, or otherwise, the said Foresters Rulers Walkers or Farmers, after Knowledge to him or them given, have likewise unlawfully used to seize and take the same Beast or Cattle as his or their own, and mark them with the Mark of their Forest there used, and so seized marked taken and them retain as Cattle forfeited unto their own use; by reason whereof the Owner and Owners of the same Cattle

have been clear without Remedy for the having again of the said Cattle, except only by way of Redemption or buying again of their own Cattle, contrary to all Equity and Conscience"; In Consideration whereof, it may please the King's Highness, with the Assent of the Lords Spiritual and Temporal, and the Commons, in this present Parliament assembled, and by the Authority of the same, to enact, ordain, and establish, That from the Feast of the Nativity of St. John Baptist next coming, which will be in the Year of our Lord God 1536, all the said unlawful Customs be determined void and had for naught throughout all and every of the said Forests within WALES and the Marches of the same.

4. And that it shall be lawful from thenceforth to all and every the King's true Subjects, and all other Person or Persons being in League and Amity with our Sovereign Lord the King, his Heirs and Successors, Kings of England, freely quietly and in Peace to pass and repass travel and go into and through the said Forests, and every of them, both on Horseback and on Foot, as well following and driving of Cattle, as with carrying of Wares, or otherwise about their lawful Business and Affairs, without any Fine Forfeiture Toll Custom Exaction or other Imposition to be taken exacted or demanded of them, by the said Foresters Rulers Walkers Farmers or their Assigns, And if it shall chance or happen any of the said Foresters Rulers Walkers Farmers or their Assigns, or any of them, at any Time after the said Feast of St. John Baptist, to take any Person or Persons, being the King's true Subjects, or otherwise in League and Amity with our said Sovereign Lord, his Heirs or Successors, Kings of England, as is aforesaid, and exact and take from them, or any of them, any of the said Forfeitures Fines Tolls Customs and Exactions, as is above mentioned, and be thereof lawfully convicted, that then he or they so doing and offending contrary to this Act, to incur and stand in the Dangers of the Statute heretofore provided for Robberies by the King's Highway, and the same to be tried before the Justices of the Peace in their next Shire adjoinant, according to the Law of this Realm of England.

5. And further be it enacted by the Authority aforesaid, That if any Manner of Beast or quick Cattle of any of the King's true Subjects, or others of the King's Friends, at any time after the said Feast of the Nativity of St. John Baptist, do come into any of the said Forests by Strays, Thiefstolen or otherwise and there be marked

and seized by any of the said Foresters Rulers Walkers Farmers or their Assigns, or any of them; and the Owner and Owners of the same Cattle, within one Year and a Day next ensuing, chance to find the said Cattle so taken, and lawfully prove the same to be his or their own proper Cattle, that then the same Cattle to be redelivered to the Owner or Owners thereof, according to the ancient Law of this Realm of England; the said Owner and Owners reasonably paying for the keeping of such Cattle after the Rate of the Time that such Cattle shall have been in the Custody and keeping of any such Foresters Rulers Walkers and Farmers, or his or their Assigns, in such Manner and Form as heretofore hath been in like Case used to be done by the Law of this Realm, of estrayed Cattle claimed and proved by the Owners within a Year and a Day next after the seizing of the same Cattle; and if any of the said Foresters Rulers Walkers Farmers their Assigns, or any of them do deny the Deliverance of any such Cattle, by them or any of them so seized or marked within any of the said Forests, after the Owner or Owners of them shall have duly and lawfully proved them to be his or their own proper Goods and Chattels as is aforesaid, that then every such Forester Ruler Walker Farmer or their Assigns, so doing and offending contrary to this Act, to forfeit and pay unto the Party grieved the double Value of all such Cattle as shall be so taken and marked, and not re-delivered to the Owner or Owners as is aforesaid; And that the Party grieved may have his Action of Detinue at the Common Law, of and for the same Cattle, against every such Offender or Offenders, and the same to be tried in the next Shire adjoinant; in which Action the Defendant shall not be admitted to wage his Law, nor Essoin nor Protection shall be allowed for them: And like Process of Outlawry to be had and made in the said Action of Detinue in the next Shire adjoinant, against every Forester Ruler Walker Farmer or their Assigns, so offending contrary to the Tenor of this Act, as in an Action of Trespass at the Common Law of this Realm is used.

A.D. 1535] **27 Henry 8, c. 10, s. 16.**

AN ACT CONCERNING USES AND WILLS.

16. Provided also, that this act, nor anything therein contained, be in anywise prejudicial or hurtful to any person or persons born in

WALES, or the marches of the same, which shall have any estate to them executed by authority of this act, in any lands, tenements, or other hereditaments within this realm, whereof any other person or persons now stand or be seised to the use of any such person or persons born in WALES, or the marches of the same; but that the same person or persons born in WALES, or the marches of the same shall or may lawfully have, retain and keep the same lands, tenements, or other hereditaments, whereof estate shall be so unto them executed by the authority of this act, according to the tenor of the same; any thing in this act contained, or any other act or provision heretofore had or made to the contrary notwithstanding.

A.D. 1535] 27 Henry 8, c. 14, s. 7.

AN ACT CONCERNING THE CUSTOM OF LEATHER.

7. Provided always, That Hides untanned of any beasts being killed within WALES or the Marches thereof may be conveyed and carried into outward parts by any person or persons from time to time Except only by Tanners and such as have Tan Houses, in such and like manner as they might have been before the making of this Act, anything in the same mentioned to the contrary notwithstanding.

A.D. 1535] 27 Henry 8, c. 24, ss. 1, 2, 3, 18.

AN ACT FOR RE-CONTINUING LIBERTIES IN THE CROWN.

"Where divers of the most ancient Prerogatives and Authorities of Justice, appertaining to the Imperial Crown of this Realm, have been severed and taken from the same by sundry Gifts of the King's most noble Progenitors, Kings of this Realm, to the great Diminution and Detriment of the Royal Estate of the same, and to the Hindrance and great Delay of Justice": for Reformation whereof, be it enacted by Authority of this present Parliament, That no Person or Persons, of what Estate or Degree soever they be, from the first Day of July, which shall be in the Year of our Lord God 1536, shall have any Power or Authority to pardon or remit any Treasons, Murders, Manslaughters, or any Kinds of

Felonies, whatsoever they be; nor any Accessaries to any Treasons, Murders, Manslaughters, or Felonies; or any Outlawries for any such Offences afore rehearsed, committed, perpetrated, done or divulged, or hereafter to be committed, done or divulged, by or against any Person or Persons in any Part of this Realm, WALES, or to the Marches of the same; but that the King's Highness, his Heirs and Successors, Kings of this Realm, shall have the whole and sole Power and Authority, thereof united and knit to the Imperial Crown of this Realm as of good Right and Equity it appertaineth; any Grants, Usages, Prescriptions, Allowances, Act or Acts of Parliament, or any other Thing to the contrary hereof notwithstanding.

2. And be it also enacted by Authority aforesaid, That no Person or Persons, of what Estate, Degree or Condition soever they be, from the said first Day of July, shall have any Power or Authority to make any Justices of Eyre, Justices of Assise, Justices of Peace, or Justices of Gaol Delivery; but that all such Officers and Ministers shall be made by Letters Patents under the King's Great Seal, in the Name and by Authority of the King's Highness and his Heirs, King's of this Realm, in all Shires, Counties, Counties Palatine, and other Places of this Realm, WALES, and the Marches of the same, or in any other his Dominions, at their Pleasure and Wills, in such Manner and Form as Justices of Eyre, Justices of Assise, Justices of Peace, and Justices of Gaol Delivery, be commonly made in every Shire of this Realm; any Grants, Usages, Prescriptions, Allowances, Act or Acts of Parliament, or any other Thing or Things to the contrary thereof notwithstanding.

3. And be it further enacted by Authority of this present Parliament, That all original Writs and judicial Writs, and all manner of Indictments of Treason, Felony and Trespass, and all manner of Process to be made upon the same, in every County Palatine, and other Liberty within this Realm of England, WALES, and Marches of the same, shall from the said first Day of July be made only in the Name of our said Sovereign Lord the King, and his Heirs Kings of England; and that every Person or Persons, having such County Palatine, or any other such Liberty to make such originals, Judicials, or other Process of Justice, shall make the *Teste* in the said original Writs and Judicial, in the Name of that same Person or Persons that have such County Palatine or Liberty.

18. Provided always, That this Act, nor any Thing therein contained, be in any wise hurtful or prejudicial unto Sir Thomas Englefield, Knight, Justice of the County Palatine of Chester and Flint, nor to his Deputy or Deputies, nor to any of them, of, for or concerning the Office of Justice or Justicer of the said County Palatine and Flint, nor for or concerning any Fees, Profits or Advantages to the same Office in any Manner wise appertaining or belonging; but that the said Sir Thomas, his Deputy and Deputies, and every of them, may lawfully have, occupy and exercise the said Office, and also receive and take to their own Use all manner Profits, Commodities and Advantages to the said Office belonging or appertaining, according to the Tenor, Purport and Effect of such Letters Patents, as before this Time were unto the same Sir Thomas made under the Seal of the said County Palatine, or under any other Seal, by our said Sovereign Lord the King that now is, of, for or concerning the said Office and other the Premises, or any Parcel thereof, in as ample and large manner as though this Act had never been had nor made; any Thing in this Act contained to the contrary in any wise notwithstanding.

A.D. 1535] **27 Henry 8, c. 26.**

AN ACT FOR LAWS AND JUSTICE TO BE MINISTERED IN WALES IN LIKE FORM AS IT IS IN THIS REALM.

"Albeit the Dominion Principality and Country of WALES justly and righteously is, and ever hath been incorporated annexed united and subject to and under the Imperial Crown of this Realm, as a very Member and Joint of the same, whereof the King's most Royal Majesty of Meer Droit, and very Right, is very Head King Lord and Ruler; yet notwithstanding, because that in the same Country Principality and Dominion divers Rights Usages Laws and Customs be far discrepant from the Laws and Customs of this Realm, and also because that the People of the same Dominion have and do daily use a Speech nothing like, nor consonant to the natural Mother Tongue used within this Realm, some rude and ignorant People have made Distinction and Diversity between the King's Subjects of this Realm, and his Subjects of the said Dominion and Principality of WALES, whereby great Discord Variance Debate Division Murmur and Sedition hath grown between his said Subjects"; His Highness therefore, of a singular Zeal Love and Favour that he beareth towards his Subjects of his said Dominion of WALES, minding and intending to reduce them to the perfect Order Notice and Knowledge of his Laws of this his Realm, and utterly to extirp all and singular the sinister Usages and Customs differing from the same, and to bring the said Subjects of this his Realm, and of his said Dominion of WALES, to an amicable Concord and Unity, hath by the deliberate Advice Consent and Agreement of the Lords Spiritual and Temporal, and the Commons in this present Parliament assembled, and by the Authority of the same, ordained enacted and established, That his said Country or Dominion of WALES shall be, stand and continue for ever from henceforth incorporated united and annexed to and with this his Realm of England; and that all and singular Person and Persons, born or to be born in the said Principality Country or Dominion of WALES, shall have enjoy and inherit all and singular Freedoms Liberties Rights Privileges and Laws within this his Realm, and other the King's Dominions, as other the King's Subjects naturally born within the same have, enjoy and inherit.

2. And that all and singular Person and Persons inheritable to any Manors Lands Tenements Rents Reversions Services or other Hereditaments, which shall descend after the Feast of *All Saints* next coming, within the said Principality Country or Dominion of WALES, or within any particular Lordship, Part or Parcel of the said Country or Dominion of WALES, shall for ever, from and after the said Feast of *All Saints*, inherit and be inheritable to the same Manors Lands Rents Tenements Reversions and Hereditaments, after the English Tenure, without Division or Partition, and after the Form of the Laws of this Realm of England, and not after any Welsh Tenure, nor after the Form of any Welsh Laws or Customs; and that the Laws Ordinances and Statutes of this Realm of England, for ever, and none other Laws Ordinances nor Statutes, from and after the said Feast of *All-Saints* next coming, shall be had used practised and executed in the said Country or Dominion of WALES, and every Part thereof, in like Manner Form and Order as they be and shall be had, used, practised and executed in this Realm, and in such like Manner and Form as hereafter by this Act shall be further established and ordained; any Act Statute Usage Custom Precedent Liberty Privilege or other Thing had made used granted or suffered to the contrary in any wise notwithstanding.

3. "And forasmuch as there be many and divers Lordships Marchers within the said Country or Dominion of WALES, lying between the Shires of England and the Shires of the said Country or Dominion of WALES, and being no Parcel of any other Shires where the Laws and due Correction is used and had, by reason whereof hath ensued, and hath been practised perpetrated committed and done, within and among the said Lordships and Countries to them adjoining, manifold and divers detestable Murthers brenning of Houses Robberies Thefts Trespasses Routs Riots unlawful Assemblies Embraceries Maintenances receiving of Felons Oppressions Ruptures of the Peace, and manifold other Malefacts, contrary to all Laws and Justice; and the said Offenders thereupon making their Refuge from Lordship to Lordship, were and continued without Punishment or Correction; for due Reformation whereof, and forasmuch as divers and many of the said Lordships Marchers be now in the Hands and Possession of our Sovereign Lord the King, and the smallest Number of them in the Possession of other Lords," It is therefore enacted by the Authority aforesaid, That divers of the said Lordships Marchers shall be united annexed and joined to divers of the Shires of England, and divers of the said Lordships Marchers shall be united annexed and joined to divers of the Shires of the said Country or Dominion of WALES, in Manner and Form hereinafter following; and that all the Residue of the said Lordships Marchers within the said Country or Dominion of WALES, shall be severed and divided into certain particular Counties or Shires, that is to say, the County or Shire of Monmouth, the County or Shire of Brecknock, the County or Shire of Radnor, the County or Shire of Montgomery, the County or Shire of Denbigh; and that the Lordships Townships Parishes Commotes and Cantreds of Monmouth, Chepstow, Matherne, Llanvihangel, Magour, Goldecliffe, Newport, Wenllonge, Llanwerne, Caerlion, Usk, Treleck, Tintern, Skynfreth, Gronsmont, Witecastle, Reglan, Calicote, Biston, Abergevenny, Penrose, Greenfield, Maghen, and Hochuyslade in the Country of WALES, and all and singular Honours Lordships Castles Manors Lands Tenements and Hereditaments lying or being within the Compass or Precinct of the said Lordships Townships Hamlets Parishes Commotes and Cantreds, and every of them, in whose Possession soever they be or shall be, and every Part thereof, shall stand and be from and after the said Feast of Al-Saints guildable, and shall be reputed accepted named and taken as Parts and

Members of the said Shire of Monmouth ; and that the said Town of Monmouth shall be named accepted reputed used had and taken Head and Shire-town of the said County or Shire of Monmouth ; and that the Sheriffs County or Shire-court of and for the said Shire and County of Monmouth, shall be holden and kept one Time at the said Town of Monmouth, and the next Time at the Town of Newport, in the same County or Shire, and so to be kept in the same two Towns *alternis vicibus*, and according to the Laws of this Realm of England for ever, and in none other Places.

4. And it is further enacted by the Authority aforesaid, That all Actions reals that hereafter shall be conceived perpetrated or sued for any Lands Tenements or Hereditaments, or any other Thing within the said County or Shire of Monmouth and all Actions personals within the same Shire or County of the sum of 40.s. or above, and all Actions mixt, shall be sued by original Writ out of the King's High Court of Chancery in England, and heard determined and tried before the King's Justices in England, or by Assise or *Nisi prius* within the said County of Monmouth, in such like Manner Form and Wise as all other Actions reals personals and Actions mixt be sued heard determined and tried in or for any Shire of this Realm of England ; and that the King's Justices of his Bench, or of his common Bench of Westminster, shall have full Power and Authority to direct all manner Process to the Sheriff and all other Officers of the said County of Monmouth, and also to direct Writs of *Venire facias* to the same Sheriff, for the Trial of every Issue joined before them ; and also to award Commissions of *Nisi prius* into the said County of Monmouth, for the Trial of such Issues joined before them, in like Manner and Form as they do into every Shire of this Realm of England ; and all and every the King's Subjects and Inhabitants within the said County of Monmouth shall be for ever, from and after the said Feast of *All-Saints*, obliged and bounden to be obedient and attendant to the Lord Chancellor of England, the King's Justices, and other of the King's most honourable Council, and unto all Laws Customs Ordinances and Statutes of this Realm of England, in like Manner Form and Wise as all other the King's Subjects within every Shire of this Realm of England be obliged and bounden ; any Act Statute Usage Custom Liberty Privilege or any other Thing to the contrary in anywise notwithstanding ; and that the Sheriff of the said County shall hold Plea of *Replegiare*, and all other Suits and

Plaints under Forty Shillings, in his County or Shire-court, in like Manner and Form as all other Sheriffs do within this Realm of England; and that the Sheriff Escheators and Coroners that hereafter shall be within the said County or Shire of Monmouth, shall be obliged and bounden to execute all the King's Processes, and to make due Returns thereof, and to use and exercise their Offices according to the Laws and Statutes of this Realm of England, in all and every Thing as the Sheriffs Escheators and Coroners be obliged and bounden to do in all and every other Shire of this Realm of England; and that the Sheriffs and Escheators of the said Shire or County of Monmouth, that hereafter shall be appointed by our Sovereign Lord the King, make their Accounts for their said Offices in the King's Exchequer in England, in like Manner and Form as other Sheriffs and Escheators do within this Realm of England, and upon such like Pain and Penalty as is upon other Sheriffs and Escheators in every other Shire within this Realm of England.

5. And it is enacted by the Authority aforesaid, That the Lordships Townships Parishes Commotes and Cantreds of Brecknock, Creckhowel, Tretowre, Penkelly, English-talgarth, Welsh-talgarth, Dynas, the Haye, Glynebough, Broynlles, Cantercely, Lando, Blaynllinby, Estrodew, Buelthe, and Lingors, in the said Country or Dominion of WALES, and all and singular Honours Lordships Castles Manors Lands Tenements and Hereditaments, lying or being within the Compass or Precinct of the said Lordships Parishes Commotes and Cantreds, or any of them, in whose Possession soever they be or shall be, and every Part thereof, shall stand and be for ever, from the said Feast of *All-Saints*, guildable, and shall be reputed accepted named and taken as Parts and Members of the said County or Shire of Brecknock; and that the said Town of Brecknock shall be named accepted reputed used had and taken Head and Shire-town of the said Shire or County of Brecknock; and that the Shire-court or County of and for the said Shire or County of Brecknock shall be holden and kept in the said Town of Brecknock.

6. And it is enacted by the Authority aforesaid, That the Lordships Townships Parishes Commotes and Cantreds of New Radnor, Elistherman, Elue-les, Bonghred, Glasebery, Glawdistre, Mihelles Church, Meleneth, Blewagh, Knighton, Norton, Preston, Commothuder, Rayder, Gwethronyon, and Stanage, in the said Country of WALES, and every of them, and all and singular Honours Lordships

Castles Manors Lands Tenements and Hereditaments lying or being within the Compass or Precinct of the said Lordships Townships Parishes Commotes and Cantreds, or any of them, in whose Possessions soever they be or shall be, and every Part thereof, shall stand and be for ever, from the said Feast of *All-Saints*, guildable, and shall be reputed accepted named and taken as Parts and Members of the said County or Shire of Radnor; and that the said Town of New Radnor shall be named accepted reputed used had and taken Head and Shire-town of the said County or Shire of Radnor; and that the Shire-court or County of and for the said County or Shire of Radnor, shall be holden and kept one Time at the said Town of New Radnor, and the next Time at the Town of Rothergowy, in the same County or Shire, and so to be kept in the said two Towns *alternis vicibus* for ever, and in none other Place.

7. And it is enacted by the Authority aforesaid, That the Lordships Townships Parishes Commotes and Cantreds of Mountgomery, Kedewenkerry, Cawrsland, Arustely, Keviliock, Doythur, Powesland, Clunesland, Balesley, Tempcester, and Alcester, in the said Country of WALES, and every of them, and all and singular Honours Lordships Castles Manors Lands Tenements and Hereditaments, lying or being within the Compass or Precinct of the said Lordships Parishes Townships Commotes and Cantreds, or in any of them, in whose Possession soever they be or shall be, and every Part thereof, shall stand and be for ever, from the said Feast of *All-Saints*, guildable, and shall be reputed accepted named and taken as Parts and Members of the said County or Shire of Mountgomery; and that the said Town of Mountgomery shall be named accepted reputed used had and taken Head and Shire-town of the said County of Montgomery; and that the County or Shire-court of and for the said County or Shire of Mountgomery, shall be holden and kept the first Time at the said Town of Mountgomery and the next Time at the Town of Maghenleth, in the same Shire or County, and so to be kept in the same two Towns *alternis vicibus* for ever, and in none other Place.

8. And also it is enacted by the Authority aforesaid, That the Lordships Townships Parishes Commotes and Cantreds of Denbighland, Ruthin, Saint Taffe, Kinllethowen, Bromfilde, Yale, Chirke and Chirkeland, Molesdale, and Hopesdale, in the said Country of WALES, and every of them, and all and singular Honours Lordships Castles Manors Lands Tenements and Hereditaments lying or being

within the Compass or Precinct of the said Lordships Townships Commotes and Cantreds, or any of them, in whose Possession soever they be or shall be, and every Part thereof, shall stand and be for ever, from the said Feast of *All-Saints*, guildable, and shall be reputed accepted named and taken as Parts and Members of the said County or Shire of Denbigh; and that the said Town of Denbigh shall be named accepted reputed used had and taken Head and Shire-town of the County or Shire of Denbigh; and that the County or Shire-court of and for the said County or Shire of Denbigh, shall be holden and kept the first Time at the said Town of Denbigh, and the next Time at the Town of Wrixham in the said Shire or County, and so to be kept in the same two Towns *alternis vicibus* for ever, and in none other Place.

9. "And forasmuch as the Counties and Shires of Brecknock, Radnor, Mountgomery, and Denbigh be far distant from the City of London, where the Laws of England be commonly used ministered exercised and executed; and for that the Inhabitants of the said Shires of Brecknock, Radnor, Mountgomery, and Denbigh be not of Substance Power and Ability to travel out of their Countries to seek the Administration of Justice"; It is therefore enacted by the Authority aforesaid, That the King our Sovereign Lord shall have one Chancery and Exchequer at his Castle of Brecknock, and one other at his Town and Castle of Denbigh; and that the Sheriff's Escheators and other Officers Accomptants of the Counties of Brecknock, Radnor, Mountgomery, and Denbigh, from and after the said Feast of *All-Saints*, shall be yearly appointed by our Sovereign Lord the King, for and within every of the said Shires of Brecknock, Radnor, Mountgomery, and Denbigh; and that the Sheriffs Escheators and other Officers Accomptants of the Counties of Brecknock and Radnor, from and after the said Feast of *All-Saints*, shall yearly make their Accompts before the King's Auditors, and such Chamberlain or Baron of the said Exchequer, as shall be thereunto appointed by our said Sovereign Lord the King, in such like Manner and Form as Sheriffs Escheators and other Officers Accomptants do yearly make their Accompts in the King's Exchequer at Westminster within this Realm of England. And that the Sheriff's Escheators and other Officers Accomptants of the Counties of Mountgomery and Denbigh, from and after the said Feast of *All-Saints*, shall yearly make their Accompts before the King's Auditors, and such Chamberlain or Baron of the said

Exchequer as shall be thereunto appointed by our said Sovereign Lord the King, in such like Manner and Form as Sheriffs Escheators and other Officers Accomptants do yearly make their Accompts in the King's Exchequer at Westminster within this Realm of England.

10. And that Justice shall be ministered used exercised and executed unto the King's Subjects and Inhabitants in every of the said Shires of Brecknock, Radnor, Mountgomery, and Denbigh, according to the Laws and Statutes of this Realm of England, and according to such other Customs and Laws now used in WALES aforesaid, as the King our Sovereign Lord and his most honourable Council shall allow and think expedient requisite and necessary, by such Justicer or Justicers as shall be thereunto appointed by our said Sovereign Lord the King, and after such Form and Fashion as Justice is used and ministered to the King's Subjects within the three Shires of North WALES.

11. And also it is enacted by the Authority aforesaid, That the Lordships Towns Parishes Commotes Hundreds and Cantreds of Oswester, Whetington, Masbroke, Knoking, Ellesmer, Downe, and Churbury Hundred in the Marches of WALES aforesaid, and every of them, and all and singular Honours Lordships Castles Manors Towns Hamlets Lands Tenements and Hereditaments lying or being within the Compass or Precinct of the said Lordships Towns Parishes Commotes Hundreds and Cantreds, or any of them, in whose Possession soever they be or shall be, and every Part thereof, shall stand and be for ever, from and after the said Feast of *All-Saints*, guildable, and shall be united annexed and joined to and with the County of Salop, as a Member Part or Parcel of the same; and that the said Lordships of Oswester, Whetington, Masbroke, and Knoking, with their Members, shall be taken named and known by the Name of the Hundred of Oswester in the County of Salop; and the Inhabitants thereof shall be attendant and do every Thing and Things at every Sessions Assise and Gaol-delivery to be holden within the County of Salop, as the Inhabitants of all other Hundreds do within the said County of Salop, according to the Laws of this Realm of England. And that the Lordship of Ellesmer, with the Members of the same, shall be united joined and knit to the Hundred of Pymhill in the County of Salop, and shall be taken named and known to be Parcel of the same Hundred; and the Inhabitants thereof shall be attendant and do every Thing and Things with the Inhabitants of the same Hundred of Pymhill

as the Inhabitants of the same Hundred now do and use, according to the Laws of this Realm of England. And that the Lordship of Downe, with the Members, shall be united joined and knit to the Hundred of Churbury in the County of Salop; and that the Inhabitants of the said Hundred of Churbury and Lordship of Downe shall be attendant and do every Thing and Things at every Sessions Assise and Gaol-delivery to be holden within the said County of Salop, as the Inhabitants of all other Hundreds do within the said County of Salop, according to the Laws of this Realm of England. And that the said Hundred of Churbury, after the said Feast of *All-Saints*, nor the said Hundred of Oswester, nor yet the Lordship of Ellesmer, shall be in nowise otherwise privileged, nor have no other Liberty nor Privilege, but as Hundreds united annexed and knit to the said County of Salop, as other Hundreds be within the said County.

12. And that the Lordships Towns Parishes Commotes Hundreds and Cantreds of Ewyas Lacy, Ewyas Harold, Clifford, Wynforton, Yerdesley, Huntington, Whytney, Wygmore, Logharneys, and Stepulton, in the said Marches of WALES, and every of them, and all and singular Honours Lordships Castles Manors Lands Tenements and Hereditaments, lying or being within the Compass or Precinct of the said Lordships Towns Parishes Commotes Hundreds and Cantreds, or any of them, in whose Possession soever they be or shall be, and every Part thereof, shall stand and be for ever, from and after the said Feast of *All-Saints*, guildable, and shall be united annexed and joined to and with the County of Hereford, as a Member Part or Parcel of the same County of Hereford; and that the Lordships of Wygmore and Logharneys, with their Members, shall be taken named and known by the Name of the Hundred of Wygmore in the County of Hereford aforesaid; and that the Inhabitants thereof shall be attendant and do every Thing and Things at every Sessions Assise and Gaol-delivery to be holden within the said County of Hereford, as the Inhabitants of all other Hundreds do within the said County of Hereford, according to the Laws of this Realm of England. And that the whole Lordship of Ewyas Lacy, with the Members, shall be taken named and known by the Name of the Hundred of Ewyas Lacy within the said County of Hereford; and the Inhabitants thereof shall be attendant and do every Thing and Things at every Sessions Assise and Gaol-delivery to be holden within the said County of Hereford, as the Inhabitants of all other Hundreds do within the said County of Hereford, according to the Laws of this Realm of England. And that the Lordship of Ewyas Harold, with the Members, shall be united joined and knit to the Hundred of Webtree in the said County of Hereford, and shall be taken named and known to be Parcel of the said Hundred of Webtree; and the Inhabitants thereof shall be attendant and do every Thing and Things with the Inhabitants of the same Hundred of Webtree, as the Inhabitants of the same Hundred now do, according to the Laws of this Realm of England. And that the Lordships of Clifford, Wynforton, Yerdesley, Whitney, and Huntington, with their Members, shall be taken named and known by the Name of the Hundred of Huntington, within the County of Hereford aforesaid, and that the Inhabitants thereof shall be attendant and do every Thing and Things at every Sessions Assise and Gaol-delivery to be holden within the said County of Hereford, as the Inhabitants of all other Hundreds do within the said County of Hereford, according to the Laws of this Realm of England. And that the said Hundred of Wygmore, with the Members, and the said Hundred of Ewyas Lacy, and the said Hundred of Huntington, and the said Lordship of Ewyas Harold, annexed unto the Hundred of Webtree, after the said Feast of *All-Saints*, shall be in nowise otherwise privileged, nor have no other Liberty Franchises nor Privilege, but as Hundreds united and annexed to the said County of Hereford, and as other Hundreds be within the said County of Hereford.

13. And that the Lordships Towns and Parishes of Wollastone, Tidnam, and Bechley, in the said Marches of WALES, and all Honours Lordships Castles Manors Lands Tenements and Hereditaments, lying or being between Chepstow Bridge in the said Marches of WALES and Gloucestershire, in whose Possession soever they be or shall be, and every Part thereof, shall stand and be guildable from and after the said Feast of *All-Saints*, and shall be united annexed and joined to and with the said County or Shire of Gloucester, as a Member Part or Parcel of the same. And that the said Lordships Towns and Parishes of Wollastone, Tidnam, and Bechley, and all Honours, Lordships Castles Manors Lands Tenements and Hereditaments, lying or being between Chepstow Bridge and the Shire of Gloucester as is aforesaid, shall be united joined and knit to the Hundred of Wesebery within the said Shire of Gloucester and shall be taken named and known to be Part and

Parcel of the same Hundred, and the Inhabitants thereof shall be attendant and do every Thing and Things with the Inhabitants of the said Hundred of Wesebery, as the Inhabitants of the same Hundred now do, according to the Laws of this Realm of England. And that the said Lordships of Wollastone, Tidnam, and Bechley, after the said Feast of *All-Saints*, shall be in nowise privileged, nor have any other Liberty Franchise nor Privilege, but as Parcel of the said Hundred of Wesebery, in the said County of Gloucester.

14. And that the Lordships Towns Parishes Commotes Hundreds and Cantreds of Gower, Kilvey, Bishops Town, Landaffe, Singhnithe supra, Singhnithe subtus, Maskin, Ogmore, Glynerotheney, Tallagarney, Ruthien, Tallavan, Lanblethyan, Lantwid, Tyeryal, Avan, Nethe, Landewey, and the Clays, in the said Country of WALES, and every of them, and all Honours, Lordships Castles Manors Lands Tenements and Hereditaments, lying or being within the Compass or Precinct of the said Lordships Towns Parishes Commotes Hundreds and Cantreds, or any of them, in whose Possession soever they be or shall be, and every Part thereof, shall stand and be guildable for ever from and after the said Feast of *All-Saints*, and shall be united annexed and joined to and with the County of Glamorgan, as a Member Part or Parcel of the same. And that the said Shire of Glamorgan and Morgandoke and all the aforesaid Lordships Towns Parishes Commotes Hundreds and Cantreds united and annexed to the said County of Glamorgan, shall, from and after the said Feast of *All-Saints*, be reputed named accepted and known by the Name and Shire of Glamorgan only, and by none other Name.

15. And that from and after the said Feast of *All-Saints*, Justice shall be ministered and executed to the King's Subjects and Inhabitants of the said County of Glamorgan, according to the Laws Customs and Statutes of this Realm of England, and after no Welsh Laws, and in such Form and Fashion as Justice is ministered and used to the King's Subjects within the three Shires of North WALES.

16. And that the Lordships Towns Parishes Commotes Hundreds and Cantreds of Lanemthevery, Abermerlese, Kedwely, Eskenning, Corneowlthou, Newcastle, Emel, Abergoyly, in the said Country of WALES, and every of them, and all Honours Lordships Castles Manors Lands Tenements and Hereditaments, lying or being within the Compass or Precinct of the said Lordships Towns Parishes

Commotes Hundreds and Cantreds, or any of them, in whose Possession soever they be or shall be, and every Part thereof shall stand and be guildable for ever, from and after the said Feast of *All-Saints*, and shall be united annexed and joined to and with the County of Kayermarthen, as a Member Part or Parcel of the same; and that from and after the said Feast of *All-Saints*, Justice shall be ministered and executed to the King's Subjects and Inhabitants of the said County of Kayermarthen, according to the Laws Customs and Statutes of this Realm of England, and after no Welsh Laws, and in such Form and Fashion as Justice is ministered and used to the King's Subjects within the three Shires of North WALES.

17. And that the Lordships Towns Parishes Commotes Hundreds and Cantreds of Haverfordwest, Kilgarran, Lansteffan, Langeharne otherwise called Tallangherne, Walwynscastle, Dewysland, Lannehadein, Lanfey, Herberth, Slebeche, Rosmarket, Castellan, and Landofleure, in the said Country of WALES, and every of them, and all Honours Lordships Castles Manors Lands Tenements and Hereditaments, lying and being within the Compass or Precinct of the said Lordships Towns Parishes Commotes Hundreds and Cantreds, or any of them, in whose Possession soever they be or shall be and every Part thereof, shall stand and be guildable for ever, from and after the said Feast of *All-Saints*, and shall be united annexed and joined to and with the County of Pembroke; and that from and after the said Feast of *All-Saints*, Justice shall be ministered and executed to the King's Subjects and Inhabitants of the said County of Pembroke, according to the Laws Customs and Statutes of this Realm of England, and after no Welsh Laws, and in such Form and Fashion as Justice is ministered and used to the King's Subjects within the three Shires of North WALES.

18. And that the Lordships Towns Parishes Commotes Hundreds and Cantreds of Tregaron, Glenergine, Landway, Ureny, in the said Country of WALES, and every of them, and all Honours Lordships Castles Manors Lands Tenements and Hereditaments, lying or being within the Compass or Precinct of the said Lordships Towns Parishes Commotes Hundreds and Cantreds, or any of them, in whose possession soever they be or shall be, and every Part thereof, shall stand and be guildable for ever, from and after the said Feast of *All-Saints*, and shall be united annexed and joined to and with the County of Cardigan, as a Member Part and Parcel of the same; and that from and after the said Feast of *All-Saints*, Justice shall be

ministered and executed to the King's Subjects and Inhabitants of the said County of Cardigan, according to the Laws Customs and Statutes of this Realm of England, and after no Welsh Laws, and in such Form and Fashion as Justice is ministered and used to the King's Subjects within the three Shires of North WALES.

19. And that the Lordship Town and Parish of Mouthway, in the said Country of WALES, in whose Possession soever it be, and all Lands Tenements and Hereditaments now lying or being within the Compass or Precinct of the said Lordship Town and Parish of Mouthway, or any of them, in whose Possession soever they be or shall be, and every Part thereof, shall stand and be guildable for ever, from and after the said Feast of *All-Saints*, and shall be united annexed and joined to and with the County of Merioneth in North WALES, as a Commote Member Part or Parcel of the same.

20. Also be it enacted by the Authority aforesaid, That all Justices Commissioners Sheriffs Coroners Escheators Stewards and their Lieutenants, and all other Officers and Ministers of the Law, shall proclaim and keep the Sessions Courts Hundreds Leets, Sheriffs Courts, and all other Courts in the English Tongue; and all Oaths of Officers Juries and Inquests, and all other Affidavits Verdicts and Wagers of Law, to be given and done in the English Tongue; and also that from henceforth no Person or Persons that use the Welsh Speech or Language shall have or enjoy any Manner Office or Fees within this Realm of England, WALES, or other the King's Dominion, upon Pain of forfeiting the same Offices or Fees, unless he or they use and exercise the English Speech or Language.

21. And it is further enacted by the Authority aforesaid, That it shall be lawful to the Sheriff of every of the foresaid Shires of Monmouth, Brecknock, Radnor, Mountgomery, and Denbigh, and every of them, to put every misruled and suspect Person within their Sheriffwick, under Common Mainprise and Surety of their personal Appearance, as the Sheriffs do within every of the three Shires of North WALES, and that the Recognizances of such common Mainprise and Surety of Appearance taken before any of the said Sheriffs, shall be as good and effectual as if it were taken by any Justice of Record.

22. And that the Sheriff of the County of Monmouth shall certify such Recognizances, common Mainprise or Surety of Appearance, at every Quarter Sessions, before the Justices of the Peace of the said County of Monmouth; and that every Person or Persons within the said County of Monmouth, put under Common Mainprise, and bound to his personal Appearance, shall keep their personal Appearance at the Sessions holden within the said Shire of Monmouth, next after the Clause of Easter, and at the Sessions to be holden within the said Shire next after the Feast of Saint Michael the Archangel, until such Time that they be thereof released after the Form of the Law.

23. And that every of the Sheriffs of the said Counties of Brecknock, Radnor, Mountgomery, and Denbigh, and every of them shall certify such Recognizances, common Mainprise or Surety of Appearance by them taken, before such Justice as shall be appointed by our Sovereign Lord the King within every of the said Shires, at every Sessions to be holden in any of the said Shires before the same Justice.

24. And that every Person and Persons within the said Counties of Brecknock, Radnor, Mountgomery, and Denbigh, and also within the above named Counties of Glamorgan, Kayermarthen, Pembroke, and Cardigan, or any of them, put under common Mainprise, and bound to his or their personal Appearance, as well by the aforesaid Sheriffs, as by the Justice of any of the said Counties, shall keep their Appearances before the said Justices at every Sessions within the said Counties to be holden, in such like Manner and Form as is used in the three Shires of North WALES.

25. "And for that the Lords Marchers before this present Parliament have used to put their Tenants within their Lordships Marchers, under such common Mainprise and Surety of Appearance, and have had the Forfeitures thereof, which for ever from and after the said Feast of *All-Saints*, shall utterly cease and determine": Therefore be it enacted by the Authority aforesaid, That after the said Feast of *All-Saints*, every lay and temporal Person now being a Lord Marcher, shall have the Moiety or Half of every Forfeiture of all and every common Mainprise, Recognizance for the Peace or Appearance, forfeited by any of their Tenants inhabiting within any of their Lordships Marchers; and they to be paid the same Moiety or Half by the Hands of the Sheriffs of every of the said Counties where such Forfeitures shall be, if the Sheriff can levy the same; and the same Sheriff to account to our Sovereign Lord the King for the other Half or Moiety in such Exchequer as they be bound to be accomptant.

26. Be it further enacted by the Authority aforesaid, That immediately upon the Prorogation or Dissolution of this present Parliament, the Lord Chancellor of England shall direct the King's Commission under his Grace's Great Seal, to such Persons as to him shall be thought convenient, to inquire and view all the said Shires of Kayermarthen, Pembroke, Cardigan, Monmouth, Brecknock, Radnor, Mountgomery, Glamorgan, and Denbigh, and every Part and Parcel of them; and upon such View and Search, to divide them and every of them into so many Hundreds as they shall think most meet and convenient; and the Hundreds so divided shall return and certify with the said Commission into the High Court of Chancery before the said Feast of *All-Saints*, and the same to remain of Record, and to be of such Force and Effect as it were by Act of Parliament; and that the said Hundreds, after the said Certificate, shall be used and taken as other Hundreds be in every other Shire within this Realm of England.

27. Furthermore it is enacted by the Authority aforesaid, That immediately after the Prorogation or Dissolution of this present Parliament, the Lord Chancellor of England shall direct the King's Commission under his Grace's Great Seal to such Persons as to him shall be thought convenient, to enquire and search out, by all Ways and Means that they can, all and singular Laws Usages and Customs used within the said Dominion and Country of WALES; and the same shall return and certify to the King's Highness, and his most honourable Council, before the said Feast of *All-Saints* next coming; and that upon deliberate Advice thereof had and taken, all such Laws Usages and Customs as the King's Highness and his said most honourable Council shall think expedient requisite and necessary to be had used and exercised in the before rehearsed Shires, or any of them, or in any other Shire of the Dominion or Country of WALES, shall stand and be of full Strength, Virtue and Effect, and shall be for ever inviolably observed had used and executed in the same Shires, as if this Act had never been had nor made; any Thing in the same Act contained to the contrary in any wise notwithstanding.

28. And it is further enacted by the Authority aforesaid, That for this present Parliament, and all other Parliaments to be holden and kept for this Realm, two Knights shall be chosen and elected to the same Parliament for the Shire of Monmouth, and one Burgess for the Borough of Monmouth, in like Manner Form and Order, as

Knights and Burgesses of the Parliament be elected and chosen in all other Shires of this Realm of England, and that the same Knights and Burgesses shall have like Dignity Pre-eminence and Privilege, and shall be allowed such Fees, as other Knights and Burgesses of the Parliament have been allowed; and the Knights' Fees to be levied perceived received gathered and paid in such Manner Form and Order, as such Fees be gathered levied perceived received and paid in other Shires of this Realm of England; and the Burgesses' Fees to be levied as well within the Borough of Monmouth as within all other ancient Boroughs within the said Shire of Monmouth.

29. And that for this present Parliament, and all other Parliaments to be holden and kept up for this Realm one Knight shall be chosen and elected to the same Parliaments for every of the Shires of Brecknock, Radnor, Mountgomery, and Denbigh, and for every other Shire within the said Country or Dominion of WALES; and for every Borough being a Shire-town within the said Country or Dominion of WALES, except the Shire-town of the foresaid County of Mereoneth, one Burgess; and the Election to be in like Manner Form and Order, as Knights and Burgesses of the Parliament be elected and chosen in other Shires of this Realm; and that the Knights and Burgesses, and every of them, shall have like Dignity Pre-eminence and Privilege, and shall be allowed such Fees, as other Knights of the Parliament have and be allowed; and the Knights' Fees to be levied and gathered of the Commons of the Shire that they be elected in; and the Burgesses' Fees to be levied and gathered as well of the Boroughs and Shire-towns as they be Burgesses of, as of all other ancient Boroughs within the same Shires.

30. And it is further enacted by the Authority aforesaid, That all and every lay and temporal Person and Persons, now being Lords Marchers, and having any Lordships Marchers or Lordships Royal, shall from and after the said Feast of *All-Saints* have all such Myses and Profits of their Tenants, as they have had or used to have at the first Entry into their Lands in Times past, and also shall have hold and keep within the Precinct of their Lordships Courts Baron Court Leets and Law-days, and all and every Thing to the same Courts belonging; and also shall have, within the Precinct of their said Lordships or Law-days Waife Straife Infanthef Outfanthef Treasuretrove Deodands Goods and Chattels of Felons and of Persons condemned or outlawed of Felony or Murther, or put in

Exigent for Felony or Murther, and also Wreck de Mer, Wharfage and Customs of Strangers, as they have had in Times past, and as though such Privileges were granted unto them by our Sovereign Lord the King by Point of Charter; any Thing in this present Act to the contrary notwithstanding.

31. Provided alway, That this present Act, nor any Thing therein contained, shall take away or derogate any Laws Usages or laudable Customs now used within the three Shires of North WALES; nor shall not deprive nor take away the whole Liberties of the Duchy of Lancaster, but that the said Liberties shall continue and be used in every Lordship, Parcel of the said Duchy, within the Dominion and Country of WALES, as the Liberties of the said Duchy be used in Shire Ground, and not County Palatine, within this Realm of England.

32. Provided also, That this Act, nor any Thing therein contained, do not extend nor be prejudicial to any Person or Persons, to avoid any Patent joint Patent of any Office Fees Annuities or Reversion of any Office Fees or Annuities to them granted for Term of their Life or Lives, by our Sovereign Lord the King, or by any other Person or Persons, either for the using exercising or occupying any Manner of Office or otherwise; but that they shall have and enjoy their said Fees and all other Offices or Constableships Portерships Stewardships of Leets Law-days Court Barons and other Offices, being not repugnant against this Act; and in case any such Offices be repugnant against this Act, that then the Grantees to have and enjoy their Fees during their Life or Lives; any Article or Clause in this present Act to the contrary in any wise notwithstanding.

33. Provided also, that this Act nor anything therein contained be not in any wise prejudicial to the Right Honourable Henry, Earl of Worcester, for the exercising, using and occupying of the Office of the Justice of the whole County of Glamorgan; any Thing in this present Act contained to the contrary in any wise notwithstanding.

34. Provided also, That this Act, nor any Thing therein contained, extend not to deprive take away or derogate any other Acts before this Time made for the Trial of Treason Murther or Felonies, or Accessaries of the same committed and done in any Lordship Marcher in WALES, in the next Shires of England adjoining to the said Lordship Marcher.

35. Provided alway, That Lands Tenements and Hereditaments lying in the said Country and Dominion of WALES, which have been used Time out of Mind, by the laudable Customs of the said Country, to be departed and departable among Issues and Heirs Males, shall still so continue and be used in like Form, Fashion and Condition, as if this Act had never been had nor made; any Thing in this Act to the contrary thereof notwithstanding.

36. Provided also, and be it enacted by the Authority aforesaid that the King's Highness notwithstanding this Act or any Thing therein contained shall have Power and Authority for the Term of three Years next after the end and Dissolution of this present Parliament, to suspend for such Time as shall please his Grace or utterly to repeal, revoke and abrogate, this whole Act or any Part thereof, from Time to Time, as shall stand with his most gracious Pleasure, so that every such suspending, repeal and revocation from Time to Time as often as any such Case shall happen, shall be made in writing under the Great Seal of England, and be annexed to the Roll of this present Parliament wherein this Act shall be enrolled and Proclamations thereupon to be made in every Shire, within the said Country and Dominion of WALES; and that every such suspending, repeal and revocation, so to be had and made by the King's Highness, shall be as good and effectual to all Intents and Purposes, as if the same had been done by Authority of this present Parliament; this Act, or anything therein contained to the contrary thereof notwithstanding.

37. And whereas by this present Act there is appointed one Chancery and one Exchequer at Brecknock and another Chancery and Exchequer at Denbigh, it is enacted by Authority aforesaid, That the King's Highness, from Time to Time, within the Term of five Years next after the End of this Parliament, for the due Ministration of Justice in the said Country of WALES shall have Power and Authority to erect, make and ordain such Court or Courts, and so many Courts of Record and such and so many Justices, Ministers, Officers and Clerks, as by his Highness within the Time of five Years next after the End of this present Parliament shall be thought sufficient and convenient, as well for the due execution of this Act, or of any Thing or Things that shall be had done or made by Authority of the same as for the good Governance and Rule of the said Country of WALES.

38. Provided alway, That this Act, or any Thing or Things to be

done by Authority thereof, shall not be prejudicial to any Person or Persons which now have by the King's Letters Patent any Office or Offices of Prothonotary or Clerk of the Crown in the said Country or Dominion of WALES; but that they and every of them shall and may still have and use their Offices in as large and ample Manner Form, Fashion, and Condition, as if this Act, nor any Thing to be done by Authority thereof, had never been had or made; any Thing in this Act to the contrary thereof notwithstanding.

39. Provided also, That this Act, or any Thing therein contained, extend not or in any wise be prejudicial or hurtful to Sir Walter Devereux, Knight of the noble Order of the Garter, and Lord Ferrers of Chartley of, for and concerning the Offices of Chief Justice of South WALES, the Office of Chamberlain of South WALES, and of the Counties of Caermarthen and Cardigan in South WALES aforesaid, and of and for the Office of the Stewardship of the Lordship of Bealth in the Marches of South WALES, and of and for the Office of Receivership of the said Lordship of Bealth, or of, for and concerning any of the said Offices; but that the said Lord Ferrers may have, use, exercise and enjoy the said Offices, and every of them with all Fees, Wages, Emoluments, Commodities and Profits to the same Offices, or to any of them in any wise belonging or appertaining in as large and ample Manner, Form and Condition, as if the said Act had never been had or made.

A.D. 1536] 28 Henry 8, c. 3.

AN ACT GIVING THE KING'S HIGHNESS AUTHORITY TO ALLOT THE TOWNSHIPS OF WALES AT ANY TIME WITHIN THREE YEARS NEXT ENSUING.

Where in the Parliament begun and holden at London the third day of November in the 21st year of the reign of our most dread Sovereign Lord King Henry the Eighth and from thence adjourned to Westminster and there holden and continued by divers prorogations unto the fourth day of February in the 27th year of the reign of our said Sovereign Lord, and then and there holden and continued unto the dissolution thereof, one act and ordinance was made in the Session of the said Parliament holden the said 4th day of February, whereby amongst other things divers Shires and Counties were newly made and named within the Dominion and Principality of WALES, and divers Towns Parishes Lordships Commotes and Cantreds within the said Dominion and Principality were allotted appointed and limited to the said several Shires and Counties as by the same Act more plainly and particularly amongst other things appeareth: And forasmuch as by credible information it is common to the King's knowledge since the making of the said Act that some Lordships Towns Parishes Counties Hundreds and Cantreds be not indifferently allotted and limited to the Shires named in the said Act for the commodity of the King's Subjects therein inhabited; Be it therefore enacted by authority of this present Parliament, that the King's Highness, during the time of three years next after the end of this present parliament shall have power and authority by writing under his great seal to allot appoint assign and limit to every of the Shires named in the said Act such and so many Lordships Towns Parishes Hamlets Hundreds Commotes and Cantreds as his Majesty by his most high wisdom shall think most convenient and agreeable for the ease and commodity of his loving subjects the inhabitants of his said Dominion and Principality; And shall likewise have power and authority to name and assign the Shire Towns in every of the said Shires named in the said Act, and that every such limitation appointment nomination and assignment to be made by the King's Highness in that behalf by authority of this Act shall be as good and effectual to all intents and purposes as though it had been done and made plainly and particularly by authority of Parliament; any thing contained in the said Act made in the last parliament or any other thing or things to the contrary thereof notwithstanding.

A.D. 1536] **28 Henry 8, c. 6.**

AN ACT FOR THE CONTINUING OF THE STATUTES FOR BEGGARS AND VAGABONDS; AND AGAINST CONVEYANCE OF HORSES AND MARES OUT OF THIS REALM; AGAINST WELSHMEN MAKING AFFRAYS IN THE COUNTIES OF HEREFORD GLOUCESTER AND SALOP.

And where at the parliament continued and prorogued unto the third day of November in the 26th year of the reign of our said

Sovereign Lord, there was in that Session of the said Parliament an other Act made and established for punishment of Welshmen attempting assaults or affrays upon any the inhabitants of Hereford Gloucester or Shropshire, which Act was also made to endure to the last day of the next Parliament as by the said Act more plainly appeareth.

Forasmuch as the said Acts be beneficial and profitable for the Commonwealth of this Realm: Be it therefore enacted by authority of this present Parliament that the said Acts and every of them and all clauses articles and provisions therein contained shall from henceforth be observed and kept and continue and endure unto the last day of the next parliament.

A.D. 1539] **31 Henry 8, c. 11.**

An Act for the allotting of certain Townships in Wales.

(Recites 27 Henry 8, c. 26, and 28 Henry 8, c. 3, and proceeds) And forasmuch as the time of three years limited to the King's Majesty by the said Act made in the 28th year of his Grace's reign is nigh expired, and that his Highness hath had such great affairs and urgent causes to do concerning the state and wealth of this Realm, that by occasion thereof his Majesty hath had no convenient time nor leisure to accomplish and execute the power and authority committed to his Highness by the said Act made in the said 28th year of his reign: Be it therefore enacted by authority of this present Parliament that his Majesty, during the space of other three years next after the first day of this present Parliament shall have like power and authority to do use execute and accomplish all and every thing and things limited and appointed to his Majesty to be done used and accomplished by the same Act made in the said 28th year of his Grace's reign, in as large and ample manner in every condition as his Majesty might have done used and accomplished within the said time of three years limited by the said Act as is aforesaid, And that every such limitation appointment nomination and assignment to be made by the King's Highness in that behalf by authority of this present Act during the space of the said other three years next after the first day of this present Parliament shall be as good and effectual to all intents and purposes as though it been done and made plainly and particularly by authority of Parliament.

A.D. 1540]

32 Henry 8, c. 4.

TRIAL OF TREASONS IN WALES.

For the speedy trial and punishment of such persons as have committed and done or hereafter shall commit and perpetrate any manner of treasons and misprisions of treasons within the principality and dominion of WALES and Marches of the same or elsewhere within any the King's dominion where his Grace's original writs in his Chancery of England commonly runneth not, Be it enacted by authority of this present parliament, that all such treasons and misprisions of treasons as is aforesaid shall be presented and tried by the oaths of 12 men inhabiting or which shall inhabit within any such Shires, and before such Commissioners as the King's Majesty from time to time in such cases shall assign and appoint by his Commission or Commissions of Oyer and determiner, in like manner and form as if such treasons or misprisions of treasons had been done and committed within such the said Shires into the which the said Commissions of Oyer and determiner shall be directed as is aforesaid; And that all presentments trials processes judgments executions and forfeitures hereafter made had or done by virtue of such commissions shall be good and effectual in the law to all purposes and intents any grant custom or usage heretofore made or used to the contrary notwithstanding.

Provided alway that trials of Peers of the Realm concerning Treasons shall be done and had as heretofore hath been used and accustomed; any usage in this Act contained notwithstanding.

A.D. 1540]

32 Henry 8, c. 27.

FOR THE RESUMPTION AT CALAIS BERWICK AND WALES.

. . . .

. . . And where also divers of the King's Subjects, of their sinister and subtle means have likewise obtained of the King's Majesty for term of life and lives divers grants unto them made by the King's Graces letters patents of divers offices of sheriffwicks within the King's dominions of WALES, contrary to the Commonwealth of the Country there; not only to the great unsuertie of the said towns and places above rehearsed but also to the great disquieting vexation and trouble of the King's loving and obedient subjects: For reformation whereof be it enacted ordained and established by the authority of this present parliament that all and singular such letters patents warrants and licenses heretofore granted or made by the King's Majesty to any person or persons as is aforesaid and every of them shall by the authority aforesaid from and after the first day of September next coming be clearly void frustrated and of none effect to all intents constructions and purposes; And also that all and singular grants of the reversion or reversions of any office or offices in the Towns above rehearsed and Marches of the same shall by the authority aforesaid be likewise void frustrated and of none effect to all intents and purposes.

A.D. 1540] **32 Henry 8, c. 37, s. 2.**

FOR RECOVERY OF ARREARAGES OF RENTS BY EXECUTORS OF TENANT IN FEE SIMPLE.

Provided alway, that this Act, nor anything therein contained, shall not extend to any such manor, lordship, or dominion in WALES, or in the Marches of the same, whereof the inhabitants have used, time out of the mind of man, to pay unto every lord, or owner of such lordship, manor, or dominion, at his or their first entry into the same, any sum or sums of money, for the redemption and discharge of all duties, forfeitures and penalties, where with the said inhabitants were chargeable to any of their said lords, ancestors, or predecessors before his said entry.

A.D. 1541] **32-33 Henry 8, c. 3.**

THE BILL FOR FOLDING OF CLOTHS IN NORTH WALES.

Where a certain kind and Sort of WELSH Cloths called Whites, Russets, and Kennets, made and wrought in North WALES and Orcester Hundred, adjoining to North WALES, of long Time have been and be so craftily and hard rolled together, that the buyer

8

thereof cannot perceive nor discern the untrue making and breadth thereof to the great Hurt Deceit and Impoverishing of the King's true and loving Subjects; for Remedy whereof be it enacted, ordained and established by the King our Sovereign Lord his Lords Spiritual and Temporal and the Commons in this present Parliament assembled and by Authority of the same, That all and every the said Cloths from and after the Feast of the Nativity of St. John Baptist next coming, that shall be brought to any common Market and Fairs to be uttered and sold shall be folded either in pleats or Cuttles as the cloths of all other Countries of this Realm commonly have been used and be used, to the Intent that the Buyers thereof may plainly see and perceive the Breadth and Goodness of such Cloth and Cloths as he shall buy; and that every piece of the said Cloths, which after the said Feast shall be brought to any Market or Fair to be uttered and sold contrary to the Form aforesaid, shall be forfeited; that is to say, the Moiety or one half thereof to the Use of our said Sovereign Lord the King, and the other Moiety thereof to any of the King's Subjects which will sue for the same in any of the King's Courts of Record by Action of Debt, Bill, Plaint, Information or otherwise, wherein the Defendant shall not be admitted to wage his Law, nor any Protection nor Essoin nor any other dilatory Plea admitted or allowed.

A.D. 1541] **33 Henry 8, c. 13. ss. 3, 4.**

AN ACT CONCERNING CERTAIN LORDSHIPS TRANSLATED FROM THE COUNTY OF DENBIGH TO THE COUNTY OF FLINT.

"3. And where the Lordships Towns and Hamlets of Hope and Asaph, have of old Time been reputed accepted and taken as Part and Parcel of the County of Flint, and so have been continued until now of late, that by an Act of Parliament made in the 27th Year of the Reign of our most dread Sovereign Lord the King's Majesty that now is, the same were assigned to the County of Denbigh; and also where Parcel of the Parish of Hawarden is at this Day and of old Time hath been accepted taken and used as Part of the said County of Flint, and the Residue of the said Parish of Hawarden is and always hath been without the Precincts Limits and Jurisdiction of the same County"; Be it also enacted by the Authority aforesaid, that as well as the said Lordships Towns and Hamlets of Hope, Asaph, and the said whole Parish of Hawarden, together with the Lordship of the same, as also the Lordships Townships and Parishes of Molesdale, Mereforde, and Oseley, and all the Lands Tenements Hereditaments within the Precinct and Limits of the same or any of them shall from henceforth be reputed accepted taken and adjudged to be within the said County of Flint, as a Member Part and Parcel of the same County of Flint and not of or within any other County or Shire, any Statute Ordinance Law or custom heretofore had or used to the contrary thereof in any wise notwithstanding.

4. Provided always that the Inhabitants and Tenants of the said Lordships Towns Hamlets and Parishes of Hope, Asaph, Moldesdale, Mereforde, Oseleye and Hawarden, shall pay their Mises and Tallages when and as often as the same shall be due, with the Inhabitants of such Shire or Shires as before Time hath been accustomed; and that the said Lordships of Hope, Moldesdale, Mereforde, Oseleye and Hawarden with the whole and entire Parish of Hawarden, and all the Grounds Lands Tenements and Hereditaments within the Precinct and Limits of the same shall from henceforth be called taken and accepted the Hundreds of Moldesdale in the County of Flint; and that the said Lordship of Asaph with all the Grounds Lands Tenements and Hereditaments within the Precinct and Limits of the same shall be taken accepted and adjudged to be as Part and Parcel of the Hundred of Ruthlande in the same County.

A.D. 1542-3] **34 & 35 Henry 8, c. 11.**

AN ACT FOR THE TRUE MAKING OF FRISES AND COTTONS IN WALES.

Forasmuch as the inhabitants clothmakers that dwell within the Towns and Boroughs of Carmarthenshire Cardiganshire and Pembrokeshire have used in times past to make their cloth called Welsh frise and cotton called Welsh cotton, to the great profit of all the King's Subjects of this Realm, that is to say; every piece called a high frise raw should be made of 54 pound yarn and should contain in length 46 yards and in breadth one yard one quarter and every half piece high frise should weigh 27 pound and contain in length 23 yards raw, and in breadth one yard one quarter and that every piece cotton should weigh being raw, 68 pound of avoirdupois and contain in length 48 yards and in breadth five quarters one nail, without any straining; and that every half piece cotton should weigh 34 pound and contain in length 24 yards and in breadth five quarters and one nail; which true and good making of frises and cottons hath been of long time decayed and extinguished and yet is, to the great decay and ruin of all the said towns and boroughs and also to the great slander and hindrance of all good true clothiers inhabiting within the same, and also to the great hurt and prejudice of all the King's Subjects which do buy the same; and the principal ground and occasion thereof is that the Clothiers Tuckers Weavers and such others that were wont to inhabit within the said towns and boroughs, and there to make true frises and cottons both in length and breadth, be now come foreigners husbandmen and grasiers dwelling in the Country, out of the said towns of Carmarthen, Cardigan and Pembroke and other borough towns aforesaid and there do make their own wool in frises and cottons after the most false and deceitful manner that may be, and the same do carry from place to place to be sold to the great disquiet and hindrance of all the King's loving Subjects, and to the great slander of all true cloth makers within all the said towns and boroughs: For remedy and reformation whereof, be it enacted by the King our Sovereign Lord the Lords Spiritual and temporal and the Commons in this present parliament assembled and by authority of the same, that after the first day of June next coming which shall be in the year of our Lord God a thousand five hundred forty and three, no manner of person make any raw frises called Welsh frise, or any cottons called Welsh cottons to be sold in any fair or market or elsewhere in any other place, unless every piece frise called a high frise raw be made of clean wool without flux or throome weighing in yarn 54 pound of avoirdupois at the least, and containing in length 46 yards raw and in breadth one yard one quarter, and that every half piece frise high shall weigh 27 pound, and contain in length 23 yards and in breadth one yard one quarter; and that every piece cotton raw shall weigh 68 pound of yarn at the least without flux or throome and contain in length 48 yards and in breadth one yard one quarter and one nail; And that every half piece cotton shall weigh 34 pound of yarn without flux or throome and contain in length 24 yards and in breadth five quarters and one nail; upon pain to forfeit every piece and half piece frise, and every piece cotton and half piece cotton so put to sale contrary to the true meaning intent and purpose of this present Act, the one half of which forfeiture to be to the King our Sovereign Lord and the other half to him and them that will sue for the same in any of the King's Courts, wherein no essoin wager of law nor protection shall be allowed.

Provided alway that this Act shall take effect after the feast of the Purification of our Lady next coming and not before.

A.D. 1542–3] **34 & 35 Henry 8, c. 26.**

An Act for certain Ordinances in the King's Dominion and Principality of WALES.

Our Sovereign Lord the King's Majesty, of his tender Zeal and Affection that he beareth towards his loving and obedient Subjects of his Dominion, Principality and Country of WALES, for good Rule and Order to be from henceforth kept and maintained within the same, whereby his said Subjects may grow and arise to more Wealth and Prosperity, hath devised and made divers sundry good and necessary Ordinances, which his Majesty of his most abundant Goodness, at the humble Suit and Petition of his said Subjects of WALES, is pleased and contented to be enacted by the Assent of the Lords Spiritual and Temporal, and the Commons, in this present Parliament assembled, and by the Authority of the same, in Manner and Form as hereafter ensueth.

2. First, That his Grace's said Dominion, Principality and Country of WALES, be from henceforth divided into twelve Shires; of the which eight have been Shires of long and ancient Time, That is to say, The Shires of Glamorgan, Caermarthen, Pembroke, Cardigan, Flint, Caernarvan, Anglesey and Merioneth; and four of the said twelve Shires be newly made and ordained to be Shires, by an Act made at the Parliament holden at Westminster in the twenty-seventh Year of our said Sovereign Lord's most noble Reign, that is to say, the Shires of Radnor, Brecknock, Montgomery and Denbigh, over and besides the Shire of Monmouth, and divers other Dominions, Lordships and Manors in the Marches of WALES, united and annexed to the Shires of Salop, Hereford and Glocester, as by the said late Act more plainly appeareth.

3. Item, That the Limitations of the Hundreds, of late made within the said Shires by Virtue of his Grace's Commissions directed out of his Highness Court of Chancery, and again returned into the same, shall stand in full Strength, Force and Effect, according to the said Limitation; except such of the same as sith that Time hath been altered or changed by Virtue of any Act or Acts of Parliament already made, or that shall be altered or changed by any Act or Acts in this present Session to be made.

4. Item, That there shall be and remain a President and Council in the said Dominion and Principality of WALES, and the Marches of the same, with all Officers, Clerks and Incidents to the same, in Manner and Form as hath been heretofore used and accustomed; which President and Council shall have Power and Authority to hear and determine, by their Wisdoms and Discretions, such Causes and Matters as be or hereafter shall be assigned to them by the King's Majesty, as heretofore hath been accustomed and used.

5. Item, That there shall be holden and kept Sessions twice in every Year, in every of the said Shires in the said Dominion and Principality of WALES, that is to say, in the Shires of Glamorgan, Brecknock, Radnor, Caermarthen, Pembroke, Cardigan, Montgomery, Denbigh, Flint, Caernarvan, Merioneth and Anglesey; the which Sessions shall be called the King's great Sessions in WALES.

6. Item, That the Justice of Chester for the Time being shall hold and keep Sessions twice in every Year, in the Shires of Denbigh, Flint and Montgomery, and have nothing but his old Fee of an hundred Pounds yearly for the same.

7. Item, That the Justices of North WALES shall in likewise hold and keep Sessions twice every Year, in every of the said Shires of Caernarvan, Merioneth and Anglesey, and shall have yearly of the King's Majesty a yearly Fee of fifty Pounds for the same.

8. Item, That one Person learned in the Laws of this Realm of England, by the King's Majesty to be named and appointed, shall be Justice of the Shires of Radnor, Brecknock and Glamorgan, and shall in likewise hold and keep Sessions twice in every Year, in every of the same Shires, and shall have yearly of the King's Majesty fifty Pounds for his Fee.

9. Item, That one other Person learned in the Laws of this

Realm, to be appointed as is aforesaid, shall be Justice of the Shires of Caermarthen, Pembroke and Cardigan, and shall in likewise hold and keep Sessions twice in every Year, in every of the same Shires, and shall also have yearly of the King's Majesty fifty Pounds for his Fee.

10. Item, The said Persons or Justices, and every of them now being, or that hereafter shall be, shall have several Letters Patents and Commissions for their Offices, under the King's Seal of England, to be exercised by themselves or their sufficient Deputies, according to the Purposes and Intents in these Ordinances specified.

11. Provided always, That their Commissions to them already granted under the said Great Seal, shall stand in Force and Effect according to the Tenor of the same, unless it shall please the King's Majesty hereafter to alter or change them or any of them; this present article last before expressed in any wise notwithstanding.

12. Item, That every of the said Justices, within the Limits of their Commissions and Authorities to them appointed as is aforesaid, shall hold all manner of Pleas of the Crown at and in the said Sessions, in as large and ample manner as the King's Chief Justice in England, and other the King's Justices of the King's Bench there, or any of them, may do in their Places, or elsewhere within the Realm of England; and also to hold Pleas of Assises, and all other Pleas and Actions real, personal and mixt, in as large and ample Manner as the King's Chief Justice of the Common-place in England, and other Justices of the same Place, or any of them, may do in the Realm of England.

13. Item, That every of the said Justices of WALES shall have Power and Authority to enquire of all Treasons, Murders, Felonies, Riots, Routs, unlawful Assemblies, Extortions, Embraceries. Maintenances, Retainers, Concealments, Contempts, and all other Offences and evil Deeds, of what Natures, Names or Qualities soever they be, done, committed or perpetrated within the Limits of their Commissions and Authorities, against the Form of the Common Law of the Realm of England, or of any Statutes of the same, and to hear and determine the Premisses, and every of them, and generally to minister common Justice to all and singular the King's Subjects within the Limits of their Commissions and Authorities, according to the Laws, Statutes and Customs of the Realm of England, and according to this present Ordinance.

14. Item, That every of the said Sessions shall be kept and continued by the Space of six Days in every of the said Shires at either of the said Times, as is or hath been used within the said three Shires of North WALES; and that the said Justices shall cause open Proclamations to be made in the Shire-towns what Time and Place they purpose to keep their said Sessions, fifteen Days at the least before they keep the same, to the Intent the King's Subjects may have Knowledge thereof.

15. Item, That Days shall be given in all Pleas, Plaints, Process and Adjournments, from Day to Day and Sessions to Sessions, by the Discretion of the said Justices within the Limits of their Authorities, for the good and speedy Ministration of Justice to all and singular the King's Subjects, as is or hath been used in North WALES.

16. Item, That one original Seal, devised by the King's Highness for Justice to be ministered in the said three Shires of North WALES, that is to say, the Shires of Merioneth, Caernarvan and Anglesey, shall be and remain in the Charge, Keeping and Custody of the Chamberlain of North WALES.

17. And that one other original Seal, devised by the King's Majesty for Ministration of Justice, to be used in the said three Shires of Caermarthen, Pembroke and Cardigan, shall be and remain in the Charge and Keeping of the Chamberlain of South WALES.

18. And that likewise one other original Seal, devised by the King's Majesty for Administration of Justice, to be used in the said three Shires of Brecknock, Radnor and Glamorgan, shall be and remain in the Charge and Custody of the Steward and Chamberlain of Brecknock.

19. And that also one other original Seal, devised by the King's Majesty for Ministration of Justice, to be ministered within the said Shires of Denbigh and Montgomery, shall be and remain in the Charge, Keeping and Custody of the Steward and Chamberlain of Denbigh.

20. And that the original Seal of Chester shall be and stand for the original Seal of Flint, for Justice to be ministered in the said Shire of Flint, and shall be and remain in the Charge, Keeping and Custody of the Chamberlain of Chester.

21. Item, That the said Stewards and Chamberlains shall seal with the said Seals, that is to say, every one of them shall seal with

the Seal to his Charge committed, all manner of original Writs and Process, returnable before the said Justices at the Sessions to be holden in every of the said Shires, in Manner and Form as is aforesaid, and shall severally account and answer the King's Majesty for the Profits of the same Seal: And that none of the said Stewards, Chamberlains or Chancellors, having the Charge and Keeping of the said Seals, shall by Occasion thereof, or by Colour of any of their Offices, compel or cause any Person or Persons inhabiting within any of the said twelve Shires, to appear before themselves or their Deputies, nor shall have Power and Authority to hear and determine any Pleas of the Crown, nor other Causes or Matters of Justice, otherwise than in this Ordinance is limited and expressed; but shall have the Charge and Keeping of the said Seals, to seal all such original Writs and Process as shall be returnable before the said Justices in their said Sessions, as is before specified, and as hereafter shall be declared; which Writs and Process shall be used, made, sealed and returned, in Manner and Form as hath been used before the Justice of North WALES.

22. Item, That all such Persons as now be or hereafter shall be the King's Highness Stewards, Chamberlains or Chancellors, within any of the said twelve Shires, which by reason of their said Offices have Charges for the Receipt, Collection or Accompt, of and for the King's Rents, Revenues, Farms or Profits, to be due to his Majesty within the said Dominion of WALES, may direct Process under the said Seal, being in their Charge and Custody, within the Limits of their Authorities, only against Bailiffs, Reeves, Farmers and other Ministers Accomptant, to appear before themselves, to answer to and for any the King's Revenues, Farms, Rents or Profits, and for none other Causes, nor against any other Person or Persons, in like Manner and Form as they have been accustomed in that Case to do.

23. Item, That all Stewards of any Lordships or Manors in WALES shall and may keep and hold such Leets, Lawdays or Court Barons, as appertaineth and belongeth to the Lordships and Manors whereof they be Stewards, and hold Pleas by Plaint under the Sum of 40/- in every such Court Baron, and have and enjoy all other Authorities, Commodities and Profits as Stewards of Leets, Lawdays and Court Barons in England commonly have and been used to have by reason of the said Offices, and none other; any

Law, Usage or Custom in the said Dominion of WALES heretofore had to the contrary hereof notwithstanding.

24. Item, Provided always, and be it enacted, That the said Stewards, nor any of them, nor the Sheriff of the said Counties in WALES, shall have any Power or Authority to enquire of any manner of Felony in any such Leet, Lawday or Torn, within the said Dominion to be holden.

25. And that from henceforth no Leet nor Lawday be kept by the Steward or other Officer of any Lordship or Manor in the said Dominion of WALES, but in such Lordships and Places where it was accustomed to be kept before the making of the Act of Parliament concerning WALES, made in the twenty-sixth Year of our said Sovereign Lord's Reign; so always the Place where such Court shall be kept, be meet and convenient for that Purpose.

26. Item, That all Mayors, Bailiffs and Head Officers of Corporate Towns in WALES, may hold Pleas and determine Actions, and do every other thing concerning common Justice, according to their lawful Grants and laudable Customs of such Towns; so always they follow the Course, Trade and Fashion of the Laws and Customs of the Realm of England, and not of any WELSH Laws or Customs. And that in every of the said Towns they may try all Issues joined, or hereafter to be joined, in any Action personal, by six Men, according as heretofore in divers Places in the said Country it hath been used; any Thing contained in this Act to the contrary notwithstanding.

27. Provided always, and be it enacted by the Authority aforesaid, That forasmuch as there be divers and many small Boroughs and Towns Corporate within the said Dominion of WALES, whereof many have their Commencement by Grants made from the Lords Marchers, and some by other Means, our said Sovereign Lord shall from henceforth, by Virtue of this Act, have full Power and Authority, by his Letters Patents, to be inrolled in his Grace's High Court of Chancery, at any Time within seven Years hereafter next ensuing to the End of this present Parliament, to repel, annihilate and dissolve such and as many of the said Boroughs and Towns Corporate, and all Liberties and Customs of the same, as to his Highness shall be thought expedient to the Intent his Majesty, at his Grace's Pleasure, may duly erect, ordain and make such and as many other Boroughs and Towns Corporate within the said Dominion, being more apt and convenient for that Purpose, and

endue them with such Liberties and Franchises, as to his most excellent Wisdom shall be thought necessary for the Wealth of the said Country.

28. Item, the King's Majesty is pleased and contented of his most gracious Goodness, that such as have Patents of any Office of Stewardships, Chamberlainships, Chancellorships or Justiceships within the said Dominion of WALES, for Term of their Lives, shall have and enjoy their certain, ordinary and annual Fees of Money, used and accustomed to be paid and borne by the King's Highness, by Virtue of any their Letters Patents, during their Interest therein, but in no wise to take or claim any casual Fees claimed by colour of their Offices, contrary to this present Ordinance; any Custom in WALES, or any Thing in this Act to the contrary notwithstanding.

29. Item, Over and besides the said original Seals, there shall be four judicial Seals devised by the King's Majesty, whereof one shall remain with the Justice of Chester, which is appointed by this Act to be Justice of the Shires of Flint, Denbigh and Montgomery, to be used within the said Shires, to seal all judicial Process and Bills that shall be sued before the said Justice, in the Sessions to be holden within the same Shires: And that one other of the said judicial Seals shall likewise remain and be in the Charge and Custody of the said Justice of North WALES: And that the third of the said Seals shall be and remain in the Custody and Charge of the Justice of the three Shires of Glamorgan, Brecknock and Radnor: And the fourth of the said Seals shall remain in the Charge and Custody of the Justice of the said three Shires of Pembroke, Caermarthen and Cardigan: And the said Justices shall seal with the said judicial Seals, that is to say, every of them with the Seal committed to his Charge and Custody, as well all Bills, as all other judicial Process, that shall be sued before them in the said Sessions, upon any original Bills or Writs; and all other Process that shall be awarded from any of the said Justices shall be sealed with the said judicial Seal.

30. Item, That every of the said Justices shall account and answer to the King's Majesty for the Profits of the said Seal being in his Charge and Custody, in Manner and Form as hereafter shall be declared.

31. Item, That the Teste of every Bill and judicial Process that shall pass under the said judicial Seal, shall be under the Name of such of the said Justices from whom such Bill or judicial Process shall pass, in like Manner and Form as is used in the Common Place in England.

32. Item, That all Actions real and mixt, Attaints, Conspiracies, Assises and Quare impedit, Appeals of Murder and Felony, and all Actions grounded upon any Statutes, shall be sued by original Writs, to be obtained and sealed with the said original Seal, returnable before the said Justices at their Sessions, within the Limits of their Authorities, in Manner and Form as is afore mentioned.

33. Item, That all manner of personal Actions, as Debt, Detinue, Trespass, Accompt and such like, amounting to the sum of 40/- or above, shall be sued by Writs original, to be obtained and sealed as is aforesaid, or by Bills, at the Pleasure of the Party suing the same, before the said Justices within the Limits of their Authorities, as is used in North WALES.

34. And that all personal Actions under the Sum of 40/- that is to say, Debt, Trespass, Detinue, Accompt and such like, shall and may be sued before any of the said Justices in the said Sessions, by Bill, as it is used in North WALES.

35. And that every original Bill concerning Actions personal, shall be sealed with the King's judicial Seal, being in the Custody of the said Justice before whom such personal Actions by Bill shall be brought and commenced.

36. And that such Fees shall be paid for the writing and sealing of such original Writs and Bills as hereafter shall be expressed, that is to say, For the sealing of every original Writ to be sued in and upon the Causes aforesaid, and for every Bill to be pursued in Actions personal, whereof the Debt and Damage amounteth to the Sum of 40/- or above, the Parties pursuing the same shall pay for the Seal of every such Writ or Bill, 6d. And for every judicial Process to be sued upon any such original Writ or Bill, the Parties pursuing such judicial Process shall pay for the sealing thereof 7d. whereof the King's Majesty shall have 6d. and the Justice sealing such judicial Process shall have 1d.

37. Item, That every Bill in personal Action, whereof the Debt, Duty or Damage amounteth not to 40/- and all manner judicial Process to be sued upon the same, shall also be sealed with the King's said judicial Seal; and the Parties pursuing the same shall pay for the Seal of every such Bill and judicial Process thereupon

to be sued, 3d. whereof the King's Majesty to have 2d. and the Justice sealing such Process to have 1d.

38. Item, That all Writs of *Scire facias*, and Writs of good Abearing, or for the Peace, or Writs of *Supersedeas* upon the same, and all other Process to be sued from the said Justices upon any Record or Suggestion admitted by any of the said Justices within the Limits of their Authorities, shall also be sealed with the said Judicial Seal; and that the Parties pursuing the same, shall pay for the Seal of every such Writ or Process 7d. whereof the King's Highness shall have 6d. and the Justice by whom such Process shall be sealed 1d.

39. And that every Exemplification upon any Record before any of the said Justices, shall be sealed with the King's said judicial Seal; and the Parties pursuing the same shall pay for the Seal thereof 20d. whereof the King's Highness shall have 16d. and the Justices sealing the same 4d.

40. Item, That Recoveries and Fines of Record, and Warrants of Attorney for the same, shall and may be taken before every of the said Justices, of Lands, Tenements and Hereditaments within his Authority, by Force of his general Commission, without any Writ of *Dedimus potestatem* to be sued for the same, in like Manner and Form as is used to be taken before the King's Chief Justice of his Common Place in England.

41. Item, That all Fines hereafter to be levied before any of the said Justices, with Proclamation made the same Sessions that the said Fine shall be engrossed, and in two other great Sessions then next to be holden within the same County, shall be of the same Force and Strength to all Purposes, as Fines levied with Proclamations be of, that be levied before the Justices of the Common Place in England.

42. Item, That every Person suing Writs of Entry in the *Post*, or Writs of Covenant, or any other Writs, for any Recovery to be had by Assent of Parties, or otherwise, or for any Fine to be levied, shall pay such Fines to the King's Use for the same, as well *Fines pro licentia concordandi*, as all other Manner of Fines, as is used in the King's Chancery, or elsewhere in any of the King's Courts of England, which Fines shall be paid to such Persons as shall seal the original Writs for that Purpose, and that they shall account for the same in like Form as they shall do for the Profits of the said original Seal, as is aforesaid.

43. Item, That the King's Silver upon every Fine to be levied, shall be paid as is used in the Common Place in England, that is to say, 2/-. which King's Silver shall be paid to the Justice afore whom such Fine shall be levied; whereof the King's Highness shall have 20d. and the Prenotary entering the same shall have 2d. and the Justice afore whom such Fine shall be levied other 2d. and that the same Justice shall account for the King's Part thereof, like as he shall for the Profits of the King's judicial Seal committed to his Charge, in Manner and Form as is aforesaid.

44. Item, There shall be four Prenotaries for the making of all judicial Process, and for the Entring of all Pleas, Process, and Matters of Record, in the Sessions to be holden before the said Justices, whereof one of the said Prenotaries shall attend upon the said Justice appointed for the three Shires of North WALES, and one other shall attend upon the Justice assigned for the three Shires of Flint, Denbigh and Montgomery; and the third shall attend upon the Justice assigned for the three Shires of Caermarthen, Cardigan and Pembroke; and the fourth of the said Prenotaries shall attend upon the Justice assigned for the three Shires of Glamorgan, Brecknock and Radnor: And these four Prenotaries, as often as their said Offices shall be void, shall be named and appointed by the King's Highness, by his Majesty's Letters Patents under his great Seal of England. And where one John Arnold, Gentleman, hath the Office of Prenotary and Clerkship of the Crown, by the King's Highness Letters Patents, within the said three Shires of North WALES; and that one John Breckenhead hath the Office of the Prenotary, and Clerkship of the Crown by the King's Letters Patents, within the said Shire of Flint; and that likewise one John Leonard hath the Office of the Prenotary and Clerkship of the Crown, by the King's Letters Patents, within all the Residue of the said Dominion of WALES; the King's Majesty is pleased and contented, that the said three Prenotaries shall have, use, and enjoy their said Offices according to the Effect of the said Letters Patents to them thereof made, doing their Duties and Attendance by themselves or their sufficient Deputies, at every of the said Sessions to be kept within the Shires whereunto they be so appointed.

45. Item, There shall be a Marshal and a Crier in every of the said Circuits and Limits allotted to the said Justices, which shall be named by the said Justices within the Limits of their Authority and Commission, in like Manner and Form as Justices of Assise do

in England: And the said Officers shall attend upon the said Justices in their Circuits in their own proper Persons, and not by their Deputies.

46. And that the Marshal shall have, upon every Judgment and every Fine, 4d. and the Crier 1d. And upon the Acquittals of Felons, and of them that shall be delivered by Proclamation or delivered out of common Mainprise before any of the said Justices, the Marshal shall have 4d. and the Crier 1d.

47. Item, That every of the said Prenotaries, within the Limits of their Offices, shall take such Fees as hereafter shall be expressed; that is to say, For the writing of Pleas, and engrossing of Writs of Entry, in the Post, Writs of Right, *Quod ei deforceat*, or any other Writs pursued by the Assent of the Parties, 5s. and if it be with a double Voucher, than 6s. 8d. and for the Exemplification thereof 2s. and for the engrossing of Fines, to have for every Fine 3s. 4d. and if it be with Proclamations, then 4s.

48. Item, for every Bill of Debt, Detinue, Trespass, and all other Actions Personal sued before the said Justices in their Circuits, under the Sum of 40s. the Prenotaries shall have for the first Bill 4d. for the second Bill 4d. and for the third Bill 4d. and for the Entry of every Declaration, Plea and Bar, Replication, and Rejoinder in and upon every such Action, so that he do inroll the same in Parchment, 4d. and for every *Venire fac'*, *Tales*, *Habeas corpora*, and *Distring'*, for every of them 4d. and for the Judgment 8d. and for every Writ of Execution in every such Action 6d. and for every Warrant of Attorney in every such Action, as well for the Plaintiffs as for the Defendants 4d.

49. Item, In all Actions of Detinue, Trespass, and all other Actions Personal, wherein the Duty, Debt, or Damage amounteth to the Sum of 40s. or above, which shall be sued by Bills before the said Justices, the Prenotary shall have for the first Bill 4d. for the second Bill 4d. and for the third 4d. and for every of the Declaration, the Answer, Replication and Rejoinder, if it be enrolled in Parchment, 8d. and for the *Venire fac'*, *Tales*, *Habeas corpora*, and *Distring'*, for every of them 6d. and for the Judgment 8d. and for the Warrant of Attorney, 4d. and for every Writ of Execution upon the Judgments in such Bills 6d.

50. Item, In original Writs sued upon every Action Personal returnable before the said Justices, the Prenotaries shall have for every *Iterum sum'*, 6d. for every Distress in Trespass 6d. and for the

Declaration 8d. for the Answer, Replication and Rejoinder, for every of them, if they be inrolled and ingrossed as is aforesaid, 12d. For the *Venire fac'*, *Tales*, *Habeas corpora* and *Distring'*, for every of them 6d. and the Prenotaries to have for the Entry of the Judgments in every such Action 12d. and for every Writ of Execution sued upon the same 6d. for the Exemplification of every Record in any of the said Actions, 2s. for every Warrant of Attorney 4d. In all Actions real and mixt, Assises, *Quare impedit*, Appeals of Felony, Murder or Maim, the Prenotary to have for the Declaration or Plaint, 2s. and for the Plea in Bar, Replication, Rejoinder, Surrejoynder, for every of them, if they be inrolled as is aforesaid, 1s. and for the Writing of every *Venire fac'*, *Tales*, *Habeas corp'*, and *Distring'* upon the same, for every of them 6d. and for the Entry of the Judgment, in every of the said Actions and Appeals, 2s. and for the writing the Writs of Execution made upon every of the said Actions, Appeals and Assises, 1s. And for Writs of *grand Cape* and *petit Cape*, and Writs of View, Writs upon Voucher, and all other Writs in every such Action or Actions, 12d. and for every Warrant of Attorney for the Defendants, or for the Demandants or Plaintiffs, in every such Action Real, Assise, Appeal and *Quare Impedit* 4d. and for the Essoins in every such Action 4d. and for the Adjournment 2d. and for the Bail of every Person of Felony 12d. and for the Bail for Trespass 6d. and for the Appearance and Bailing of common Mainprise 2d.

51. Item, For writing Writs for the Peace and good Abearing, granted by any of the said Justices in their Sessions, 6d. and for the entering of every Recognisance to be had and taken before the said Justices, for every Cause or Causes, other than before is expressed, 12d. and if it be with Condition, than 2s. and upon every Acquittal and Deliverance of Felons or Murderers, by Verdict or by Allowance or Pardon, the Prenotaries to have 2s. and if it be upon Indictments certified from the Justices of the Peace, afore the Justices in the great Sessions, the Clerk of the Peace to have also 12d. and upon the Delivery of any suspect of Felony or Murder by Proclamation, the said Prenotary to have 12d.

52. Item, That the King's Majesty shall have all Fines, Issues, Amerciaments, and all Forfeitures of Recognisances, lost or forfeited before any of the said Justices in the Session aforesaid; and that the said Prenotaries, within the Limits of their Offices, shall yearly estreat the same into the Exchequer appointed for that

Limit, to the Intent that Process from thence may be awarded to the Sheriffs to levy the same to the King's Use, as appertaineth, which Sheriffs shall yearly make their accompts before the King's Auditors thereunto to be assigned and appointed.

53. Item, Over and besides the said President and Council, and Justices, there shall be Justices of Peace and Quorum, and also one *Custos Rotulorum*, in every of the said twelve Shires.

54. Item, that the said Justices of Peace, Justices of Quorum, and *Custos Rotulorum* in the said Shires, shall be named and appointed by the Chancellor of England, by Commission under the King's great Seal of England, by the Advice of the President, Council, and Justices aforesaid, or three of them, of the which the said President to be one, from Time to Time as the Case shall require.

55. Item, That there shall not exceed the Number of eight Justices of the Peace in any of the said Shires, over and besides the President, Council, and Justices aforesaid, and the King's Attorney and Solicitor; which President, Council, Justices, and the King's Attorney and Solicitor, shall be put in every Commission of Peace in every of the said twelve Shires.

56. Item, That such Persons as shall be named to be Justices of Peace within every of the said Shires, shall be of good Name and Fame; and after they be assigned by Commission, may use and exercise the Office of the Justice of Peace, albeit they may not dispend twenty Pound, nor be learned in the Laws of the Lands, without any Loss, Damage, or Penalties for Insufficiency of their Lands: And that every of the said Justices of Peace, before they shall execute their Commission, shall take their Oaths before the Chancellor of England, or else before the said President, or one of the said Justices in WALES, by Virtue of the King's Writ of *Dedimus potestatem*, or before any other Person to be limited by the Lord Chancellor of England for that Purpose, the Contents of which Oath shall be after the Form as Justices of Peace in England use to make.

57. Item, That the said Justices of Peace, or two of them at the least, whereof one to be of the Quorum, shall and may keep their Sessions, within the Limits of their Commissions, four Times in the Year, and at other Times upon urgent Causes, as Justices of Peace in England use to do; and shall have like Power and Authority in all Things, and Fees of the King's Majesty for the Time of their sitting, as well for themselves as for their Clerks,

and shall be bound to use and do their Offices, in like Manner as is used in England.

58. Item, That no Justices of Peace, Clerk of the Peace, nor other Clerk of any Justice of Peace in WALES, shall take for the writing of any Warrant of the Peace, or good Abearing, above 6d. and for entering of Pledges or Boroughs to pay the King's Fine upon any Indictment, 9d. and if it be with Protestation, then to take 12d. and for a Supersedeas not above 8d. and for a Recognisance 12d. And that all the said Justices of Peace shall certify all Recognisances taken before any of them for the Peace or good Abearing, into their Sessions next to be holden after the taking thereof; and Recognisance taken before any of them, for Suspicions of any Manner of Felony, shall be certified before the Justices of the great Sessions next to be holden after the taking thereof, without Concealment, Detaining or Imbezling of the same, upon such Penalties and Damages as be therefore ordained and established.

59. Item, That all Fines and Amerciaments, before the said Justices of Peace lost, and hereafter to be lost, shall be taxed and affered by two Justices of the Peace at the least, whereof one to be of the Quorum, and that all such Fines and Amerciaments shall be set truly and duly, according to the Quantity of the Offences, without Partiality or Affection.

60. Item, That the said Fines and Amerciaments, and also all Issues lost before the said Justices of Peace, and all Forfeitures of Recognisances and other Forfeitures, before the same Justices, shall be yearly estreated by the Clerks of the Peace into the Exchequer appointed for that Limit, to the Intent that Process from thence may be awarded for the levying of the same Forfeitures and Sums of Money to the King's Use, to the Sheriff of every County as shall appertain, who shall make thereof their Accompts before such Auditors as thereunto shall be assigned, so that the King's Majesty may thereof be truly and duly answered and satisfied; which Auditors shall make due Allowance to the same Sheriffs, for the Fees of the Justices and Clerks of the Peace, upon their said Accompts, as is used in the Realm of England.

61. Item, That there shall be Sheriffs in every of the said Shires yearly appointed by the King's Majesty; and that none of the said Sheriffs shall have their said Office of Sheriffwick any longer Time than is used by the Laws and Statutes of England. And for

the yearly Nomination of the said Sheriffs, the said Lord President, Council, and Justices of WALES, or three of them at the least, where, of the said President to be one, shall yearly nominate three substantial Persons in every of the said twelve Shires, to be Sheriffs of the same, and shall certify their Names to the Lords of the King's most honourable Council, attending upon his Grace's Person, *Crastino Animarum*, to the Intent the King's Majesty, being thereof advertised, may appoint one of them in every of the said Shires to be Sheriff for that Year, at his most gracious Will and Pleasure, like as his Highness doth for his Realm of England; and thereupon the said Sheriffs shall have their Patents and Commissions under the Great Seal of England, as Sheriffs of England have, and shall make and take Oaths and Knowledges of Recognisances before the President and Justices, or one of them, by Virtue of the King's Writ of *Dedimus potestatem* to be directed for the same, for the due Execution of their Offices, and for their just and true Accounts before the King's Auditor or Auditors assigned for WALES.

62. Item, That every of the said Sheriffs shall have full Power and Authority, within the Limits of their Sheriffwick, to do and use their Offices as Sheriffs in England, and shall accomplish and execute, without any Favour, Dread or Corruption, all Manner of Writs, Process, Judgments and Executions, and all manner common Justice appertaining to their Offices of Sheriffs, and all lawful Commandments and Precepts of the said President, Council and Justices of WALES, and also of the Justices of the Peace, Escheators and Coroners, and every of them, in all Things appertaining to their Offices and Authorities.

63. Item, That the said Sheriffs shall do, and be bound to do, all and every other Thing and Things for the Ministration of Justice, and for the Conservation of the King's Peace, and the Apprehension and Repress of Traytors, Murderers, Thieves, Felons and other Offenders, as Sheriffs of England do use and be bound to do within the Realm of England.

64. Item, That the said Sheriffs shall yearly account before such the King's Auditor or Auditors, as shall be assigned and appointed by the King's Majesty for his said Dominion of WALES; and that every of the said Sheriffs shall have yearly for his Fee £5.

65. Item, That all Mayors, Sheriffs, Stewards, Bailiffs and other

Ministers and Officers of Justice of every County, Lordship, Town and Place within the said Dominion of WALES, and all and singular the King's Subjects of the same shall be always obedient, attendant and assisting to the said President Council and Justices of WALES, and every of them, and shall obey the King's Commandments and Process from them or any of them directed, and all the lawful and reasonable Precepts of the said President, Council and Justices, and every of them, and also shall be obedient to all the said Justices of Peace, Sheriffs and Escheators within the Limits of their said Authorities, as well for common Administration and due Execution of Justice, as in all other Things appertaining to their Duties and Offices.

66. Item, That Escheators shall be named in every of the said Shires by the Lord Treasurer of England, by the Advice of the said President, Council and Justices, or three of them at the least, whereof the said President to be one; which Escheators shall make and take their Oaths, and knowledge their Recognisances, before the said President, or one of the said Justices, by Virtue of the King's Writ of *Dedimus potestatem* to be directed for the same, for the due Execution of their Offices, and for their true Account to be made before the King's Auditor or Auditors to be assigned for the same; which Oath and Recognizance shall be agreable to the Oath and Recognizance used for the Escheators in England; and the Escheators shall yearly have their Patents and Commissions under the Great Seal of England, and shall have Power and Authority to exercise their Offices in like Manner and Form as Escheators in England, and shall be bound to all Laws and Statutes of England.

67. Item, That all such Persons as shall be appointed to the said Offices, shall and may exercise their Offices, if they may dispend yearly £5 of Freehold, any Statutes of England to the contrary thereof notwithstanding; and that every of the said Escheators shall make their Accompts yearly before such Auditor or Auditors as shall be assigned by the King's Majesty, to hear and determine his Highness Account for his Revenues and Profits of the said Dominion of WALES.

68. Item, There shall be two Coroners to be elected in every of the said twelve Shires, as is used in England, by Virtue of the King's Writ *De Coronatore eligendo*, to be awarded out of the King's Chancery of England; and that the said Coroners shall have like

Power and Authority to do and exercise their Offices, and have like Fees, as is limited by the Laws and Statutes of England.

69. Provided always, That the Writ *De Coronatore eligendo*, to choose the Coroners within the said County of Flint, shall be directed out of the Exchequer of Chester.

70. Item, That the said Justices of the Peace, or two of them at the least, whereof one of them to be of the Quorum, shall appoint and name, in every hundred within the Limits of their Commissions, two substantial Gentlemen or Yeomen, to be the chief Constables of the Hundred wherein they inhabit: which two Constables of every Hundred shall have a special Regard to the Conservation of the King's Peace, and shall and may do and use their Offices in all and singular Things, as is used by the High Constables of the Hundreds in England, and shall be bound to all Things as the High Constables of the Hundreds in England be bound to do.

71. Item, That every of the said Sheriffs shall have a Gaol for Prisoners within some convenient Place of the Castles of the Shire-towns where he is Sheriff, or in such other convenient Place, as by the said President, Council and Justices, or three of them, whereof the said President to be one, shall be appointed: any Patent or Grant heretofore made to any Person or Persons of the Constable-ship or Keeping of any of the said Castles in any wise notwith-standing. And that the Sheriff shall make the Bailiffs of the Hundreds, and they to attend upon the Justices in every of their Courts and Sessions.

72. Provided always, That the Constables of the King's Castles within every of the said Shire-towns of WALES shall not be charged with the Gaols, and of all the Prisoners that shall be committed to their Ward, like as they have heretofore been, until such Time, convenient Places for that Purpose be assigned to the said Sheriff.

73. Item, The said Sheriffs shall keep their Counties monthly, and their Hundred Courts for Pleas under 40s., as is used in England; and shall take for the entering of Plaints, Process, Pleas and Judgments in the said Shire-courts and Hundreds, such small Fees as is used to be taken in Shires and Hundreds in England, and not above.

74. Item, That all manner of Trials before them in their said Courts, or before any Stewards in Court-Barons, shall be by Wager of Law, or Verdict of six Men, at the Pleasure of the Party Plaintiff or Defendant that pleaded the Plea.

75. And that every of the said Sheriffs shall keep and hold their Torns yearly after Easter and Michaelmas, as they have been used in England.

76. Item, the King's Highness shall have all manner of Fines, Issues, Amerciaments, and Forfeitures lost or forfeited in any of the said Counties, Hundreds, Courts and Torns, to his own Use, and the Sheriff to account for the same accordingly.

77. Item, That the Estreats of the said Torns, Counties and Hundreds shall be viewed, and the Fines, Issues and Amerciaments afferred by the said Justices of Assises of that Circuit, before the levying of the same Amerciaments or other Forfeitures; and that no Sheriff, or any of his Officers, presume to gather or levy any such Amerciament, or other Forfeiture, before the said Estreat be so affered, upon Pain to forfeit to the King's Use 40s. And that the Sheriff upon every Judgment had before him in his County or Hundred Court, in any Plaint under 40s. shall and may award a *Capias ad satisfaciendum*, to arrest the Party condemned, or else a *Fieri fac'*, at the Liberty of the Party pursuant.

78. Item, That all Bills sued before the said Justices in personal Actions, whereof the Debt, Duty or Damage is under 40s. the Sheriffs shall have for the return of every Bill 2d. and every *Venire fac'*, *Tales*, *Habeas corp'*, *and Distr'*, 2d. and for Writs of Execution upon the Judgment in any such Bill, 12d.

79. Item, In Bills sued before the said Justices in Actions personal above the sum of 40s. the Sheriff shall have, for the Return of every such Bill, 4d. and for the Return of every *Venire fac'*, *Habeas corp'*, *Distr'*, and *Tales*, 4d. and for every Writ of Execution 2s. And in all personal Actions sued by original Writs returnable before the said Justices, the Sheriff shall have for every *Iterum sum' Distr'* and *alias Distr'*, 4d. and for every *Venire fac' Habeas corp'*, *Distr'* and *Tales*, 6d. and for every Writ of Execution tobe executed upon the Judgment in such Actions, 2s. For the serving of every *Writ of Eligit*, 6s. 8d. And in all real Actions, or mixt, pursued before the said Justices by original Writ, for Return of every Original, 2s. and for the Return of every other Writ and judicial Process depending upon the same, before Judgment, 2s. and for every Writ of Execution after Judgment, upon every original, in Actions real or mixt, 2s. and for the serving of every Writ of *Haberi fac' seisinam*, 6s. 8d.

80. Item, For Attachments upon *Capias*, or other Process sued

before the said Justices by original or judicial Writ, if he return *Cepi Corpus*, 2s. and for a *Reddit se*, upon an Exigent of Felony, in Appeal of Murder or Maim, or upon any Indictment of Felony or Murder, 2s. and upon a *Reddit se*, upon an Exigent of Debt, Trespass, Detinue, and all other Actions personal, 1s. and for the making of *Replegiar'*, 1s. and *Withernam* upon the same, 1s. For the Return of every Writ of Appeal of Murder or Felony, or Maim, 1s. and upon all other Process grown upon the same, as *Venire fac'*, *Tales*, *Habeas corp'* and *Distr'*, 1s. and in every Action taken before the Sheriff by Justices, for the Summons thereof, 4d. and for every other Process thereupon, 4d. and for every Prisoner delivered by Acquittal, or by Proclamation, for any manner of Felony, 1s.

81. Item, That every Sheriff, within the Limits of his Authority, may and shall put such Persons under common Mainprise, as they have reasonable Cause of Suspect, according to the said Act made for WALES, binding such as they shall so put to common Mainprise with two sufficient Sureties with them, by Recognisance, to appear before the said Justices within the Limits of their Authorities, at the next great Sessions, to be holden next after the taking of such Bonds, and shall certify the Names of them that be bound, before the said Justices at the said Sessions accordingly, without Concealment thereof, at their Pleasure.

82. Item, That every Person that the Sheriff taketh to common Mainprise, to appear before the said Justices as is aforesaid, shall pay for his Mainprise 2d. and not above; and the said Sheriffs to put no Man to common Mainprise, but such as be suspect, and as shall be returned by them before the said Justices at their Sessions as is aforesaid. And also the said Sheriff shall have, for the Return of a Writ of false Judgment, out of a base Court, before the said Justices, 2s. and that the said Sheriffs shall take no manner of Fees for the Return of any of the said Writs of Execution afore expressed, unless he return the same executed.

83. Item, That in all and every such Writs, Original or Judicial, or other Process, Pleas or Writings, which be not expressed in this Ordinance, the Fees thereof, as well for the Seals as Writing, shall be rated by the said President, Council and Justices, or three of them, whereof the said President to be one, by their Discretions from Time to Time, as the Case shall require; and that they shall have full Power and Authority from Time to Time to assess and appoint what Fee the said Sheriffs, Escheators and Coroners

and their Ministers, Prenotaries and their Clerks, and other Ministers of Justice in the said Shires, shall have, take and receive of the King's Subjects for any manner Writs, Plaints, Pleas, Process, Returns, or any other Matter or Thing concerning or belonging to the Execution of their Offices and Rooms, and to augment or diminish any Fee or Fees above declared, as shall be thought by their Discretions to be convenient and meet for the Commonwealth of the King's Subjects of those Parts of WALES; any Thing contained in this Act to the contrary thereof notwithstanding.

84. Item, That from henceforth no manner of Person or Persons, for Murder or for Felony shall be put to his Fine, but suffer according to the Laws of the Realm of England, except it please the King's Majesty to pardon him or them; and if the said Justices see Cause of Pity, or other Consideration, they may reprieve the Prisoner till they have advertised the King's Majesty of the Matter.

85. Item, That the Act made in the Parliament holden in the twenty-sixth Year of the most Royal Reign of the King's Majesty, concerning (among other Things) Inquisitions and Trials of counterfeiting, washing, clipping and minishing of the King's Coin, Murders, Felons and Accessaries to the same, perpetrated or done within WALES, to be had, made and determined in the next Shire or County within England adjoining, where the King's Writ runneth, and every Article therein contained, shall stand in his full Strength and Force, according to the Tenor and Effect of the same; any Thing in this said Ordinance, or any other Act, Cause or Matter heretofore had or made to the contrary thereof notwithstanding.

86. "And albeit the same Act as yet was never put in Execution for any of the said Offences heretofore done or committed within any of the said three Shires of North WALES; that is to say, the Counties of Anglesey, Caernarvan and Merioneth," be it now declared and enacted by the Authority aforesaid, That the said Act, and every Article therein contained, shall from henceforth take Effect, and be executed in all Points for and concerning any of the said Offences perpetrated and done, or that hereafter shall be perpetrated or done, within the said County of Merioneth, to be enquired of, heard and determined within the County of Salop, in like Manner and Form as commonly is and hath been used for any of the same or like Offences committed or done within any

other County of South WALES; any Matter or Cause heretofore risen or grown to the contrary thereof notwithstanding.

87. Item, That the Town and Hamlet of *Abertannad*, and all the Grounds and the Soil within the same, which afore this Time hath been taken, reputed and used as Parcel of the said County of Merioneth, shall from the Feast of Easter next coming, by Virtue of this Act, be united, annexed and made Parcel of the said County of Salop; and so from thenceforth to be reputed, taken and used for ever, and not to be of any other Shire or County of WALES; and that the same Town or Hamlet, and all the Ground and Soil within the same Town or Hamlet, be from and after the said Feast accepted and taken us Part and Parcel of the Hundred of Oswestre; and that the Inhabitants thereof from the said Feast shall be attendant, and do every Thing and Things with the Inhabitants of the said Hundred of Oswestre, as the same Inhabitants do or be bound to do; any Laws or Customs to the contrary thereof notwithstanding.

88. Item, In case any foreign Plea or Voucher be hereafter pleaded or made before any of the said Justices of WALES, between Party and Party, triable in any other Shire within WALES, than where the same Plea is pleaded or Voucher made; that then the said Justices, afore whom the same Plea or Voucher is or shall be pleaded or made, shall and may send the King's Writ, with a Transcript of the Record mentioning the same foreign Matter of Plea or Voucher, under the Seal to him committed, unto the Justice of the County where the same Matter is or shall be triable, commanding the said Justice, by Virtue of the said Writ, to proceed to the Trial thereof according to the King's Laws and Statutes; which Trial so before him had, he shall remand with the whole Record unto the Justice before whom the said Plea or Voucher was pleaded or made, who thereupon shall proceed to Judgment, as the Case shall require.

89. Item, In case the same foreign Plea, Voucher or other Matter so pleaded, be triable within this Realm of England, that then in every such Case the Justice, afore whom the same Plea or Voucher is or shall be pleaded, had or made, shall and may proceed to the Trial thereof, as shall appertain, within the same Shire of WALES, where the same Plea, Voucher or Matter was pleaded; the said foreign Plea, Voucher, or any other Thing or Matter to the contrary thereof notwithstanding.

90. Item, That no Manner of Person or Persons from henceforth without lawful Authority, shall make any Rumours, Tumults, unlawful Assemblies or Outcries at any of the said Courts or Sessions, nor any Outcries and unlawful Assemblies in great Numbers at any other Time or Times, except it be for the Apprehension or pursuing of Murtherers or Felons; upon Pain of Imprisonment and grievous Fine to be taxed and set upon them by the said President and Council, or by the Justices or other Officer before whom such Misdemeanour shall happen to be committed.

91. Item, That all Manors, Lands, Tenements, Messuages and other Hereditaments, and all Rights and Titles to the same, in any of the said Shires of WALES, descended to any Manner Person or Persons sith the Feast of the Nativity of St. John Baptist in the thirty-third Year of our said Sovereign Lord's Reign, or that hereafter shall descend, be taken, enjoyed, used, and holden as English Tenure, to all Intents according to the Common Laws of this Realm of England, and not to be partable among Heirs Males, after the Custom of Gavelkind, as heretofore in divers Parts of WALES hath been used and accustomed. And that the same Law, from and after the said Feast of St. John Baptist, in the said thirty-third Year, be used, taken, and exercised in the said County of Monmouth, and in all such Lordships and other Places as by Virtue of the said Act made in the said twenty-seventh Year, or by any other Act or Acts made or to be made, were and shall be annexed, united, or knit to any of the Shires of Salop, Hereford, Gloucester, or other Shire; any Laws, Usages, or Customs heretofore had or used to the contrary thereof notwithstanding.

92. Item, That no Mortgages of Lands, Tenements, or Hereditaments made or had after the said Feast of St. John Baptist, which was in the said thirty-third Year of the Reign of our said Sovereign Lord, or that hereafter shall be had or made within any of the said Shires or Places, shall be hereafter allowed or admitted, otherwise than after the Course of the Common Laws or Statutes of the Realm of England; any Usage or Custom heretofore had to the contrary thereof notwithstanding.

93. Item, It shall be lawful to all Persons to aliene, sell, or otherwise put away their Lands, Tenements, and Hereditaments within the said Country or Dominion of WALES, the County of Monmouth, and other Places annexed to any of the Shires of England, from them and their Heirs, to any Person or Persons in Fee-simple or

Fee-tail, for Term of Life, or for Term of Years, after the Manner and according as is used by the Laws of the Realm of England; and Welsh Law or Custom heretofore used in the said Country or Dominion of WALES to the contrary thereof notwithstanding. This Article to take Effect from and after the said Feast of the Nativity of St. John Baptist, which was in the said thirty-third Year of our said Sovereign Lord's Reign.

94. Item, If any Person or Persons having Lands, or Tenements within the said Dominion of WALES, been, or hereafter shall be bound within the Realm of England, by Obligation upon the Statute of the Staple, or by Recognizance, and pay not the Debt as shall appertain, that then upon Certificate thereof made unto the King's Chancery of England, by the Clerk of the Staple, or by any Justice of Record before whom such Recognizance shall be knowledged, Process shall be made to the Sheriffs of WALES out of the Chancery of England after the Form as is used to be made upon Statutes and Recognizances by the Course of the Laws of England, for the due levying and paying of the said Debt.

95. Provided always, and be it enacted by the Authority aforesaid, That for such Recognizances as be or hereafter shall be taken and knowledged before the King's Justices of his Highness Bench or Common-place in England, Process shall be had and pursued immediately out from the said Justices, as is used upon Recognizances taken before the said Justices by the common Course of the Laws of England.

96. Item, That all such Writs, Bills, Plaints, Pleas, Process, Challenges and Trials, shall be used throughout all the Shires aforesaid, before the said Justices in their Sessions, as is used in North WALES, or as shall be devised by the said President, Council and Justices, or three of them, whereof the said President to be one, for the good Ministration of Justice to be had in every of the said Shires.

"97. Item, Where the Lordship of Hope, with divers other Lordships, Parishes, Towns and Hamlets, were by an Act of Parliament made in the thirty-third Year of the Reign of our said Sovereign Lord appointed and translated from the said County of Denbigh to the County of Flint, and by the same Act were made Part, Parcel, and Members of the same County of Flint, afore which Appointment or Translation divers Indictments and Presentments, as well of Felony as other Offences, were had and taken for the

King's Highness, before the Justice of the said County of Denbigh, in the great Sessions there, and some before the Justices of the Peace within the same County, for Offences supposed to be done within divers of the said Lordships so translated, and also divers Judgments given at the Suit of the Parties before the said Justices; and some before the Sheriff of the said County of Denbigh, for Matters risen and grown within the Precinct of the said Lordships or other Places, before the Translation of the same": It is now ordained and enacted, that all the said Indictments and Presentments shall be heard, tried, and determined within the said County of Denbigh, by Persons as well of the said Lordship or Place where the said Offences were done or committed, as of other Place or Places within the said County of Denbigh, in Manner and Form, as though the said Translations had never been had nor made: And also that the said Judgments as before given or had between Party and Parties, before any Justice of Record or other Officer within the said County of Denbigh, for any Matter or Cause, appearing by the Record of the same to be grown and risen within any of the said Lordships, Parishes, Towns, or Hamlets so translated, shall and may be executed by the Sheriff of the said County of Denbigh within any of the same Lordships, or other Place so translated; the said Translation, or any other Cause or Matter to the contrary thereof notwithstanding.

98. Item, Like Law and Order to be kept and ministered upon all other like Translations of any other Lordships, Manors, Towns, Parishes, and other Places within WALES, had, made or done in this present Parliament, or any other afore or after the same Translations, or any other Cause or Matter to the contrary thereof notwithstanding.

99. Item, Where there shall be divers and many Suits taken before the said Justices in Pleas personal, which (as it is thought) cannot be tried before them in the Time of the said great Sessions, for Brevity of Time; Therefore, and for the speedy Trial of these Matters, the Issues taken in the said Suits shall and may be tried at a Petty Sessions, before the Deputy Justices there, as is and hath been used in the said three Shires of North WALES; except such of the said Suits, as by the Discretion of the said Justices shall be thought necessary to be tried before themselves, within their Limits; and that there shall be no Suit taken before any of the said Justices by Bill, under the Sum of twenty Shillings.

100. Item, If any Murder or Felony hereafter be committed or done within WALES, that then the Party or Parties to whom any such Offence shall hap to be committed, shall in no wise make any End or Agreement with the Offenders in that Behalf, nor with any other in his Name or Behalf, unless the said Party first make the said President and Council, or one of the said Justices, privy unto the same, upon Pain of Imprisonment, and grievous Fine to be set and adjudged at the Discretion of the said President, Council and Justices, or two of them, whereof the said President to be one; the same Pain and Penalty to extend as well to and against such as shall labour, move, or procure any such End or Agreement made, although the same Labour, Motion, or Procurement never take Effect, to make any End or Agreement, as against him or them with whom such End or Agreement shall be made, if the same happen to take Effect.

101. Item, "Where divers Lordships Marches, as well in WALES, as in the borders of the same, now being by Act of Parliament annexed to divers shires of ENGLAND, be lately come to the King's hands by suppression of Houses, by purchase or attainders, and now be under the survey of the Court of Augmentations, or of the King's general surveyors, the liberties, franchises and customs of all which Lordships be lately revived by Act of parliament made in the 32nd year of his most gracious reign"; nevertheless his Majesty willeth and commandeth, That no other liberties franchises or customs shall from henceforth be used claimed or exercised within the said Lordships, nor any other Lordships within WALES, or the county of MONMOUTH, whosoever be Lord or owner of the same, but only such liberties, franchises, and customs as be given and commanded to the Lords of the same Lordships, by force and virtue of the said Act of Parliament made for WALES, in the said 27th year of his Grace's reign, and not altered nor taken away by this Ordinance; the said Act made in the said 32nd year, or any other Act grant law or custom to the contrary thereof notwithstanding.

102. Item, That if any person or persons, their ancestors, or they whose estate the same person or persons have or hath, in peaceable possession of any lands or tenements in Wales, by the space of five years, without let, interruption or lawful claim: That then the same person or persons shall still continue their possession, until such time as it shall be lawfully recovered against them by the order of the King's laws, or by decree of the President and Council there.

103. Item, in actions personal, taken and pursued before the said Justices in Wales, by original writ or Bill if nine of the Jury be sworn to try the issue between the party Plaintiff and the Defendant, and the residue of the said Jury make default, or be tried out: Then the Sheriffs shall and may immediately return other names in the said jury, *de circumstantibus*, unto such time there be twelve men sworn to try the issue between them, as before the Justices of North Wales hath been afore used and accustomed in such cases.

104. Item, That if any goods or chattels be stolen by any person or persons, and sold in any fair or market within the said Dominion of Wales, that no such sale shall change the property thereof from the owner of the same, but that he may lawfully seize take and have the same again, upon proof thereof made, the said sale notwithstanding.

105. Item, That no person or persons bargain or buy any manner of beast or other quick cattle in any place within Wales, out of the Market or Fair, unless he can bring forth sufficient and credible witness of the name of the person, what place and time he bought the same, upon pain and danger of such punishment and fine as shall be set upon him by the said President and Council, or any of the said Justices in his Circuit, for the said offence, and as he will therefore answer at his further peril.

106. Item, If any goods or chattels be stolen within the limits of any of the said Shires of Wales, that then upon suit thereof had and made, the track shall be followed from Township to Township, or Lordship to Lordship, according to the laws and customs in that behalf heretofore used in Wales, upon such penalty and danger as heretofore hath been accustomed.

107. Item, That every person that hath any lands or tenements in fee-simple or fee-tail, or for term of life, or for term of any other man's life, being freehold, shall and may pass in all manner juries and Trials, as well in case of felony or murder, as in all actions real, personal and mixed, whatsoever they be, Attaint only except; and also may be impannelled, and inquire of all concealments, forcible entries, and other causes of inquiry for the King's Majesty, albeit he may not dispend forty shillings by the year; saving to every man his lawful challenge for any other cause, according to the Laws of this Realm of England.

108. Item, That no Juror shall pass in Attaint, unless he may dispend forty shillings by the year of estate of freehold.

109. Item, The tenants and resiants in Wales shall pay their Tallage at the change of their Lords in such places, and after such form, as hath been heretofore accustomed in Wales.

110. Item, That all the King's subjects and resiants in WALES, shall find, at all Parliaments hereafter to be holden in England, Knights for the Shires, and Citizens and Burgesses for Cities and Towns, to be named and chosen by authority of the King's Writ under the Great Seal of England, according to the Act in that case provided, and shall be charged and chargeable to all subsidies and other charges to be granted by the Commons of any of the said Parliaments, and pay all other their Rents Farms Customs and Duties to the King's Highness, as they have been accustomed heretofore; Fines for redemption of Sessions only excepted, which the King's Majesty of his most gracious goodness and liberality is contented and pleased to remit at the humble suit of his said loving subjects of his said Dominion of Wales.

111. Item, That the town of Haverfordwest shall after the end of this present Parliament for ever find one burgess for the said town, at every Parliament after that time to be holden: And the charges of the same Burgess to be always born by the Mayor Burgesses and inhabitants of the said town, and none other.

112. Item, That the King's Majesty shall have all felons goods, and goods of persons outlawed, Waifs, Strays and all other forfeitures and escheats whatsoever they be, answered thereof by the hands of the Sheriffs: saving always the rights and interests of every of his subjects having lawful title to have the same.

113. That all errors and Judgments before any of the said Justices at any time of the Great Sessions, in pleas real or mixed, shall be redressed by writ of error, to be sued out of the King's Chancery of England, returnable before the King's Justices of his Bench in England, as other writs of error be in England. And that all errors in pleas personal shall be reformed by Bills to be sued before the said President and Council of Wales, from time to time as the party grieved will sue for the same. And if in case the judgment be affirmed good in any of the said writs of Error or Bills, then there to make execution, and all other process thereupon, as is used in the King's Bench of England; And that the pursuants in every such writ of Error or Bill do pay like fees therefore as is used in England.

114. Item, That no execution of any judgment given or to be given in any base Court be stayed or deferred by reason of any Writ of False Judgment, but that execution shall and may be had and made at all times before the reversal of the said judgment, the pursuit of the said writ notwithstanding. And in case the said judgment happen after to be reversed, then the party pursuant to be restored to all that he hath lost by the said judgment, according to the Laws of the Realm of England.

115. Item, That all process for urgent and weighty causes shall be made and directed into Wales by the special commandment of the Chancellor of England for the time being, or any of the King's Council in England, as heretofore hath been used: any thing in this Act to the contrary thereof notwithstanding.

116. Item, That the town of Bewdley, which is within the parish of RIBBESFORD in the County of Wigorn, and all the ground and soil of the same town, shall from henceforth be united annexed and made parcel of the county of WIGORN, and to be within the Hundred of DODINGTRE. And that all the inhabitants of the said town and parish shall from henceforth be attendant, and do every thing and things with the inhabitants of the said Hundred, as the same inhabitants be now bound to do by the laws of this realm of England. Saving always to the Burgesses and inhabitants of the said town of BEWDLEY all such liberties and franchises as they lawfully had and exercised within the said town before the making of this Act, in like manner and form as though this Act had never been had nor made.

117. Item, That the Lordship of LLANSTIFFAN, USTERLOYS, and LANGHAM, and the members of the same, and all manors lands tenements and other hereditaments in the same Lordship, and the members of the same, be from henceforth united annexed joined named accepted and taken as part and parcel of the County of CAERMARTHEN, and reputed joined united named accepted and taken as part and parcel of the Hundred of DERLES in the said County of CAERMARTHEN. And that the tenants and inhabitants of the said lordships and members be attendant, and do every thing and things with the tenants and inhabitants of the said Hundred of DERLES, as the said inhabitants now be bound to do, according to the laws there used.

118. Item, That the County or Shire Court of the County of RADNOR shall from henceforth be holden one time at NEW RADNOR, and one other time at PRESTON, *alternis vicibus*, and

never from henceforth to be kept or holden at RATHER GOWEY; any former Act or other thing to the contrary thereof notwithstanding.

119. Item, It is further enacted by the Authority aforesaid, That the King's Most Royal Majesty shall and may, at all Times hereafter from Time to Time, change, add, alter, order, minish and reform all manner of Things afore rehearsed, as to his most excellent Wisdom and Discretion shall be thought convenient; and also to make Laws and Ordinances for the common Wealth and good Quiet of his said Dominion of WALES and his Subjects of the same, from Time to Time, at his Majesty's Pleasure; any Thing contained in this Act, or in the said Act made for the said Shire-ground of WALES, or any other Act or Acts, Thing or Things, to the contrary thereof heretofore made in any wise notwithstanding.

120. And that all such Alterations of the Premisses, or any Part thereof, and all such Laws and Ordinances to be hereafter made, devised and published by Authority of this Act, by the King's Majesty, in writing under his Highness Great Seal, shall be of as good Strength, Virtue and Effect, as if they had been had and made by Authority of Parliament.

121. Item, Be it further enacted and ordained by Authority aforesaid, That where the King's Majesty that now is, by his Letters Patents bearing date the first day of May in the 34th Year of his most prosperous Reign, demised and granted to William Webbe, the subsidy and usage of all woollen cloths made or to be made in the County of Monmouth, and in the twelve Shires of WALES, that is to say, in the County of Brecknock, Radnor, Montgomery, Caermarthen, Glamorgan, Pembroke, Cardigan, Anglesey, Flint, Denbigh, Caernarvan and Merioneth, and in all and singular Towns and other Places whatsoever they be, within the Precincts and Limits of the said Counties, and elsewhere within the Dominion of WALES; to have and hold to the said William Webbe and his Assigns, for certain Years yet enduring, that the said William Webbe his Deputies and Assigns, shall have from henceforth full Power and Authority, by Force of this Act, to take for the sealing of every woollen cloth hereafter to be made in the said twelve Shires, and elsewhere within the said Dominion of WALES, as hereafter is declared, and none otherwise; that is to say, for every whole piece of Frieze, 1d. every half piece of Frieze *ob.* every piece of Cotton and Lining being 24 yards and under, *ob.* and for every Piece of the same being above

24 yards 1d. of every Broadcloth 1d. of every piece of Kersey being 18 yards and above 1d. of every piece of Kersey being under 18 yards *ob.*

122. Provided always, That this Act, nor nothing therein contained, extend not to charge any Manner of Person or Persons, being or that hereafter shall be inhabitants in any of the said twelve Shires or elsewhere within the Dominion of WALES, for any Cloths, Friezes, Kerseys, or Linings made or hereafter to be made and occupied within their houses, and not to put to sale to any Person or Persons, but to their Servants for their wearing.

123. And further be it enacted by the Authority aforesaid, that the said Aulnager in WALES, by himself, or by his sufficient Deputy or Deputies shall in all Things to his Office appertaining, do and be bound to do and answer in every Case like and according as all and every other Aulnager in the Realm of England doth or ought to do according to the Laws and Statutes of the Realm of England; and for the contrary doing or exercising of the said Office, shall in every case and degree suffer, as by the said Laws and Statutes is ordained, established or enacted for Aulnagers under the Lord Treasurer of England for the Time being.

124. And furthermore the King's Majesty is contented and pleased, notwithstanding the Statute made in the 27th year of his most gracious reign, That where there should be but twelve shires in WALES that the town of HAVERFORDWEST shall be a county in itself as it hath been before this time used, at the will and pleasure of the King's said Majesty: and that it shall be separated from the county of PEMBROKE at the KING'S said pleasure. And that the King's High Justice of the said county of PEMBROKE shall be High Justice of the said county and town of HAVERFORDWEST, and shall have like power and authority, to and for the administration of Justice within the said county and town of HAVERFORDWEST as is limited and appointed to the said Justice to and for the administration of Justice in the said county of PEMBROKE. And that the Mayor Sheriff Bailiffs and Burgesses of the said county and town of HAVERFORDWEST, from time to time, shall be as well attendant, and obey all precepts and commandments of the President and Council of our said Sovereign Lord the King in his Marches of WALES as also shall be attendant to all precepts and process awarded or directed by the said High Justice unto the Sheriff of the said County and Town of HAVERFORDWEST, and to make return thereof.

And the said Sheriff of the said county and town shall serve all precepts and process directed from the said High Justice, in like manner and form as the Sheriff of the said county of Pembroke is bound to do, and according to the effect and purport of the King's Ordinance in that behalf had made and provided. And that it shall be lawful unto the said Mayor Sheriff Bailiffs and Burgesses of the said county and town of HAVERFORDWEST aforesaid, to use and exercise all lawful liberties and grants by the King's Majesty or his noble progenitors to them granted and confirmed at the King's Majesty's will and pleasure, according to the laws of the realm of England and not otherwise. And that the judicial seal of the said shires of PEMBROKE, CAERMARTHEN, and CARDIGAN, being in the custody and keeping of the King's High Justice there for the time being, shall be used in the said county and town of HAVERFORDWEST, as the original and judicial seal of the said town and county. And that the said Justice of the said shires of PEMBROKE CAERMARTHEN, and CARDIGAN, shall have like power and authority, by virtue of the King's letters patents to him made, as well to do all and every thing and things concerning common Justice to be ministered within the said town and county of HAVERFORDWEST, as he hath in his said letters patents within any of the said shires of PEMBROKE, CAERMARTHEN, and CARDIGAN.

125. Provided alway, That this article touching and concerning the county and town of HAVERFORDWEST, and all things therein contained, shall stand and endure but only at the King's Majesty's Will and pleasure, and none otherwise.

126. Provided alway, That this Act or any thing therein contained shall not be prejudicial nor hurtful to any person or persons, or bodies politick, for or concerning any lands tenements rents services bondmen tolls or other hereditaments; but that they and every of them, their heirs, successors and assigns, and the heirs successors and assigns of every of them, shall have hold and enjoy their lands tenements rents services bondmen and other their hereditaments, in such like manner, form and condition, as they had the same before the making of this Act, and as if this Act had never been had nor made.

127. Provided also, That this Act nor any thing therein contained shall be hurtful or prejudicial to any person or persons, for or concerning any office or offices, which they or any of them have by virtue of any of the King's letters patents, being now in force

before the making of this Act, nor to the fees of money used and accustomed to be paid for the exercise of any such offices; but that every person and persons having such offices and fees, and their substitutes and deputies, shall and may have and exercise their said offices as is limited by this Act, and as they might have done before the making of this Act, and shall also have and perceive all such fees for the exercise of the said offices, in as large and ample manner form and condition as they might afore the making of this Act, and as if this Act had never been had nor made.

128. Provided always, That all lands tenements and hereditaments, within the said Dominion of Wales, shall descend to the heirs, according to the course of the Common laws of the Realm of England, according to the tenor and effect of this Act, and not to be used as Gavelkind; any thing contained in these provisions or any of them to the contrary thereof notwithstanding.

129. Provided always, That this Act, nor any Clause, Article or Thing therein contained, be in any wise prejudicial or hurtful to George Blunt Esquire, Son and Heir of Sir John Blunt Knight, deceased, for or concerning the Offices of Stewardships of the King's Lordships, or Manors of Bewdly and Clebury, or any other Office or Offices heretofore granted unto the said George Blunt by the King's Letters Patents, sealed under the Great Seal of England, for Term of Life of the same George, or for or concerning any Fees, Wages, Rewards, Annuities, Profits, Commodities, Advantages or Emoluments, appertaining or belonging unto the said Offices or any of them; but that the said George, his Deputy and Deputies, shall and may at all Time and Times, during the Life of the same George, have, hold exercise and enjoy the same Offices, and every of them, and also perceive, levy and take the Fees, Wages, Rewards, and all other Profits and Commodities to the same Offices, and every of them, or to any of them belonging, or in any wise appertaining, in as large and ample Manner, Form, and Condition, to all Intents, Constructions and Purposes, as though this Act had never been had or made; any Thing before in this Act contained to the contrary notwithstanding.

130. Provided always, That all liberties, franchises and privileges of the Duchy of Lancaster, or in anywise appertaining to the same, shall be of the same force plight quality goodness and condition, and may be used in as large and ample manner, as they were before the making of this Act, and as if this Act had never been had nor

made; any thing in this Act to the contrary thereof notwithstanding.

A.D. 1543]

35 Henry 8, c. 11.

AN ACT FOR THE DUE PAYMENT OF THE FEES AND WAGES OF KNIGHTS AND BURGESSES FOR THE PARLIAMENT IN WALES.

Where the Knights of all and every Shire of this Realm of England and WALES and the Burgesses of all Cities, Towns and Boroughs of the same be named elected and chosen for their assembly in the King's High Court of Parliament, as by ancient laudable laws and customs of this Realm hath been used and accustomed at and by the King's Majesty's high commandments, unto the which Knights and Burgesses their fees and wages be assigned certainly, that is to say, to every Knight by the day 4/- unto every Citizen Burgess by the day 2/- or more as heretofore hath been accustomed accounting for the same so many days as the said High Court of Parliament endureth with addition thereunto of so many days as every such Knight and Burgess may reasonably journey and resort from their habitations or dwelling places to the said High Court of Parliament and from the said High Court to return to their habitations or dwelling places, together with their costs of writs and other ordinary fees and charges; which wages fees and charges at all times ought to be levied and collected by the Sheriffs and by the Mayors Bailiffs and other head officers of and in the Cities Boroughs and Towns aforesaid, wherein some of the said Sheriffs Mayors Bailiffs and other head officers have been negligent and laches nor endeavouring themselves in accomplishment of their duties in collection and payment of the same in due form and according to Justice to the great injury and delay of the King's said subjects; Be it therefore enacted by the authority of this present Parliament that the Sheriff for the time being of every of the twelve Shires in WALES and in the County of Monmouth from the beginning of this present Parliament shall have full power and authority by force of this Act to gather and levy or cause to be gathered and levied the said Knight's fees and wages of the inhabitants of the said 12 Shires and of the said County of Monmouth which ought to pay the same; and the same so gathered shall pay or cause to be paid to every such Knight or

Knights or to his or their assigns within the term of two months after that any such Knight or Knights shall deliver or cause to be delivered the King's Writ *de solutione feodi militis parliamenti* to any such Sheriff; and every such Sheriff making default of payment of the said fees or wages in manner and form as aforesaid to lose and forfeit £20 whereof the one moiety to be to the King's use and the other to his or their use that will sue for the same in any of the King's Courts of Record by information bill or plaint or otherwise afore any of the King's Officers wherein no essoin protection nor wager of law shall be admitted. And if it shall happen any Sheriff in any of the said twelve Shires and County of Monmouth do make default of payment of the said wages or fees by a longer time than two months then every said Sheriff to forfeit for every month that he or they shall make default £20 to be forfeited and levied in manner and form as is aforesaid.

2. And that every Mayor and Bailiff and other head officers of cities boroughs and towns in every the said twelve Shires and in the said County of Monmouth within the like term and space of two months after the receipt of the King's Majesty's Writ *De Solutione feodi Burgensi Parliamenti* like as is before mentioned for gathering or levying of the Knight's Fees shall levy gather and pay the wages and fees to their Burgesses in like manner and form as is aforesaid and in and under like pains and forfeitures as be afore-mentioned to be levied on the goods and chattels of every such mayor bailiff and other officer to whom the King's said Writ shall be directed for the levying of such fees making default of payment of the said fees and wages to the Burgesses in manner and form as is aforesaid.

3. And be it further enacted by the authority aforesaid forasmuch as the inhabitants of all cities and Boroughs in every the said twelve Shires within WALES and in the said County of Monmouth not finding Burgesses for the Parliament themselves, must bear and pay the Burgesses' Wages within the Shire towns of and in every of the said twelve Shires in WALES and in the said County of Monmouth, that from the beginning of the said Parliament the Burgesses of all and every of the said cities boroughs and towns which be and shall be contributory to the payment of the Burgesses wages of the said shire towns shall be lawfully admonished by proclamation or otherwise by the Mayors Bailiffs or other head officers of the said towns or by one of them to come and to give their

elections for the electing of the said Burgesses, at such time and place lawful and reasonable as shall be assigned for the same intent by the said Mayors Bailiffs and other head officers of the said Shire towns, or by one of them ; in which elections the Burgesses shall have like voice and authority to elect, name and choose the Burgesses of every the said Shire towns, like and in such manner as the Burgesses of the said Shire towns have or use.

4. Provided always that two Justices of the Peace in every the Shires in WALES and in the said County of Monmouth by force of this Act shall have full power and authority indifferently to allot and tax every City Borough and town within the Shires in WALES wherein they do inhabit and in the said County of Monmouth for the portions and rates that every of the said cities and Boroughs shall bear and pay towards the said Burgesses within the said Shire towns of every of the said Shires in WALES and the County of Monmouth ; which rates so rated and taxed in gross by the said two Justices of the Peace as aforesaid shall be again rated and taxed on the inhabitants of every the said Cities and Boroughs by four or six discreet and substantial Burgesses of every the said cities and boroughs in WALES thereunto named and assigned by the Mayor Bailiffs or other head officers of the said cities towns and boroughs for the time being ; and thereupon the Mayors Bailiffs and other head officers of every such City, Borough and town to collect and gather the same and thereof to make payment in manner and form as is aforesaid to the Burgesses of the Parliament for the time being within like time and upon the like pains and forfeitures as is above mentioned.

A.D. 1547] **1 Edward 6, c. 10.**

AN ACT FOR EXIGENTS AND PROCLAMATIONS IN WALES, AND IN THE COUNTY PALATINE OF CHESTER, AND ALSO IN THE CITY OF CHESTER.

Where in the High Court of Parliament holden at Westminster in the seven and twentieth Year of the most prosperous Reign of the late famous King HENRY the Eighth, by the Assent of the Lords Spiritual and Temporal, and the Commons, assembled in the said High Court of Parliament, it was enacted and established by Authority of the same Parliament,

That his Highness Dominion and Principality of WALES, and all Manors, Lands, Tenements and other Dominions within the said Dominion and Principality of WALES, should be divided into twelve Shires or Counties, that is to say, the Shires or Counties of Glamorgan, Radnor, Brecknock, Caermarthen, Pembroke, Cardigan, Merioneth, Montgomery, Flint, Caernarvon, Anglesey, and Denbigh; in every of which said Counties and Shires, amongst the Officers yearly appointed, it was then ordained, that there should be distinct and several Sheriffs yearly; and also where the Counties Palatine of Chester, and of the City of Chester, be ancient and several Counties Palatine of themselves, in all which said Counties the King's Writ hath not nor yet doth run; so that the Proclamation awarded upon any Exigent against any Person or Persons in any Action wherein Process of Outlawry doth lie, according to the Statute made in the sixth Year of the Reign of the said late King, cannot be directed unto the Sheriff or Sheriffs of any of the said Shires or Counties, but unto the Sheriff of the County next adjoining; so that the Party dwelling in any of the said Shires or Counties against whom any such Exigent and Proclamation shall be so awarded, shall not nor can have any Knowledge of the same Suit or Process, by Reason whereof many of the Persons inhabiting in the said Shires and Counties, without Knowledge or Cause of Suit, have been wrongfully and unjustly outlawed to their utter Undoing.

2. Be it therefore, and for divers other good Considerations, by the King our Sovereign Lord, with the Assent of the Lords Spiritual and Temporal, and the Commons, in this present Parliament assembled, and by the Authority of the same, enacted, ordained and established, That if and whensoever, any Writ of Exigent at any Time after the first Day of April next coming, shall be awarded at the suit of the King, or of any Person or Persons, Plaintiff or Plaintiffs in any Action or Suit in any of the Courts of our said Sovereign Lord the King, his Heirs or Successors, commonly called the King's Bench and the Common Place, against any Person or Persons dwelling in any of the aforesaid Counties in WALES, or in the said Counties Palatine of Chester or of the City of Chester or in any of them, that then immediately upon the awarding of every such Exigent, the Justice or Justices before whom any such Writ of Exigent upon such Suit or Action shall be sued, shall have full Power and Authority to award one Writ of Proclamation according to the Tenor and Effect of Proclamations awarded upon

Exigents, and directed out of any of the said Courts into London against any Persons dwelling in any other Shire where the King's Writ is current, according to the Order and Form of the said Statute made in the sixth Year of the said late King, to be directed to such of the aforesaid Sheriffs of any of the aforesaid Counties in WALES, and of the Counties Palatine of Chester, and of the City of Chester for the Time being, where it shall happen the said Defendant, against whom any such Action shall be sued as is aforesaid, to be dwelling: And that every such Writ of Proclamation shall have the same Teste and Day of Return, as the Exigents whereupon every such Writ of Proclamation shall be awarded shall have; and that every such Sheriff to whom any such Writ of Proclamation shall be directed, shall make Proclamation of the said Writ of Proclamation according to the Tenor of the same, and shall make true Return of the same in such Court, and before such Justices as the Tenor of the same Writ shall require and demand. And that all Outlawries hereafter to be promulged or pronounced against any Person or Persons upon any such Exigent or Exigents awarded against any Person or Persons dwelling in any of the said Counties of Wales, Counties Palatine of Chester and the City of Chester, and no Writ of Proclamation awarded in Form abovesaid to the Sheriff or Sheriffs of the County where the Party Defendant shall be as is abovesaid dwelling, or not returned, to be clearly void and of none Effect or Force in the Law.

3. And be it further enacted by the Authority aforesaid That all and every Sheriff and Sheriffs of every of the said Counties of WALES, and of the Counties Palatine of Chester, and of the City of Chester aforesaid, shall have in every of the said Courts of the King's Bench, and of the Common Place one sufficient Deputy at the least to receive all Writs directed to such Sheriff or Sheriffs for whom the same Deputy or Deputies shall be appointed, in like Manner or Form, and upon like Pains, as by the former Statutes and Laws of this Realm, other Sheriffs of other Shires or Counties within this Realm of England be bounden to have in either of the same Courts. And that all Writs of Proclamation aforesaid shall be delivered unto every such Deputy of Record in the same Courts; and also like Fees shall be paid for making every such Writ of Proclamation, and for enrolling the same of Record, as is limited in the said Statute made in the said sixth Year of the Reign of our said late Sovereign Lord King HENRY the Eighth.

4. And be it further enacted by the Authority aforesaid, That if any Person dwelling in any of the said Counties of WALES after the aforesaid first Day of April, shall be outlawed in any Suit or Action aforesaid, that then Writs of Special *Capias utlagatum* single *capias utlagatum*, *non molestand'* and all other Process for or against any Person outlawed, shall and may from henceforth be directed to the Sheriff of any of the said Counties in WALES, as immediate Officers to the King's said Courts of the King's Bench or Common Place in that Behalf: And that every such Writ may be delivered of Record to the Deputy of such of the said Sheriffs to whom any such Writ or Process shall be directed, and that every such Sheriff shall make Execution and Return of every such Writ or Process to him directed, upon like Pain and Penalty as is above limited.

5. And be it further enacted and established, That if any such Writ or Writs of Proclamation hereafter directed to any of the Sheriffs of any of the said Shires in WALES or Counties Palatine of Chester, or of the City of Chester be delivered unto any of the said Sheriffs for the Time being, or to his or their Deputy in Manner and Form aforesaid, and the same Sheriff or Sheriffs do not make true Return of every such Writ or Writs of Proclamation into such Court and Courts out of which the said Writ or Writs of Proclamation shall be awarded; that for every such Default or Non-return, every such Sheriff for the Time being shall lose and forfeit five Pound; the one Half thereof shall be to our Sovereign Lord the King, his Heirs and Successors, the other Half to any such Person or Persons as will sue for the same in an Action of Debt grounded upon this Act, in any of the King's Courts of Record, wherein no Essoign, Protection or Wager of Law shall be allowed or admitted.

6. Provided always, That this Act, or any thing therein contained shall not in any wise extend or be prejudicial to the same Counties of WALES, or to the same Counties Palatine of Chester, or of the City of Chester for or concerning such Liberties Franchises or Privileges as belong to them or any of them, or to any Ministers or Officers of them or any of them, otherwise or in any other Manner than by the true Meaning of this Act is before provided and declared; any Thing in this Act mentioned to the contrary notwithstanding.

7. Provided always and be it enacted by the Authority aforesaid, That this Act, nor any Thing therein contained, shall not in any

wise be prejudicial or hurtful to any Lord Marcher in WALES, but that they and every of them, and their Heirs, and the Heirs of every of them, shall and may have like Liberty Interest and Preeminence, as they and every of them had might or ought to have had before the making of this Act, and as though this Act had never been had nor made; any Thing in this Act mentioned to the contrary in any wise notwithstanding.

A.D. 1548] **2-3 Edward 6, c. 13, s. 16.**

TITHES OF MARRIAGE GOODS IN WALES ABOLISHED.

Provided nevertheless where heretofore such a custom hath been in many parts of WALES that on such cattle and other goods as hath been given with the marriage of any person their tithes have been exacted and levied by the parsons and curates in those parts, which custom being dissonant from any other part of this Realm as it seemed when the said country of WALES was through civil dissension uncultivated for want of other sufficient profits that might otherwise grow to the curates and ministers there to have been for that time tolerable; So now the country being well manured and husbanded and that tithe is duly paid there of corn hay wool and cheese and of other increase of all manner of cattle as it is commonly in all other parts of this Realm, the same custom seems to be grievous and unreasonable especially where the benefices are else sufficient for the finding of the said Ministers and Curates; that it be therefore enacted by the authority aforesaid that from and after the first day of May next coming no such tithes of marriage goods be exacted or required of any person within the said Dominion of WALES or Marches of the same; anything in this Act contained or any other Act custom or prescription had or made to the contrary hereof notwithstanding.

A.D. 1554] **1 Mary (session 3), c. 11.**

AN ACT TOUCHING THE SEA SANDS IN GLAMORGANSHIRE.

Where in the xxiii. year of the Reign of the Excellent Prince of famous memory King Henry the Eighth, It was enacted and established, That Commissions of Sewers from time to time when need should require, should be directed to such substantial and indifferent persons as should be named by the Lord Chancellor of England, the Lord Treasurer, the Lord Privy Seal, and the two Chief Justices or three of them, whereof the Lord Chancellor to be one, authorising them or six of them to survey Walls Streams Dykes Banks Gutters Sewers Gouts Causeways Bridges Trenches Mills Mill-dams Floodgates Pounds Cocks Ebbing Weirs and other Lets and Nuisances, by reason of the outrageous course and rage of the Sea in and upon Marshes and other low Places; Which good Law doth not extend nor is not taken to give authority and power unto the said Commissioners of Sewers to reform the great hurt nuisance and losses that cometh and chanceth to the Queen's Highness and her Subjects, by reason of Sand rising out of the Sea and driven to Land by Storms and Winds, whereby much good Ground lying on the Sea coasts in sundry Places of this Realm and especially in the County of Glamorgan, be covered with such Sand rising out of the Sea that there cometh no Profit of the same, to the great loss of the Queen's Highness and her loving Subjects, and more is like to ensue if speedy Remedy be not therein provided: May it therefore please the Queen's Highness with the assent of the Lords Spiritual and Temporal and the Commons in this present Parliament assembled, and by authority of the same, Be It Enacted, That as well the said Act of Sewers made in the said xxiii.rd year, as all Commissions of Sewers hereafter to be directed according to the tenor of the said Act, may extend and give authority that the Commissioners therein named for the County of Glamorgan, or six of them, whereof three to be of the Quorum, shall by this Act and the said former Act and Commission to them directed, have full power and authority from time to time to make such Laws Provisions Ordinances Judgments and Decrees within the said County of Glamorgan, for the redress and saving the said Grounds from hurt or destruction by reason of the said Sands, as they might or may do by the said former Act and Commission, for the withstanding and avoiding of the outrageous course and rage of the Sea, or other Waters; Any Usage or Custom to the contrary notwithstanding.

A.D. 1554] 1-2 Philip and Mary, c. 15.

An Act to confirm the Liberties of the Lords Marchers in WALES.

Humbly beseeching your Excellent Majesties your true and faithful Subjects the Lords Marchers both Spiritual and Temporal within your Highness's Dominion of WALES, That Whereas in the Parliament holden at Westminster the 27th year of the reign of King Henry the Eighth, father unto you our natural Sovereign Lady, amongst other things One Act was made and established for Laws and Justice to be ministered in the said Dominion of WALES in like form as it is in this Realm of England ; In the which Act one Article is, that for that the Lords Marchers before the Parliament had used to put their tenants within their Lordships Marchers under Common Mainprise and Surety of Appearance, and have had the forfeitures thereof, which for ever from and after the feast of All Saints then next ensuing the said Parliament should utterly cease and be determined; It was enacted that after the said Feast of All Saints every lay and temporal person then being a Lord Marcher should have the moiety or half of every forfeiture of all and every Common Mainprise Recognisance for the Peace or Appearance forfeited by any of their Tenants inhabiting within any of their Lordships Marchers, and they to be paid the same moiety or half by the hands of the Sheriff of every of the Counties where such forfeiture shall be if the Sheriff can levy the same, and the same Sheriff to account to Our said late Sovereign Lord the King for the other half or moiety in such Exchequer as they be accountant; And further it was enacted by the authority aforesaid that all and every Lay and Temporal person and persons then being Lords Marchers, and having any Lordships Marchers, or Lordships Royal, should from and after the said Feast of All Saints have all such mises and profits of their Tenants as they have had or used to have at the first entry into their lands in times past ; And also should have hold and keep within the precincts of their Lordships, Courts Baron Courts Leet and Lawdays, and all and every thing to the said Courts belonging and also should have within the precinct of their said Lordships or Lawday, Waif, Straif, Infangthefe Outfangthefe Treasure trove Deodands Goods and Chattels of Felons and of persons condemned or outlawed of Felony or Murder, put in Exigent for Felony or Murder and also Wreck de Mer Wharfage and Customs of Strangers as they have had in times past, and as though such privileges had been granted unto them by point of Charter any thing in that Act to the contrary notwithstanding, as in the said Act of Parliament more at large it may appear: And forasmuch as Bishops and other Ecclesiastical persons being Lords Marchers, having the like Liberties, Casualties Profits and Commodities within their Lordships Marchers and Lordships Royal within the said Dominion or Principality of WALES, were not provided for by the express Letter of the said Statute, in like sort as the Lay and Temporal Lords Marchers were, but rather of purpose as it should seem forgotten and left out of the said Act, against all Reason and good Equity: And forasmuch also as the heirs and successors of the Lay and Temporal Lords Marchers then being, were not provided for by the limitation and express words of the said Act as well as their Ancestors and Predecessors were, as reason would they should have been; It may please your Majesties of your most gracious favour and benignity at the humble suit and supplication of your said faithful Subjects the Lords Marchers that now are in the said Dominion of WALES, both Spiritual and Temporal, to grant that it may by the assent of the Lords Spiritual and Temporal and the Commons in this present Parliament assembled, Be ordained, established and enacted by the Authority of this present Parliament, That as well your said Spiritual and Ecclesiastical Subjects Lords Marchers now having Lordships Marchers or Lordships Royal in WALES aforesaid and their successors and the successors of every of them, As also the heirs and successors of the Lords Temporal Marchers that then were or now be, and the heirs and successors of every of them, being or which hereafter shall be Lords Marchers, within their Lordships Marchers and Lordships Royal in the Dominion or Principality of WALES, shall have and enjoy to them and to their heirs and successors respectively and severally for ever the moiety and half of every forfeiture of all and every Common Mainprise Recognisance for the Peace or Appearance forfeited by any of their tenants inhabiting within any their Lordships Marchers or Lordships Royal, and they to be paid the same moiety or half by the hands of the Sheriff of the County for the time being, after such form and sort as the said Lay or Temporal Lords Marchers have been or ought to have been paid the same by force of the said Statute: And further shall have all such Mises and profits of their tenants as the Lords Marchers Spiritual or Temporal respectively or severally had or used to have at their first entry into their lands in times past before the making of the said Act or Statute ; And also shall have hold and keep within the precincts of their said Lordships all such Courts Baron, Courts Leet, and Law-days, and all and every thing and things to the same Courts belonging, and also shall have within the precinct of their said several Lordships or Lawdays, all such Waif, Straif, Infangthefe, Outfangthefe Treasure trove Deodands Goods and Chattels of Felons and of persons condemned or outlawed of Felony or Murder, put in Exigent for Felony or Murder, And also all such Wreck de Mer Wharfage and Customs of Strangers, as the Lords Marchers Spiritual and Temporal respectively and severally had and used in times past before the making of the said Statute.

A.D. 1557] **4-5 Philip and Mary, c. 2, ss. 18, 19.**

AN ACT FOR THE HAVING OF HORSE ARMOUR AND WEAPON.

18. Provided always that this Act nor any thing therein contained shall extend to charge any person or persons dwelling or abiding within the Countries of North WALES and South WALES, and within the County Palatine of Lancaster and Chester or either of them with the finding or having of any Haquebutt ; but that they and every of them shall and may at their will liberty and pleasure, have and keep, in stead and place of every Haquebutt charged by this Act, one Long-bow and one Sheaf of Arrows, over and besides such other Armour and Munition as is by the Laws of this Realm limited and appointed ; any thing in this Act to the contrary notwithstanding.

19. Commissioners to view Armour may be appointed "as well in England as in WALES."

A.D. 1558] **1 Elizabeth, c. 11, s. 11.**

AN ACT LIMITING THE TIME FOR LAYING ON LAND MERCHANDISE FROM BEYOND THE SEAS.

Provided always, that this Act or anything therein contained, be not prejudicial or hurtful to the Isle of Anglesea, the shires of

Carnarvon, and Flint in North Wales; but that the inhabitants thereof and every of them may receive lade and discharge according to their old ancient use customs or liberties granted to them or any of their predecessors by the late King of famous memory King Henry the Eighth, or any of his progenitors; so that they and every of them pay the customs and subsidies that shall be due, and discharge and load within the times and hours before mentioned; anything in this present Act to the contrary notwithstanding.

A.D. 1562] **5 Elizabeth, c. 5, s. 31.**

An Act touching certain Politique Constitutions made for the maintenance of the Navy.

Provided also, that it shall and may be lawful to and for any person or persons being strangers born, to bring yearly in any ship, vessel or bottom, whereof any stranger or strangers born is or shall be owner or owners, into the havens, ports and towns of Cardiff Carnarvon Beaumarris and other havens, ports and towns in South Wales and North Wales, or any of them, and into the haven, port and town of Newport in the said county of Monmouth, any of the said wines made in any of the said dominions or countries belonging to the said Crown of France, over and besides all Rochell Wines heretofore in this act allowed to be brought; and in and at the same ports and towns, or any of them, to discharge the said wines so to be brought; so that there be not brought and discharged by the same strangers in any such strangers ships, bottoms or vessels in any one year in or at the said havens, ports and towns, or any of them, above one hundred tons at the most; this act or anything therein contained to the contrary thereof notwithstanding.

A.D. 1562] **5 Elizabeth, c. 23, s. 6.**

An Act for the due Execution of the Writ de Excommunicato Capiendo.

6. Provided always, that in Wales, the counties palatines of Lancaster, Chester, Durham and Ely, and in the cinque ports, being jurisdictions and places exempt, where the queen's majesty's

writ doth not run, and process of capias from thence not returnable into the said court of the King's bench, after any significavit being of record in the said court of chancery, the tenor of such significavit by mittimus shall be sent to such of the head officers of the said counties of WALES, counties palatines and places exempt, within whose offices, charge or jurisdiction the offenders shall be resiant; that is to say, to the chancellor or chamberlain for the said county palatine of Lancaster, and Chester, and for the cinque ports to the lord warden of the same, and for WALES and Ely, and the county palatine of Durham, to the chief justice or justices there: and thereupon every of the said justices and officers to whom such tenor of significavit with mittimus shall be directed and delivered, shall by virtue of this estatute have power and authority to make like process to the inferior officer and officers to whom the execution of process there doth appertain, returnable before the justices there at their next sessions or courts, two months at the least after the teste of every such process: so always as in every degree they shall proceed in their sessions and courts against the offenders, as the justices of the said court of king's bench are limited by the tenor of this Act in term times to do and execute.

A.D. 1562] **5 Elizabeth, c. 25.**

AN ACT TO FILL UP JURIES DE CIRCUMSTANTIBUS LACKING IN WALES.

Where in the Parliament holden at Westminster in the 35th year of the Reign of our late Sovereign Lord King Henry the Eighth, Father to our most dear Sovereign Lady the Queen's Majesty that now is, one wholesome and profitable Act and Statute amongst others was then established and enacted, intituled by the name of an Act concerning the appearance of Juries in Nisi Prius, where amongst other things in the Act, it was established that where a full Jury returned betwixt party and party did not appear before the Justices of Assize or Nisi Prius, or else after Appearance of a full Jury by challenge of any of the parties the Jury was like to remain untaken for default of Jurors, that the same Justices upon request made by the party Plaintiff or Demandant should have authority, by virtue of the same Act, to command the Sheriff, or other Minister or Ministers to whom the making of the said Return should appertain, to name and appoint as often as need should require, so many of such other able persons of the said County then present at the said Assize or Nisi Prius as should make up a full Jury, which persons so to be named and impanelled by such Sheriff or other Minister or Ministers, should be added to the former Panel, and their Names annexed to the same; and further as in the same Act more plainly may appear; Which said beneficial Act doth not extend unto the Twelve Shires of WALES, nor to the County Palatine of Chester, nor to the County Palatine of Lancaster, nor to the County Palatine of Durham; By reason whereof many Juries remain untaken betwixt the parties, what for lack of appearance of Jurors, and some because of challenges, to the great hindrance of Justice and great Expenses and charges to the parties: For Reformation whereof be it enacted by the Queen our Sovereign Lady, with the assent of the Lords Spiritual and Temporal and the Commons in this present Parliament assembled and by the authority of the same, That in every of the Shires of WALES that is to say, Pembroke Carmarthen Cardigan Brecknock Radnor Glamorgan Montgomery Denbigh Flint Merioneth Anglesea Carnarvon and in the County Palatine of Chester, and in the said County Palatine of Durham, and in the said County Palatine of Lancaster, where a full jury shall not appear before the Justices of the Great Session in any of the said Shires or County Palatines, or their Deputies there, or else after appearance of a full Jury by challenge of any of the parties the Jury is like to remain untaken for default of Jurors, that then the same Justices, in every of the said Shires and County Palatines for the time being or their Deputy or Deputies, upon request made by the party Plaintiff or demandant, shall have full authority by virtue of this Act to command the Sheriff or other Minister or Ministers to whom the making of the said Return shall appertain, to name and appoint as often as need shall require, so many of such other able persons of the said Counties then present at the said Great Session as shall make up a full Jury, which persons so to be named and impanelled by such Sheriff or other Minister or Ministers, shall be added to the former Panel, and their Names annexed to the same, And that every of the parties shall and may have his or their Challenge to the Jurors so named added and annexed to the said former Panel by the said Sheriff or other Minister or Ministers, in such wise as if they had been impanelled upon the Venire facias awarded to try the said Issue: And that the said Justices and every of them, and their Deputy or Deputies shall and may proceed to the trial of every such Issue with those persons that were before empanelled and returned and with those newly added and annexed to the said former Panel by virtue of this Act, in such wise as they might or ought to have done if all the said Jurors had been returned upon the writ of Venire facias awarded to try the said Issue: And that all and every such Trial had, shall be as good and effectual in the Law to all Intents Constructions and Purposes, as if such trial had been had and tried by 12 of the Jurors impanelled and returned upon the Writ of Venire facias awarded to try such Issue; And in case such persons as the said Sheriff Minister or Ministers shall name and appoint as is aforesaid or any of them, after they shall be called be present and do not appear, or after his or their Appearance do wilfully withdraw him or themselves from the presence of the Court, that then such Justices or their Deputies shall and may set such Fine upon every such Juror making default or wilfully withdrawing himself as aforesaid as they shall think good by their discretions, the said Fine to be levied in such manner and form as Issues forfeited and lost by Jurors for default of their Appearance, as is provided by the Law and Custom of the said Counties of WALES and Counties Palatines aforesaid where such Issues are forfeited.

2. And be it further enacted by the Authority aforesaid That where any Jury that shall be returned by the Sheriff or other Minister or Ministers, shall be made full by the commandment of the said Justices or their Deputies by virtue of this present Act, that yet nevertheless such persons as were returned in the said Panel by the Sheriff or other Minister or Ministers to try any such Issue, that shall not appear but make default, shall lose the issues upon them returned in such wise as though the same Jury had remained for default of Jurors.

3. Provided always and be it further enacted, That upon a reasonable excuse for the default of Appearance of any Juror or Jurors, sufficiently proved before the Justices of the Great Sessions or their Deputies in the Counties and Counties Palatines aforesaid at the day of their Appearance by the oaths of two lawful and honest witnesses, that the same Justices shall have authority by their discretions to discharge every such Juror of every such forfeiture of Issues upon him returned; and that the said Sheriff or Sheriffs

or other Minister or Ministers having commandment by the said Justices to omit the returning of such Issues as is aforesaid upon such Juror or Jurors, shall be therein discharged of the Penalties aforesaid for the non returning of the said Issues, and that yet notwithstanding the said Return to be good and effectual in the Law; any Law Usage Ordinance or Custom to the contrary notwithstanding.

4. Provided also and be it enacted by the authority aforesaid, That if the said Justices or their Deputies afore whom any such Jury should appear in the Shires or Counties Palatine where such Issue is to be tried, do not come at the Day and Place appointed, That then every one of the same Jurors shall be discharged for forfeiting of any Issues upon him returned in the same Writ; And the Sheriff or other Minister or Ministers shall be likewise discharged of the Penalties of this Statute for the non returning of such Issues as are before limited in this Act; any Article or Sentence herein contained to the contrary notwithstanding.

5. And also be it further enacted by the authority aforesaid That if upon any such Writ of Habeas Corpora or Distringas, Issues be returned upon any Hundredors Juror or Jurors by the Sheriff, or other Minister or Ministers to whom the execution of the same Writ or Writs shall appertain, where as the same Hundredors and Jurors shall not be lawfully summoned warned or distrained in that behalf, That then every such Sheriff or other Minister or Ministers aforesaid shall lose for every such Offence so committed double so much as the said Issues returned upon such Hundredors or Jurors not lawfully summoned warned or distrained shall amount unto; The moiety of all which forfeitures contained in this present Act, other than the issues to be returned upon the Jurors as is aforesaid, shall be to the Queen our Sovereign Lady her Heirs and Successors, and the other half to him that will sue for the same by Action of Debt Bill Plaint or Information, in the Queen her Grace's Great Court within the said County where such forfeiture shall happen to be, before the said Justices his or their Deputy or Deputies, in which no Wager of law Essoin or Protection shall be allowed nor admitted.

6. Saving to all manner of Persons Bodies Politic and Corporate their Heirs and Successors, having lawful Right Title and Interest to have such Issues to be before any such Justices or their Deputies at any time or times hereafter lost and forfeited, all such Right

Title and Interest as they or any of them should or ought to have had to such Issues to be lost and forfeited, as though this Act had never been had or made.

7. Provided also, That this Act nor anything therein contained shall not extend to any City or Town Corporate, or to any Sheriff Minister or Ministers in the same, for the return of any Inquest or Panel to be made and returned of Persons inhabiting in the said Cities or Towns Corporate; but that they and every of them shall and may return such persons in every such Inquest or Panel as before this time they might and have been accustomed to do, and as if this Act had never been had or made; so that the same Sheriff Minister or Ministers return upon such Persons as shall be impanelled such like and reasonable Issues as they ought to return; any thing in the same contained to the contrary notwithstanding.

A.D. 1562]

5 Elizabeth, c. 28.

An Act for the Translating of the Bible and the Divine Service into the WELSH Tongue.

"Whereas the Queen's most Excellent Majesty, like a most godly and virtuous Princess, having chief Respect and Regard to the Honour and Glory of God, and the Souls Health of her Subjects, did in the First Year of her Reign, by the Authority of her High Court of Parliament, chiefly for that Purpose called, set forth a Book of Common Prayer and Order of the Administration of Sacraments in the vulgar English Tongue, to be used through all her Realm of England, Wales and the Marches of the same, that thereby her Highness' most loving Subjects understanding in their own Language the terrible and fearful Threatenings rehearsed in the Book of God against the Wicked and Malefactors, the pleasant and infallible Promises made to the elect and chosen Flock, with a Just Order to rule and Guide their Lives according to the Commandments of God, might much better learn to love and fear God, to serve and obey their Prince, and to know their Duties towards their Neighbours; which Book being received as a most precious Jewel with an inspeakable Joy of all such her Subjects as did and do understand the English Tongue, the which Tongue is not understanded of the most and greatest Number of all her Majesty's most loving and obedient Subjects inhabiting within her Highness

Dominion and Country of WALES, being no small Part of this Realm, who therefore are utterly destituted of God's Holy Word, and do remain in the like or rather more Darkness and Ignorance than they were, in the Time of Papistry": Be it therefore enacted by the Queen our Sovereign Lady, the Lords Spiritual and Temporal, and the Commons, in this present Parliament assembled, and by the Authority of the same, That the Bishops of Hereford, Saint David's, Asaph, Bangor and Landaff, and their Successors, shall take such Order amongst themselves for the Souls Health of the Flocks committed to their Charge within WALES, that the whole Bible, containing the New Testament and the Old, with the Book of Common Prayer and Administration of the Sacraments, as is now used within this Realm in English, to be truly and exactly translated into the British or WELSH Tongue; and that the same so translated, being by them viewed, perused and allowed, be imprinted to such Number at the least, that one of either Sort may be had for every Cathedral, Collegiate and Parish Church, and Chapel of Ease, in such Places and Countries of every the said Dioceses where that Tongue is commonly spoken or used, before the First Day of March, Anno Dom. One thousand five hundred sixty six. And that from that Day forth, the whole Divine Service shall be used and said by the Curates and Ministers throughout all the said Dioceses where the WELSH Tongue is commonly used, in the said British or WELSH Tongue, in such Manner and Form as is now used in the English Tongue, and differing nothing in any Order or Form from the English Book; for the which Books so imprinted, the Parishioners of every of the said Parishes shall pay the one Half or Moiety, and the Parson and Vicar of every of the said Parishes (where both be) or else the one of them where there is but one, shall pay the other Half or Moiety; the Prices of which Books shall be appointed and rated by the said Bishops and their Successors, or by Three of them at the least; the which Things if the said Bishops or their Successors neglect to do, then every one of them shall forfeit to the Queen's Majesty, her Heirs and Successors, the Sum of Forty Pounds, to be levied of their Goods and Chattels.

2. Be it further enacted by the Authority aforesaid, That every Minister and Curate within the Dioceses before said, where the WELSH Tongue is commonly used, shall from the Feast of Whitsuntide next ensuing until the aforesaid Day of March, which shall be

in the Year One thousand five hundred sixty and six, at all Times of Communion declare or read the Epistle and Gospel of the Day in the WELSH Tongue, to his or their Parishioners in every of the said Churches and Chapels; and also once every Week at the least, shall read or declare to their said Parishioners in the said Churches the Lord's Prayer, the Articles of the Christian Faith, the Ten Commandments, and the Litany, as they are set forth in the English Tongue, in the said WELSH Tongue, with such other Part of the Common Prayer and Divine Service as shall be appointed by the Bishop of the Diocese for the Time being.

3. And one Book containing the Bible, and one other Book of Common Prayer, in the English Tongue, shall be bought and had in every Church thoughout WALES in which the Bible and Book of Common Prayer in WELSH is to be had by Force of this Act (if there be none already) before the first Day of March which shall be in the Year of our Lord God One thousand five hundred sixty six; and the same Books to remain in such convenient Places within the said Churches, that such as understand them may resort at all convenient Times to read and peruse the same; and also such as do not understand the said Language, may by conferring both Tongues together, the sooner attain to the Knowledge of the English Tongue; any Thing in this Act to the contrary notwithstanding.

A.D. 1566] **8 Elizabeth, c. 20.**

AN ACT FOR THE REPEAL OF A BRANCH OF A STATUTE MADE 26 HENRY 8 TOUCHING TRIAL OF OFFENCES IN THE COUNTY OF MERIONETH IN NORTH WALES.

Where in the Parliament holden at Westminster in the 26th year of the Reign of our late King Henry the Eighth, amongst other Things it was enacted, That all Murders Robberies Felonies and other felonious Offences which should from that time be committed in any Lordships Marchers or other Place in WALES, might be inquired of, heard, tried and examined in the next English Shire thereunto adjoining; and also by one other Branch contained in the Statute it is ordained that such of the same Offences as should be committed within the County of Merioneth, one of the Three Old Shires of North WALES, might at the Discretion of the Justices there, be inquired of, heard tried and determined in the Counties of Anglesea and Carnarvon, being two other Counties of North WALES; as by the same Act more plainly doth appear; And yet nevertheless in the Parliament holden at Westminster in the 34th and 35th year of the Reign of the said late King Henry the Eighth, by one Act and Statute there made touching certain Ordinances in WALES, it is by one Branch thereof amongst other Things enacted and established, that all Offences, Murders, Robberies and other Felonies which from henceforth should be committed in the said County of Merioneth should and might be inquired of heard and determined before the Justices within the said County of Merioneth, or else in the County of Salop being the next English County adjoining thereunto, in such manner and form as the like Offences committed in other the said Counties in WALES should or might be inquired of heard and determined, as by the said Act more at large doth appear; By reason of which said several Branches contained in the said several Statutes, the said County of Merioneth standeth now not only chargeable to such like Trial, in the next English Shire, for the said Offences as other Counties of WALES at this present be, but also by force of the said Statute made in the said 26th year of the said King Henry the Eighth, the said County of Merioneth is also subject to such Inquiry and Trial to be had within the said Counties of Carnarvon and Anglesea, being both Welsh Shires, much to the discredit of the Inhabitants of the said County of Merioneth, for that no other Counties of WALES for such Offences are chargeable with the like Trial.

2. Wherefore be it enacted by the Authority of this present Parliament That so much of the said Act and Statute made in the said 26th year of the Reign of the said late King Henry the 8th as doth limit or appoint any of the said Offences before mentioned committed within the said County of Merioneth, to be inquired of tried heard and determined within the said Counties of Carnarvon and Anglesea, or either of them, shall from henceforth be utterly repealed void and of none effect.

A.D. 1576] **18 Elizabeth, c. 8.**

AN ACT FOR THE APPOINTING AND AUTHORISING OF JUSTICES OF ASSIZES IN THE SHIRES OF WALES.

Whereas by divers laudable Statutes Usages and Laws of this Realm for the good Government and Administration of Justice within the Principality and Dominion of WALES and the County Palatine of Chester, it hath been established used and enacted amongst other Things that there shall be holden and kept Sessions twice in every year in every of the shires in the said Dominion and Principality of WALES, that is to say, in the Shires of Glamorgan Brecknock Radnor Carmarthen Pembroke the Town and County of Haverfordwest Cardigan Montgomery Denbigh Flint Carnarvon Merioneth and Anglesea and in the said County Palatine of Chester, the which Sessions are called the King's Great Sessions; and that the Justice of Chester for the time being shall hold and keep Sessions twice in every year in the Shires of Chester Denbigh Flint and Montgomery; And likewise that the Justice of North WALES shall hold and keep Sessions twice in every year in every of the said Shires of Carnarvon Merioneth and Anglesea; And that also one person learned in the Laws of this Realm of England, by the Queen's Majesty to be appointed, shall be Justice of the Shires of Radnor Brecknock and Glamorgan, and shall in likewise hold and keep Sessions twice in every year in every of the same Shires; And that one other person learned in the Laws of this Realm to be appointed as is aforesaid shall be Justice of the Shires of Carmarthen Pembroke and Cardigan, and the Town and County of Haverfordwest, and shall likewise hold and keep Sessions twice in every year in every of the same Shires; And that the said persons or Justices and every of them then being or that thereafter should be should have several letters Patents and Commissions for their Offices under the Great Seal of England, to be exercised by themselves or their sufficient Deputies, according to the Purports and Intents in the Ordinances specified.

2. Forasmuch as by the good Administration of Justice within the said Shires and Counties the same Principality and Dominion of WALES, and the said County Palatine of Chester, are reduced to great Obedience of Her Majesty's laws and the same greatly inhabited manured and peopled; And for that all and all manner Causes Pleas Actions as well Real Personal and Mixed, Treasons, Pleas of the Crown, Attaints Conspiracies Assizes Quare Impedit Appeals of Murder Mayhems and Felony and trial upon all Murders Manslaughters and Felonies whatsoever arising within the said several Circuits, are by the said Laws Usages and Statutes impleadable impleaded and determinable before One only Justice as is aforesaid; And for that many great and weighty Causes Matters

Questions Demurrers and Ambiguities in Law do thereupon daily arise increase and are like daily more and more to increase within the said Shires, to the infinite trouble of such one Justice within every of the said several Circuits, and to the great Delay and Hindrance of Administration of Justice.

3. For the better and more speedy Remedy whereof her Majesty's Subjects of the said Principality and Dominion of WALES and County Palatine of Chester have made their most humble Petition and Suit to her Highness, to have two Justices learned in the Laws in every of the said several Circuits: And Forasmuch as some Question Ambiguity and Doubt hath been heretofore made, whether her Highness by her letters Patents under the Great Seal of England might or may authorise constitute or appoint two persons or more to be Her Highness's Justices in every of the said several Circuits, or grant Commission or Commissions of Association or Associations to or with every or any such several Justice and Justices or no; And also whether after such grant the Administration of Justice in those Offices and Function done by Two may be sufficiently warranted by Law or no; For plain explanation whereof and for the better Redress and more speedy Administration of Justice to be had touching the Premisses, Be it declared explained enacted and established by the Queen's most excellent Majesty, by the assent of the Lords Spiritual and Temporal and the Commons in this present Parliament assembled, and by the authority of the same, That the Queen's Highness her Heirs and Successors may and shall, at her or their Will and Pleasure, have full Power Prerogative and Authority from time to time to constitute authorise name or appoint Two or more, learned as aforesaid in the Laws of this Realm, to be Justices of and for the said Counties of Chester Flint Denbigh and Montgomery; and Two or more, learned as aforesaid, to be Justices of NORTH WALES, viz. of and for the said Shires of Anglesea Carnarvon and Merioneth; And likewise two or more, learned as aforesaid, to be Justices of and for the said Circuits and Shires of Radnor Glamorgan and Brecknock; and also two or more, learned as aforesaid, to be Justices of and for the said Circuit and Shires of Cardigan Carmarthen and Pembroke and the Town and County of Haverfordwest; Any Law Usage Opinion or Statute to the contrary notwithstanding.

4. And that her Majesty her Heirs and Successors may and shall, at her and their good will and pleasure, from time to time associate and grant Commission and Commissions of Association or Associa-

tions under the Great Seal of England, to any person or persons, learned as aforesaid, to be associate to or with every or any such several Justice or Justices for the time being of the said several Circuits and Counties aforesaid, or in any of the said Counties: And that all and every such two Justices or more within every of the said several Circuits and Counties, and also that every such Justice or Justices together with such person or persons associate, if any such Association or Associations shall happen to be as aforesaid, during such Association and after such Association ended, or without such Association, such Justice or Justices shall have the like full Power Pre-eminence Authority and Jurisdiction from henceforth, to all Intents and Constructions Purposes and Effects, as any one Justice within any of the said Circuits or Shires aforesaid now hath or at any time heretofore had or ought to have; And also shall have like Power Authority Pre-eminence and Jurisdiction to keep and hold the several Sessions aforesaid twice in every Year in every of the said Shires within their several Circuits aforesaid; and to hear determine order award adjudge receive take knowledge of and execute, all and singular Causes Matters Pleas of Assises Treasons Murders Felonies Indictments Appeals of Murder Felony and Mayhems, Actions Real Personal and Mixed, Suits Plaints Informations Quarrels Attaints Conspiracies Quare Impedit and all Actions grounded upon any Statute or Statutes, Writs Processes, Returns Essoigns Verdicts Judgments Fines Acknowledgments Confessions Warrants and Executions Actions and Acts whatsoever, And to do perform observe accomplish and make all and every other Act and Acts Matter and Matters Thing and Things whatsoever in like and in as ample beneficial lawful and effectual manner and form, to all Constructions Qualities Intents and Purposes, as any of the now several Justices, or any One of the now Justice or Justices, within the same several Circuit or Circuits and Counties aforesaid may ought hath or might lawfully do by force of any Law Usage or Statute heretofore had made or used before the making of this Act: And that from henceforth all and singular Writs and Processes Returns Essoigns Verdicts Judgments Fines Recoveries Recognizances Acknowledgments Confession Act and Acts Thing and Things Matter and Matters as aforesaid, had made taken done returned heard determined awarded adjudged or executed by or before any such two Justices or more, or any such Justice or Justices and Associate or Associates as aforesaid to be appointed, nominated authorised or constituted as aforesaid, shall be allowed taken construed expounded and adjudged as good effectual and available to all Intents Constructions and Purposes as if the same had been had made taken done returned heard determined awarded adjudged or executed by or before any such One Justice, or One of the Justices now or late being Justice or Justices of the same Circuit or several Circuits aforesaid; Any Law Usage Statute Act Ordinance or Prescription to the contrary in any wise notwithstanding.

A.D. 1584] 27 Elizabeth, c. 6, s. 6.

AN ACT FOR RETURNING OF SUFFICIENT JURORS, ETC.

6. Provided also, that this Act shall not extend to any Juries or issues to be returned in any city or town corporate or other town or place privileged to hold Plea, or in the twelve Shires of Wales; but that they shall and may be returned as heretofore they lawfully might have been; this Act or anything therein contained to the contrary in any wise notwithstanding.

A.D. 1584.] 27 Elizabeth, c. 9.

AN ACT FOR REFORMATION OF ERRORS IN FINES AND RECOVERIES IN THE 12 SHIRES OF WALES, TOWN AND COUNTY OF HAVERFORDWEST WITH THE COUNTIES PALATINE.

Whereas in the Parliament by Prorogation holden at Westminster in the 23rd year of her Majesty's Reign that now is One good and beneficial Statute was made and ordained for the appeasing of Suits, the avoiding of False practices Deceits Devices and Misdemeanours and for helping of Negligences and Misprisions of Clerks and Officers, dangerous to Assurances of Men's Lands and Hereditaments, entituled An Act for the Reformation of Errors in Fines and Recoveries; Forasmuch as the said Statute, or sundry good and necessary Clauses and parts thereof, doth not extend to Fines and Recoveries levied had and suffered in the 12 Shires of WALES, that is to say, Glamorgan Brecknock Radnor Carmarthen Pembroke Cardigan Montgomery Denbigh Flint Carnarvon Anglesea and Merioneth, the Town and County of Haverfordwest, and the Counties Palatine of Chester Lancaster and Duresme: Be it therefore enacted by our Sovereign Lady the Queen's most Excellent Majesty the Lords Spiritual and Temporal and the Commons in this present Parliament assembled and by the authority of the same, That every Writ of Covenant, and other Writ whereupon any Fine heretofore hath been levied or hereafter shall be levied, the Return thereof, the Writ of Dedimus potestatem made for the acknowledging of any of the same Fines, the Return thereof, the Concord Note and Foot of every such Fine, the Proclamations made thereupon and the King's Silver, And also every original Writ of Entry in the Post, or other Writ whereupon any common Recovery hath been suffered, or hereafter shall be suffered or passed, the Writs of Summons Ad Warrantizandum, the Returns of the said originals and Writs of Summons Ad Warrantizandum, and every Warrant of Attorney had or to be had, as well of every Demandant and Tenant as Vouchee extant and remaining, or that shall be extant and in being, in the Courts of Assizes or Great Sessions within the said 12 Shires of WALES, Town and County of Haverfordwest, and Counties Palatines, or in the custody of the Officers to whom the charge of Keeping thereof doth appertain, may upon the Request or Election of any person or persons be inrolled in Rolls of Parchment, by such persons and for such Considerations as hereafter in this Act shall be mentioned; And that the Inrollments of the same or any part thereof, shall be of as good force and Validity in Law, to all intents respects and purposes, for so much of any of them so inrolled, as the same being extant and remaining were or ought by Law to be.

2. Be it further enacted by the Authority aforesaid, That no Fine, Proclamations upon Fines, or common Recovery, heretofore had levied suffered or passed, or hereafter to be had levied suffered or passed, in any of the said 12 Shires of WALES, Town and County of Haverfordwest, or Counties Palatine, shall be reversed or reversable by any Writ of Error for false or incongruous Latin, erasure, interlining, misentering of any Warrant of Attorney or of any Proclamation, misreturning or not returning of the Sheriff, or other Want of form in Words, and not in Matter of Substance.

3. Provided always, That neither this Act nor any Thing therein contained, shall bar or exclude any person or persons from any Writ of Error, which shall be had taken or pursued within Five years next after the end of this Session of this present Parliament, upon any Fine or Recovery heretofore had or suffered in any of the Courts

aforesaid; Nor from any Writ of Error which shall be had taken or pursued, upon any fine or Recovery heretofore levied acknowledged or had in any of the Courts aforesaid within any of the said 12 Shires of WALES or Town and County of Haverfordwest, which Fine or Recovery or any part or parcel thereof now is or at any time before the first day of June which shall be in the year of our Lord God 1585, shall be exemplified under the judicial Seal of the said Courts, at or by the Suit of any person that is or may be entitled to have or sue any Writ of Error upon any the same Fines or Recoveries so heretofore passed; Nor from any Writ of Error which shall be had taken or pursued, upon any Fine or Recovery heretofore levied, acknowledged or had in any of the Courts aforesaid within any of the said Counties Palatine, which Fine or Recovery, or any part or parcel thereof now is or at any time before the said first day of June which shall be in the year of our Lord God 1585 shall be exemplified under the Seal of the same County Palatine where the same Fine or Recovery shall be so levied knowledged or had, at or by the Suit of any person that is or may be entitled to have or sue any Writ of Error upon the same Fine or Recovery so heretofore passed; Nor to bar any Feme Coverte, or any person within the age of 21 years, or any person that is non compos mentis, in prison, or beyond the Seas, of or from any Writ of Error to be had or prosecuted for the reversing of any Fine or Recovery, heretofore passed levied or suffered in any of the said 12 Shires of WALES Town and County of Haverfordwest or Counties Palatine, so that such Feme Coverte or her Heirs within seven years next after that she become sole, and such person within the age of 21 years or his Heirs within seven years next after he shall come and be of full age of 21 years, and such person that is non compos mentis within seven years next after he shall become of *Sanæ Memoriæ* and in default thereof the Heirs of such person that is non compos mentis within seven years next after the death of any such person being non compos mentis, And such person in prison or his Heirs within seven years next after the same person shall be at liberty, and such person beyond the Seas or his Heirs within seven years next after the return of such person into this Realm of England or the death of the said person, if he shall before his Return die in any foreign country, shall sue take and prosecute their Writs of Error, as their Causes shall severally require, for reversing of any of the said Fines or Recoveries heretofore passed levied or suffered.

4. Provided always and be it further enacted by the authority aforesaid, That if any person or persons shall within the time and years aforesaid, commence or sue his or their Writs of Error for the reversing of any of the said Fines or Recoveries heretofore passed, which Suit shall fortune to abate by the Death of any of the parties to the same, that then it shall and may be lawful for his and their Heirs, at any time within one year next after the said seven years expired, to have sue and take their Writ of Error for the reversing of every such Fine and Recovery; And if such Heir be an infant within the age of 21 years, then within one year next after the full age of such Infant; Any thing in this present Act contained to the contrary thereof in any wise notwithstanding.

5. And be it further enacted by the authority of this present Parliament, That every person that shall at any time hereafter take the knowledge of any Fine or Warrant of Attorney of any Tenant or Vouchee for suffering any Common Recovery, to be levied, knowledged, passed or had within any of the said 12 Shires of WALES, Town and County of Haverfordwest or Counties Palatine, or shall certify them or any of them, shall with the Certificate of the Concord or Warrant of Attorney certify also the day and year wherein the same was acknowledged: And that no person that taketh any such knowledge of any Fine or Warrant for any Recovery, shall be bound or by any means inforced to certify any such knowledge or Warrant, except it be within one year next after the said knowledge taken.

6. And that no Clerk or Officer in any of the said 12 Shires of WALES, Town or County of Haverfordwest, or Counties Palatine, shall receive any Writ of Covenant or Writ of Entry, or any other Writ whereupon any Fine or Common Recovery is hereafter to pass, unless the day of the knowledge of the same Fine and Warrant shall appear in or by such Certificate; upon pain that every Clerk that shall receive any such Writ shall forfeit for every time that he shall so offend the sum of forty shillings; And that no Attornment in or upon any such Fine in any of the Courts aforesaid be entered upon Record, except the Party mentioned to attorn therein first have appeared in the Court, in person or by Attorney warranted by the Hands of one of the Justices of the same Court, upon a Writ of Quid juris clamat, quem Redditum reddit, or per quæ servitia, as the cause requireth; And that every Entry of Attornment hereafter to be made in any of the Courts aforesaid wherein there shall be no

Appearance as aforesaid, shall be utterly void and of none effect without any Writ of Error or other means to be used for avoiding thereof.

7. And be it further enacted by the authority aforesaid, That there shall be for ever an Office for the Inrolments aforesaid, in every of the said 12 Shires of WALES, Town and County of Haverfordwest and the Counties Palatine, which shall be and continue an Office for ever, called the Office of the Inrolments of Fines and Recoveries; And that the Justices of the said 12 Shires of WALES, Town and County of Haverfordwest, and Counties Palatine for the time being, that is to wit, every of them within the Limits and Precincts of their several Authorities and Commissions, shall have and take the Care and Charge of and for the Inrolments aforesaid, and shall have and enjoy the said Office and the disposition thereof, and carefully see and look to the execution thereof; And in consideration of their Charges Pain and Travail therein, shall have and take the sums of Money hereafter following and no more, that is to say; for the Inrolment and Examination of every Fine and the parts thereof 5s., and for the Inrolment and Examination of every Recovery and the parts thereof 5s. and for every Exemplification of the Inrolment of every Fine and the parts thereof 3s. 4d., and for every Exemplification of the Inrolment of every Recovery and the parts thereof 3s. 4d., and for the Search of the Rolls for one Year, 4d., and for the Copy of one Sheet of Paper containing 14 lines 4d. And that the Justices of the said Courts of Assizes or Great Sessions for the time being within the said 12 Shires of WALES, Town and County of Haverfordwest, and Counties Palatine, or any one of them within the several Limits and Precincts of their said several Commissions, shall examine the Inrolment of every such Fine and Recovery and of the parts thereof, And after such Examination of the Inrolment of every such Fine and Recovery and of the parts thereof, shall immediately write his name that so examineth with his own hand in the Roll thereof; upon pain that the said Justices shall forfeit to our Sovereign Lady the Queen's Majesty the sum of Forty Shillings for every time that they or one of them shall make default of such Examination or writing of his or their Name as is aforesaid; And that it shall and may be lawful for the said Justices or any of them for the time being to take order in all things that shall be convenient and needful for the Inrolments aforesaid; And upon Examination in the said Courts to assess such Fine or Amerciament,

upon any Clerk Sheriff Deputy Attorney or any other person for his and their Misprision Contempt and Negligence for not doing or misdoing in any thing of in or concerning the said Fines or Recoveries, or any part of them or either of them, as by the said Justices for the time being or any one of them shall be thought meet and convenient; The said Fine and Amerciament to be estreated amongst other Fines and Amerciaments of that Court where such Offence or Misprision shall be committed.

8. And be it further enacted by the Authority aforesaid, That the Exemplification of any such Inrolment of any Fine or Recovery or of any part thereof within any of the said twelve Shires of WALES, or the said Town and County of Haverfordwest, under the Judicial Seal of the said Shire Town or County where such Fine or Recovery was levied had or passed, and the Exemplification of any such Inrolment of any Fine or Recovery or of any part thereof within any of the said Counties Palatine, under the Seal of that County Palatine where such Fine or Recovery was levied had or passed, shall be of as good Force and Validity in the Law to all Intents Respects and Purposes, for such part and so much of any of them as shall be so exemplified, as the very original Record itself, being extant and remaining, were or ought by Law to be.

9. Provided always and be it enacted by the Authority aforesaid, That it shall be lawful for the Justices Clerks authorised by their Warrant in the said several Offices and Places where the same Records or any of them do or shall remain, to write out or enrol, the same Records and every part thereof; And that the said Records nor any of them for the writing out or making the Rolls thereof by the Clerk of the said Justices shall be brought or carried forth of the said Offices or Places.

10. And be it further enacted by the Authority aforesaid, That none of the said Fines or Recoveries aforesaid, heretofore levied passed or suffered, which shall be exemplified under any Judicial Seal of any of the said Shires of WALES or Town or County of Haverfordwest or under the Seal of any of the said Counties Palatine, according to the form of this Act, shall after such Exemplifications had, be in any case amended.

11. Provided always that this Act or any thing therein contained shall not in any wise extend to the prejudice of the Heirs of Sir Edward Gray Knight Lord Powys deceased, or of Sir Edward Herbert Knight or his Heirs or Assigns, Henry Vernon or John

Vernon Esquires or their Heirs or Assigns, for or concerning any Fine levied or Recovery suffered by or against the said Lord Powys, of any Baronies Honours Manors Lands Tenements or Hereditaments in the County of Montgomery, or any Exemplification thereof, or for or concerning any Writ of Error brought or to be brought for the reversing of any such Fine or Recovery; but that they and every of them shall have and enjoy the same Right Title Benefit and Advantage to all Intents and Purposes as if this Act had never been had or made.

12. And forasmuch as upon great Examination it appeareth that divers Fines and Recoveries have been heretofore levied and suffered, of divers Castles Manors Messuages, Lands, Tenements, and Hereditaments which sometime were the Inheritance of George sometime Earl of Kent, Great Grandfather to Henry now Earl of Kent, in Use Possession Reversion or Remainder, whereunto the said now Earl of Kent pretendeth Title in Use Possession Reversion or Remainder, which if they be erroneous, as is pretended, do much vary from the general Cause and Mischief for which this Statute meaneth to provide: Be it therefore enacted by the Authority aforesaid, That neither this Statute nor any Thing therein contained shall extend to take away any Writ of Error whereunto any person or persons is now or hereafter shall be lawfully entitled to have for the reversing of the said Fines and Recoveries or any of them heretofore levied or suffered of any of the said Castles Manors Messuages Lands Tenements or Hereditaments which late were any part or parcel of the Inheritance of the said George sometime Earl of Kent in Use Possession Reversion or Remainder; Any Thing in this Statute contained to the contrary in any wise notwithstanding.

A.D. 1605] **3 James 1, c. 17.**

AN ACT CONCERNING WELSH COTTONS.

Whereas in a Statute made at the first Session of Parliament holden at Westminster in the first year of his Majesty's Reign, amongst other things it was provided and enacted, "That no person or persons should incur any penalty for want of length breadth or weight of Welsh Cottons under the price of Fifteen Pence the yard and Two Shillings the goade so as they be not mixed with Hair or other deceitful stuff, nor for any other above that price, except they be mixed as aforesaid, or shall shrink above half a yard in twelve yards of length or weigh less than fourteen ounces the yard or hold not full three quarters of a yard broad, as by the same Statute appeareth"; which Proviso in the construction of divers persons doth not preserve such as make or sell coarse Welsh Cottons from the penalty and danger of not adding or affixing a Seal to contain the length breadth or weight of the said Cottons, which affixion of a seal is needless when there is no length breadth or weight prescribed for them: And moreover for that in all antecedent Ages the said Cottons being commonly used for Linings were never seized as forfeited for want of the Seal of the makers put unto them, nor used to be searched or tried by water, but only by the buyer: Be it therefore enacted by our Sovereign Lord the King and by the Lords Spiritual and Temporal and Commons in this present Parliament assembled and by the Authority of the same, That from henceforth no person or persons shall incur any penalty for want of any Content Seal to contain the breadth length or weight of any Welsh Cottons; and that no Welsh Cottons shall at any time or times hereafter be searched or tried in the Water by any person or persons other than by the buyer thereof; upon pain to forfeit for every such Offence by the party who shall make any such search or trial contrary to the intent of this Statute, Five pounds of lawful money of England; the one moiety thereof to the King's Majesty his Heirs and Successors, the other moiety to the party grieved, to be recovered by Action of Debt Bill Plaint or Information, wherein no Essoign Protection or Wager of Law shall be allowed.

A.D. 1623-4]

21 James 1, c. 9.

AN ACT FOR THE FREE TRADE OF WELSH CLOTHS.

Whereas the Trade of making WELSH Cloths Cottons Frizes Linings and Plains within the Principality and Dominion of WALES is and hath been of long Continuance, in the using and exercising whereof many Thousands of the poorer Sort of the Inhabitants there in precedent Ages have been set on work in Spinning Carding Weaving Frilling Cottoning and Shering (whereby they (having free Liberty to sell them to whom and where they would), not only relieved and maintained themselves and their Families in good Sort, but also grew to such Wealth and Means of Living as they were thereby enabled to pay and Discharge all Duties Mizes Charges Subsidies and Taxations which were upon them imposed or rated in their several Counties Parishes and Places wherein they dwelled for the Relief of the Poor, and for the service of the King and the Commonwealth; And whereas also the Drapers of the Town of Shrewsbury, in the County of Salop, have of late obtained some Orders of Restraint whereby the Inhabitants of WALES find themselves much prejudiced in the Freedom of their Markets for buying and selling of their Cloths, to their great damage as was verified by the general Voice of the Knights and Burgesses of the Twelve Shires of WALES and of the County of Monmouth: For remedy whereof be it declared and enacted by the King's most excellent Majesty the Lords Spiritual and Temporal, and Commons in this present Parliament assembled, and by the Authority of the same, That it shall and may be lawful to and for all and every his Majesty's Subjects inhabiting or dwelling, or which at any Time hereafter shall inhabit or dwell within the said Dominion of WALES, or any part thereof, freely to sell by way of a Barter or otherwise, all or any their WELSH Cloths Cottons Frizes Linings or Plains, at their Wills and Pleasures, to any person or persons who lawfully by the Laws and Statutes of this Realm may buy the same; And that it shall and may also be lawful for any person and persons who by the Laws or Statutes of this Realm may lawfully buy such Cloths and other the premisses, freely to buy the same of any person or persons inhabiting or dwelling or which hereafter shall inhabit or dwell within the Dominion of WALES: Any Charter, Grant, Act, Order or any Thing else heretofore made or done, or hereafter to be made or done to the contrary notwithstanding.

2. And be it further enacted by the Authority aforesaid, That it shall and may be lawful to and for any person or persons using or which shall use the Trade of Merchandise, to transport into any the parts beyond the Seas any of the said WELSH Cloths Cottons Frizes Linings and Plains, out of any Ports or Havens within this Realm of England or Dominion of WALES, or out of any the Members thereof where his Majesty his Heirs or Successors have or shall then have Officers attending to search view and control the same, and to receive the King's Majesty's Customs and other Duties due and payable for the same; So as always the Customs and other Duties payable for such Cloths and other the premisses so to be transported, shall be justly and duly paid for the same; And so as

always the said WELSH Cloths Cottons Frizes Linings and Plains before the transporting thereof, shall be frilled cottoned and sheared as in former times they have used to be; And that no person shall transport the said Cloths in other manner than as aforesaid, upon pain to forfeit the whole Value of such Cloths so to be transported contrary to the true meaning of this Act, the one half of all which Forfeitures to be to his Majesty, his Heirs and Successors, and the other half to such person or persons as will sue for the same by Information Bill Plaint Action of Debt or otherwise, in any of his Majesty's Courts of Record, wherein no Essoign Protection Privilege or Ley Gager shall be allowed to the Defendant.

3. This Act to endure and continue for the term of Seven years from the end of this Session of Parliament, and from thenceforth to the end of the next Session of Parliament ensuing after the end of those Seven years.

4. Provided always, That this Act or any thing therein contained, shall not give Power or Authority to any Foreigner or Foreigners to buy and sell by way of Retail any of the said WELSH Cloths Cottons Frizes Linings or Plains within the Town of Shrewsbury, or in any other Corporate Town or privileged Place, contrary to any lawful Charter Grant Custom Privilege or Liberty in the same Town or Place now being or used.

A.D. 1623-4]

21 James 1, c. 10.

AN ACT OF REPEAL OF ONE BRANCH OF THE STATUTE MADE IN THE 34TH YEAR OF KING HENRY THE EIGHTH (C. 26), GIVING THE KING POWER TO ALTER THE LAWS OF WALES.

Whereas the Subjects of the Country and Dominion of WALES have been constantly loyal and obedient, and have lived in all dutiful subjection to the Crown of England; And whereas by an Act of Parliament made in the four and thirtieth year of the Reign of the late King HENRY 8, entituled an Act for certain Ordinances in the King's Majesty's Dominion and Principality of WALES, amongst other Things it is enacted and ordained in these Words: Item, it is further enacted by the authority aforesaid, That the King's most Royal Majesty shall and may at all times hereafter from time to time change add alter order minish and reform all manner of Things afore rehearsed as to his most excellent Wisdom and Discretion shall be thought convenient, and also to make Laws and Ordinances for the Commonwealth and good Quiet of his said Dominion of WALES, and his Subjects of the same, from time to time at his Majesty's Pleasure; Any thing contained in this Act or in the said Act made for the Shire Grounds of WALES, or any other Act or Acts, Thing or Things to the contrary thereof heretofore made in any wise notwithstanding; And that all such Alterations of the premisses, or any part thereof, and all such Laws and Ordinances to be hereafter made devised and published by authority of this Act, by the King's Majesty in Writing under his Highness's Great Seal, shall be of as good Strength, Virtue and Effect as if they had been had and made by authority of Parliament; And Forasmuch as it is manifest by long Experience that the Laws and Statutes already ordained for the said Country are in effect and for the most part agreeable to the Laws and Statutes of this his Highness's Kingdom of England, and all and every of the same obeyed with great alacrity; And for that after so long a Quiet amongst them any future Change or Innovation herein would be dangerous and for the Abolition of distinction and difference between the Subjects of England and WALES, his most excellent Majesty tendering the common and constant good of the said Country and Dominion of WALES, and of their Posterity for ever hereafter is graciously pleased, that it may be enacted by his Majesty with the Assent of the Lords Spiritual and Temporal and the Commons in this present Parliament assembled, And be it enacted by the authority of the same, That the said recited Branch of the said Act of Parliament, and every Article, Word and Sentence in that Branch contained, be utterly repealed and made void and of none effect to all Intents Constructions and Purposes, as if the said Branch had never been made or contained in the said Act: And that the King's Majesty his Heirs or Successors shall not by Virtue of the said Clause or Branch of the said Act, at any time hereafter alter change or reform any Laws Usage or Custom, or make any new Laws for or concerning the said Dominion or Principality of WALES.

2. Provided always and be it enacted by the Authority aforesaid, That all and every Clause Article and thing contained in the aforesaid Act of Parliament, other than the aforesaid Branch before recited, shall stand remain and be in as full Force and Effect to all Intents Constructions and Purposes as if this present Act had never been had or made.

A.D. 1623-4] 21 James 1, c. 28, ss. 5, 11.

An Act concerning Welsh Cottons and repealing laws of Henry 4 and Henry 6 against Welshmen.

5. Provided also and be it enacted, That no person or persons shall incur any penalty for want of Length Breadth or Weight of Welsh Cottons under the price of Fifteen pence the yard or two shillings the Goad, so as they be not mixed with Hair or other deceitful Stuff, nor for any others above that price, except they be mixed as aforesaid, or shall shrink above the rate of half a yard in twelve yards in length, or weigh less than fourteen ounces the yard, or hold not full three quarters of a yard broad.

11. . . . And one Statute made in the second year of the Reign of the late King Henry 4, by which it is enacted, That no Welshman whole born in Wales and having Father and Mother born in Wales, shall purchase Lands and Tenements within the Town of Chester and other places named in that Act; and that no Welshman shall be chosen a Citizen or Burgess in any City Borough or Merchant Town, and that Welshmen be not put in certain Offices, nor bear Arms, and every Clause thereof; And one other Statute made in the same year, concerning Arrests made by the Inhabitants of Wales, and driving of Distresses into Wales; And one other Statute made in the same year, concerning Welshmen entering into the Counties adjoining, and in the same do burn kill ravish or commit any other Felony or Trespass; And one other Statute made in the same year, by which it is enacted, That the Lords of the Marches of Wales shall ordain and set sufficient Stuffing and Ward in their Castles and Seigniories of Wales; And one other Statute made in the same year, by which it is established, That no Welshman be received to purchase Lands or Tenements within England nor within the Boroughs or English Towns of Wales, Nor that no Welshman should be accepted Burgess nor to have any other Liberty within the Realm nor within the Boroughs and Towns aforesaid, and every Clause in every the said Statutes made in the said second year; And one Statute made in the fourth year of the Reign of the late King Henry 4, whereby it is ordained, That no Englishman liege to the King be convicted by any Welshman, nor that English Burgesses which have married Welsh women, have Franchises with English Burgesses; And one other Statute made in the same year, by which

it is ordained, That no Congregations be made or suffered to be made by the WELSHMEN but as in the said Statute is appointed: And one other Statute made in the same year, concerning sending and bringing Merchandise and Armour into WALES; And one other Statute made in the same year, concerning WELSHMEN not having of Castle Fortress or House of Defence to keep; And one other Statute made in the same year, That WELSHMEN shall not be made Justice Chamberlain nor have certain other Offices in the said Statute mentioned; And one other Statute made in the same year, concerning storing of the Castles and Towns in WALES with English; And one other Statute made in the same year, That Englishmen marrying WELSH Women shall not be put in Offices, and every Clause of the said Statute made in the said fourth year; And one Statute made in the ninth year of the Reign of the said late King HENRY 4, concerning Felonies and Robberies done within any Seigniory of SOUTH WALES; And so much of one Statute made in the five and twentieth year of the Reign of the late King HENRY 6 as concerneth the confirming of Statutes made before that time against WELSHMEN and making void grants of Franchise made to WELSHMEN, and concerning Villains in WALES; . . . shall be by virtue of this Act repealed.

A.D. 1640–1] **16 Charles 1, c. 10, ss. 4, 9.**

AN ACT FOR REGULATING THE PRIVY COUNCIL AND FOR TAKING AWAY THE STAR CHAMBER JURISDICTION EXERCISED BEFORE THE COUNCIL IN WALES.

4. And be it likewise enacted, That the like Jurisdiction now used and exercised in the Court before the President and Council in the Marches of WALES and also in the Court before the President and Council established in the Northern parts And also in the Court commonly called the Court of the Duchy of Lancaster held &c. . . . shall from the said first day of August One thousand six hundred forty and one be also repealed and absolutely revoked and made void, Any Law &c. to the contrary thereof and any wise notwithstanding And that from henceforth no Court Council or place of Judicature shall be erected ordained constituted or appointed within this Realm of England or Dominion of WALES which shall have, use or exercise the same or the like jurisdiction as is or

hath been used practised or exercised in the said Court of Star Chamber.

9. Provided always and be it enacted, That this Act and the several Clauses therein contained shall be taken and expounded to extend only to the Court of Star Chamber and to the said Courts holden before the President and Council in the Marches of WALES and before the President and Council in the Northern parts and also to the Court commonly called the Court of the Duchy of Lancaster holden &c., &c.

A.D. 1648] **Commonwealth Statute.**

AN ACT CONCERNING THE SEQUESTRATION OF SOUTH WALES AND COUNTY OF MONMOUTH.

Whereas the several Counties of South WALES, viz. :—Glamorgan, Pembroke, Carmarthen, Cardigan, Radnor, Brecon and the County of Monmouth were at the beginning of these Wars under the command of the King's Forces and so continued for many years ; By which means the generality of the said Counties according to several Ordinances made this present Parliament, are liable to Sequestration for aiding and assisting the Forces raised against the Parliament : And whereas there be in the said Counties divers desperate malignants that have maliciously endeavoured the subversion of Parliaments and the freedom of the People ; And there being also many people that have been forced in some things to comply with them, to preserve themselves and families from spoil and ruin ; Now to the end some distinction may be made whereby exemplary Justice may be done on the most capital Offenders, and the more moderate punishment be inflicted on the lesser, now involved in a general guilt ; The Commons assembled in this present Parliament, taking the same into their consideration, Do hereby enact, And be it enacted by this present Parliament, and by Authority of the same, in relation to the said lesser Offenders, That a fine be imposed on the said several Counties for their respective Delinquencies : viz., on the County of Pembroke £3500. On the County of Cardigan £3000. On the County of Carmarthen the sum of £4000. On the County of Glamorgan the sum of £3500. On the County of Brecon the sum of £2000. On the County of Monmouth the sum of £3000. On the County of Radnor the sum of £1500. Which said sums are to be paid by the respective

Counties in manner and form following, viz:—The first moiety amounting to the sum of Ten thousand two hundred and fifty pounds within ten weeks after the passing of this Act, and the moiety of the said Fine being Ten thousand two hundred and fifty pounds of the said Fine within Ten weeks next following the payment of the said first moiety To be paid to the Treasurers at Wars for the Army who are hereby authorized to receive the same, and any two of them to give Receipts under their Hands and Seals, which Receipts shall be a sufficient Discharge to the said respective Counties, for payment of the said sums of money imposed on them by virtue of this Act for their Delinquencies: And that the said moneys may be the better levied, raised and paid, and with most equality, according to the Estates and Delinquencies of persons, and that the innocent and well affected may not be molested, Be it enacted by the Authority aforesaid, That Sir Erasmus Philips, Baronet, Thomas Horton, Henry Herbert, Michael Owldesworth, Thomas Wogan, William Herbert, Busey Mancell, Edward Prichard, William Jones, Thomas Morgan, Philip Jones, Edmond Morgan, Rowland Dawkins, John Price, John Herbert, Edward Stradling, Christopher Catchmay, Walter Cuney, William Barber, Edward Herbert, Silvanus Taylor, Peter Price, Ralph Grundy, Henry Bowen, Roger Williams, Edward Games, Henry Williams, William Fleming, Roger Lort, James Phillips, Sampson Lort, James Lewis, John Williams, Lewis Jones, John Danzy, William Watkins of Sheaphouse, John Elliot, Griffith Lloyd, Esqs., and William Sudgon, Gent., be appointed Commissioners for the several Counties and places herein mentioned, who, or any three of them, have hereby full power and authority to remove all obstructions that may hinder the carrying on of the said work, and to supervise and regulate proceedings to their best judgement, according to the true intent and meaning of this Act: Provided, That no person well affected, be Rated, or Taxed, or compelled to pay any Rate or Tax towards raising the said Fines; But if any Delinquent, or person liable to Sequestration within the said Counties, shall refuse to pay his or their proportion towards raising the said Fines set on the several Counties by virtue of this Act, and according to the time limited for payment of the same, he or they so refusing, are not to have any benefit or immunity by this Act, but are left to be proceeded with according to the Ordinance of Sequestrations. And it is further Enacted and Provided, That this Act shall not extend to discharge or pardon any person excepted from pardon in the Propositions presented to the King at Hampton Court. Provided also this shall not extend to free or pardon for their several Delinquencies against the Parliament, Edward Earl of Worcester, Lord of Bergavenny, Richard Lord of Cherbury, Sir Trevor Williams, Baronet, Sir Philip Jones, Knight, Sir George Probert, Knight, Sir Hugh Owen, Knight, Edward Kemys of Kemis, William Morgan of Pencrigge, Henry Probert, Roger Williams of Kevenhiley, Esqs. Thomas Hughes of Llanfethrin, Major Lewis Thomas, James Jones of Llanvihangel Lanternam, Gent., Of the County of Monmouth, Sir Charles Kemeis, Knight and Baronet, Sir John Awbrey, Knight, Sir Richard Basset, Knight, Sir Henry Stradling, Knight, Sir Edward Thomas, Baronet, Miles Button, Humphrey Matthews, Henry Mauncel, Thomas Stradling, Robert Thomas, John Thomas of Merthwr of the County of Glamorgan, Esqs., Sir John Stepney, Baronet, Sir Rice Rudd, Baronet, Sir George Vaughan, Knight, Henry Floid, Walter Floid, and Thomas Phillips, Esquires, Of the County of Carmarthen, Sir Walter Floid, Sir Francis Floid, Knights, and John Floid of Crunrin, Esquires, Of the County of Cardigan, Herbert Price, Hoe Gaines, John Jeffreys, John Williams of the Park, John Herbert, Lewis Morgan, Lewis Floid, Thomas Price, John Price, Sir Francis Fane, Knight, Marmaduke Floid, Esq, William Floid, William Saunders, Gent, Of the County of Brecon, Major General Laughorn, Colonel Powell, Colonel Poyer, John Barton of Slebitch, Lewis Barlow and William Philips, Esqs, Of the County of Pembroke, Sir John Culpepper, Bryan Crowther, Hugh Floid, Banyham, Vaughan, Howell Floid, Esqs., Sir Edmond Sawyer, Knight, and Robert Martin, of the County of Radnor, Esquires: Provided also, this shall not extend to free or pardon any Clergyman that for Scandal or Delinquency is sequestered or liable to Sequestration. Provided, this shall not extend to set at liberty any person that is a prisoner of war. Provided also That this shall not extend to make any person capable to bear Office in the Commonwealth, contrary to any former Ordinances of Parliament, without the consent of Parliament. Provided also, That such persons as are not worth Eight pounds per annum, or One hundred pounds in personal estate be not liable to pay towards the said Fines imposed on the said several Counties, but are hereby freely pardoned and discharged for their said Delinquencies. And it is further Enacted and Declared by the Authority aforesaid, That all persons inhabiting in the said Counties of Glamorgan, Pembroke, Carmarthen, Cardigan, Brecon, Radnor and Monmouth are hereby pardoned for any Delinquency or Offence committed against the Parliament to the time of the passing of this Act, and are hereby fully acquitted and discharged from all Sequestrations or other Molestations whatsoever by reason thereof, and are to be restored to their respective Estates, and are also to be discharged of all Bonds and Securities entered into to the Commissioners appointed by Ordinance of Parliament bearing date the 19th of June 1648 or any acting by or under them, for payment of any moneys by reason of their said Delinquency (except such persons as are by this Act excepted and provided against and except such Counties as shall not pay in their said Fines according to the appointment of this Act). And it is further Enacted by the Authority aforesaid That if any person or persons within the said Counties shall after the passing of this Act, contrary to his and their duties, and to the disturbance of the Peace of the Kingdom, raise any Forces tending to the levying of a new War, without Authority of this present Parliament, or Commission from the Lord General, or shall join with any such person or Forces, or shall be aiding or assisting to any Forces whatsoever contrary to the aforesaid Authorities, he or they are hereby declared Traitors and uncapable of any Pardon, and their Estates confiscated to the use of the Commonwealth: And be it enacted by the Authority aforesaid That the power given to the Commissioners named in the said Ordinance of Parliament bearing date the 19th of June last, shall from henceforth extend no further than to the Sequestrations of such Delinquents Estates as are excepted in this Act.

A.D. 1649] **Commonwealth Statute.**

"An Act for the better Propagation and Preaching of the Gospel in WALES, and Redress of some Grievances.

"The Parliament of England, taking into their serious consideration the great duty and trust that lies on them to use all lawful ways and means for the propagation of the Gospel of Jesus Christ in this Commonwealth, in order thereunto, do enact and ordain, and be it enacted and ordained by this present Parliament, and by the authority thereof, that Col. Thomas Harrison, Col. Philip Jones, Col. John Jones, Sir John Trevor, Knight, Henry Herbert, Esq., William Herbert, William Parker, William Blethin, Christopher Catchmay, Reese Williams, John Nicholas, Edward Herbert, Robert Jones, Bussey Mansel, Edward Prichard, John Price, Rowland Dawkins, William Botteler, Edward Stradling, John Herbert, Richard Jones, Jenkin Franklyn, John James, Wroth Rogers, John Herring, Stephen Winthrop, Esqrs.; Sir Erasmus Phillips, Samson Lort, Henry Williams, Silvanus Taylor, Richard King, John Williams, John Dancy, Thomas Watkins, James Phillips, John Lewis, William Barber, Esqrs.; John Daniel, John Bowen, Gent., John Puleston, one of the Justices of the Court of Common Pleas, Humphrey Mackworth, William Littleton, Robert Duckenfield, Thomas Baker, Hugh Price, Evan Lloyd, Richard Price, Robert Griffith, Edward Owens, George Twistleton, George Carter, Thomas Mason, Lighton Owens, Rice Vaughan, Thomas Ball, Hugh Courtney, Edward Taylor, Roger Soutley, Esqrs.; Daniel Lloyd, David Morris, William Wynne, Gentlemen; Thomas Swift, Esq.; Hugh Richard, Gent.; John Saddler, John Peck, Luke Lloyd, Andrew Ellis, Ralph Crechley, Esqrs.; Lewis Price, of Llanwenog, Henry Williams, John Brown, Gent., are hereby constituted and appointed to be Commissioners in the counties of Montgomery, Denbigh, Flint, Caernarvon, Merioneth, Anglesea, Monmouth, Glamorgan, Pembroke, Caermarthen, Cardigan, Brecknock, and Radnor, and every one of them, to put in execution the several powers and authorities hereinafter mentioned and directed (that is to say), that they, the said Commissioners, or any five or more of them, shall have full power and authority, and are hereby enabled and authorized to receive all articles or charges which shall be exhibited against any parson, vicar, curate, schoolmaster, or any other now having, or that shall have, any ecclesiastical benefit or promotion within the said counties or any of them, for any delinquency, scandal, malignancy, or non-residency, and upon such articles so exhibited to grant out warrants in writing under the hands and seals of the said Commissioners, or any five or more of them, to be directed to the party against whom such articles shall be exhibited, requiring his appearance before such Commissioners at a certain day and place in the said warrant mentioned, to answer the said charge or articles respectively, and after notice of the said warrant personally made or given to the said party articled against, or left at his dwelling-house or ordinary place of abode, and that notice proved by oath to be made by the space of ten days before the day of appearance in the said warrant mentioned (no just cause being made and proved to excuse the not appearing), and likewise after answer made by such as shall appear according to summons, then the said Commissioners, or any five or more of them, are hereby enabled and authorized to proceed to examination of witnesses on oath; the said examinations and depositions of such witnesses to be put in writing, as well on the behalf of the Commonwealth to prove such articles, as on the behalf of the parties articled against to make good their answers; which oaths the said Commissioners, or any two or more of them, have hereby power to administer; and after due examination and proof made by confession of the party complained of, or by the oath of two credible witnesses, actually to amove, discharge, and eject all such ministers and other persons from their respective cures, benefices, places, and charges, as they the said Commissioners, or any five or more of them, upon such hearing shall adjudge to be guilty of any of the crimes aforesaid, in the said articles contained and comprised; and after such judgment given, in case any person shall find himself aggrieved with such judgment so given, then it shall and may be lawful to and for any twelve or more of the said Commissioners, upon petition preferred to them by the party grieved, to review, examine, and reverse the same, if they or the greater part of them see just cause so to do; and if notwithstanding the said ejected person shall not find relief within six weeks after his petition so preferred, then the said Commissioners, or any five or more of them, shall at the request of the parties aggrieved respectively, certify the respective proceedings and proofs in such cases respectively, to the Committee of Parliament for Plundered Ministers; who are hereby authorized, upon the return of such certificates, and view of such proceedings and proofs, without further examination of witnesses in such cases, to examine the grounds of the said respective judgments appealed from, and to affirm or revoke the same, as they shall find it most agreeable to justice, and the tenor of this Act.

"And be it further enacted and declared, that the said Commissioners, or any five or more of them, have hereby power and authority to allow the wife and children of such minister or ministers so ejected and amoved, for their maintenance, a proportion not exceeding a fifth part of the living, parsonage, benefice, vicarage, charge, or other place, out of which the said ministers shall be respectively removed (all parish charges, public taxes, and other duties being first deducted out of the whole).

"And be it further enacted by the authority aforesaid, that if any Parson or Vicar holdeth or enjoyeth, or which shall hold or enjoy, plurality of benefices or ecclesiastical promotions (one or more of which being within the counties aforesaid), and upon a warrant directed to him under the hands of the said Commissioners, or any five of them, requiring him at a certain day and place in the said warrant mentioned, to make choice and elect which of the said benefices and ecclesiastical promotions he desires to hold; and upon notice of the said warrant, shall not within forty days after the said notice make his election, testified under his hand before five or more of the said Commissioners, which of the said benefices or promotions he desires to hold, then from and after such default (no just cause being proved to excuse the same) all his right, title, or interest in and to all such benefices and promotions, to cease, determine, and be utterly void. And to the end that godly and painful men, of able gifts and knowledge for the work of the ministry, and of approved conversation for piety, may be employed to preach the Gospel in the counties aforesaid (which heretofore abounded in ignorance and profaneness); and that fit persons, of approved piety and learning, may have encouragement to employ themselves in the education of children in piety and good literature;

"Be it enacted by the authority aforesaid, that the said Commissioners, or any five or more of them, be and are authorized and enabled to grant certificates by way of approbation to such persons as shall be recommended and approved of by Henry Walter, Walter Cradock, Richard Simonds, Roger Charnock, Jenkin Lloyd, Morris Bidwel, David Walter, William Seaborn, Edmond Ellis, Jenkin Jones, George Robinson, Richard Powel, Robert Powel, Thomas Ewen, John Miles, Oliver Thomas, Doctor John Ellis, Ambrose Moston, Stephen Lewis, Morgan Lloyd, William Jones, Richard Edwards, Vavasour Powel, Richard Swain, Rowland Nevet, ministers of the Gospel, or any five or more of them, for the preaching of the Gospel in the said counties, as well in settled congregations and parochial charges, as in an itinerary course, as the said Commissioners (by the advice of such of the said ministers as shall recommend and approve of the said persons respectively), shall adjudge to be most for the advancement of the Gospel, or for the keeping of schools and education of children. And to the end that a fitting maintenance may be provided for such persons as shall be so recommended and approved of, as also for such others approved by godly and painful ministers now residing within the said counties, for whose support and maintenance there is little or no settlement made or provided;

"Be it therefore enacted and ordained by the authority aforesaid, that in order to the said maintenance, and in the regulating, ordering, and disposal thereof, they, the said Commissioners, or any twelve or more of them, are hereby authorized and enabled by themselves, or others deriving authority from them, to receive and dispose of all and singular the rents, issues, and profits of all and every the Rectories, Vicarages, Donatives, Sine Curas, portion of tenths, and other ecclesiastical livings, which now are or hereafter shall be in the disposing of the Parliament, or any other deriving authority from them: as also to receive and dispose of the rents, issues, and profits of all impropriations and glebe lands within the said counties which now are or hereafter shall be under the sequestration or in the disposal of the Parliament, by virtue of any former statute, or any Act or ordinance of this present Parliament.

"And be it further enacted by the authority aforesaid, that the said Commissioners, or any five or more of them, shall and may out of the said rents, issues, and profits of the said Rectories, Vicarages, Donatives, Sine Curas, portion of tenths and other ecclesiastical promotions; as also out of the rents, issues, and profits of the said impropriations and glebe lands, order and appoint a constant yearly maintenance for such persons as shall be recommended and approved of as aforesaid for the work of the ministry or the education of children; as also for such other ministers as aforesaid, now residing within the said counties; provided that the yearly maintenance of a minister does not exceed one hundred pounds, and the yearly maintenance of a schoolmaster exceed not forty pounds. And that godly ministers who have or shall have wife or children, may not too much be taken off from their duties in the ministry, with the care and consideration of maintenance for their wives and children, after their decease, but that some care thereof may be had by others, whereby a greater encouragement may be given to them to set themselves the closer to the work of the said ministry;

"Be it enacted by the authority aforesaid, that the said Commissioners, or any twelve or more of them, are hereby enabled and authorized to make such yearly allowance to the wife and children of such godly minister after his decease, as to the said Commissioners, or any twelve of them, shall seem reasonable, for the necessary support and maintenance of the said wife and children, or any of them: provided always that such allowance so to be made to such wife and children do not exceed the yearly sum of thirty pounds: and if any person or persons, being tenants, occupier of any lands, tenements, or hereditaments, liable and subject to the payment of any tenths, or other duties, in right payable or belonging to any Parsonage, Vicarage, or any the abovesaid ecclesiastical promotions, shall refuse payment thereof, then the said Commissioners, or any two or more of them, are hereby authorized and enabled to put in execution against every person and persons so refusing, the powers and authorities vested and settled by this present Parliament in the Justices of the Peace for the relief of ministers from whom such tenths and duties are detained and subtracted.

"And be it further enacted by the authority aforesaid, that the said Commissioners, or any twelve or more of them, out of the said tenths, rents, and profits, by them receivable by force of this Act, shall and may allow such moderate salary or wages to such person or persons who shall be employed in the receiving, keeping and disposal thereof, or any part thereof, as they shall conceive to be necessary and reasonable.

"And be it further enacted by the authority aforesaid, and all and every person or persons qualified and approved of as abovesaid, for the preaching of the Gospel as aforesaid, who shall be vested or settled by the said Commissioners, or any twelve or more of them, in any Rectory, Vicarage, or parochial charge, which the said Commissioners or any twelve or more of them have hereby power to do, shall be deemed and adjudged to be seized of the same, as fully and amply to all intents and purposes, as if such person and persons were presented, instituted, and inducted to and in the same, according to former laws in such cases used and provided. And whereas the remoteness of the said counties from the Courts of Justice at Westminster, occasioneth many acts of high misdemeanours, oppression, and injury to be committed there, which oftentimes escape unpunished, and the parties aggrieved thereby, for want of means to seek relief by due course of law, left remediless; to the end therefore that such misdemeanours, oppressions, and injuries, may the better be inquired after, and the parties aggrieved thereby, without much expense of moneys, or loss of time, may be in some way of relief;

"Be it enacted by the authority aforesaid, that the said Commissioners, or any five or more of them, shall have and hereby have full power and authority to receive all complaints which shall be brought before them, of any such misdemeanours, oppression, or injury, committed by any person or persons within the said counties or any of them; and by warrant directed to the party complained of, under the hands and seals of the said Commissioners, or any five or more of them, to appear before them at a certain day and place in the said warrant mentioned, requiring an answer to the said complaints: and after answer made, then, with the consent of both parties, testified under their hands and seals, to proceed to hear and determine the same. And whereas sufferings of that nature generally fall upon persons well affected to the Parliament, and such as have acted in and for their service, which said persons are not of ability to travel to London, to be relieved by the Committee of Parliament commonly called the Committee of Indemnity;

"Be it therefore enacted and ordained by the authority aforesaid, that the said Commissioners, or any five or more of them, shall be and are hereby made and constituted a Committee of Indemnity, to all intents and purposes, within the counties aforesaid, for the hearing and determining of all matters and things properly relievable and determinable by the said Committee of Indemnity. Provided always, that if any person or persons shall find him or themselves aggrieved at the proceedings of the said Commissioners acting as a Committee of Indemnity, then the said person or persons so aggrieved shall and may prosecute his and their petition or appeal for relief, in such manner and form as in and by this Act is prescribed in the cases of ejected ministers, and bring the same to a final determination, before the said Committee of Indemnity sitting at Westminster, which said Committee are hereby authorized to hear and determine the same, as they shall see just cause.

"And be it further enacted, that all power and authority formerly vested in any Committee within the said counties, or any of them, for the placing of ministers in ecclesiastical livings or promotions, be from henceforth determined: and that no person or persons shall be from henceforth vested and settled in any Rectory, Vicarage, or any ecclesiastical promotion within any of the said counties, unless such person or persons so to be vested or settled, be recommended and approved of for the work of the ministry, according to the tenor and true meaning of this Act: and that this Act shall continue and be in force for the space of three years, from the Five-and-twentieth day of March, One thousand six hundred and fifty, and no longer.

"Die Veneris, 22 Februarii, 1649. Ordered by the Parliament, that this Act be forthwith printed and published."

A.D. 1649] Commonwealth Statute.

AN ACT FOR THE ADMITTING OF THE SIX COUNTIES OF NORTH WALES TO A GENERAL COMPOSITION FOR THEIR DELINQUENCY.

Whereas the five Counties of NORTH WALES; viz:—Montgomery, Denbigh, Flint, Merioneth and Carnarvon, with the Island of Anglesey, have been for many years together, since the beginning of these late Wars, wholly under the power of the late King's Army and Forces; by reason whereof many well affected persons to the Parliament within the said Counties have been forced through compulsion or fear, for the avoiding of present ruin to themselves and families, to comply with the said Forces in unwarrantable acts and engagements, whereby they are become involved in a general guilt and defection from the Parliament and the authority thereof: The Commons of England assembled in Parliament (at the humble and earnest Request of divers of the Inhabitants of the said Counties) taking the same into serious consideration, and being willing that some distinction may be made between such persons as have been eminently active in the raising and promoting of the said War and those that were moved by constraint or fear to a compliance with the Enemy being under their power and are now resolved to adhere to the Interest of this Commonwealth, as it is now established; and being likewise willing that such money as is by any Ordinance or Order of Parliament charged upon the Estates of new Delinquents in NORTH WALES, and payable to persons well affected to the Parliament, and to the present Constitution of this Commonwealth should be paid accordingly, Do Declare and Ordain, and be it Ordained and Enacted by this present Parliament and the Authority of the same, that the Inhabitants of the said five Counties of NORTH WALES, viz:—Montgomery, Denbigh, Flint,

Carnarvon and Merioneth and of the said Island and County of Anglesey, and every of them (except such persons as are hereafter in this Act excepted) be and are hereby admitted to a general Composition; and that the sum of Four and Twenty Thousand pounds be raised upon the said five Counties and the said Island and County of Anglesey; that is to say, On the County of Montgomery, the sum of Three thousand pounds; on the County of Denbigh, the sum of Three thousand pounds; on the County of Flint, the sum of Two thousand pounds; on the County of Carnarvon, the sum of Four thousand pounds; on the County of Merioneth, the sum of Three thousand pounds; on the Island and County of Anglesey the sum of Nine thousand pounds, to be paid in manner and form following, that is to say, the first moiety amounting to the sum of Twelve thousand pounds within Ten weeks after the passing of this Act, and the other moiety being Twelve thousand pounds to be paid within Ten weeks then next ensuing, which said sum of Four and Twenty thousand pounds is to be paid to the Treasurers at War for the Army, who are hereby authorized to receive the same, and any two of them to give receipts and acquittances under their hands and seals for the same; which said receipts or acquittances shall be a sufficient discharge to all intents and purposes to the said respective Counties and Island, and unto such as they shall appoint to pay the same according to the true intent of this Act: And to the end the said sum of Four and Twenty thousand pounds may be equally and indifferently taxed, proportioned and levied upon the respective Inhabitants of the said Counties unto whom the benefit of this Act is to extend; Be it further Enacted by the Authority aforesaid, That Thomas Mitton, John Jones, John Carter, George Twisleton, Thomas Mason, Thomas Madrin, Edmund Glyn, Esqs., Robert Soutley, Esq., Thomas Bale, Esq., John Peck, Esq., Richard Bassnet, Gent.; Edward Wyn, Esq., Thomas Crichley, Gent., Daniel Lloid, Gent., Watkin Kyffin, Gent., William Wyn, Gent., Gerard Barbour, Esq., Gruffith Glin, Gent., Richard Anwil, Esq., Captain Thomas Pugh, Lewis Lloid, Esq., Peter Marick, Esq., Major Edward Moor, Roger Haumer, Esq., Sir John Trevor, Knight, John Puleston, Esq., one of the Justices of the Common Pleas, Thomas Ravenscroft, Esq., John Aldersey, Esq., Luke Lloid, Humphrey Dymmock, Esqs., Andrew Ellis, Esq , Thomas Dymmock, Esquire, Daniel Matthews, Gent., Hugh Courtney, Gent., Sir John Wittewrong, Knight, Evan

Lloid, Hugh Price, Richard Price, Richard Gruffith, Robert Gruffith, Rice Vaughan, Esqs., Samuel Big, Gent., Edward Owen of Castle-Dail, Owen Salusbury, Esq., Gruffith Hanney, John Lloyd, Lewis Owen, Robert Vaughan, Esqs., Robert Owen, Thomas Michael, Gent., William Williams, Esquire, be and hereby are constituted and appointed Commissioners for the said several and respective Counties and Island; which said Commissioners or any five of them have hereby full power and authority to do all and every such Act and Acts as may further the rating and collecting of the said sum of Twenty four Thousand pounds upon the said respective Counties and Island in the manner and proportion aforesaid; and to remove all lets and obstructions and determine all differences that may hinder the effectual prosecution of this Work, and to supervise and regulate proceedings to the best of their Judgments, according to the true intent and meaning of this Act.

Provided always, That no well affected person in any of the said Counties and Island be compelled to pay any Rate or Tax towards the raising of the said sums or any of them. Provided also, That this Act shall not extend to discharge or pardon any person excepted from pardon, or from Composition for his Estate, by the Propositions sent to the late King at Newcastle, nor by any Act, Order or Vote of Parliament not yet repealed.

2. Nor any Member of Parliament that hath deserted his Trust and adhered to the Enemy.

3. Nor any person that hath assisted the Irish Rebellion, or held correspondency or Intelligence with the Rebels in Ireland.

4. Nor any person that having been in Arms against the Parliament, doth reside in France or Ireland, or in any other Parts beyond the Seas.

5. Nor any person that hath given Intelligence to, or held correspondency in any thing against the Parliament, with Charles Stuart, the late King's son, or his Adherents in any of the parts beyond the seas.

6. Nor any Delinquent, or otherwise scandalous Minister or Clergyman (as to Ecclesiastical Promotions only) that is already duly sequestered or sequestrable nor at all to pardon such of them as have plotted or contrived the Revolt of the said Island of Anglesey.

7. Nor any Papists in arms, nor any other Papists for the two thirds of their Estates sequestered or sequesterable, according

to former Orders or Ordinances of Parliament for their Nonconformity.

8. Nor any persons that are now Prisoners of War.

9. Nor any person that hath public money in his hands for which he ought to accompt, and shall not discover and pay the same to the Treasurers for the Army, for the use of the Commonwealth, within three months after the passing of this Act. Provided further that this Act shall not extend to discharge any person that hath his Fine set at Goldsmith's Hall, from the payment of the same to the Treasurers there accordingly. Provided also That this Act shall not extend to make any person capable to bear any Office in the Commonwealth, contrary to any former Act or Ordinance of Parliament, without consent of Parliament.

Provided likewise, and be it further Enacted by the authority aforesaid That all persons within the said respective Counties and Island that have been engaged against the Parliament (not comprised within the former Exceptions, Qualifications or Crimes, to the discharging or pardoning whereof this Act is not to extend), that are not worth in Lands Four pounds per annum, or in personal Estate Forty pounds, and shall declare unto the said Commissioners or any five of them their firm resolutions faithfully to adhere to the interest of this Commonwealth, shall not be taxed or compelled to pay any part of the said sum of Twenty four thousand pounds, but are hereby freely pardoned and discharged of their Delinquency: And be it further Enacted by the Authority aforesaid, That all the Inhabitants in the said several and respective Counties of Montgomery, Denbigh, Flint, Merioneth and Carnarvon, and in the said Island of Anglesey, (that have Estates above the Values aforesaid in the said respective Counties) or any of them (except the persons before excepted and comprised in the said former Qualifications, and unto whom the benefit of this Act is not to extend) and shall duly pay their proportions of the said sum of Twenty four thousand pounds, according to the true meaning of this Act, and constantly and faithfully adhere to the present established interest of this Nation, be and are pardoned and acquitted of and for any Act of Delinquency or Offence committed or done by them, or any of them against the Parliament to the time of the passing of this Act; And are hereby permitted to enjoy all their several and respective estates without molestation to all intents and purposes whatsoever, free from any Act done or to be done against them or any of them by virtue colour or pretence of any Act Ordinance or Order of Parliament for Sequestration of Delinquents estates. Provided moreover And be it Enacted and Ordained by the authority aforesaid That if any person or persons that have complyed with the late King's Forces, or are lyable to Sequestration within the said several and respective Counties and Island of Anglesey, or any of them, shall refuse to pay his or their proportion, as the same shall be rated or taxed and approved of by the said Commissioners or any five of them (towards the raising of the aforesaid fine) within the time herein limited for the payment of the same, such person and persons so refusing are not to have any benefit or immunity by this Act, but are left to be effectually proceeded against according to the several Ordinances of Sequestrations. And be it further Enacted by the Authority aforesaid, That such sum and sums of money as are by Ordinance or Order of Parliament charged upon the estates of New Delinquents in NORTH WALES, and payable to persons well affected to the Parliament and to the present Constitution of this Commonwealth (not exceeding in the whole the sum of Four thousand pounds) be according to the true intent and meaning of the said several Ordinances and Orders, paid and discharged out of the said sum of Twenty four thousand pounds. And the Treasurers at Wars are authorized and required to pay and discharge the same accordingly; And to the end this present Act, and the several former Ordinances of Sequestrations may be better put in execution, Be it further Enacted by the Authority aforesaid That the said Thomas Mitton, John Jones, John Carter, George Twisleton, Thomas Mason, Thomas Madrin, Edmond Glyn, Robert Soutley, Thomas Bale, John Peck, Richard Bassnet, Edward Wyn, Thomas Crichley, Daniel Lloyd, Watkin Kyffin, William Wyn, Gerard Barbour, Gruffith Glyn, Richard Anwyl, Captain Thomas Pugh, Lewis Lloyd, Peter Meirick, Major Edward Moor, Roger Haumer, Sir John Trevor, John Puleston, Thomas Ravenscroft, John Aldersey, Luke Lloyd, Humphrey Dymmock, Andrew Ellice, Thomas Dymmock, Daniel Matthews, Hugh Courtney, Sir John Wittewrong, Evan Lloyd, Hugh Price, Richard Price, Richard Gruffith, Robert Gruffith, Rice Vaughan, Samuel Big, Edward Owen of Castle Dail, Owen Salusbury, Gruffith Hanney, John Lloyd, Lewis Owen, Robert Vaughan, Robert Owen, Thomas Michael, William Williams or any three or more of them shall be and hereby are constituted and appointed to be a Committee for the putting in execution all and every the Ordinances of Sequestrations of Delinquents and Papists estates, according to the true intent and meaning of this Act and of the said several Ordinances; which said Committee, or any three or more of them are hereby authorized and required to Sequester or cause to be Sequestered the estates Real and Personal of all and every person and persons (being Delinquents or Papists) within the said several Counties and Island, whose estates by the true meaning of this Act ought to be sequestred and unto whom the benefit of this Act is not extended; And the said estates so sequestered to dispose of as by the several Ordinances or Orders of Parliament in that behalf is required; observing in the execution of the premises such further Orders and Directions as they shall from time to time receive from the Committee of Goldsmith's Hall. And be it further Enacted by the Authority aforesaid that the said Commissioners or any five of them shall have and hereby have full power and authority to hear and examine Complaints as well touching the inequality of Assessments of former and future Taxes levied or to be levied in the said respective Counties, or any of them for the Service of the Parliament as also touching allowance to be made by Landlords to their Tenants in respect of Taxes and to order such relief therein as shall be agreeable to Equity and Justice, and to the true intent and meaning of the several Ordinances of Parliament in that behalf made: And be it further Enacted by the Authority aforesaid That the said Commissioners or any five of them in the said respective Counties shall have power and are hereby authorized to collect and receive of the persons that are to have benefit by this Act so much money as shall defray the necessary charge of prosecuting this service: Provided that the same exceed not the sum of One hundred pounds in each County: And that no one Commissioner be allowed for his charges in attending the said Service above the rate of five shillings per diem for every day that he shall be actually employed in the said service: And be it further Enacted by the Authority aforesaid That all former Suspensions of Sequestrations made by Sir Thomas Middleton by virtue of an Ordinance of Parliament authorising him so to do, or made by any other person or persons imployed in the service of the Parliament in the said Counties not authorized thereunto by any Act, Ordinance or Order of Parliament be from henceforth void and of none effect. And be it further Declared and Enacted by the Authority aforesaid,

That the payment of any part of the said Fine or of any other sum of money by any of the Inhabitants of the said Counties in pursuance of this Act shall not be construed or taken to be a sufficient matter of evidence or confession for the conviction of such person to have acted anything against the Parliament: And whereas Col. Thomas Mason, Capt. Richard Price, Capt. Thomas Bell and Richard Cheadle, Esq. have done very good and faithful service to the Commonwealth, some of them having had their houses burnt, and their whole estates kept from them for divers years by the Enemy (to their total ruin) for their affection to the Parliament; by reason whereof they are become incapable of serving the Commonwealth, according to the Trust reposed in them unless they receive some reasonable supply and reparation towards their Arrears, Disbursements and Sufferings; Be it therefore Enacted by the Authority aforesaid That the sum of Two thousand pounds out of the first money that shall be raised by Sequestration of, or Composition with, any new Delinquents in the said Counties not pardoned by this Act, shall be disposed of towards Satisfaction of the Arrears, Disbursement, and Reparation of the losses and sufferings of the said persons, as the Parliament shall hereafter order and appoint; And likewise That the debts and engagements of William Lloid, Esq., late High Sheriff of the County of Carnarvon, now deceased, not exceeding One thousand pounds be according to a vote of the Commons assembled in Parliament of the tenth of June One thousand six hundred forty eight, discharged out of the Rents, Fines or Compositions of the said New Delinquents not pardoned by this Act.

Die Veneris, 10th August, 1649. Ordered by the Commons in Parliament assembled, That this Act be forthwith printed and published. HEN. SCOBELL, Cleric. Parliament.

A.D. 1659] **Commonwealth Statute.**

AN ACT FOR TAKING THE ACCOMPTS, AND REDRESSING OF GRIEVANCES CONCERNING THE TITHES AND CHURCH LIVINGS IN WALES; AND FOR ADVANCEMENT OF RELIGION AND LEARNING THERE.

Be it Enacted and Ordained by this present Parliament, That the Council of State be, and are hereby Impowered by Letters,

Commissions, or Instructions from them directed, under the Seal of the Council, to Authorise and Appoint such person and persons as they shall think fit within the respective Counties of WALES and County of Monmouth, thereby Impowering them, or any three or more of them, to take and receive the Accompts of the Commissioners named in an Act of the two and twentieth day of February One thousand six hundred forty nine, Entituled, An Act for the better Propagation and Preaching of the Gospel in WALES, And to take the Accompts of all other person and persons that have been Instructed and Imployed, or have any ways Intermedled with the Letting, Setting, Receiving, Collecting, Sequestring or Disposing of all or any Church-livings with Care of Souls, Donatives, Rectories, Vicaridges, Impropriations, Rents rescued sine Curis, Colledge Pensions and Portions of Tithes, and other Ecclesiastical Livings, Benefices, Procurations, Promotions, and public Revenues whatsoever, Sequestred or Sequestrable, or in the Disposal of the Parliament, or which did or do any ways belong or appertain to the Commonwealth within the said respective Counties of WALES and County of Monmouth ever since the two and twentieth day of February One thousand six hundred forty nine: And to examine and certify all Deceipts, Frauds, Under Valuations, Concealments, Mis-imployments, and Breaches of Trust of any person or persons that have had the Letting, Setting, Collecting, Sequestring, Receiving or Disposing of the said Church-Livings, Rectories Impropriations, and other the Premises, or have any ways intermedled therewith.

And for the better discovery of the truth thereof, the said Commissioners, or any three of them are hereby Impowered to send for Persons, Papers, Witnesses, Books and Accompts and to examine the Accomptants, And all such Witnesses as shall be produced before them on Oath, which the said Commissioners or any three of them are hereby Impowered to administer: And to use all other lawful Ways and Means, and execute all such further Powers as were heretofore given to any Committee or Commissioners, for taking the Accompts of the Kingdom, by any former Acts or Ordinances of Parliament, for the better performance and discharge of the Service aforesaid. And the said Commissioners or any three of them are hereby further Authorized and Required to examine and certify the true and real Valuations of the said Rectories, Vicarages, Impropriations, Tithes, Church-Livings and other the Premises within the said respective Counties, as the same were farmed, Estimated, Received or Accompted, for in the year One thousand six hundred forty nine, and so *Communibus Annis* to this time. And how many Ministers and School Masters have been at any time since the year aforesaid Ejected and Amoved: And how many of them are fit to be restored, what Churches, Vicaradges, Rectories and Places have since become void and for how long time they so remained by the Death, Ejection or Removal of the former Incumbents, Ministers and School-Masters To whom the presentation and right of patronage to such vacant Places did and doth belong. How the respective Churches and Parishes have been supplied since the said two and twentieth day of February, One thousand six hundred forty nine, And by whom and how the persons are qualified that supplied the same; And the said Commissioners, or any three or more of them, are hereby further Impowered and Required to examine and certify, by whom the said Church-Livings, Rectories, and Vicarages, Impropriations, and other the Premises, since the time aforesaid, have been sequestred, farmed, received, collected or disposed of. And to what real value the same did and doth amount unto, and how Accompted; And how much thereof doth remain in the hands of any person or persons within the said respective Counties, due and unaccompted for to the Commonwealth; And to certify the same with all other their proceedings by virtue of this Act. And the Commissions and Instructions aforesaid to the Council of State, and one other part thereof to the Court of Exchequer at Westminster, with a Schedule of the Debtors and Accomptants sum and sums of money due, and payable from them and every of them to the Commonwealth, whereby the same may be proceeded upon according to the Course of Exchequer, against like Accomptants, to force the payment thereof, without any further Commission, Inquiry or Inquisition thereon to be had, which they are hereby enabled to do: Any former Act or Ordinance concerning the same to the contrary thereof notwithstanding.

And the Council of State from time to time are hereby enabled to give further Instructions and Directions for the carrying on of the Service aforesaid, and to give such allowances to the persons by them to be imployed therein as they shall think fit.

And the Council of State are hereby further impowered and required, That in all Cases where the Presentation doth or shall belong to the State either of meer right or by lapse, That they shall take speedy care for the supply of them.

And it is hereby Enacted and Declared, That all Grants or Leases of any Glebes or Titles belonging to any Parsonage or Vicarage with Cure of Souls within the Counties aforesaid, made by the Patron and Incumbent since the Two and twentieth day of February One thousand six hundred forty nine to any person or persons whatsoever, shall be absolutely void to all intents and purposes against the Successor of such Incumbent, such Successor coming in upon Death, Cession, Sequestration or otherwise.

And be it further Enacted, That where upon the Certificates of the said Commissioners, there shall appear any Profits of Livings within the Counties aforesaid, to be remaining in the hands of any person or persons, That the Council is further impowered to allow and dispose of the same to the present or succeeding Incumbent, allowing for the serving of the Cure during the Vacancy what they shall think fit.

Friday, March 16, 1659. Ordered by the Parliament That this Act be forthwith printed and published.

THOMAS H. NICHOLAS, Clerk of the Parliament.

A.D. 1662] **13 and 14 Charles 2, c. 4, s. 27.**

BOOK OF COMMON PRAYER TO BE TRANSLATED INTO THE WELSH TONGUE.

27. Provided always, and be it enacted by the Authority aforesaid that the Bishops of Hereford, St. Davids, Asaph, Bangor and Landaff, and their Successors, shall take such Order among themselves, for the Souls Health of the Flocks committed to their Charge within WALES, that the Book hereunto annexed be truly and exactly translated into the British or Welsh Tongue; and that the same so, translated, and being by them, or any Three of them at the least viewed, perused and allowed, be imprinted to such Number at least, so that one of the said Books so translated and imprinted, may be had for every Cathedral, Collegiate and Parish Church, and Chapel of Ease, in the said respective Dioceses and Places in WALES, where the Welsh is commonly spoken or used, before the first Day of May one thousand six hundred sixty-five; and that from and after the imprinting and publishing of the said Book so translated, the whole Divine Service shall be used and said by the Ministers and Curates throughout all WALES within the said Dioceses where the Welsh

Tongue is commonly used, in the British or Welsh Tongue, in such Manner and Form as is prescribed according to the Book hereunto annexed to be used in the English Tongue, differing nothing in any Order or Form from the said English Book; for which Book, so translated and imprinted, the Church-wardens of every the said Parishes shall out of the Parish Money in their Hands for the Use of the respective Churches, and be allowed the same on their Account; and that the said Bishops and their Successors, or any Three of them at the least, shall set and appoint the Price for which the said Book shall be sold: And one other Book of Common Prayer in the English Tongue shall be bought and had in every Church throughout WALES, in which the Book of Common Prayer in Welsh is to be had by Force of this Act, before the first Day of May One thousand six hundred sixty and four, and the same Books to remain in such convenient Places within the said Churches, that such as understand them may resort at all convenient Times to read and peruse the same, and also such as do not understand the said Language, may by conferring both Tongues together, the sooner attain to the Knowledge of the English Tongue; any Thing in this Act to the contrary notwithstanding: And until printed Copies of the said Book so to be translated may be had and provided, the Form of Common Prayer established by Parliament before the making of this Act, shall be used as formerly in such Parts of WALES where the English Tongue is not commonly understood.

A.D. 1667] **19 Charles 2, c. 5.**

An Act extending Replevins and Avowries to the Principality of WALES.

Whereas by an Act of Parliament, intituled, An Act for the more speedy and effectual Proceeding upon Distresses and Avowries for Rents, Provision is made where any Plaintiff shall be non-suit before Issue joined in any Suit or Replevin by Plaint or Writ lawfully returned, removed, or depending in any of the King's Courts at Westminster; be it enacted, that the said Act and all the Powers and Provisions thereby made for Causes of Replevins depending in his Majesty's Courts of Westminster shall be extended and be of the same force and efficacy in all Causes of Replevin which are or shall be depending in the Courts of the Great Sessions of his Majesty's Principality of WALES, as fully and as amply for and during the Continuance of the said Act as if the said Courts had been mentioned therein.

A.D. 1670] **22 Charles 2, c. 6, s. 8.**

AN ACT FOR ADVANCING THE SALE OF FEE-FARM AND OTHER RENTS. PROVISO FOR WALES.

Provided always That neither this Act nor anything therein contained shall extend or be construed to extend to the Sale of any the Fee-Farm Rents, Tenths Chauntry Rents, Rents Secke or any dry or other Rents whatsoever due or payable to his Majesty, or the Prince of Wales for the time being, issuing or arising within the Principality and Dominion of WALES; This Act or anything therein contained to the contrary in any wise notwithstanding.

A.D. 1688] **1 William and Mary, c. 27.**

AN ACT FOR TAKING AWAY THE COURT HOLDEN BEFORE THE PRESIDENT AND COUNCIL OF THE MARCHES OF WALES.

1. WHEREAS by the Statute made in the 34 & 35 year of KING HENRY 8th intituled an act for certain ordinances in the King's MAJESTY'S Dominion and Principality of WALES it is enacted that there shall be and remain a President and Council in the said Dominion and Principality of WALES and the Marches of the same, with all officers clerks and incidents to the same in manner and form as hath been heretofore used and accustomed, which President and Council shall have power and authority to hear and determine by their wisdoms and discretions such causes and matters as be or hereafter shall be assigned to them by the King's Majesty as heretofore hath been accustomed and used, and for as much as the proceedings and decrees of that Court have by experience been found to be an intolerable burthen to the subject within the said Principality contrary to the Great Charter the known laws of the Land and the birthright of the subject and the means to introduce an arbitrary power and government; and forasmuch as all matters examinable or determinable or pretended to be examinable or determinable before the said Court of President

and Council may have their proper redress in the ordinary Courts of Justice provided and settled in the several shires within the said Principality and Dominion for remedy whereof

2. Be it enacted by the King and Queen's most excellent Majesties, and by the Lords Spiritual and Temporal and Commons in this present Parliament assembled and by the authority of the same, that the before recited clause in the said Statute made in the 34 & 35 year of KING HENRY 8th shall be and is hereby repealed and that the said Court commonly called the Court before the President and Council in the Marches of WALES and all jurisdiction power and authority belonging unto or exercised in the same Court or by any of the Judges officers or ministers thereof to be clearly and absolutely dissolved taken away and determined.

3. And be it further enacted by the authority aforesaid that the Justices of the Great Sessions in WALES respectively for the time being shall yearly nominate three substantial persons for each shire in their respective circuits to be Sheriffs of the same and shall certify their names to the Lords of the Most Honorable Privy Council *crastino animarum* to the intent the King's and Queen's Majesties and the survivors of them and their successors being thereof advertised may appoint one of the persons so certified in every of the said shires to be Sheriff for that year.

4. And be it further enacted that all arrears in pleas personal within the said Principality or Dominion of WALES shall be redressed by Writ of Error in the same manner as errors in Pleas real and mixed are appointed to be redressed by the said Statute made in the 34 & 35 year of KING HENRY 8th.

5. Provided always that no Judgments nor Decrees passed in the said Court before the first day of June 1689 shall be by this Act repealed or annulled but all and every of them shall remain in the same force, and all executions upon them in the same state in which they were before the making of this Act, anything in this Act contained to the contrary notwithstanding.

A.D. 1692] **4 and 5 William and Mary, c. 24, ss. 15, 19.**

AS TO THE QUALIFICATION OF JURORS IN WALES.

15. And whereas a certain Act made at the Session of Parliament held in the 16th and 17th years of the Reign of the late

King CHARLES 2 intituled An Act for returning of able and sufficient Jurors, is expired; Be it enacted by the Authority aforesaid, That all Jurors (other than Strangers upon Trials per Medietatem Linguae) who are to be returned for Trials of Issues joined in any of the Courts of King's Bench, Common Pleas, or Exchequer, or before Justices of Assize, or Nisi Prius, Oyer and Terminer, Gaol Delivery or General Quarter Sessions of the Peace, from and after the First day of May One thousand six hundred ninety three in any County of this Realm of England, shall every of them have in their own Name or in Trust for them, within the same County, Ten Pounds by the Year at least above Reprizes, of Freehold or Copyhold Lands or Tenements, or of Lands and Tenements of ancient Demesne, or in Rents, or in all or any of the said Lands, Tenements or Rents in Fee-simple, Fee-tail, or for the life of themselves or some other person: And that in every County of the Dominion of WALES, every other Juror shall then have within the same County six Pounds by the Year at least, in Manner aforesaid above Reprizes, All which persons, having such Estates as aforesaid, are hereby enabled and made liable to be returned and serve as Jurors for the trial of Issues before the Courts and Justices aforesaid; any Law or Statute to the contrary in any wise notwithstanding. And if any of a lesser Estate and Value shall be respectively returned upon any such Jury it shall be a good cause of challenge, and the Party returned shall be discharged upon the said challenge, or upon his own Oath of the truth of the said matter, &c., &c.

19. Provided nevertheless, that it shall be lawful to return any Person to serve upon the Tales in any County within the Dominion of WALES, who shall have within the same County three Pounds by the Year, above Reprizes, in Manner aforesaid and not otherwise.

A.D. 1693] **5 and 6 William and Mary, c. 4.**

AN ACT TO REPEAL A CLAUSE IN THE STATUTE MADE IN THE FOUR AND THIRTIETH AND FIVE AND THIRTIETH YEARS OF KING HENRY THE EIGHTH, BY WHICH JUSTICES OF PEACE IN WALES ARE LIMITED TO EIGHT IN EACH COUNTY.

" Whereas in a Statute made in the thirty-fourth and thirty-fifth Years of the Reign of King Henry the Eighth, intituled, An Act for certain Ordinances in the King's Majesty's Dominion and Principality of WALES, there is a Clause or Article contained in these Words, that is to say, Item, That there shall not exceed the Number of eight Justices of the Peace in any of the said Shires, over and besides the President, Council, and Justices aforesaid, and the King's Attorney and Solicitor, which President, Council Justices, and the King's Attorney and Solicitor, shall be put in every Commission of Peace, in every of the said twelve shires:" "And whereas the Law contained in this clause or Article is by Experience found to be inconvenient":

2. Be it therefore enacted by the King's and Queen's Most Excellent Majesties, by and with the Advice and Consent of the Lords Spiritual and Temporal, and Commons, in Parliament assembled, and by Authority of the same, That the said Clause or Article be from henceforth absolutely repealed and vacated to all Intents and Purposes; and that it shall and may be lawful to and for the King's and Queen's Most Excellent Majesties, Their Heirs and Successors, by Commission under the Great Seal of England, to constitute, nominate, and appoint, from Time to Time, any such Number of Persons to be justices of Peace in any of the said Counties of WALES, as they shall think fitting and convenient according to such Ways and Methods as are commonly used for the constituting, nominating, and appointing of Justices of the Peace in and for any County of England; and that the Persons so constituted, nominated and appointed, shall have Power and Authority to act and to do any Manner of Thing pertaining to the Office of a Justice of Peace, in as large and ample Manner as any Justice or Justices of Peace within the Dominion of WALES might or ought to have done before the making of this Act; any Law, Statute, Usage, or Ordinance, to the contrary in any wise notwithstanding.

A.D. 1695] 7 and 8 William 3, c. 38.

AN ACT TO TAKE AWAY THE CUSTOM OF WALES WHICH HINDERS PERSONS FROM DISPOSING THEIR PERSONAL ESTATES BY THEIR WILLS.

Whereas in several Counties and places within the Principality of WALES and Marches thereof the widows and younger children of persons dying inhabitants therein have often claimed and pretended to be entitled to a part of the goods and chattels of their late husbands or fathers called her and their reasonable part by virtue or colour of a custom or other usage within the said Principality and Marches thereof, notwithstanding any disposition of the same by the husband's and father's last Wills and testaments or by deed in their lives time and notwithstanding a competent jointure according to the agreement made for the livelihood of the said widows by their husbands which have often occasioned great troubles disputes and expenses about and concerning such custom and usage, whereby many persons have been and are disabled from making sufficient provision for their families younger children and relations and great disputes troubles and expenses have often happened concerning the same to the great damage or ruin of many; for remedy whereof and for preventing of questions doubts and difficulties for the future touching the said custom and usage; be it enacted by the King's Most Excellent Majesty by and with the advice and consent of the Lords Spiritual and Temporal and Commons in this present Parliament assembled and by the authority of the same that from and after the twenty-fourth day of June 1696 it shall and may be lawful for any person or persons inhabitant or residing or who shall have any goods or chattels within the Principality of WALES or Marches thereof by their last Wills and Testaments to give bequeath and dispose of all and singular their goods chattels debts and other personal Estate to their Executor or Executors or to such other person or persons as the said Testator or Testators shall think fit in as large and ample manner as by the laws and Statutes of this Realm any person or persons may give and dispose of the same within any part of the Province of Canterbury or elsewhere; and that from and after the said twenty-fourth day of June 1696 the widows children and other the kindred of such Testator or Testators shall be barred to claim or demand any part of the goods chattels or other personal Estate of all such testator or testators in any other manner than such by the last Wills and Testaments is limited and appointed, any law said custom or usage to the contrary in any wise notwithstanding.

2. Provided always that nothing in this Act contained shall extend to take away any right or title which any woman now married or younger children may have to the reasonable part of their husband's or father's Estate by virtue or colour of the said custom or usage.

A.D. 1697]

9-10 William 3, c. 16.

An Act to execute Judgments and Decrees saved in a Clause in an Act of the first year of the Reign of King William and Queen Mary intituled An Act for taking away the Court holden before the President and Council of the Marches of WALES.

Whereas in a Statute made in the First Year of the Reign of His Majesty and the late Queen MARY intituled An Act for taking away the Court holden before the President and Council of the Marches of WALES It is provided That no Judgment nor Decrees passed in the said Court before the First Day of June One Thousand six hundred eighty nine shall be by that Act repealed or annulled but all and every of them shall remain in the same force and all Executions upon them in the same state in which they were before the making of that Act, Any thing in that Act contained to the contrary notwithstanding, But Forasmuch as no Provision is made in the said Act to authorise His Majesty's Courts of Westminster and Great Sessions of WALES or any other Court to order or issue out any Executions upon the said Judgments and Decrees the said Clause is become fruitless and ineffectual to the great and manifest Damage and Injuries of the Parties on whose behalfs such Judgments and Decrees passed, For remedy whereof Be it enacted by the King's most Excellent Majesty by and with the Advice and Consent of the Lords Spiritual and Temporal and Commons in this present Parliament assembled and by Authority of the same, That it shall and may be lawful to and for His Majesty's High Court of Chancery Court of Exchequer at Westminster or His Majesty's Court of Great Sessions in the respective Counties within the Principality of WALES where the Cause or Causes originally arose to issue forth Execution or Executions and other Processes upon every Judgment or Decree given or made in the said Court held before the President and Council of the Marches of WALES before the First Day of June in the Year of Our Lord God One thousand six hundred eighty nine in the same Manner and to the same intent and purpose as if such Judgment or Decree had been given or made in either of the said Courts of the Exchequer or Grand Sessions.

2. Provided also And it is hereby further enacted by the Authority aforesaid That the Courts before mentioned respectively

shall have Power and Authority and are hereby empowered to review rehear reverse or affirm the said Judgments and Decrees.

A.D. 1698-9] 11 and 12 William 3, c. 9.

AN ACT FOR PREVENTING OF FRIVOLOUS AND VEXATIOUS SUITS IN THE PRINCIPALITY OF WALES AND THE COUNTIES PALATINE.

Whereas by a Clause in an Act made in the 22nd and 23rd Years of King CHARLES 2, intituled An Act for laying Impositions on Proceedings at Law, it is enacted That in all Actions of Trespass, Assault and Battery, and other personal Actions, the Plaintiff in such Actions, in case the Jury shall find the Damages to be under the Value of forty Shillings, shall not recover or obtain more Costs of Suit than the Damages so found shall amount unto; which Clause having Reference to an Act made in the 43rd Year of Queen ELIZABETH, for avoiding infinite Numbers of small and trifling Suits commenced in the Courts at Westminster, hath been understood to relate only to the said Courts; Be it therefore enacted by the King's most excellent Majesty, by and with the Advice and Consent of the Lords Spiritual and Temporal, and Commons, in this present Parliament assembled, and by the Authority of the same, That as well the said Clause, and all the Powers and Provisions thereby, or by any other Law now in Force, made for Prevention of Frivolous and Vexatious Suits in Law commenced in the Courts at Westminster, shall from and after the first Day of May which shall be in the Year One thousand and seven hundred, be extended to, and be of the same Force and Efficacy in all such Suits, to be commenced or prosecuted in the Court of Great Sessions for the Principality of WALES, the Court of Great Sessions for the County Palatine of Chester, the Court of Common Pleas for the County Palatine of Lancaster, and the Court of Pleas for the County Palatine of Durham, as fully and as amply as if the said Courts had been mentioned therein.

2. And whereas the holding of Persons inhabiting within the said Principality of WALES and Counties Palatine, to special Bail in small Actions, is oppressive and Vexatious to the Subject: For Remedy whereof be it further enacted by the Authority aforesaid, That no Sheriff or other Officer within the said Principality or Counties

Palatine, upon any Writ or Process issuing out of any of his Majesty's Courts of Record at Westminster shall hold any Person to Special Bail, unless an Affidavit be first made in Writing, and filed in that Court, out of which such Writ or Process is to issue signifying the Cause of Action, and that the same is Twenty Pounds and upwards; and where the Cause of Action is Twenty Pounds and upwards, Bail shall not be taken for more than the Sum expressed in such Affidavit.

A.D. 1705] 4 Anne, c. 16, s. 24.

AN ACT FOR THE AMENDMENT OF THE LAW, AND THE BETTER ADVANCEMENT OF JUSTICE.

24. And be it further enacted by the Authority aforesaid, That from and after the said first Day of Trinity Term, this Act, and all the Statutes of Jeofails shall extend to all Suits in any of her Majesty's Courts of Record at Westminster, for Recovery of any Debt immediately owing, or any Revenue belonging to her Majesty, her Heirs or Successors; and shall also extend to all Courts of Record in the Counties Palatine of Lancaster, Chester, and Durham, and the Principality of WALES, and to all other Courts of Record within the Kingdom.

A.D. 1713] 13 Anne, c. 6.

AN ACT FOR TAKING AWAY MORTUARIES WITHIN THE DIOCESES OF BANGOR LANDAFF ST. DAVIDS AND ST. ASAPH AND GIVING A RECOMPENSE THEREFORE TO THE BISHOPS OF THE SAID RESPECTIVE DIOCESES, ETC., ETC.

Whereas by Act of Parliament passed in the one and twentieth year of the reign of the late King HENRY the Eighth, intituled, An Act where mortuaries ought to be paid, for what persons, and how much and in what case none is due, and by a proviso or clause therein contained, it is provided (among other things) that it shall be lawful to the Bishops of Bangor Landaff St. Davids and St. Asaph to take such mortuaries of the priests within their dioceses and jurisdictions as thentofore had been accustomed; and the Bishops of the said dioceses for the time being have accordingly used to demand and take and continue to demand and take mortuaries upon the death of any clergyman within their said dioceses and jurisdictions which said mortuaries consisting of several of the best goods of the deceased do oftentimes amount to a very considerable part of his estate, and the payment thereof does very much lessen that small provision which generally the clergy of those dioceses are able to make for the support of their families, and tends to the great impoverishing of the same: for the remedying whereof for the future, and for abolishing and taking away all mortuaries or corse presents and the custom or usage of taking and paying mortuaries or corse presents upon the death of clergymen within the said dioceses and jurisdictions; and to the end a reasonable recompense and satisfaction for the same may be provided and established for the bishops of the said dioceses for ever: Be it therefore enacted by the Queen's most excellent Majesty, by and with the advice and consent of the Lords spiritual and temporal, and of the Commons, in this present Parliament assembled, and by the authority of the same, that the said proviso or clause in the said Act, and all and every proviso or clause in the same Act, so far as the same do or doth relate to the taking of any mortuary or corse present upon the death of any clergyman within the said respective dioceses or jurisdictions, shall immediately, from and after the respective times herein after mentioned, that is to say, within the said diocese of St. Asaph from and after the four and twentieth day of June in the year of our Lord one thousand seven hundred and fourteen and within the said diocese of Bangor, immediately from and after such time any rectory *sine curâ* shall next happen to be void and be in the collation of the present bishop of the said diocese of Bangor, or of any of his successors and within the said diocese of Landaff, immediately from and after such time as the treasurership, with the prebend thereto annexed, founded in the cathedral church of Landaff, shall next happen to be void, such treasurership and prebend being in the collation of the bishop of the said diocese of Landaff: and within the said diocese of St. Davids, immediately from and after such time as the prebend of Langamarch founded in the collegiate church of Brecon now enjoyed by John Medley arch deacon of St. Davids shall next happen to be void the same being in the collation of the bishop of St. Davids stand and be absolutely repealed annulled and void and all and every and any custom and usage of and for paying demanding or taking any mortuary or corse present or any goods thing or things for or in the name of a mortuary or corse present upon the death of any clergyman within the said respective dioceses or jurisdictions shall from the respective times aforesaid for ever be absolutely abolished and void and no mortuary or corse present or sum or sums of money for or in lieu of the same or in the name thereof shall be yielded paid answered or satisfied or be due or payable by any person or persons to any bishop of either of the said dioceses or other person or persons claiming by from or under any such bishop, And that from and after the respective times aforesaid it shall not be lawful to or for the respective bishops of the said dioceses or any of them their or any or either of their successors farmers bailiffs or lessees or any of them or any other person or persons whatever claiming by or under such bishops or any or either of them to take receive or demand of any person or persons any manner of mortuary or corse present or any sum or sums of money or other thing for or in the name lieu or stead of any mortuary or corse present or to convene cite sue or prosecute any person or persons before any judge spiritual or in any of her Majesties courts of law or other court whatsoever for the recovery of or for touching or concerning any mortuary or corse present or any thing in lieu thereof for or by reason or on account of the death of any priest or clergyman within the said respective dioceses or jurisdictions at any time after the respective times aforesaid any thing in the said recited Act or any law custom or usage whatever to the contrary notwithstanding.

2. And be it further enacted by the Authority aforesaid, That in Recompense and Satisfaction to the Bishop of St. Asaph and his Successors, for such Mortuaries as might arise or become due or payable to the said Bishop of St. Asaph, or his Successors, by Virtue of the said recited Act, upon the Death of any Priest or Clergyman, the Rectory *Sine Cura*, which shall first after the said four and twentieth Day of June one thousand seven hundred and fourteen, happen to be void, and be in the Collation of the Bishop of the said Diocese of St. Asaph, or any of his Successors, shall immediately upon such Vacancy, and from thenceforth be annexed and united to the said Bishoprick of Bangor for ever; and all and every the Profits, Rights, Dues, Benefits, and Advantages whatsoever, of the same Rectory, or thereto in any wise belonging or appertaining, shall or may be had, received, taken, and enjoyed

by the Bishop of the said Diocese and his Successors for ever.

3. And be it further enacted by the Authority aforesaid, That in Recompense and Satisfaction to the Bishop of Bangor and his Successors, for such Mortuaries as might arise or become due or payable to the said Bishop of Bangor or his Successors, by virtue of the said recited Act, upon the Death of any Priest or Clergyman, the Rectory *Sine Cura*, which shall next happen to be void, and be in the Collation of the Bishop of the said Diocese of Bangor, or any of his Successors, shall, immediately upon such Vacancy, and from thenceforth be annexed and united to the said Bishoprick of Bangor for ever; and all and every the Profits, Rights, Dues, Benefits, and Advantages whatsoever, of the same Rectory, or thereto in any wise belonging or appertaining, shall or may be had, received, taken, and enjoyed by the Bishop of the said Diocese of Bangor and his Successors for ever.

4. Provided always, That nothing in this Act shall extend to enable any Bishop in either of the said Dioceses of St. Asaph and Bangor, to demise, let or set; and that it shall not be lawful to or for the Bishops of either of the said Dioceses, or any of their Successors, to demise, lease, set, or let to Farm, or otherwise, either of such Rectories *Sine Cura*, annexed and united to the respective Bishopricks of St. Asaph and Bangor, as afore-mentioned, or any the Rights, Dues, Benefits or Profits thereof, for any longer Time than such Bishop, by whom any Lease of either of the said Rectories *Sine Cura* shall be made, shall continue Bishop of the said Diocese; any Statute, Law, or Usage whatsoever to the contrary notwithstanding.

5. And be it further enacted by the Authority aforesaid, That in Recompense and Satisfaction to the Bishop of Llandaff and his Successors, for such Mortuaries as might arise or become due or payable to the said Bishop of Llandaff, or his Successors, by virtue of the said recited Act, upon the Death of any Priest or Clergyman, whensoever the Treasurership with the Prebend thereto annexed, founded in the Cathedral Church of Landaff, shall next happen to be void, the said Treasurership and Prebend shall, immediately upon such Vacancy, and from thenceforth be annexed and united to the said Bishoprick of Landaff for ever; and all and every the Profits, Rights, Dues, Benefits and Advantages whatsoever, of the said Treasurership and Prebend, or thereto in any wise belonging

or appertaining, shall or may be had, received, taken and enjoyed by the Bishop of the said Diocese of Landaff and his Successors for ever.

6. And be it further enacted by the Authority aforesaid, That in Recompense and Satisfaction to the Bishop of St. David's, and his Successors, for such Mortuaries as might arise or become due or payable to the said Bishop of St. David's, or his Successors, by virtue of the said recited Act, upon the Death of any Priest or Clergyman, whensoever the said Prebend of Langamarch shall next happen to be void, the said Prebend shall, immediately upon such Vacancy, and from henceforth be annexed and united to the said Bishoprick of St. David's for ever; and all and every the Profits, Rights, Dues, Benefits and Advantages whatsoever, of the same Prebend, or thereto in any wise belonging or appertaining, shall or may be had, received, taken and enjoyed by the Bishop of the said Diocese of St. David's, and his Successors for ever, in as full and ample Manner as the said John Medley now hath or enjoyeth, or might or ought to have and enjoy the same.

9. Saving nevertheless, and always reserved unto her Majesty, her Heirs and Successors, all and singular First-fruits and Tenths, in any wise due or payable to her Majesty, her Heirs and Successors, for or in respect of such Rectories *Sine Cura*, and Treasurership, and Prebend thereunto annexed, founded in the Cathedral Church of Landaff, and the said Prebend of Langamarch, and all such Right and Title, as her said Majesty hath in or to such First-fruits and Tenths, or any of them, and which shall continue to be levied and paid in like Manner as heretofore; any Thing herein contained to the contrary in any wise notwithstanding.

10. Saving also to the Queen's Majesty, her Heirs and Successors, and to the respective Lessee or Lessees of the said Treasurership, and Prebend thereunto annexed, founded in the Cathedral Church of Landaff, and to the said Prebend of Langamarch, and to all and every other Person or Persons whatsoever, all such Estate, Right, Title, and Interest, in, to, or out of the said Treasurership and Prebend thereunto annexed, and the said Prebend of Langamarch, as any such Lessee or Lessees, or other Person or Persons, have or might have or claim, in, to, or out of the said Treasurership and Prebend thereunto annexed, and the said Prebend of Langamarch if this Act had not passed.

A.D. 1715] 1 George 1, Stat. 2, c. 37.

AN ACT TO ENABLE HIS MAJESTY TO GRANT THE REGALITIES AND LANDS NOW REMAINING IN THE CROWN IN NORTH WALES AND SOUTH WALES, AND COUNTY OF CHESTER, TO HIS ROYAL HIGHNESS THE PRINCE OF WALES, IN SUCH MANNER AND FORM AS THE PRINCIPALITY OF WALES AND EARLDOM OF CHESTER HAVE FORMERLY BEEN GRANTED TO THE PRINCES OF WALES; AND ALSO TO ENABLE HIS SAID ROYAL HIGHNESS TO MAKE LEASES OF LANDS, PARCEL OF HIS ROYAL HIGHNESS'S DUCHY OF CORNWALL, OR ANNEXED TO THE SAME.

It shall be lawful for his Majesty to grant to the Prince, all the honours, castles, &c. belonging to the Crown, in WALES, MONMOUTH, and the County Palatine of CHESTER His Majesty may grant to the said Prince the like jurisdiction, &c. as King JAMES I. granted to Prince HENRY, &c. The Prince may make leases, &c. of the premises, for 31 years or three lives. All leases and grants made by his Royal Highness, of any manors, &c. in the Duchy of CORNWALL shall be good. Proviso that such leases, &c. be made only for 31 years or three lives, and not dispunishable by waste, and that the usual rent be reserved, and where there has been no such rent, the twentieth part of the value shall be reserved.

A.D. 1716] 3 George 1, c. 15, ss. 20, 22.

SHERIFFS OF WALES AND CHESTER TO TAKE THE OLD OATH.

20. Provided that the Sheriffs of WALES and the County Palatine of Chester, shall not be obliged to take the aforesaid Oaths or either of them but shall still take the usual and accustomed Oaths as they have formerly done (except the words following "Ye shall be dwelling in your own proper Person within your Bailiwick, for the Time ye shall continue in the same Office, except ye be otherwise licensed by the King") which words shall hereafter be left out of the said Oaths.

SHERIFFS IN WALES TO ACCOUNT BEFORE AUDITORS IN WALES.

22. And whereas by 34 and 35 HENRY 8th c. 26 it is enacted, that there shall be Sheriffs in every of the twelve Shires of WALES, yearly appointed by the King's Majesty; and that the said Sheriffs shall yearly account before such the King's Auditor or Auditors as shall be assigned and appointed by the King's Majesty for the Dominion of WALES; Be it therefore enacted, that the said Sheriffs of WALES shall not be compelled to appear to be apposed in his Majesty's Court of Exchequer but shall account before his Majesty's said Auditor or Auditors for the Principality of WALES and not elsewhere; any Law Statute Custom or Usage to the contrary notwithstanding, and that the Quietus of the said Sheriffs under the Auditor's Hand or his Deputy shall be a sufficient Discharge for the said Sheriffs in that behalf.

A.D 1721] **8 George 1, c. 25, s. 6.**

AN ACT FOR SETTING DOWN THE TIME OF SIGNING JUDGMENTS IN THE PRINCIPALITY OF WALES, AND COUNTIES PALATINE.

6. And whereas the Provision made by 29 CHARLES 2, c. 3, intituled An Act for Prevention of Frauds and Perjuries was made for setting down the day of the Month and Year of signing Judgments in his Majesty's Courts at Westminster, hath proved very beneficial to purchasers, but hath not yet been extended to the Courts of the Principality of WALES, or of the Counties Palatine: Be it therefore enacted by the Authority aforesaid, That from and after the 24th day of June 1722, any Judge or Officer of any of the Courts of Great Session in the Principality of WALES, or Courts of Session in the Counties Palatine of Chester, Lancaster and Durham, that shall sign any Judgments, shall at the signing of the same, without Fee for doing the same, set down the Day of the Month and Year of his so doing, upon the Paper Book, Docket or Record which he shall sign, which Day of the Month and Year shall be also entered upon the Margent of the Roll of the Record where the said Judgment shall be entered, and that such Judgments, as against Purchasers bona fide for Valuable Consideration of Lands, Tenements or Hereditaments, to be charged thereby, shall in consideration of Law be Judgments only from such times as they shall be so signed, and shall not relate to the first Day of the Session whereof they are entered, or the Day of the Return of the Original or Filing the Bill; any Law, Usage or Course of any Court to the contrary notwithstanding.

A.D. 1730] **3 George 2, c. 25, s. 9.**

AN ACT FOR THE BETTER REGULATION OF JURIES.

Returns of Jurors in WALES.

9. And be it further enacted, that every Sheriff or other Officer, to whom the return of Juries for the trial of causes in the Court of Grand Sessions in any county of WALES do or shall belong, shall, at least eight days before every Grand Sessions, summon a competent number of persons qualified to serve on Juries, out of every Hundred and Commote within every such county, so as such number be not less than ten or more than fifteen, without the directions of the Judge or Judges of the Grand Sessions held for such county, who is and are hereby impowered, if he or they shall see cause, by rule or order of Court, to direct a greater or lesser number to be summoned out of every such Hundred and Commote respectively; and that the said Officer and Officers who shall summon such persons, shall return a list containing the christian and surnames, additions and places of abode of the persons so summoned to serve on Juries, the first Court of the second day of every Grand Sessions; and that the persons so summoned or a competent number of them, as the Judge or Judges of such Grand Sessions shall direct, and no other, shall be named in every panel to be annexed to every writ of *Venire facias juratores*, *Habeas corpora juratorum*, and *Distringas*, and shall be issued out and returnable for the Trial of causes in such Grand Sessions.

A.D. 1732-3] **6 George 2, c. 14, ss. 1, 3.**

AN ACT FOR THE MORE EFFECTUAL PREVENTING FRIVOLOUS AND VEXATIOUS ARRESTS, AND FOR THE MORE EASY RECOVERY OF DEBTS AND DAMAGES, IN THE COURTS OF GREAT SESSIONS IN THE PRINCIPALITY OF WALES, AND IN THE COURT OF ASSIZE IN THE COUNTY PALATINE OF CHESTER, AND FOR THE OBVIATING A DOUBT WHICH HAS ARISEN UPON AN ACT MADE IN THE FOURTH YEAR OF HIS PRESENT MAJESTY'S REIGN, INTITULED, AN ACT THAT ALL PROCEEDINGS IN COURTS OF JUSTICE, WITHIN THAT PART OF GREAT BRITAIN CALLED ENGLAND, AND IN THE COURT OF EXCHEQUER IN SCOTLAND, SHALL BE IN THE ENGLISH LANGUAGE, SO FAR AS THE SAME

ACT DOTH OR MAY RELATE TO THE COURTS OF JUSTICE HOLDEN WITHIN THE SAID PRINCIPALITY, AND FOR EXPLAINING AND AMENDING THE SAID ACT.

1. Whereas in and by an Act made in the fifth year of his present Majesty's Reign, intituled an Act to explain, amend and render more effectual an Act made in the twelfth Year of the Reign of his late Majesty King George the First, intituled An Act to prevent Vexatious Arrests, it is (inter alia) enacted That where the Cause of Action should not amount to the Sum of Ten Pounds or upwards, in any Superior Court, the Writ, Process, Declaration and all other Proceedings should be in the English Tongue, and written in Words at length, in a common legible Hand and Character, and the Defendant or Defendants in such Cases (a Copy of such Process in English having been served, as by the said Act is directed) shall appear at the Return thereof, or within eight days after such Return: And whereas the Courts of Great Sessions in the Principality of WALES, and the Court of Assize in the County Palatine of Chester are held only for and during the Space of six days, Therefore for the more effectual and speedy Determination of all Actions personal, to be commenced in the said Courts of Great Sessions, and the said Court of Assize respectively, where the Debt or Damages expressed in the said Process, or declared for, do not amount to the sum of Ten Pounds, Be it enacted therefore by the King's most Excellent Majesty, by and with the Advice and Consent of the Lords Spiritual and Temporal, and Commons, in this present Parliament assembled, and by the Authority of the same, That in all such personal Actions where the Debt or Damages as aforesaid shall not amount to the sum of Ten pounds, to be commenced in the said Courts of Great Sessions and Assize, and where the Plaintiff or Plaintiffs, in such Action or Actions, shall sue out an original Writ or Process, and serve the Defendant or Defendants with a true copy thereof, by a literate Person, at least Eight days before the commencement of the said Courts of Great Sessions and Assize respectively, and shall cause on every copy of such Process to be written the Notice in the said Act specified and directed, the Defendant or Defendants in such Cases shall appear at the Return of such original Writ or Process, or at or before the third Court to be held in the same respective Courts of Great Sessions and Assize, and in Case the said Defendant or Defendants shall not appear at

the Return of the said original Writ or Process, or at or before the said third Court, that then it shall and may be lawful to and for the Plaintiff or Plaintiffs, or his or their Attorney, upon affidavit being made and filed in the proper Court, of the personal service of such Writ or Process as aforesaid (which said affidavit shall be filed in the said Court, and for the filing whereof there shall be paid the sum of one shilling to the proper Officer and no more) to enter an Appearance for such Defendant or Defendants, and to proceed thereon as if the Defendant or Defendants had entered his, her or their Appearance to such Action or Actions, any Law or Usage in the said Courts of Great Sessions or of Assize to the contrary notwithstanding.

3. And whereas Doubts have arisen whether An Act made in the fourth Year of his present Majesty's Reign, intituled An Act that all Proceedings in Courts of Justice within that part of Great Britain called England, and in the Court of Exchequer in Scotland, shall be in the English Language, doth extend to the said Courts of Great Sessions and other Courts in the Principality of WALES, the said Courts of Great Sessions, and the said other Courts in the said Principality not being therein mentioned: For the removing and obviating of such Doubts, be it further enacted, and it is hereby declared, That the said last mentioned Act, and all Clauses and Directions therein, shall be deemed and taken, and is and are hereby directed to be deemed and taken to extend to the said Courts of Great Sessions, and all other Courts within the said Principality of Wales, in as large, ample and beneficial Manner as if the said Courts of Great Sessions, and the said other Courts in the said Principality had been particularly mentioned and expressed in the said Act.

A.D. 1746] **20 George 2, c. 42, s. 3.**

WALES TO BE INCLUDED IN ENGLAND.

And it is hereby further declared and enacted by the Authority aforesaid, That in all Cases where the Kingdom of England, or that Part of Great Britain called England, hath been or shall be mentioned in any Act of Parliament, the same has been and shall from henceforth be deemed and taken to comprehend and include the Dominion of WALES, and Town of Berwick upon Tweed.

A.D. 1758–9] 32 George 2, c. 28, s. 11.

An Act for the relief of Debtors.

11. And for the more speedy punishing Gaolers, Bailiffs and others employed in the execution of Process, for Extortion or other abuses in their respective Offices and Places, Be it enacted that, upon the Petition, in Term Time, of any Prisoner or Person being or having been in arrest or in custody, complaining of any Exaction or Extortion by any Gaoler, Bailiff or other Officer or Person in or employed in the keeping or taking care of any Gaol or Prison or other Place where any such Prisoner or Person under or having been under arrest or in custody by any Process or Action is or shall have been carried, or in respect of the arresting or apprehending any Person or Persons by Virtue of any Process, Action, or Warrant or if any other abuse whatsoever committed or done in their respective Offices or Places, unto any of His Majesty's Courts of Record at Westminster from whence the Process issued, by which any Person who shall so petition was arrested, or under whose Power or Jurisdiction any such Gaol, Prison, or Place is; . . . and if within the Principality of Wales, . . . then to the Justices at some great Sessions to be holden for the County in the Principality of Wales, where any such Prisoner or Person being or having been under arrest or in custody was arrested or in custody in the said Principality of Wales . . .; every such Court . . . and Justices of Great Sessions, are to hear and determine the same in a summary way and may make such Order thereupon for redressing the Abuse and punishing the offender as they shall think just; and may inforce Obedience to such Orders.

A.D. 1768] 8 George 3, c. 14.

An Act for providing proper Accommodations for his Majesty's Justices of the Great Sessions in WALES, during the Time of holding such Sessions.

"Whereas certain Accommodations are provided for his Majesty's Justices of Assize upon their Circuits in England, by the Sheriffs of the respective Counties, who are allowed the Expences thereby occasioned in their Bills of Cravings in each Year: And whereas it is proper that the like Accommodations should be provided for his Majesty's Justices of the Great Sessions in the Principality of WALES, during their respective Sessions, by the Sheriffs there; and that such Sheriffs should be reimbursed the Expences of providing such Accommodations out of the Land Revenues of the Crown arising within the said Principality, in Manner herein after mentioned; but some Doubts having arisen, whether, since the Act made in the First Year of the Reign of his present Majesty, intituled, An Act for the Support of his Majesty's Household, and of the Honour and Dignity of the Crown of Great Britain, any Part of the said Revenues can be applied for the said Purpose without the Authority of Parliament": May it therefore please your Majesty that it may be enacted; and be it enacted by the King's most Excellent Majesty, by and with the Advice and Consent of the Lords Spiritual and Temporal, and Commons, in this present Parliament assembled, and by the Authority of the same, That the Sheriffs of the several Counties in WALES shall, from henceforth, in each of their respective Counties, provide necessary Lodging and other Accommodations for his Majesty's Justices of the Great Sessions, during the Time of each respective Session, in like Manner as has been usually provided by the Sheriffs within the several Counties in England, for the Justices of Assize there; and that his Majesty may, by any Warrant or Warrants under his Royal Sign Manual, countersigned by the High Treasurer, or any Three or more of the Commissioners of the Treasury for the Time being, authorize, during the Continuance of the said Act made in the First Year of his Majesty's Reign, the Auditor for the Time being of the Land Revenues of the Crown arising within the Principality of WALES, to allow and pass all or any of such Charges as shall, from Time to Time, be made by the respective Sheriffs of the Counties within the said Principality, in the Accounts by them to be delivered into the Office of the said Auditor, of Expences incurred by them respectively in providing necessary Accommodations for his Majesty's Justices of the Great Sessions of WALES, during their Sessions; and to direct that Certificates shall be delivered by the said Auditor to the said Sheriffs of the Sums so allowed and passed in their Accounts respectively; and also to authorize, during the aforesaid Term, the Receiver or Receivers General of the said Revenues to pay the Sums so, from Time to Time, certified upon the Production and Delivery to him or them of such respective Certificates, without any Fee,

Deduction, or Reward whatsoever, to be paid by the Sheriff either to such Auditor or Receiver.

2. Provided nevertheless, and it is hereby enacted, That no greater or larger Sum shall be allowed, passed, certified, and paid, than the Sum of Ten Pounds for or in respect of such Accommodations in any one County, during or upon Account of any one such Session.

A.D. 1772] 12 George 3, c. 30.

An Act for the further Augmentation of the Salaries of the Justices of Chester, and the Great Sessions for the Counties in WALES.

"Whereas it is highly reasonable and expedient that a further Augmentation should be made to the Salaries of the Justices of Chester, and of the Great Sessions for the Counties in Wales: And whereas the several Stamp-duties, granted by divers Acts of Parliament made in the thirty-second Year of the Reign of his late Majesty King George the Second, and in the Second and Fifth Years of his present Majesty's Reign, and appropriated for the Payment of the augmented Salaries of the respective Judges therein mentioned, have for the last four Years, produced annually a considerable Surplus; and the same is, by the said several Acts, reserved for the Disposition of Parliament"; be it therefore enacted by the King's most Excellent Majesty, by and with the Advice and Consent of the Lords Spiritual and Temporal, and Commons, in this present Parliament assembled, and by the Authority of the same, That, from and after the fifth day of April, one thousand seven hundred and seventy-two, there shall be issued, paid, and applied, in every Year, and out of any of the Surplusses which shall arise upon the several Stamp-duties granted by the Acts aforesaid, after the Payment already charged thereupon, shall, from Time to Time, have been satisfied, the Sums of Money following to the several Justices herein after mentioned, as an Addition to, and in further Augmentation of, their respective Salaries; that is to say, The annual Sum of three hundred Pounds, to the Chief Justice of Chester for the Time being; the annual Sum of two hundred Pounds to the second Justice of Chester for the Time being; and to each of the Justices for the Time being of the Great Sessions for the

Counties in WALES: Which said several and respective Sums of Money shall be, and are hereby charged upon the Surplusses of the several Stamp-duties aforesaid, and shall be paid thereout, in every Year, at such Time or Times, and in such Manner, as the Salaries of the said Justices now are or have been used to be paid.

2. Provided always, and be it further enacted by the Authority aforesaid, That if the Surplusses of the said Duties shall prove insufficient, in any Year, to make good and answer the Sums herein-before appointed to be paid and applied yearly, in further Augmentation of the Salaries of the said Justices; then, and in every such Year, a rateable Abatement or Deduction, in Proportion to such Deficiency, shall be made out of the several annual Sums hereby directed and appointed to be paid for that Year to such Justices respectively; and if any Surplus shall remain, in any Year, of the Produce of the said Duties, after Payment of the Monies hereby charged thereon, the same shall be reserved for the Disposition of Parliament, in the same Manner as it was directed to be reserved before the making of this Act.

A.D. 1773.] **13 George 3, c. 51.**

AN ACT TO DISCOURAGE THE PRACTICE OF COMMENCING FRIVOLOUS AND VEXATIOUS SUITS IN HIS MAJESTY'S COURTS AT WESTMINSTER, IN CAUSES OF ACTION ARISING WITHIN THE DOMINION OF WALES; AND FOR FURTHER REGULATING THE PROCEEDINGS IN THE COURTS OF GREAT SESSIONS IN WALES.

"Whereas, to the intolerable Vexation and Charge of his Majesty's Subjects in the Dominion of WALES, it hath been the Practice to commence trifling and frivolous Suits in the Courts at Westminster, upon Causes of Action arising within the said Dominion of WALES: In order that the same may be tried in the nearest adjoining English County to that Part of the Dominion of WALES in which the Cause of Action has arisen, to discourage the like Practices for the future"; may it please your Majesty that it may be enacted; and be it enacted by the King's most Excellent Majesty, by and with the Advice and Consent of the Lords Spiritual and Temporal, and Commons, in this present Parliament assembled, and by the Authority of the same, That, from and after the first Day of January, one thousand seven hundred and seventy-four, in case the Plaintiff in any Action upon the Case for Words, Action of Debt, Trespass on the Case, Assault and Battery, or other personal Action, where the Cause of such Action shall arise within the Dominion of WALES, and which shall be tried at the Assizes, at the nearest English County to that Part of the said Dominion of WALES, in which the Cause of Action shall be laid to arise, shall not recover, by Verdict, a Debt or Damages to the Amount of ten Pounds; in such Case, if the Judge who tried the Cause on Evidence appearing before him, shall certify on the Back of the Record of Nisi Prius, that the Defendant or Defendants was or were resident in the Dominion of WALES at the Time of the Service of the Writ, or other mesne Process served on him, her, or them, in such Action, on such Fact being suggested on the Record or Judgement Roll, a Judgement of Nonsuit shall be entered against the Plaintiff, and such Defendant or Defendants shall be intitled to, and have like Judgement and remedy thereon, to recover such and the like Costs, against the Plaintiff or Plaintiffs, in every such Action, as if a Verdict had been given by the Jury for the Defendant or Defendants, unless the Judge, before whom such Cause shall be tried, shall certify on the Back of the Record, that the Freehold or Title of the Land mentioned in the Plaintiff's Declaration was chiefly in question, or that such Cause was proper to be tried in such English County.

2. And, in order to prevent transitory Actions, where the Cause of Action does not amount to ten Pounds, arising within the Principality of WALES, from being brought in any of his Majesty's Courts of Record out of the said Principality, be it further enacted, That in all transitory Actions arising within the said Principality, which from and after the first Day of January, one thousand seven hundred and seventy-four, shall be brought in any of his Majesty's Courts of Record out of the said Principality of WALES, and the Venue therein, shall be laid in any County or Place out of the said Principality, and the Debt or Damages found by the Jury, shall not amount to the Sum of ten Pounds, and it shall appear upon the Evidence given on the trial of the said Cause, that the Cause of Action arose in the said Principality of WALES, and that the Defendant or Defendants were resident in the Dominion of WALES at the Time of the Service of any Writ, or other mesne Process served on him, her, or them, in such Action, and it shall be so

certified, under the Hand of the Judge who tried such Cause, upon the Back of the Record of Nisi Prius (on such Facts being suggested on the Record or Judgement Roll), a Judgement or Nonsuit shall be entered thereon against the Plaintiff, and the Plaintiff or Plaintiffs shall pay to the Defendant or Defendants, in such Action, his or their Costs of Suit; and the Defendant and Defendants shall have like Remedy to recover the same as in the Case of a Verdict given for the Defendant or Defendants in such Action; and, in the Taxation of all Costs allowed and given to the Defendant or Defendants by and in pursuance of this Act, the proper Officer shall allow to the Plaintiff or Plaintiffs, out of the Defendant's Costs, the full Sum given by the Verdict to the Plaintiff or Plaintiffs for his or their Debt or Damages; and, although no Judgement shall be entered for the Plaintiff or Plaintiffs upon such Verdict, yet nevertheless such Verdict, without any Judgement entered thereon, shall be an effectual Bar to any Action or Actions commenced by the Plaintiff or Plaintiffs for the same.

"3. And whereas by an Act made in the thirty-fourth and thirty-fifth Years of the Reign of his late Majesty King HENRY the Eighth, intituled, An Act for certain Ordinances in the King's Dominion and Principality of WALES, it is (amongst other Things) enacted, That there shall be holden and kept Sessions, twice in every Year, in every of the Shires of the said Dominion and Principality of WALES, the which Sessions shall be called the King's Great Sessions in WALES; and that the Justice of Chester, shall hold and keep Sessions, twice in every Year, in the Shires of Denbigh, Flint, and Montgomery; and likewise that the Justice of NORTH WALES shall hold and keep Sessions, twice in every Year, in the Shires of Caernarvon, Merioneth, and Anglesey; and also that one Person, learned in the Laws of this Realm, by the King's Majesty to be named and appointed, shall be Justice of the Shires of Radnor, Brecknock, and Glamorgan; and shall likewise hold and keep Sessions, twice in every Year, in every of the same Shires; and likewise that one other Person, learned in the Laws of this Realm, to be appointed as aforesaid, shall be Justice of the Shires of Caermarthen, Pembroke, and Cardigan, and shall in like wise hold and keep Sessions, twice in every Year, in every of the same Shires; and that the said Persons, or Justices, and every of them, then being, or that thereafter shall be, shall have several Letters Patents and Commissions for their Offices under the King's Great Seal of England, to be exercised by themselves, or their sufficient Deputies, according to the Purposes and Intents in the said Ordinances specified: And whereas by one other Act, made in the eighteenth Year of the Reign of her late Majesty Queen ELIZABETH, intituled, An Act for the appointing of Justices in the Shires of WALES, it is (amongst other Things) enacted, That the Queen's Highness, her Heirs and Successors, may and shall have full Power and Authority, from Time to Time, to constitute, name, or appoint, two or more Persons, learned in the Laws of this Realm of England, to be Justices of and for the said Counties of Chester, Flint, Denbigh, and Montgomery; and two or more, learned as aforesaid, to be Justices of North WALES; (videlicet) of and for the said Shires of Anglesey, Caernarvon, and Merioneth; and likewise two or more, learned as aforesaid, to be Justices of and for the Circuits and Shires of Radnor, Glamorgan, and Brecknock; and also two or more, learned as aforesaid, to be Justices of and for the Circuits and Shires of Cardigan, Caermarthen, Pembroke, and the Town and County of Haverfordwest: And whereas the exercising the Power of appointing Deputies by such Justices may be attended with Inconvenience; for preventing thereof," be it further enacted, That no Justice now appointed, or at any time hereafter to be appointed, of or for the said County of Chester, or of or for any County, Circuit, or Shire, within the said Principality or Dominion of WALES, shall have any Power or Authority of exercising his Office by Deputy, save and except for the Purpose of calling and adjourning any Court or Courts, and receiving any Motion or Motions appointed, or especially directed to be made at such Court, and for the further Purpose of taking and proclaiming Fines and arraigning Recoveries, in such Court or Courts of each respective Great Session and Assizes, within the Circuit of such Justice; any Law, Statute, or Usage to the contrary notwithstanding.

4. Provided always nevertheless, and be it further enacted by the Authority aforesaid, That from henceforth it shall and may be lawful to and for the several and respective Justices of and for the said several and respective Circuits and Counties for the Time being, from Time to Time, and at any Time, as Occasion may require, by writing under the Hand and Seal, or Hands and Seals, of such Justice or Justices respectively, to nominate, constitute, or appoint, any Person or Persons to be his or their Deputy or Deputies, for the Intent and Purpose of calling and adjourning any Court or Courts, and receiving any Motion or Motions, appointed or especially

directed to be made at such Court, and for the further Purpose of taking and proclaiming Fines, and arraigning Recoveries in such Court or Courts of each respective Great Session and Assizes, within their several and respective Circuits and Counties aforesaid, which Person or Persons so appointed shall have full Power and lawful Authority so to do.

5. Provided always, and be it further enacted, That his Majesty, his Heirs and Successors, shall and may, under his and their Royal Sign Manual, appoint one or more Person or Persons, learned as aforesaid, to execute the said Office of Justice in the said County Palatine of Chester, or in any of the said Counties of WALES, for the then next ensuing Great Sessions, in the Place and Stead of any of the said Justices, who shall, by Illness, be prevented attending upon such Great Sessions, and so often as the Necessity of the Case shall require; any Law, Usage, or Custom, to the contrary thereof in any wise notwithstanding.

"6. And whereas it is conceived that the Suitors in the Court of the King's Great Sessions in the Dominion and Principality of WALES will, in many cases, experience great Benefit and Advantage by having their Suits tried by Special Juries"; be it therefore further enacted by the Authority aforesaid, That the Justices of his Majesty's Great Sessions in WALES, upon Motion made on Behalf of his Majesty, his Heirs or Successors, or on Motion of any Prosecutor or Defendant in any Indictment or Information of any Misdemeanour, or on the Motion of any Plaintiff or Plaintiffs, Defendant or Defendants, in any Action, Cause, or Suit whatsoever, depending, or to be brought and carried on, in any of his Majesty's Courts of Great Sessions in WALES, shall and may, in case such Justices in their Discretion shall think fit, order and appoint a Jury to be struck before the proper Officer of such Courts, for the Trial of any Issue joined in any of the said Cases, in such Manner as Special Juries have been usually struck in the Courts of Law at Westminster, upon Trials at Bar had in the said Courts; which Jury so struck as aforesaid shall be the Jury returned for the trial of such Issue as aforesaid.

7. Provided always, and be it further enacted by the Authority aforesaid, That the Person or Party who shall, by virtue of this Act, apply for such Special Jury, shall not only bear and pay the Fees for striking such Jury, but shall also bear, pay, and discharge all the Expences occasioned by the Trial of the Cause by such Special

Jury, and shall not have any further or other Allowance for the same, upon Taxation of Costs, than such Person or Party would be intitled unto in case the Cause had been tried by a common Jury, unless the Justices or Justice before whom the Cause is tried shall, immediately after the Trial, certify in open Court, under his or their Hand or Hands, upon the Back of the Record, that the same was a Cause proper to be tried by a Special Jury.

"8. And to prevent the Demand or Payment of extravagant Fees of Jurymen returned under the Authority of this Act," be it further enacted by the Authority aforesaid, That no Person who shall serve upon any Jury, appointed or returned by Authority of this Act, shall be allowed, or take, for serving on any such Jury, More than the Sum of Money which the Justices or Justice who tries the Issue or Issues shall think just and reasonable, not exceeding the Sum of one Pound one Shilling, except in Causes where a View hath been or shall be directed.

"9. And, for the greater Ease and Benefit of all Persons whomsoever in the taking of Affidavits to be made use of and read in the Courts of his Majesty's Great Sessions in WALES, in all Matters and Causes whatsoever depending, or to be depending, in all or any of the Courts aforesaid, or in anywise concerning the Proceedings of or in the same," be it enacted by the Authority aforesaid, That the Justices of the respective Courts of Great Sessions in WALES for the Time being shall and may, by one or more Commission or Commissions, under the Seal of the said respective Courts, from Time to Time, as Need shall require, impower such and so many Persons as they shall think fit and necessary, in all and every the several Shires and Counties within their respective Circuits in the said Dominion of WALES, to take and receive all and every such Affidavit and Affidavits as any Person or Persons shall be willing and desirous to make before any of the Persons so impowered in, or concerning any Cause, Matter, or Thing depending, or hereafter to be depending, or in any wise concerning any of the Proceedings to be in their respective Circuits of Great Sessions, as the Justices of his Majesty's Court of King's Bench, or Common Pleas, or the Lord Treasurer, Chancellor, and Barons of the Court of Exchequer for the Time being, do use to do; which said Affidavits, taken as aforesaid, shall be filed in the several and respective Offices of the said several and respective Courts of Great Sessions, and the same shall and may be read and made use of in the said respective Courts to all Intents and

Purposes, as other Affidavits taken in the said respective Courts now are; And that all and every affidavit and Affidavits, taken as aforesaid, shall be of the same Force as Affidavits taken in the said respective Courts now are; and all and every Person and Persons forswearing him, her, or themselves, in such Affidavit or Affidavits, shall incur and be liable unto the same Penalties, as if such Affidavit or Affidavits had been made and taken in open Court: which said several Commissions shall be made out by the Prothonotary, upon a Fiat or Warrant from the said Justices for the Time being of the said respective Courts of Great Sessions in WALES; and the said Prothonotary shall cause an Entry to be made in a Book to be kept for that Purpose of the Names of the Persons to whom such Commissions are, from Time to Time, granted, and the respective Times when issued; and the following Fees shall be paid for each Commission, and no more; (to wit,) the Sum of two Shillings for the Fiat or Warrant; the Sum of four Shillings for making out the said Commission, besides the King's Duty, and Value of the Parchment; and the Sum of four Shillings for sealing the same; and every Commissioner, or Person so impowered, shall take and receive, for the swearing of every affidavit before him, the Sum or Fee of one Shilling, and no more.

10. Provided nevertheless, That no Person appointed a Commissioner as aforesaid shall take or receive any affidavit during the Time of holding the Great Sessions, or Assizes, for the County or Place in which such Cause, Matter, or Thing, shall be depending.

11. Provided always, and it is hereby enacted, That such Officers of the said several and respective Courts of Great Sessions in WALES, as have heretofore taken or sworn Affidavits, shall and may continue so to do, in the same Manner as if this Act had not been made; any Thing herein contained to the contrary notwithstanding.

12. And, to give greater Ease and Benefit to all Persons within the said Dominion of WALES, in taking the Recognizances of Special Bails upon all Actions and Suits depending, or to be depending in any of the Courts of his Majesty's Great Sessions in WALES"; be it further enacted by the Authority aforesaid, That the Justices of the respective Courts of Great Sessions in WALES for the Time being shall and may, by one or more Commission or Commissions, under the Seal of the said respective Courts, from Time to Time, as need shall require, impower such and so many Persons (other than common Attorneys or Solicitors) as they shall think fit and necessary in all and every the several Shires and Counties within their respective Circuits in the said Dominion of WALES, to take and receive all and every such Recognizance or Recognizances of Bail or Bails, as any Person or Persons shall be willing or desirous to acknowledge or make before any of the Persons so impowered in any Action or Suit depending, or hereafter to be depending, in the said respective Courts, or any of them, in such Manner and Form, and by such Recognizance or Bail Piece, as the Justices of the said Courts of Great Sessions respectively have used to take the same; which said Recognizance or Recognizances, Bail Piece or Bail Pieces, so taken as aforesaid, together with an affidavit made of the due taking of the Recognizances of such Bail or Bail Piece, by some credible Person present at the taking thereof, shall be transmitted to the Prothonotary's Office, there to be filed of Record, paying such Fees as have usually been received for the taking of Special Bails by the Justices' Clerks, and other Officers of the said respective Courts, which Recognizance of Bail or Bail Piece, so taken and transmitted, shall be of the like Effect, as if the same were taken before any of the said Justices; for the taking of every which Recognizance or Recognizances of Bail or Bail Piece, the Person or Persons so impowered shall receive only the Sum of, or Fee of, two Shillings, and no more.

13. And be it further enacted by the Authority aforesaid, That the said Justices of Great Sessions, in their respective Courts, shall and may make such Rules and Orders, for the justifying of such Bails, and making the same absolute, as to them shall seem meet, so as the Cognizor or Cognizors of any such Bail or Bails be not compelled to appear in Person in any of the said Courts, to justify him or themselves; but the same may be, and is hereby directed to be determined by Affidavit or Affidavits, duly taken before the said Commissioners, touching the Value of their respective Estates.

14. Provided always, That the Attorney for the Defendant or Defendants shall give Notice to the Plaintiff's Attorney of the taking of such Bail within Eight Days after the Caption thereof, and that the Plaintiff shall be at Liberty, within Eight Days after such Notice, to take Exception to such Bail, and enter the same in the Prothonotary's Office; and such Exception having been taken, the Bail shall be justified before the Justices, before the Rising of the Second Court at the ensuing Sessions; and the Bail Bond taken by the Sheriff, Under Sheriff, or other Officer, for the Defendant's

Appearance, shall remain in Force until such Special Bail shall have been finally justified as aforesaid; but the Plaintiff, nevertheless, shall be at liberty to file his Declaration conditionally in the Prothonotary's Office; and the Defendant, in case such Declaration shall have been delivered seven Days before the first day of the Session next ensuing the Return of such Writs, shall plead thereto, before the Rising of the Second Court of such Great Sessions, unless further Time shall be given him by the Court for that Purpose.

"15. And whereas all Writs relating to Actions depending in the Courts of Great Sessions, in the several Counties in NORTH and SOUTH WALES, are returnable at the Great Session held respectively for the said Counties, and at no other Time, by which Means no Action that is commenced (except where the Defendant or Defendants voluntarily appear) can be brought to issue, and tried before the second Session after such Action is commenced at the soonest, which is usually near a Year, and a great Delay to the Suitors of the said Courts": For Remedy whereof, and for the greater Ease and Benefit of the said Suitors, be it further enacted by the Authority aforesaid, That from and after the first Day of January, one thousand seven hundred and seventy-four, all original Writs, Bills, and all mesne Process Whatsoever, by which any Action shall be commenced or sued in the said Courts of Great Sessions for the said Counties of NORTH and SOUTH WALES, shall and may be made returnable before his Majesty's Justices respectively of the several Counties of NORTH and SOUTH WALES, on the first Wednesday in any Month, in each of the two Vacations, annually, betwixt the two Sessions, or on the first Day of the next Sessions, at the Election of the Plaintiff or Plaintiffs, his, her, or their Attorney, who shall sue out the same: And that all such Writs or Process which shall issue out of the said Courts, returnable in the Vacations as aforesaid, and whereon or wherewith the Defendant or Defendants shall be arrested or served with a Copy or Copies, such Defendant or Defendants shall appear and file Special Bail, or enter a Common Appearance, as the Case shall require, on the Day of such Return, or within fourteen Days next after; and in case of Neglect in bailable Actions, the Sheriff, Under Sheriff, or other Officer, shall, at the Request and Costs of the Plaintiff or Plaintiffs, in such Actions, his, her, or their Attorney assign to such Plaintiff or Plaintiffs the Bail Bond taken for the Defendant's Appearance upon the Arrest, by Indorsement and Attestation under his Hand, in the Presence of two or more credible Witnesses; and the Plaintiff or Plaintiffs in such Action, after such Assignment made, may bring an Action or Suit upon such Bail Bond in his, her, or their own Name or Names; and the said Courts may, by Rule or Rules thereof respectively, give such relief to the Plaintiff and Plaintiffs, Defendant and Defendants, in the original Action, and to the Bail so sued upon the Bail Bond, as is agreeable to Justice and Reason; and in case on Service of the Copy of any Writ or Process (having Notice thereunder written, purporting the Intent of such Service) returnable in the Vacation Time as aforesaid, the Defendant or Defendants so served therewith, shall not appear at the Return, or within fourteen Days next after the Return thereof, as aforesaid, it shall and may be lawful to and for the Plaintiff or Plaintiffs in such Action, upon Affidavit being made, and filed with the Prothonotary of the said respective Courts, or his Deputy, of the personal Service of such Writ or Process as aforesaid, to enter a common Appearance or Appearances for the Defendant or Defendants, and to proceed thereon as if such Defendant or Defendants had entered his, her, or their Appearance; and Special Bail having been filed, or a common Appearance entered, as the Case shall require, the Plaintiff in such Action may proceed to file his Declaration; and the Defendant or Defendants, in case such Declaration shall have been delivered seven Days before the first Day of the Session next ensuing the Return of such Writ, shall be bound to plead thereto, before the Rising of the Second Court of such Great Session, to be holden for the County or Place in which such Action shall have been brought, unless the Court shall think proper to allow further Time for that Purpose.

16. And be it further enacted by the Authority aforesaid, That from and after the first Day of January, one thousand seven hundred and seventy-four, every Officer or Clerk belonging to the several Courts of Great Sessions in the Principality of Wales, who shall sign any Original Writ or Bill, relating to Actions depending in the said Courts of Great Sessions, shall, at the signing thereof, set down upon such Original Writ or Bill the Day and Year of his signing the same, which shall be entered upon the Remembrance, or in the Book where the Abstracts of such Original Writ or Bill shall be entered, upon Pain to forfeit the Sum of five Pounds for every Offence or neglect of such Officer or Clerk aforesaid; to be recovered by any Person who shall sue for the same, by Action of Debt, Bill,

Plaint, or Information, wherein no Wager of Law, Protection, or Essoin, or more than one Imparlance shall be allowed.

"17. And whereas, by sundry Statutes, Penalties are given for Offences thereby provided against, and such Penalties are directed to be sued for and recovered in his Majesty's Courts of Westminster only, and the enabling the respective Courts of Great Session to hold Pleas, or to have Cognizance in all such Cases arising or happening within their respective Jurisdictions, would be for the Ease and Benefit of the Inhabitants of the Dominion of WALES"; be it further enacted by the Authority aforesaid, That from and after the first Day of January, one thousand seven hundred and seventy-four, in all Cases where any Penalty or Penalties is or are given by any Statute, and the same is, are, or shall be directed to be recovered in the Courts of Westminster, or either of them, excepting such as may by the Laws now in being be sued for only in his Majesty's Court of Exchequer, and the Offence for which any such Penalty or Penalties hath or shall be given shall be done or committed in any of the Counties of WALES, and the Defendant or Defendants liable to the same shall be resident within the Jurisdiction of the Great Session held for any County of WALES, it shall and may be lawful to and for the Plaintiff or Plaintiffs, Prosecutor or Prosecutors, or other Person to whom any such Penalty is given, or who shall be intitled to sue for the same, in every such Case, to sue for and recover the same in the Courts of Great Session respectively in WALES, within which such Penalties have or shall be incurred, in such Manner and Form as he, she, or they might have done in the Courts at Westminster; and that the said respective Courts of Great Session shall have Jurisdiction as fully, to all Intents and Purposes, as if the said Courts had been respectively named in all and every of the said Acts, and the Powers thereby given extended to the said respective Courts.

A.D. 1793] **33 George 3, s. 68.**

AN ACT FOR REMEDYING INCONVENIENCES ATTENDING CERTAIN PROCEEDINGS IN THE COURTS OF GREAT SESSIONS IN WALES, AND FOR THE COUNTY PALATINE OF CHESTER . . . AND IN THE COUNTY COURTS OF WALES.

Whereas Persons against whom Judgments may be obtained in the Courts of Great Sessions in WALES . . . may, in order to avoid

Execution, remove their Persons and Effects beyond the Jurisdiction of such Courts, be it enacted, That in all cases where final Judgment shall be obtained in any Action or Suit, in any of the said Courts, it shall and may be lawful to and for any of his Majesty's Courts of Record at Westminster, upon Affidavit made before a Judge, or Commissioner authorised to take Affidavits in such Court, and filed therein of such Judgment being obtained, and diligent Search and Enquiry having been made after the Person or Persons against whom such final Judgment shall be obtained, and that the Person or Persons, or Effects of such Person or Persons, are not to be found within the Jurisdiction of such Court, to cause a Transcript of the Record of the said Judgment to be removed into such Court at Westminster; and to issue Writs of Execution thereupon to the Sheriff of any County, City, Liberty or Place, against the Person or Persons, or Effects of such Person or Persons, against whom such final Judgment shall be obtained, in such Manner as upon Judgments obtained in the said Courts at Westminster; and the Sheriff upon every such Execution shall, and he is hereby authorised to detain the Person or Persons against whom such Execution shall be issued, until the sum of 40s. be paid to him, or to levy that Sum out of the Effects, according to the Nature of the Execution, for the extraordinary Costs of the Person or Persons by whom such final Judgment shall be obtained in such Court subsequent to the said Judgment, and of the Execution in the said Court at Westminster, over and above the Money for which such Execution shall be issued.

2. And whereas by 34 HENRY 8, c. 26, it is, amongst other Things, enacted, That the Sheriff of the several Counties or Shires in WALES, in the said Act mentioned, upon every Judgment had before him in his County or Hundred Court, in any Plaint under 40s. may award a *Capias ad satisfaciendum* to arrest the Party condemned; and it is also enacted, That no Execution of any Judgment given or to be given in any Court in the said Act mentioned, be stayed or deferred by reason of any Writ of False Judgment, but that Execution may be had and made at all Times before the Reversal of the said Judgment, the pursuit of the said Writ notwithstanding; be it further enacted, That the several Clauses aforesaid in the said Act shall be, from and after the passing of this Act, repealed.

3. Provided always, and be it further enacted, That no Execution

shall be stayed upon or by any Writ of False Judgment, for the reversing of any Judgment given in any County Court in WALES, unless the Person or Persons who shall prosecute the said Writ be first bound, unto the Party or Parties for whom the said Judgment shall have been given, in a Recognizance with two sufficient Sureties, such as the Sheriff in the said Court shall approve and allow, in the Sum of £10 (except when the Sum adjudged for Costs and Damages shall exceed the Sum of £10, and in such Case, in double the Sum so adjudged) to prosecute the said Writ with Effect, and also to pay and satisfy, if the said Judgment be affirmed, or the Damages awarded for the Delay of Execution; the acknowledgment of which Recognizance the said Sheriff is hereby authorised and required to take and file amongst the Proceedings of his said Court; and for the caption and filing thereof the Sum of one Shilling, and no more, shall be paid to the said Sheriff by the Person or Persons who shall prosecute the said Writ; And in case of a Breach of the Condition of such Recognizance the Conuzee or Conuzees thereof may have and maintain an Action of Debt on the same, in any of his Majesty's Courts of Record in WALES, against the Conuzors, or either of them, to recover all and singular the Damages and Costs in the said Recognizance mentioned.

A.D. 1809] **49 George 3, c. 127, s. 5.**

AN ACT FOR FURTHER AUGMENTING THE SALARIES OF THE JUSTICES IN THE GREAT SESSIONS IN WALES.

5. And be it further enacted, That from and after the passing of this Act, there shall also be issued, paid, and payable out of and charged and chargeable upon the said Consolidated Fund . . . in augmentation of their respective Salaries and Profits, and over and above any Sums of Money to which they may be entitled under any Act now in force, the several annual Sums hereinafter mentioned; that is to say, to the Chief Justice of Chester, and to the second Justice of Chester, and to each of the Justices of the Great Sessions for the Counties of WALES, the Sum of Four Hundred Pounds.

A.D. 1812]

52 George 3, c. 155, s. 10.

AN ACT TO REPEAL CERTAIN ACTS AND AMEND OTHER ACTS RELATING TO RELIGIOUS WORSHIP AND ASSEMBLIES, AND PERSONS TEACHING OR PREACHING THEREIN.

Penalty for Producing False Certificate.

10. And be it further enacted, that every person who shall produce any false or untrue certificate or paper as and for a true certificate of his having made and taken the oaths and subscribed the declarations by this Act required for the purpose of claiming any exemption from civil or military duties as aforesaid, under the provisions of this or any other Act or Acts of Parliament, shall forfeit for every such offence the sum of fifty pounds; which penalty may be recovered by and to the use of any person who will sue for the same by any action of debt, bill, plaint, or information in any of his Majesty's courts of record at Westminster, or the courts of great sessions in WALES or the courts of the counties palatine of Chester, Lancaster, and Durham (as the case shall require), wherein no essoign, privilege, protection, or wager of law, or more than one imparlance shall be allowed.

A.D. 1824]

5 George 4, c. 106.

AN ACT TO ENLARGE AND EXTEND THE POWER OF THE JUDGES OF THE SEVERAL COURTS OF GREAT SESSIONS IN WALES, AND TO AMEND THE LAWS RELATING TO THE SAME.

Whereas Difficulties have arisen in His Majesty's Courts of Great Sessions in WALES from a want of Power in the Judges of such Courts respectively to compel any Person residing out of the Jurisdiction of any such Courts respectively, to attend as a Witness on any Trial or Cause therein: And whereas Inconvenience has been experienced for Want of Power in the Judges of the said Courts of Great Sessions to issue Commissions for the taking of Answers, Examinations, and Affidavits, and for the Examination of Witnesses, at Places out of the respective Jurisdictions of the said Courts, and of administering Oaths to the Persons putting in such Answers and Examinations, and making such Affidavits, and being examined as

Witnesses: And whereas Difficulties have arisen in His Majesty's Courts of Great Sessions in WALES with respect to enforcing Rules, Orders, and Decrees of the said Courts, against Persons who have entered Appearances in Suits instituted in such Courts, or have come in as Creditors or Purchasers, and submitted to the Jurisdiction thereof, but by reason of their Residence being out of the Limits of the Jurisdiction of the said Courts, or of their having withdrawn themselves therefrom, are not amenable to the Process thereof: And whereas it is advisable that further Provisions be made for discouraging the Practice of commencing frivolous and vexatious Suits in His Majesty's Courts at Westminster, in Causes of Action arising within the Dominion and Principality of WALES, and also to expedite Suits in the said several Courts of Great Sessions, and provide for new Trials, and regulate the Practice therein: And whereas it is therefore expedient that the Powers of the Judges of the said Courts should be enlarged and extended, and the Laws and Usages relating to the same be amended: And whereas it is also expedient to regulate the Fees and King's Silver payable on Fines and Recoveries levied and suffered within the Principality of WALES, and to provide for the more effectually levying and suffering the same: May it please Your Majesty that it be enacted; and be it enacted by the King's most Excellent Majesty, by and with the Advice and Consent of the Lords Spiritual and Temporal, and Commons, in this present Parliament assembled, and by the Authority of the same, That from and after the passing of this Act, when and as often as the Attendance of any Person or Persons shall or may be deemed necessary as a Witness or Witnesses to give Evidence in, about, or concerning any Suit, Cause, Trial, Commission, or Issue, prosecuted, brought, and depending in or before any of the said Courts of Great Sessions, and such Person or Persons shall not, when his, her, or their Attendance is so deemed necessary, be resident within the Jurisdiction of the said Court of Great Sessions, where such his, her, or their Attendance may so be deemed necessary, but be resident at such Time in ENGLAND or WALES, in all and every such Cases it shall and may be lawful for any of the Parties in the said Suits, Trial, Commission, or Issue, to apply to the Proper Officer of His Majesty's Courts of Exchequer at Westminster, and such Officer is hereby authorized and required to issue a Writ or Writs of *Subpœna ad testificandum*, or any Writ or Writs of *Subpœna duces tecum*, on Demand, in like Manner as the same is or are issuable by the said Court of Exchequer in any Cause, Trial, Suit, Commission, or Issue depending therein; and such Writ or Writs of *Subpœna ad testificandum* and of *Subpœna duces tecum* shall be directed to such Person or Persons, commanding such Person or Persons to attend and give Evidence as a Witness or Witnesses in such Court of Great Sessions, upon such Cause, Trial, Commission, Suit, or Issue so prosecuted and depending therein; and such Person or Persons shall be compelled and compellable to attend the same, in like Manner and under such Penalties as if the said Writ or Writs had issued to command his, her, or their Attendance in the said Court of Exchequer, in, upon, or concerning any Suit, Cause, Trial, Commission, or Issue depending therein; and any such Party, on whose Behalf any such Writ or Writs shall be issued, in Default of Obedience to any such Writ or Writs by the Person or Persons to whom the same may be directed, and on whom the same shall be served, shall have the like Remedy against such Person or Persons for such Default, as if the said Writ or Writs had issued from the said Court of Exchequer, to compel and require such Person or Persons to attend and give Evidence there: Provided always, that in every Case where a new Cause or Issue is commenced, it shall and may be lawful for the Marshal of the said Court of Great Sessions in which such new Cause or Issue is commenced, in the Name of a Justice of such Court, to issue such Writs of *Subpœna ad testificandum* or of *Subpœna duces tecum*, as either of the Parties to the said Suit shall require; and in case of Disobedience to any such Writ, the Parties shall have the like Remedy in the said Court of Exchequer as if the said Writ or Writs had been directly issued out of that Court.

2. And whereas it may be expedient, for the better and more perfect Administration of Justice in WALES, that the Court of King's Bench, Common Pleas, and Exchequer should in certain Cases have the Power of granting new Trials of Causes which have been commenced and been tried in the said Court of Great Sessions; be it therefore enacted by the Authority aforesaid, That from and after the passing of this Act, it shall and may be lawful for any Party or Parties, who shall be dissatisfied with any Verdict given or obtained, or Nonsuit entered against him, her, or them, in any Action which shall have been tried in any of the said Courts of Great Sessions, to apply by Motion to any of the said Courts of King's Bench, Common Pleas, or Exchequer sitting *in Banco*,

for a Rule to show Cause why a New Trial of such Action should not be granted, or Nonsuit set aside and a new Trial granted, or a Verdict entered for the Plaintiff or Defendant, or a Nonsuit entered, as the Case may be, in the same Manner as hath been usually heretofore done in Actions depending in the said Courts, and tried at *Nisi Prius* before any Judge of Assize, by virtue of any Record issuing out of the said Courts; and that thereupon it shall and may be lawful for the said Courts to grant such Rule, and proceed to hear and determine the Merits of the same, in such Manner and Form as hath been heretofore done in Actions depending in the said last-mentioned Courts, and tried as aforesaid; and in Case the Courts shall make the said Rule absolute, which they are hereby authorized and empowered to do, and order a new Trial to be had between the Parties in such Action, that upon the Party or Parties who shall have obtained such Rule delivering an Office Copy of such Rule so made absolute, to the proper Officer of the Court of Great Sessions where such Cause was tried, all Proceedings upon the former Verdict or Nonsuit so obtained in the said Courts of Great Sessions shall cease, and the said Actions shall proceed to Trial at the next or some other Great Sessions, to be holden in and for the County in which the same was tried as aforesaid, in like Manner as if no Trial had been had therein; or in case of a Verdict being ordered to be entered for the Plaintiff or Defendant, or a Nonsuit being ordered to be entered, as the Case may be, Judgment shall be entered accordingly.

3. And be it further enacted by the Authority aforesaid, That a Transcript of the Record for which such new Trial shall be moved, or Motion made for altering the Verdict, or entering or setting aside a Nonsuit, certified by the Prothonotary of the said Courts of Great Sessions respectively, or his Deputy, shall be transmitted to the Court to which such Application shall be made as aforesaid, for the Purpose of such Motion for a new Trial, or setting aside such Nonsuit and granting a new Trial thereon, or entering a Verdict for the Plaintiff or Defendant, or entering a Nonsuit, and which Transcript the said Prothonotary or his Deputy is hereby authorized and required to deliver on Demand, on Payment of the usual Fee; and that the Costs of such Application for a new Trial and setting aside such Nonsuit, or entering a Verdict for Plaintiff or Defendant, or entering a Nonsuit, shall be in the Discretion of the said Court to award and order to and by which Party to such Motion the same

shall be paid: Provided always, that nothing herein contained shall be deemed or taken to prevent any of the said Courts of Great Sessions from granting any new Trial, or setting aside any Nonsuit, or entering a Nonsuit, or altering a Verdict, according to any Rule established therein.

4. And be it further enacted by the Authority aforesaid, That it shall and may be lawful for the said Court, to which such Applications shall be made, or any Commissioner appointed to take Affidavits therein, to administer an Oath to any Person or Persons making an Affidavit either to obtain such Rule, or show Cause against the same as aforesaid; and every Person or Persons forswearing him, her, or themselves in such Affidavit or Affidavits, shall incur and be liable to the same Penalties as if such Affidavit or Affidavits had been made and sworn in an Action depending in the said Court: Provided always, that nothing in this Act contained shall extend or be construed to extend to stay or delay the entering up Judgment which shall have been given or obtained in any Action in any of the said Courts of Great Sessions, and suing out Execution thereon, unless the Party or Parties intending to apply under the Provisions of this Act for a new Trial thereof, or for Alteration of the Verdict, or entering or setting aside a Nonsuit, with Two sufficient Sureties, such as the Court of Great Sessions wherein such Action shall be depending shall allow of, shall first before such Stay made be bound unto the Party or Parties for whom such Verdict or Nonsuit shall have been given or obtained, by Recognizance to be acknowledged in the same Court, in such reasonable Sum as the same Court of Great Sessions shall think fit, to make and prosecute such Application for such new Trial or Alteration of Verdict, or entering or setting aside a Nonsuit, and also to satisfy and pay, if such Application shall be refused, all and singular the Debts, Damages, and Costs adjudged and to be adjudged in consequence of the said Verdict, or Nonsuit, in the said Court of Great Sessions, and all Costs and Damages to be also awarded for the delaying of Execution thereon; and upon such Recognizance being entered into, the said Court of Great Sessions is hereby authorized to stay all Proceedings in such Action: And further, that the entering up of Judgment, in any of the said Courts of Great Sessions, in any Writ of Dower or Action of Ejectment, and suing out Execution thereon, shall not be stayed, unless the Party or Parties intending to apply for a new Trial, or to alter the Verdict or enter or set aside

a Nonsuit therein under the Provisions of this Act, shall be bound in Manner aforesaid unto the Party or Parties in whose Favour such Verdict or Judgment of Nonsuit shall have been given or obtained, in such reasonable Sums as the Court of Great Sessions in which such Action shall be depending shall think fit, with Condition, that if such Application shall not be made and prosecuted, or shall be refused, the Party or Parties so intending to make such Application shall pay such Costs, Damages, and Sum or Sums of Money as shall be awarded by the said Court of Great Sessions, in case no such Application shall have been made and prosecuted, or after such Application shall have been refused; and upon such Recognizance being entered into, the said Court of Great Sessions is hereby authorized to stay all Proceedings in such Action.

5. And to the End that the same Sum and Sums and Damages may be ascertained, it is further enacted, That the Court of Great Sessions wherein such Action shall be depending, upon such Failure to make and prosecute such Application, or such Refusal as aforesaid, shall issue a Writ (if necessary) to inquire as well of the Mesne Profits as of the Damages by any Waste committed after such Verdict or Nonsuit in such Writ of Dower or Action of Ejectment shall have been given or obtained; and upon the Return thereof, Judgment shall be given, and Execution awarded for such Mesne Profits and Damages, and also for Costs of Suit.

6. And whereas all Writs of Execution issued upon Judgments obtained in the said Courts of Great Sessions in WALES, are now returnable only at the Great Sessions held for the respective Counties; and Sheriffs frequently delay executing the same for many Months, and often refuse to make Returns to such Writs, or to pay over the Money received by them; and Sheriffs may also refuse to return bailable Processes, returnable in the Vacation, until the following Great Sessions, to the great Prejudice of the Suitors of the said Court; for Remedy whereof, and facilitating the Proceedings of the said Courts, be it enacted by the Authority aforesaid, That from and after the passing of this Act all Writs of Execution upon Judgments obtained in the said Courts of Great Sessions shall and may be made returnable before the Judges of such Courts respectively, on the common Day in each of the Two Vacations annually betwixt the Two Sessions (being the First Days of Trinity Term after the Spring Sessions, and the First Day of Hilary Term after the Autumn Sessions), or on the First Day of the next Sessions,

at the Election of the Party or Parties obtaining such Judgment, his, her, or their Attorney, who shall sue out the same; and that the Sheriffs (to whom any such Writ of Execution, or bailable Writ issued out of the said Courts, returnable in the Vacation, shall be delivered) shall make due Returns of such Writs at the Time the same shall be returnable, and file such Writs and Returns with the proper Officer of such Courts, or as soon afterwards as such Sheriff shall be called upon by a Rule of the same Courts.

7. And be it further enacted by the Authority aforesaid, That from and after the passing of this Act it shall and may be lawful to and for the respective Prothonotaries of the said Courts, or such other Officers as the Judges of the said Courts respectively shall appoint, to grant Rules for the Sheriffs in the Vacation to return such Writs of Execution and bailable Processes as shall be returnable in the Vacation, in such Manner and under such Regulations as the said Justice of the said Court shall appoint for that Purpose; and in case any Sheriff shall refuse or decline to return any Writ within Six Days after the Service of such Rule on him or his Deputy, such Sheriff shall be in the like Contempt, and answerable in the same Manner as if such Rule had been made by the said Judges at Sessions.

8. And be it further enacted, That after the passing of this Act it shall and may be lawful to and for the said Prothonotaries, or such other Officer as aforesaid, to grant Rules in the Vacation for a Particular of the Plaintiff's Demand, and of Defendant's Set-off, and for Leave to plead several Matters, or to pay Money in Stay of Proceedings, or to sign Judgment for Want of a Plea, in any Action depending in the said Court, under such Regulations as the said Judges shall appoint for that Purpose.

9. And be it further enacted by the Authority aforesaid, That from and after the passing of this Act it shall and may be lawful for the Judges of the said Courts of Great Sessions respectively, and the Judges of such Courts are hereby authorized and empowered, to issue Commissions to Persons resident out of the Jurisdiction of such Courts, for the Purpose of taking Answers, Examinations, and Affidavits, and for the Examinations of Witnesses in Causes in Equity, and also for the taking of Affidavits and the Examination of Witnesses at Law, in such Manner and in such Cases as the said Court of Exchequer has been used to issue the same, as Occasion shall require, and of administering Oaths to the Persons putting in

such Answers and Examinations, and making such Affidavits, and being examined as Witnesses.

10. And it is hereby further enacted by the Authority aforesaid, That all and every Person or Persons forswearing him, her, or themselves in any Answer or Affidavit, or in any Deposition or Examination, taken and sworn before any Commissioner appointed by virtue of this Act, shall incur and be liable to the same Penalties as if such Answer or Affidavit, Deposition or Examination, had been taken and sworn in any Suit in Equity depending in the said Court of Exchequer, or in any Action depending in the said Court.

11. And it is hereby further enacted, That from and after the passing of this Act it shall and may be lawful for the Judges of the said Courts of Great Sessions, and they are hereby authorized and empowered, in all Cases at Law, when the said Courts shall be sitting, in any County within the Limits of such Courts respectively, to make such Rules and Orders in Suits at Law, instituted and depending in the other Counties within their Jurisdiction, as to them the said Judges shall seem meet, and Occasion shall require; and such Rules and Orders shall be as valid and effectual in the Law, and as binding upon the Parties, as if the same had been made in the particular County in which suits were instituted.

12. And it is hereby further enacted, That from and after the passing of this Act it shall and may be lawful for the Judges of the said Courts of Great Sessions, and they are hereby authorized and empowered, in all Cases, both at Law and in Equity, when the said Courts shall not be sitting in WALES, to hear Motions and Petitions, and make such Rules and Orders thereon in Vacation, and out of the Jurisdiction of the said Courts, as to them the said Judges shall seem meet, and Occasion shall require; and such Rules and Orders shall be as valid in the Law, and as binding upon the Parties, as the same would or might have been in case the same had been made in WALES, within the Jurisdiction of the said Courts, and during the Sitting thereof.

13. And whereas Doubts and Difficulties arise as to serving Process in Actions within the respective Courts of Great Sessions, where the Cause of Action arises in one County, and the Defendant or Defendants reside in another County, each such Counties being within the same Jurisdiction of such Court of Great Sessions respectively; be it declared and enacted by the Authority aforesaid, That from and after the passing of this Act, whenever a Cause

of Action shall arise in one County and the Defendant or Defendants shall reside in another County, such Counties as last aforesaid being within the same Jurisdiction of the said Courts of Great Sessions respectively, it shall and may be lawful that any Writ or Writs to commence any Action within any of the Courts of Great Sessions, shall and may issue, directed to the Sheriff of such County wherein such Defendant or Defendants may reside, such last-mentioned County being within the same Jurisdiction of the said Courts of Great Sessions respectively, Notice being indorsed on such Writ of the County wherein such Action is brought, and which said Writ or Writs shall be deemed legal Process to compel such Defendant or Defendants to appear to such Action or Actions.

14. And be it further enacted, That from and after the passing of this Act, in all Cases in which Judgments shall have been obtained in the Courts of Great Sessions respectively, it shall and may be lawful for the Prothonotary of the Circuits of the said Courts of Great Sessions within which such Judgment has been obtained, and he is hereby required, upon the Application of the Person or Persons so obtaining the same, to issue a *testatum* Execution against the Defendant or Defendants, his, her, or their Goods and Chattels, directed to the Sheriff of any of the Counties within the same Jurisdiction of such Court of Great Sessions, although such County is not the County within which such Judgment was obtained, in such and the same Manner, and with the same Force and Effect as *testatum* Executions are issued from the Courts at Westminster into any County on Judgments in Actions where the Venue is laid in another County.

15. And be it further enacted by the Authority aforesaid, That in all Cases in which any Person shall have commenced any Suit, or have entered any Appearance in any Suit at Law or in Equity instituted in any of the said Courts of Great Sessions, or shall have come in as a Creditor or Purchaser, or otherwise submitted to the Jurisdiction of the said Courts of Great Sessions, but by reason of his or her Residence out of the Jurisdiction of such Courts, or having withdrawn therefrom, his or her Person or Goods cannot be made amenable to the Process thereof, it shall and may be lawful for the said Court of Exchequer in all Suits and Matters in Equity, and in all Suits and Matters at Law for the said Court of Exchequer, and also for the said Courts of King's Bench and Common Pleas, upon a Certificate from the proper Officer of the said Courts of Great

Sessions, of such Commencement of Suit, or of such Appearance having been entered or such Submission made, and upon a Transscript or Office Copy of such Rule, Order, or Decree being duly certified to the said Court of Exchequer in Matters of Equity, or in Matters of Law to the said Court of Exchequer or the said Courts of King's Bench and Common Pleas, together with an Affidavit of a due Service of a Copy of Such Rule, Order, or Decree, and of the Non-performance thereof, to issue an Attachment or other Process for enforcing Obedience to the same, in such Manner as is usual for the Purpose of enforcing Obedience to the Rules, Orders, and Decrees of such Court.

16. And whereas it is expedient that the Judges of the said Courts of Great Sessions should have full Power over the Officers thereof; be it therefore enacted by the Authority aforesaid, That from and after the passing of this Act it shall and may be lawful for the Judges of the said Courts, and they are hereby authorized to remove any Officer of the said Courts, or his Deputy, for Peculation, Extortion, or other Misconduct, and appoint a new Officer or Deputy in the Room of the Person so removed; any Law, Usage, or Custom to the contrary notwithstanding: Provided always, that nothing in this Clause contained shall authorize such Judges to dismiss on their own Authority any officer of the said Courts nominated and appointed by the Crown.

17. And whereas it is expedient that Security shall hereafter be given for any Sum or Sums of Money paid into any of the said Courts of Great Sessions for and on account of any Party or Parties to any Suit therein; be it further enacted, That from and after the passing of this Act the Judges of the said several Courts of Great Sessions shall and may, within their respective Jurisdictions, have and take, and are hereby required to have and take, from any Officer or Officers of such Courts respectively, and hereafter to be appointed, within Three Calendar Months next after such Appointment, and as often after as Occasion may require, such Security as to such Judges shall seem proper for and concerning the accounting for all and every Sum and Sums of Money which such Officer or Officers shall receive in any Cause or Suit at Law or in Equity pending in any such Court of Great Sessions, and which said Sum or Sums of Money shall be paid into any such Court by any Person in any Suit therein, and received by any such Officer or Officers as is or are or shall be accustomed or authorized to receive the same;

such Security to be given by Recognizance, or otherwise, as the said Judges shall direct, binding every such Officer or Officers, together with Two or more sufficient Sureties, in such penal Sum or Sums as to the said Judges shall seem proper, for the due accounting for all and every such Sum or Sums of Money so paid.

18. And it is hereby further enacted by the Authority aforesaid, That it shall and may be lawful for the Judges of the said Courts of Great Sessions, and they are hereby authorized and empowered, in all Cases in which they shall think fit, to order and direct any Sum or Sums of Money belonging to the Suitors of the said Courts of Great Sessions to be paid into the Bank of England, in the Name and with the Privity of the Accountant-General of his Majesty's Court of Exchequer at Westminster, subject to the Order and Decree of the Court of Great Sessions at the Instance of which it shall be so paid in; and the said Accountant-General is hereby directed to obey the Orders and Decrees of such Court of Great Sessions in regard thereto, in like Manner as he obeys the Orders and Directions of the said Court of Exchequer, and to act and do all Matters and Things relating to the delivering, securing, and investing of the Money so ordered to be paid, and the Payment, selling, and transferring of the same, and the keeping the Accounts with the Bank of England, and other Matters relating thereto, in the like Manner as he acts and does all Matters and Things relating to the Delivery, securing, and investing of the Money and Effects of the Suitors of the said Court of Exchequer, and the Payment, selling, and transferring of the same, and the keeping the Accounts or other Matters relating thereto.

19. And whereas by an Act of Parliament made in the Thirteenth Year of His late Majesty's Reign, intituled, An Act to discourage the Practice of commencing frivolous and vexatious Suits in His Majesty's Courts at Westminster, in Causes of Action arising within the Dominion of WALES, and for further regulating the Proceedings in the Courts of Great Sessions in WALES, it is enacted, that in case the Plaintiff in any Action upon the Case for Words, Action of Debt, Trespass on the Case, Assault and Battery, or other personal Action, where the Cause of such Action shall arise within the Dominion of WALES, and which shall be tried at the Assizes at the nearest English County to that Part of the said Dominion of WALES in which the Cause of Action shall be laid to arise, shall not recover by Verdict Debt or Damages to the Amount of Ten Pounds, in such Case, if the Judge who tried the Cause, on Evidence appearing before him, shall certify on the Back of the Record of *Nisi Prius*, that the Defendant or Defendants was or were resident in the Dominion of WALES at the Time of the Service of the Writ or other Mesne Process served on him, her, or them in such Action, on such Fact being suggested on the Record or Judgment Roll, Judgment of Nonsuit shall be entered against the Plaintiff; and such Defendant or Defendants shall be entitled to and have like Judgment and Remedy thereon, to recover such and the like Costs against the Plaintiff or Plaintiffs in every such Action, as if a Verdict had been given by the Jury for the Defendant or Defendants, unless the Judge before whom such Cause shall be tried shall certify on the Back of the Record that the Freehold or Title of Land was chiefly in question, or that such Cause was proper to be tried in such English County: And whereas it is expedient that so much of the said Act as is herein recited should be repealed, and other Provisions be made in lieu thereof; be it therefore enacted, That so much of the said Act as has been herein recited be and from henceforth shall stand absolutely repealed, and is hereby repealed.

20. And whereas it is also expedient that so much of the said Act of the Thirteenth Year of His late Majesty's Reign which relates to prevent transitory Actions, where the Cause of Action does not amount to Ten Pounds, arising within the said Principality, from being brought in any of His Majesty's Courts of Record out of the said Principality, be repealed, and other and further Provisions substituted in lieu thereof; be it therefore enacted by the Authority aforesaid, That so much of the said last-mentioned Act be and is hereby repealed.

21. And be it further enacted, That in all Actions upon the Case for Words, Action of Debt, Trespass on the Case, Assault and Battery, or other personal Action, and all transitory Actions, which from and after the Sixth Day of November which shall be in the Year of our Lord One thousand eight hundred and twenty-four, shall be brought in any of His Majesty's Courts of Record out of the Principality of WALES, and the Debt or Damages found by the Jury shall not amount to the Sum of Fifty Pounds, and it shall appear upon the Evidence given on the Trial of the said Cause, that the Cause of Action arose in the said Principality of WALES, and that the Defendant or Defendants was or were resident in the Dominion of WALES at the Time of the Service of any Writ, or other Mesne Process, served on him, her, or them in such Actions, and it shall be so testified under the Hand of the Judge who tried such Cause, upon the Back of the Record of Nisi Prius (on such Facts being suggested on the Record or Judgment Roll), a Judgment of Nonsuit shall be entered thereon against the Plaintiff or Plaintiffs, and the Plaintiff or Plaintiffs shall pay to the Defendant or Defendants in such Action, his, her, or their Costs of Suit, and the Defendant and Defendants shall have like Remedy to recover the same as in the Case of a Verdict given for the Defendant or Defendants in such Action; and in the Taxation of all Costs allowed and given to the Defendant or Defendants, the proper Officer shall allow to the Plaintiff or Plaintiffs, out of the Defendant's Costs, the full Sum given by the Verdict to the Plaintiff or Plaintiffs for his, her, or their Debt or Damages; and although no Judgment shall be entered for the Plaintiff or Plaintiffs upon such Verdict, yet nevertheless such Verdict, without any Judgment entered thereon, shall be an effectual Bar to any Action or Actions commenced in any Court whatsoever by the Plaintiff or Plaintiffs for the same.

22. Provided always, and be it further enacted, That nothing in this Act contained shall bar or preclude any Person or Persons from commencing and carrying on any Action, and which may be tried at the Assizes at the nearest English County to that Part of the said Dominion of WALES in which the Cause of Action shall be laid, to arise against any Defendant or Defendants so resident in the Dominion of WALES, and obtaining full Costs in such Action, if the Judge before whom the Cause shall be tried shall certify on the Back of the Record that the Title or Freehold of Land was chiefly in question, or that such Cause was proper to be tried in such English County.

23. And for the better preventing vexatious Delays and Expences occasioned by the suing forth Writs of Certiorari for the Removal of Actions, Suits, Causes, or other Proceedings at Law commenced and carried on in any of His Majesty's Courts of Great Session in WALES, and for regulating in future the issuing of such Writs; be it further enacted, That from and after the Sixth Day of November which shall be in the Year of our Lord One thousand eight hundred and twenty-four, no Writ of Certiorari shall be granted, issued forth, or allowed, to remove any Action, Bill, Plaint, Cause, Suit, or other Proceeding at Law whatsoever, originated in or commenced, carried on or had in any of His Majesty's Courts of Great Sessions in

WALES, unless it be duly proved upon Oath that the Party or Parties suing forth the same hath or have given Seven Days Notice thereof in Writing to the other Party or Parties concerned in the Action, Bill, Plaint, Cause, Suit, or other Proceeding sought to be so removed, and unless the Party or Parties so applying or suing forth such Writ shall, upon Oath, shew to the Court in which Application shall be made sufficient Cause for issuing such Writ, and so that the Party or Parties therein concerned may have an Opportunity to shew Cause, if he or they shall so think fit, against the issuing or granting such Certiorari, and that the Costs of such Application be in the Discretion of the Court wherein such Application shall be made for such Certiorari.

24. And whereas the Sum or Sums of Money now demandable and payable for Fines and Recoveries levied and suffered at the several Courts of Great Sessions in WALES, is and are unequal and uncertain in the Amount; be it further enacted, That from and after the passing of this Act, the Fees to be paid on any Fine or Recovery so levied or suffered, and the Amount of King's Silver to be paid thereon, shall be in the same Proportion, and ascertained and calculated in the same Manner by the proper Officer, as the Fees and King's Silver now usually payable on Fines and Recoveries levied and suffered in His Majesty's Courts of Common Pleas at Westminster, and shall not exceed the same.

25. Provided always, and be it further enacted, That in all and every Case where such Fees and King's Silver are now payable to any Person or Persons duly authorized to receive and compound for the same, under and by virtue of any Patent or Patents for any Term or Terms now in Existence, within the respective Courts of Great Sessions in WALES, the same Sum or Sums as is or are now demandable and payable under and by virtue of such Patent or Patents, shall be hereafter paid during the Term or Terms granted by such Patent or Patents; but that when and as often as such Term or Terms shall respectively cease, expire, and determine, the said Sum or Sums of Money thereafter payable upon levying or suffering of any such Fines and Recoveries, as King's Silver or Fees thereon, within the Limits of the Jurisdiction of the Court or Courts of Great Sessions in such Patent or Patents named, and the Term or Terms whereof shall have so ceased, expired, and determined, shall immediately after any such Expiration and Determination be thenceforth in the same Proportion, and be ascertained

and calculated in the same Manner by the proper Officer, as the Fees and King's Silver now usually payable on Fines and Recoveries levied and suffered in the said Court of Common Pleas, and shall not exceed the same.

26. And whereas Fines can now be levied in the said Courts of Great Sessions within the Dominion of WALES Twice only in the Year, and it is expedient to give to His Majesty's Subjects possessing Lands, Tenements, and Hereditaments within WALES, the Power of levying such Fines Four Times in the Year, in like Manner as the Subjects of the Realm of England can now levy the same; be it therefore further enacted, That from and after the passing of this Act it shall and may be lawful for the Cursitor of each and every Court of Great Sessions in WALES, to issue any Writ or Writs of Covenants, for the Purpose of levying any Fine or Fines within the Jurisdiction of such Courts respectively, such Writs to be issued and be tested, and bear Date Fourteen Days at least before the First Day of Hilary Term, or Fourteen Days at least before the First Day of Trinity Term in each and every year; and the several Cursitors, and each and every of them, are hereby required so to do as often as applied to for that Purpose, on Payment of the usual Fee or Fees now demandable on any Writ of Covenant; and that all and every Writ or Writs so tested or bearing Date as aforesaid be made returnable on the said First Day of Hilary Term, and the said First Day of Trinity Term respectively, in each and every such Year; and that upon an Acknowledgment of such Fine or Fines by the proper Parties to the same, taken before a Judge of such Court respectively, or by virtue of any *Dedimus Potestatem*, which the said Cursitor or Cursitors is and are hereby also required to grant, as often as the same be necessary, and on the *Allocatur* of a Judge of the Court of Great Sessions within whose Jurisdiction the Fine may be so levied, in like Manner in which such *Allocatur* is given when a Fine is acknowledged on any *Dedimus Potestatem*, or otherwise during the Sitting of such Courts of Great Sessions, and on a Certificate made on the Back of any such Writ or Writs of Covenant by the proper Officer of such Court, of the actual Payment of King's Silver payable upon every such Fine or Fines, and which Certificate such proper Officer is hereby required to make upon Payment of such King's Silver, at the Costs and Charges of any Person or Persons paying the same, such Fine or Fines shall have full Force and Effect, and be deemed to be fully completed from the said First

Day of Hilary Term, or the said First Day of Trinity Term, on which the said Writ or Writs shall be made returnable as aforesaid; and Proclamation, if necessary, shall be made of such Fine or Fines at the next ensuing Great Sessions, and at the Two following Great Sessions, according to Law; and all such Fine and Fines shall operate and enure, and shall be equally binding upon all Lands, Tenements, and Hereditaments, and upon all Parties privy thereto, from the said First Day of Hilary Term, and the said First Day of Trinity Term, in like Manner as if the same was or were levied during the Sitting of the Court of Great Sessions, within the Jurisdiction of which such Lands, Tenements, and Hereditaments are situated.

27. And be it further enacted, That all and every Fine and Fines hereafter levied in WALES, shall take effect and enure, and be deemed complete from the Date of the Caption of the Acknowledgment taken in such Fine or Fines, and on the Payment of King's Silver due thereon, notwithstanding the Death or Deaths of any Party or Parties to such Fine or Fines after such Acknowledgment.

28. And be it further enacted by the Authority aforesaid, That from and after the passing of this Act, any Person authorized to take Affidavits as a Commissioner in the Courts of King's Bench, Common Pleas, and Exchequer, or a Master Extraordinary in the High Courts of Chancery in the United Kingdom, are hereby authorized to take any Affidavit of and concerning any Matter or Matters arising, or Fines or Recoveries levied or suffered within the said respective Courts of Great Sessions, in like Manner as any Affidavit is now taken in the said last-mentioned Courts of King's Bench, Common Pleas, Exchequer, or Chancery, of and concerning any Fines or Recoveries levied or suffered, or any Cause, Matter, or Thing depending or in anywise concerning any of the Proceedings arising or being within the last-mentioned Courts.

29. And for the better Regulation of Persons hereafter serving as Petit Jurymen at any of the said Courts of Great Sessions; be it further enacted, That from and after the First Day of July which shall be in the Year One thousand eight hundred and twenty-four, no Person shall be compellable to serve on any Petit Jury at any such Court of Great Sessions, unless he possess an Estate of Freehold or Copyhold of the clear yearly Value of Eight Pounds or upward, or any Estate for the Term of any Life or Lives, or for the

Term of Ninety-nine Years from the Commencement of such Estate, of the clear yearly Value of Fifteen Pounds.

A.D. 1827] 7-8 George 4, c. 53, s. 3.

AN ACT TO CONSOLIDATE AND AMEND THE LAWS RELATING TO THE COLLECTION AND MANAGEMENT OF THE REVENUE OF EXCISE THROUGHOUT GREAT BRITAIN AND IRELAND.

3. And be it declared and enacted, that in all cases relating to the revenue under the collection and management of the Commissioners of Excise, where "England" or "Great Britain" is or shall be mentioned in this Act, or in any other Act or Acts of Parliament relating to the revenue of Excise, the same shall be deemed and taken to extend to and include WALES, and the Town of Berwick-upon-Tweed. . . .

A.D. 1830] 1 William 4, c. 70, ss. 1, 13-20, 22-34, 39.

AN ACT FOR THE MORE EFFECTUAL ADMINISTRATION OF JUSTICE IN ENGLAND AND WALES.

Whereas the Appointment of an additional Puisne Judge to each of His Majesty's superior Courts of Common Law would cause much greater Facility and Dispatch of Business therein: And whereas it is expedient to put an end to the separate Jurisdiction for the County Palatine of Chester and the Principality of WALES, and to make more effectual Provision for the Administration of Justice in England and WALES; be it therefore enacted by the King's most Excellent Majesty, by and with the Advice and Consent of the Lords Spiritual and Temporal, and Commons, in this present Parliament assembled, and by the Authority of the same, That whenever His Majesty shall be pleased to appoint an additional Puisne Judge to either of His Courts of the King's Bench, the Common Pleas, and the Exchequer, the Puisne Judges of such Court shall sit by Rotation in each Term, or otherwise, as they shall agree amongst themselves, so that no greater Number than Three of them shall sit at the same Time in Banc for the Transaction of Business in Term, unless in the Absence of the Lord Chief

Justice or Lord Chief Baron; and that it shall and may be lawful for any One of the Judges of either of the said Courts, when Occasion shall so require, while the other Judges of the same Court are sitting in Banc, to sit apart from them for the Business of adding and justifying Special Bail, discharging Insolvent Debtors, administering Oaths, receiving Declarations required by Statute, hearing and deciding upon Matters on Motion, and making Rules and Orders in Causes and Business depending in the Court to which such Judge shall belong, in the same manner and with the same Force and Validity as may be done by the Court sitting in Banc.

13. And be it further enacted That from and after the Commencement of this Act His Majesty's Writ shall be directed and obeyed, and the Jurisdiction of His Majesty's Courts of King's Bench, Common Pleas, and Exchequer respectively, and of the several Judges and Barons thereof, shall extend and be exercised over and within the County of Chester and the County of the City of Chester, and the several Counties in WALES, in like Manner, to the same Extent, and to and for all Intents and Purposes whatsoever as the Jurisdiction of such Courts respectively is now exercised in and over the Counties of England not being Counties Palatine, any Statute heretofore passed to the contrary notwithstanding; and that all original Writs to be issued into the said several Counties of Chester, City of Chester, and WALES, shall be issued by the Cursitors for London and Middlesex, and the Process and Proceedings thereon shall be issued by and transacted with such of the Officers of the several Courts of King's Bench and Common Pleas as shall be named for that Purpose by the Chief Justices of such Courts respectively, each naming for his own Court.

14. And be it further enacted, That all the Power, Authority, and Jurisdiction of His Majesty's Court of Session of the said County Palatine of Chester, and of the Judges thereof, and of His Court of Exchequer of the said County Palatine, and of the Chamberlain and Vice Chamberlain thereof, and also of His Judges and Courts of Great Sessions, both in Law and Equity, in the Principality of WALES, shall cease and determine at the Commencement of this Act; and that all Suits then depending in any of the said Courts, if in Equity, shall be transferred, with all the Proceedings thereon, to His Majesty's Court of Chancery or Court of Exchequer, as the Plaintiff or (in default of his making Choice

before the last Day of next Michaelmas Term) as any Defendant shall think fit, and if in Law, to the Court of Exchequer, there to be dealt with and decided according to the Practice of those Courts respectively, or of the Court from whence the same shall be transferred, according to the Discretion of the Court to which the same shall be transferred; which Court shall, for the Purpose of such Suits only, be deemed and taken to have all the Power and Jurisdiction, to all Intents and Purposes, possessed before the passing of this Act, by the Court from whence such Suit shall be removed.

15. Provided always, and be it enacted, That nothing in this Act contained shall be construed to abolish or affect the Obligations and Duties of the Jurisdiction or Rights now lawfully imposed upon, performed, or claimed and exercised by the Mayor and Citizens of Chester in the Courts of the County of the City of Chester or otherwise, save and except that such Writs of Error or false Judgment as may now by any Charter or Usage of the said Corporation be brought upon the Judgments of the said Courts or any of them before any of the Courts abolished by this Act, shall hereafter be issued, as in other Cases, from inferior Courts, and be returnable into His Majesty's Court of King's Bench.

16. And be it further enacted, That all Persons who on or before the passing of this Act shall have been admitted as Attornies and shall then be practising in any of the Courts of Sessions or Great Sessions in the County Palatine of Chester or in WALES respectively, shall be entitled, upon the Payment of One Shilling, to have their Names entered upon a Roll to be kept for that Purpose in each of the superior Courts of Westminster, and thereupon be allowed to practise in such Courts in all Actions and Suits against Persons residing, at the Commencement of the Suit, within the County of Chester or Principality of WALES; and that all Persons having served or now actually serving as Clerks to such Attornies under Articles, and who would otherwise be entitled to be admitted as Attornies of the said Courts of Great Sessions, may, on or before the Expiration of Six Months after the passing of this Act, be admitted as Attornies of the said Courts at Westminster, for the Purpose of practising there, in the like Matters only, without Payment of any greater Duty than would now be payable by Law upon their Admission as Attornies of such Courts of Great Sessions respectively.

17. And be it further enacted, That all Attornies and Solicitors now actually admitted and practising in any of the said Courts

of Sessions or Great Sessions may be admitted as Attornies of the said Courts at Westminster, in like Manner as is now or may be hereafter prescribed for the Admission of other Persons as Attornies therein, upon Payment of such Sum for Duty, in addition to the Sum already paid by them in that Behalf, as shall, together with such latter Sum, amount to the full Duty required upon Admission of Attornies in the said Courts at Westminster; and that all Persons having served or now actually serving under Articles as Clerks to such Attornies or Solicitors of any of the said Courts of Sessions or Great Sessions, may, at the Expiration of their respective Times of Service, be admitted as Attornies of the said Courts at Westminster, in like Manner and upon Payment of the like Duty as if they had served under Articles as Clerks to Attornies of the last-mentioned Courts.

18. And be it further enacted, That any Person who shall have been duly appointed a Commissioner for taking Affidavits, or a Master Extraordinary in Chancery of any of the Courts abolished by this Act, shall, upon producing his Appointment before the proper Officer, and upon the Payment of One Shilling, be entitled to have his Name inserted in a List to be kept for that Purpose of such Commissioners or Masters Extraordinary, as the Case may be, and to exercise, within the Limits of his existing Commission or Commissions, the same Power and Authority, and for the same Purposes, and if his Commission had issued from one of His Majesty's Courts at Westminster.

19. And be it further enacted, That from and after the Time herein appointed for the Commencement of this Act Assizes shall be held for the Trial and Dispatch of all Matters, Criminal and Civil, within the County of Chester and the several Counties and County Towns in the Principality of WALES, under and by virtue of Commissions of Assize, Oyer and Terminer, Gaol Delivery, and other Writs and Commissions, to be issued in like Manner and Form as hath been usual for the Counties in England; and all Laws and Statutes now in force relating to the Execution of such Commissions, when issued for Counties in England, shall extend and be applied to the Execution of the Commissions issued for the County of Chester and the Counties of WALES under the Authority of this Act.

20. And be it further enacted, That, until it shall be otherwise provided by Law, One of the Two Judges appointed to hold the

Sessions of Assizes under His Majesty's Commission within the County of Chester and Principality of WALES shall, in such Order and at such Times as they shall appoint, proceed to hold such Assizes at the several Places where the same have heretofore been most usually held within SOUTH WALES; and the other of such Judges shall proceed to hold such Assizes at the several Places where the same have heretofore been more usually held in North WALES; and both of such Judges shall hold the Assizes in and for the County of Chester in like Manner as in other Counties of England.

22. And be it further enacted, That a Defendant who shall hereafter be in Custody of the Gaoler of the County Gaol of any County in England or in the Principality of WALES, by virtue of any Proceeding out of any of His Majesty's superior Courts of Record may be rendered in Discharge of his Bail in any other Action depending in any of the said Courts, in the Manner herein-before provided for a Render in Discharge of Bail; and the Keeper of such Gaol, or such Sheriff or other Person responsible for the Custody of Debtors as aforesaid, shall on such Render be duly charged with the Custody of such Defendant, and the said Bail shall be thereupon wholly exonerated from Liability as such.

23. And be it further enacted, That the Salaries of the Judges of the County Palatine of Chester, and of the Judges of the several Courts of Great Sessions in the Principality of WALES, shall, upon the Termination of the said Offices respectively, make Part of the Consolidated Fund of the United Kingdom of Great Britain and Ireland, and a Sum equal to the Amount of each such Salary shall be retained in the Exchequer as Part of the Consolidated Fund, and no Part thereof shall be issued or carried to the Account of the Civil List; any thing in any Act or Acts of Parliament to the contrary notwithstanding.

24. And whereas it is expedient that due Provision should be made for the Compensation of the Judges hereinafter mentioned, and of other Persons having a Freehold in their Offices in the County of Chester or Principality of WALES, for the Losses they may sustain by the Abolition of their Offices or Reduction of their Fees by virtue of this Act; be it therefore enacted, That from and after the Commencement of this Act there shall be issued, paid, and payable, out of and charged upon the Consolidated Fund of the United Kingdom of Great Britain and Ireland, (after paying or

reserving sufficient to pay all former Charges thereon, but in preference to any Charge hereafter to be made,) to Thomas Jervis Esquire, now One of His Majesty's Justices of the Chester Circuit, the Sum of One thousand and fifteen Pounds Twelve Shillings; to Jonathan Paine, Esquire, now His Majesty's Chief Justice of the North WALES Circuit, the Sum of One thousand Pounds; and to Robert Matthew Casberd, Esquire, One of His Majesty's Judges of the Brecon Circuit, the Sum of One thousand Pounds; the said several Sums to be payable and paid, free and clear from all Taxes and Deductions whatsoever, by even Portions, on the Fifth Days of January, April, and July, and the Tenth Day of October, in each Year, the first Payment thereof to commence and be made on the first of such Days as shall occur after the Commencement of this Act; and the said Annuities respectively to continue during the Lives of the Parties respectively entitled to receive the same, or until such Time as they may respectively be appointed by His Majesty to any other Place or Office the Salary or Emoluments of which shall be of equal or greater Amount than the said Annuities respectively, or in case the Salary or Emolument of such Office shall be of less yearly Amount than the Annuity which the Party appointed to such Office is entitled by this Act to receive, then the said Annuity to be abated and reduced in proportion to the Amount of such Salary or Emoluments, so as to make the whole Sum received by the Party equal to, but not exceeding, the Amount of such Annuity.

25. And be it further enacted, That there shall in like Manner, after the Commencement of this Act, be issued, paid, and payable out of and charged upon the said Consolidated Fund, (after paying and reserving as aforesaid, and with such Preference as aforesaid,) to the several Persons having a Freehold Interest in such Offices in the County of Chester or Principality of WALES as shall be abolished or affected by virtue of this Act, free and clear of all Taxes and Deductions whatsoever, such Sums of Money, at such Times, by way of Annuity or otherwise, as shall be adjudged and determined to be due to such Persons respectively by any Commission to be appointed by His Majesty or by virtue of any Act of Parliament, for the Purpose of determining the Amount of the Compensation that ought to be due and payable in such Cases; and that in the meantime and until Compensation shall be awarded and determined in manner aforesaid, or the Time shall have elapsed that may be

appointed for claiming the same, it shall be lawful for the Commissioners of His Majesty's Treasury of the United Kingdom of Great Britain and Ireland, or any Three of them, to issue their Warrants for the Payment to such Persons as aforesaid, out of the said Consolidated Fund, of such half-yearly or quarterly Allowances as to the said Commissioners shall seem reasonable, both as to the Amount and Times of Payment, on account of such Compensation as may thereafter be awarded to the said Parties respectively.

26. Provided always, and be it further enacted, That no Person shall be entitled to such Compensation or Allowance as aforesaid, whose Appointment to his Office was qualified by any condition or Reservation expressed in his Patent or otherwise made known to such Person, that such Office or the Emoluments thereof were to be held and enjoyed subject to any future Provision to be made by Parliament touching the same, or without any claim to Compensation in case the same should cease or be subjected to any Regulation: And provided also, that no Person shall be entitled to receive any such Compensation or Allowance who shall not previously make a full and true Statement to the said Commissioners of His Majesty's Treasury, to be verified on Oath before a Judge or Master in Chancery, if they shall think fit so to direct, of the Amount of the Salary, Fees, and Emoluments of such Office, and of the Disbursements and Outgoings of the same, for the Space of Ten Years before the passing of this Act; and that such Compensation or Allowance shall cease altogether, or be reduced in Amount, as the Case may be, whenever the Party entitled to receive the same shall be placed in any other public Office of which the Salary and Emoluments shall be equal to the Whole or to Part of such Compensation or Allowance, so that in the last-mentioned Case no Person shall be entitled to receive more of such Compensation or Allowance than shall be equal to the Difference between the full Amount thereof and the Amount of the Salary and Emoluments of the Office in which he may be hereafter placed.

27. And be it further enacted, That the Records, Muniments, and Writings of the several Courts abolished by this Act shall, until otherwise provided by Law, be kept by the same Persons and in the same Places as before the passing of this Act; and that the Court of Common Pleas shall have the like Power and Authority to amend the Records of Fines and Recoveries passed heretofore in any of the Courts abolished by this Act, as if the same had been

levied, suffered, or had in the Court of Common Pleas: Provided always, that in case of the Death of any such Person before any other Provision shall have been make for keeping such Records, Muniments, and Writings, the Custody thereof shall be with the Clerks of the Peace of the several Counties to which Counties the same shall respectively belong.

28. And be it further enacted, That upon all Fines which now are or before the Commencement of this Act shall be duly acknowledged in Chester or WALES, Proclamation may be made at the successive Assizes to be holden under His Majesty's Commission within the County of Chester and Principality of WALES, before any Judge of such Assize, during the Continuance of such his Commission, in the same Manner and Form, and with the same Force and Effect, as if the same had been proclaimed before the Justices of Chester and WALES, or any of them; any Law or Usage to the contrary notwithstanding.

29. And be it further enacted, That all Fines and Recoveries to be levied and suffered after the Commencement of this Act, of Lands, Tenements, or Hereditaments in the County of Chester or County of the City of Chester or Principality of WALES, shall be levied and suffered in such and the like Manner, and the same Officers shall be employed therein, as in the Case of Fines and Recoveries now levied or suffered of Lands, Tenements, or Hereditaments in any County of England not being a County Palatine.

30. Provided always, and be it further enacted, That nothing in this Act contained shall be taken to affect the Right of any Lessee by Patent under the Crown, or of any Pensioner or other Person lawfully entitled to any Portion of the Money Payable upon Fines and recoveries of Manors, Lands, or Tenements in the County of Chester or Principality of WALES, but that the same shall be paid and payable by the proper Officer of the Court of Common Pleas who shall receive the same, to such Lessee or other Person, or his Agent, in like Manner and to the same Extent as heretofore, during the Continuance of his Interest therein.

31. And be it further enacted, That in all Cases where any Trust for charitable Uses or of a public Nature shall have been cast upon the Judges of the Courts hereby abolished, by virtue of their Offices, it shall be lawful for the Lord High Chancellor or Keeper of the Seals for the Time being, or for the Judges of Assize upon their Circuits in the County of Chester or Principality of WALES, to appoint such other Trustee or Trustees as they shall think fit, by any Writing under their Hands, in place of the former Judge or Judges; which Trustee or Trustees so named shall have the same Power and Authority, and be subject to the same Rules and Duties, as the Trustee or Trustees for whom he or they may be substituted.

32. And be it further enacted, That where by any Law, Charter, or Usage any Corporate or other Officer or Person hath been accustomed or sought to take any Oath before any of the Judges or other Officers or in any of the Courts abolished by this Act, such Officer or Person may and shall take the same Oath before any Judge during the Assizes or in open Court at the Quarter Sessions in the County where such Oath was formerly taken, and such Oath being so taken shall have the same Force and Effect to all Intents and Purposes as if taken before any of the Judges or in any of the Courts abolished by this Act.

33. And whereas it is expedient that the Accounts of the Sheriffs of the County of Chester and Principality of WALES should be passed, as nearly as Circumstances will admit, in the same Manner as heretofore; be it enacted, That the Clerk of Assize, within Ten Days after the Conclusion of the Assizes in the County of Chester and in each County in WALES, shall make out a Roll containing the Names and Places of Residence of all Persons liable to the Payment of any Fines, Issues, Amercements, Recognizances, Compositions, or other Sums imposed or forfeited during the preceding Assizes, with the Sums set opposite to each Name, and shall forthwith transmit the same to the Sheriff, with an order upon the Sheriff, signed in the Name of One of the Judges of Assize, directing the Sheriff to cause such Sums to be levied and recovered from the Parties liable to pay the same, which Order shall be of the same Force and Efficacy, and be returnable to the same Person or Persons, as any Writ or Process heretofore issued to the Sheriff for the like Purpose; and the Sheriff, upon the Receipt thereof, shall proceed to levy the Sums in the said Roll mentioned, and shall be accountable for the same, and all Arrears thereof, in the same Manner, at the same Time, and to the same Officer, and shall pass his Accounts before the same Officer or Officers, as he hath been heretofore accustomed.

34. And be it further enacted, That the several Persons holding and exercising within the several Counties of Chester and WALES the Office of His Majesty's Attorney General shall, until His

Majesty's Pleasure shall be otherwise declared, continue (within their several Places and Counties where they are now entitled to exercise such Office) to have, in Person only, and not by Deputy, the same Rank, Name of Office, and the same Privileges, Fees, and Emoluments, which by any Law or Custom they have hitherto enjoyed and held within their respective Counties, save and except such Fees as would necessarily cease with the Abolition of the Courts and Jurisdictions abolished by this Act.

39. And be it enacted, That this Act shall, as to all Matters not otherwise provided for, commence and take effect upon and from the Twelfth Day of October in this present Year.

A.D. 1832] 2-3 William 4, c. 45, ss. 4, 8, 9, 10, 15, 32.

AN ACT TO AMEND THE REPRESENTATION OF THE PEOPLE IN ENGLAND AND WALES.

4. "New Boroughs hereafter to return One Member."

And be it enacted, that each of the Places named in the Schedule marked (D) to this Act annexed, (that is to say,) . . . and Merthyr Tydfil, shall for the Purposes of this Act be a Borough, . . . and shall from and after the End of this present Parliament return One Member to serve in Parliament.

8. "Places in WALES to have a share in Elections for Shire-towns."

And be it enacted, That each of the Places named in the First Column of the Schedule (E) to this Act annexed shall have a Share in the Election of a Member to serve in all future Parliaments for the Shire-town or Borough which is mentioned in conjunction there-with and named in the Second Column of the said Schedule (E).

9. "Boundaries of Shire-towns and Places in WALES to be settled."

And be it enacted, That each of the Places named in the First Column of the said Schedule (E), and each of the Shire-towns or Boroughs named in the Second Column of the said Schedule (E), and the Borough of Brecon, shall for the Purposes of this Act include the Place or Places respectively which shall be compre-hended within the Boundaries of each of the said Places, Shire-towns, and Boroughs respectively, as such Boundaries shall be settled and described by an Act to be passed for that Purpose in this present Parliament, which Act, when passed, shall be deemed and taken to be Part of this Act as fully and effectually as if the same were incorporated herewith.

10. "Swansea, Loughor, Neath, Aberavon and Kenfig to form one Borough, and Electors thereof not to vote for a Member for Cardiff."

And be it enacted, that each of the Towns of Swansea, Loughor, Neath, Aberavon, and Kenfig shall for the Purposes of this Act include the Place or Places respectively which shall be comprehended within the Boundaries of each of the said Towns, as such Boundaries shall be settled and described by an Act to be passed for that Purpose in this present Parliament, which Act, when passed, shall be deemed and taken to be Part of this Act as fully and effectually as if the same were incorporated herewith; and that the said Five Towns, so including as aforesaid, shall for the Purposes of this Act be One Borough, and shall as such Borough, from and after the End of this present Parliament, return One Member to serve in Parliament; and that the Portreeve of Swansea shall be the Returning Officer for the said Borough; and that no Person by Reason of any Right accruing in any of the said Five Towns, shall have any Vote in the Election of a Member to serve in any future Parliament for the Borough of Cardiff.

15. "Certain Counties to return Two Knights of the Shire."

And be it enacted, That in all future Parliaments there shall be . . . Two Knights of the Shire, instead of One, to serve for each of the Counties of Carmarthen, Denbigh and Glamorgan.

32. "Provision as to the Freemen of Swansea, Loughor, Neath, Aberavon and Kenfig.

. . . Provided also, that every Person who would have been entitled, if this Act had not been passed, to vote as a Burgess or Freeman of Swansea, Loughor, Neath, Aberavon, or Kenfig, in the Election of a Member to serve in any future Parliament for the Borough of Cardiff, shall cease to vote in such Election, and shall instead thereof be entitled to vote as such Burgess or Freeman in the Election of a Member to serve in all future Parliaments for the Borough composed of the Towns of Swansea, Loughor, Neath, Aberavon and Kenfig, subject always to the Provisions herein-before contained with regard to a Burgess or Freemen of any Place sharing in the Election for any City or Borough.

SCHEDULE (D).

Merthyr Tydfil, Glamorganshire	

SCHEDULE (E).

Places sharing in the Election of Members.		Shire-Towns or Principal Boroughs.	County in which such Boroughs are situated.
Amlwch Holyhead and Llangefni	sharing with	Beaumaris	Anglesey
Aberystwyth Lampeter and Adpar	sharing with	Cardigan	Cardiganshire
Llanelly	sharing with	Caermarthen	Carmarthenshire
Pwllheli Nevin Conway Bangor Criccieth	sharing with	Caernarvon	Caernarvonshire
Ruthin Holt Town of Wrexham	sharing with	Denbigh	Denbighshire
Rhyddlan Overton Caerwis Caergwrley St. Asaph Holywell Mold	sharing with	Flint	Flintshire

SCHEDULE (E)—*Continued.*

Places sharing in the Election of Members.		Shire-Towns or Principal Boroughs.	County in which such Boroughs are situated.
Cowbridge Llantrissent	sharing with	Cardiff	Glamorganshire
Llanidloes Welsh Pool Machynlleth Llanfyllin Newtown	sharing with	Montgomery	Montgomeryshire
Narberth Fishguard	sharing with	Haverfordwest	Pembrokeshire
Tenby Wiston Town of Milford	sharing with	Pembroke	Pembrokeshire
Knighton Rhayader Kevinleece Knucklas Town of Presteigne	sharing with	Radnor	Radnorshire

A.D. 1836] 6 and 7 William 4, c. 77, ss. 11, 19.

An Act for carrying into effect the reports of the Commissioners appointed to consider the state of the Established Church in England and WALES, Etc., Etc.

After reciting the reports of the said Commissioners it was enacted—

11. That the said Commissioners shall prepare, and lay before His Majesty in Council, such scheme as shall appear to the said Commissioners to be best adapted for preventing the appointment

of any clergyman not fully conversant with the Welsh language to any benefice with cure of souls in WALES in any parish the majority of the inhabitants of which do not understand the English language.

19. That all archdeacons throughout England and WALES shall have and exercise full and equal jurisdiction within their respective archdeaconries, any usage to the contrary notwithstanding.

A.D. 1837] **7 William 4, and 1 Victoria, c. 22, s. 23.**

PROVISION FOR MARRIAGES IN THE WELSH TONGUE.

23. And be it enacted, That the Registrar-General, under the direction of one of Her MAJESTY'S Principal Secretaries of State, shall take order that the solemn declaration and form of words provided to be used in the case of marriages under the said act for marriages be truly and exactly translated in the WELSH TONGUE, and shall cause the same so translated to be furnished to every Registrar of Marriages throughout WALES, and in all places where the WELSH TONGUE is commonly used; and it shall be lawful to use the Declaration and form of words so translated, and published by authority in all places where the WELSH TONGUE is commonly used or preferred, in such manner and form and to the same intents and purposes as by the said Act is prescribed in the English Tongue.

A.D. 1838]
1 and 2 Victoria, c. 106, ss. 103, 104, 105.

AN ACT TO ABRIDGE THE HOLDING OF BENEFICES IN PLURALITY AND TO MAKE BETTER PROVISION FOR THE RESIDENCE OF THE CLERGY.

103. And whereas in many benefices in WALES and in the counties adjacent thereunto many of the inhabitants are imperfectly or not at all instructed in the English language, and it is expedient that persons to be hereafter instituted or licensed to such benefices should possess an adequate knowledge of the WELSH language: and whereas in and by an act passed in the session of parliament holden in the sixth and seventh years of his majesty's

reign, intituled "An Act for carrying into Effect the Reports of the Commissioners appointed to consider the State of the Established Church in England and WALES, with reference to Ecclesiastical Duties and Revenues, so far as they relate to Episcopal Dioceses, Revenues, and Patronage," the said Commissioners were directed to prepare and lay before his then majesty in council a scheme for preventing the appointment of any clergyman not fully conversant with the WELSH language to certain benefices with cure of souls in WALES: and whereas it is expedient to repeal such enactment, and instead thereof to enact other provisions of more general and extensive application; be it therefore enacted, that the said enactment shall be and the same is hereby repealed.

104. And be it enacted, That within the several dioceses of Saint Asaph, Bangor, Llandaff, and Saint Davids, it shall and may be lawful for the Bishop, if he shall think fit, to refuse institution or Licence to any Spiritual person who after due examination and inquiry shall be found unable to preach, administer the Sacraments, perform other pastoral duties, and converse in the WELSH language: Provided always that any such Spiritual person may, within one month after such refusal, appeal to the Archbishop of Canterbury, who shall either confirm such refusal or direct the Bishop to grant institution or licence, as shall seem to the Archbishop just and proper: Provided also, that nothing hereinbefore contained shall be construed to affect or abridge any rights which the inhabitants of any benefice within the said four Welsh dioceses may at present by Law possess of entering a caveat against or objecting in due course of law to the institution, collation, or License of any Spiritual person, or of proceeding to procure the deprivation of any such person.

105. And be it enacted, That all the provisions and powers of this Act relating to the appointment of curates where the ecclesiastical duties are inadequately performed shall within the several dioceses of Saint Asaph, Bangor, Llandaff, and Saint Davids extend and apply to cases wherein the Bishop shall see reason to believe that the ecclesiastical duties of any benefice are not satisfactorily performed by reason of the insufficient instruction in the WELSH language of the Spiritual person serving such benefice.

A.D. 1840] **3 and 4 Victoria, c. 113, ss. 1, 2, 19, 22, 38, 39, 40, 51, 62, 66.**

AN ACT TO CARRY INTO EFFECT THE REPORT OF THE ECCLESIASTICAL COMMISSIONERS.

1. That from henceforth all the members of chapter, except the dean, in every cathedral and collegiate church in England, and in the cathedral churches of Saint David and Llandaff, shall be styled canons; and the precentor of the cathedral church of Saint David . . . shall be . . . styled dean.

2. That, subject to the provisions hereinafter contained, the number of canons in the several cathedral and collegiate churches of the new foundation, and in the cathedral churches of Saint David and Llandaff, . . . shall be the number respectively specified in the Schedule hereto annexed, viz:—two in each.

19. That no appointment shall hereafter be made to any canonry in either of the cathedral churches of Saint David or Llandaff, excepting any canonry by the vacancy of which the canons shall be reduced below the number of two; and that all canonries vacant previously to such reduction shall be suspended.

22. Subject to the provisions hereinafter contained, That after the passing of this Act no presentation, collation, donation, admission, election, or other appointment to the dignity or office of sub-dean, Chancellor of the Church, Vice Chancellor, treasurer, provost, precentor, or succentor, nor to any prebend not residentiary in any cathedral or collegiate church in England, or in the cathedral churches of Saint David and Llandaff, or in the collegiate church of Brecon, shall convey any right or title whatsoever to any lands, tithes, or other hereditaments, or any other endowment or emolument whatsoever, now belonging to such dignity, office, or prebend, or enjoyed by the holder thereof in right of such dignity, office, or prebend, or any part thereof: provided that nothing herein contained shall be construed to deprive any present or future holder of any office in any cathedral or collegiate church, actually performing duties in respect of such office, of any stipend or other emolument heretofore accustomably assigned to such office, or paid to the holder thereof, according to the statutes of such church, out of the revenues thereof.

38. That the canonries of the cathedral church of Saint David

shall be in the direct patronage of the Bishop of Saint David's, and that so soon as conveniently may be the canons may be respectively instituted or licensed, as the case may be, to the cure of souls in the parish of Saint David; and the whole divisible corporate revenues shall be divided into twenty-four parts, ten of which parts shall be assigned to the dean, and five to each canon, and the remaining four parts shall be assigned as an endowment to the archdeacon of Cardigan.

39. That, so soon as conveniently may be, and by the authority hereinafter provided, due provision shall be made out of the endowments belonging to the prebends in the collegiate church of Brecon for the archdeaconries of Brecon and Carmarthen.

40. That the archdeacon of Llandaff shall from henceforth be also dean of the cathedral church of Llandaff, and that, so soon as conveniently may be, the canons of the said church may be instituted or licensed, as the case may be, to the cure of souls in the parishes of Llandaff and Whitchurch respectively; and, after the reservation to the Lord Bishop of Llandaff of one seventh part (being his present share) of the whole divisible corporate revenues, the remainder thereof shall be divided among the three members of the chapter, in the proportions of one half to the dean and one quarter to each of the canons.

51. That all lands, tithes, and other hereditaments, excepting any right of patronage, and all other the emoluments and endowments whatsoever belonging to the deanery of Brecon, and to the dignity or office of sub-dean, chancellor of the church, vice chancellor, treasurer, provost, precentor, or succentor, and to any prebend not residentiary in any cathedral or collegiate church in England, or in the cathedral churches of Saint David's and Llandaff, or in the collegiate church of Brecon, or enjoyed by the holder of any such deanery, dignity, office, or prebend as such holder, shall, as to all such of the said deaneries, dignities, offices, and prebends respectively as may be vacant at the passing of this Act immediately upon its so passing, and as to all others immediately upon the vacancies thereof respectively, without any conveyance or assurance in the law other than the provisions of this Act, accrue to and be vested absolutely in the Ecclesiastical Commissioners for England and their successors for the purposes of this Act: Provided always, that all other rights and privileges whatsoever now by law belonging to any of such dignities, offices, or prebends, except the said last-named

deaneries, shall continue to belong thereto, except so far as any of such rights or privileges may be controuled or affected by any of the provisions of this Act, respecting the right of election now exercised by any chapter; Provided always, that nothing herein contained shall in any manner apply to or affect any dignity, office, or prebend which is permanently annexed to any bishoprick, archdeanery, professorship, or lectureship, or to any school or the mastership thereof, &c.

62. That, if it be deemed fit, any part of the lands, tithes, or other hereditaments, or of the rents and profits thereof, which shall be vested in or accrue to the Ecclesiastical Commissioners for England from or in respect of the cathedral church of Saint David or the collegiate church of Brecon, may by the authority hereinafter provided be transferred to the college of Saint David's at Lampeter, in exchange for benefices with cure of souls which are now connected with the said college; and the said college is hereby empowered upon the completion of any such arrangement to convey any such benefices to such person or body corporate, and in such manner, as shall by the like authority be directed.

66. That so soon as conveniently may be, and by the authority, hereinafter provided, such other annual sums shall be determined on to be paid, and shall be accordingly paid, by the said Commissioners, or such deductions shall be allowed to be made out of the proceeds of any suspended canonry or canonries, as, after like inquiry and calculation, shall give to the dean of every cathedral and collegiate church in England an average annual income of £1,000, and to the deans of Saint David's and Llandaff respectively an average annual income of £700, and to the respective canons of every cathedral church in England an average annual income of £500, and to the canons of the said churches of Saint David and Llandaff an average annual income of £350.

A.D. 1841] **4 & 5 Victoria, c. 39, ss. 14, 28.**

AN ACT RELATING TO THE ECCLESIASTICAL COMMISSIONERS.

(*Repealing sections* 38, 39, *and* 40 *of* 3–4 *Victoria*, *c.* 113).

14. That so much of the said secondly recited Act as relates to the division and application of the existing corporate revenues of the chapters of the cathedral churches of Saint David and Llandaff

respectively, and to the application of the endowments belonging to the prebends in the collegiate church of Brecon, shall be and the same is hereby repealed.

28. That nothing in this Act contained shall, except as hereinafter specified, extend or apply to the dioceses or cathedral churches of Saint Asaph and Bangor or either of them; and that 5 & 6 WILL. 4, c. 30, 6 & 7 WILL. 4, c. 67, and such parts of 2 & 3 VICT., c. 55, as relate to the two last-mentioned Acts, so far only as the same Acts and parts of an Act apply to the said two last-mentioned dioceses and churches, or either of them, and also the temporary provisions, of the first herein recited Act, shall respectively continue and be in force until the first of August 1842, and, if Parliament shall be then sitting, until the end of the then session of Parliament: Provided always, that notwithstanding anything in the same Acts, or any or either of them, or in this Act contained, it shall be lawful for the Bishop of Bangor for the time being to collate to any vacant canonry, prebend, dignity, or office in the said cathedral church of Bangor not having any estate or endowment belonging thereto; and also that any bishop or archdeacon may hold visitations of the clergy within the limits of his diocese or archdeaconry, and at such visitations may admit churchwardens, receive presentments, and do all other acts, matters, and things by custom appertaining to the visitations of bishops and archdeacons in the places assigned to their respective jurisdiction and authority under or by virtue of the provisions of the said first or secondly recited Act; and any bishop may consecrate any new church or chapel or any new burial ground within his diocese.

A.D. 1842] **5 & 6 Victoria, c. 112.**

AN ACT FOR SUSPENDING APPOINTMENTS TO CERTAIN ECCLESIASTICAL PREFERMENTS IN THE DIOCESES OF SAINT ASAPH AND BANGOR; AND FOR SECURING CERTAIN PROPERTY TO THE SAID SEES.

By this Act,

After reciting the passing of 5 & 6 WILL. 4, c. 30, and 6 & 7 WILL. 4, c. 67, and that the said Acts, so far as they apply to the dioceses and cathedral churches of Saint Asaph and Bangor, have been and are continued until the 1st of August next, and if Parliament be then sitting until the end of the then session of Parliament; and it is expedient further to continue the same for a limited time:—

1. It is enacted, That the said Acts, so far as they apply to the said dioceses and cathedral churches of Saint Asaph and Bangor, shall continue and be in force until the 1st of October in the year 1843.

2. That all lands, tithes, tenements, and other hereditaments and endowments whatsoever, held, possessed, or received by the Right Reverend William Carey Bishop of Saint Asaph, and the Right Reverend Christopher Bethell Bishop of Bangor, respectively, as such bishops, not being so held, possessed, or received in respect of any benefice with cure of souls, shall be and be deemed to be to all intents and purposes part and parcel of the lands, tithes, tenements, and other hereditaments and endowments of the respective sees of Saint Asaph and Bangor, or of the united see of Saint Asaph and Bangor, as the case may be, and shall continue to be held, possessed, and received by the bishops of the same sees for the time being; subject nevertheless to any order in council issued under the provisions of 6 & 7 WILL. 4, c. 77, or of any other Act of Parliament.

3. That this Act may be repealed or amended during this session of Parliament.

A.D. 1843]

6 and 7 Victoria, c. 77.

AN ACT FOR REGULATING THE CATHEDRAL CHURCHES OF WALES.

Whereas an Act was passed in the Fourth Year of Her Majesty's Reign, intituled "An Act to carry into effect, with certain Modifications, the Fourth Report of the Commissioners of Ecclesiastical Duties and Revenues"; and another Act was passed in the Fifth Year of Her Majesty's Reign, intituled "An Act to explain and amend Two several Acts relating to the Ecclesiastical Commissioners for England": And whereas it is expedient to extend the Provisions of the said recited Acts to the Dioceses and Cathedral Churches of Saint Asaph and Bangor, and to alter and amend some of the said Provisions: Be it enacted by the Queen's most Excellent Majesty, by and with the Advice and Consent of the Lords Spiritual and Temporal, and Commons, in this present Parliament assembled, and by the Authority of the same, That from and after the passing of this Act all the Provisions of the said recited Acts shall, subject to the further Enactments herein-after contained, extend and apply to the said Dioceses and Cathedral Churches of Saint Asaph and Bangor, and to the Bishops of the same Dioceses, and to all Ecclesiastical Rectories without Cure of Souls, and all Benefices with Cure of Souls, and all Parishes and Places, therein, and to the Dignities, Offices, Canonries, and Prebends of the same Churches, and the respective Holders thereof.

2. And be it enacted, notwithstanding any thing in the said recited Acts contained, That in each of the Chapters of the Cathedral Churches of Saint Asaph, Bangor, Saint David's and Llandaff there shall be Four Canonries Residentiary, and no more; and such Canonries shall be in the direct Patronage of the Bishops of Saint Asaph, Bangor, Saint David's, and Llandaff respectively.

3. Provided always, and be it enacted, That, so soon as conveniently may be after the passing of this Act, Arrangements shall be made, by the Authority in the said recited Acts provided, for permanently annexing Two of such Four Canonries Residentiary, in such Cathedral Churches respectively, to Two Archdeaconries, in the respective Dioceses in which such Churches are situate.

4. And be it declared and enacted, That the Dean of each of the said Four Cathedral Churches shall be the Head of the Chapter thereof, and shall have Precedence over all other Members of such Chapter; and that such Dean and the Canons Residentiary respectively of each such Church shall possess and may exercise all the like Rights, Power, and Authority as are and may be possessed and exercised by the Dean and Canons respectively of any Cathedral Church in England founded by King HENRY the Eighth.

5. And be it enacted, That so much of the said recited Acts as relates to the Cure of Souls in the Parish of Saint David in the Diocese of Saint David's, and in the Parishes of Llandaff and Whit church in the Diocese of Llandaff, shall be repealed; and that it shall be lawful, if it be deemed expedient, by the Authority herein-before mentioned, with the Consent of the Bishop of Llandaff for the Time being, to declare and provide that the Cure of Souls in and over the respective Parishes of Llandaff and Whitchurch, or either of them, shall be vested in One Spiritual Person as Perpetual Incumbent thereof, and that such Bishop and his Successors shall

from Time to Time collate, or nominate and license, as the Case may be, a Spiritual Person to be such Incumbent, and also, with the like Consent and with the Consent of the Dean and Chapter, to endow such Parishes, or either of them, in such Manner and to such Amount as may appear expedient; and upon any such Declaration being made in the Case of the Parish of Llandaff, the respective Rights and Duties to be exercised and performed within and over the Cathedral Church by the Dean and Chapter, Dean, Canons, and Minor Canons thereof, and by such Incumbent as aforesaid, respectively, shall be defined by the like Authority, with the like Consents.

6. And be it declared and enacted, That the average annual Incomes of the Deans and Canons Residentiary of the said Four Cathedral Churches shall be of the same Amounts respectively as are fixed as the average annual Incomes of the Deans and Canons respectively of the Cathedral Churches of Saint David's and Llandaff by the said first-recited Act, and that the Provisions of the said recited Acts, respecting the Augmentation of the Incomes of Deans and Canons, shall be construed to authorize the Augmentation of the Incomes of the respective Deans and Canons Residentiary aforesaid, out of the common Fund in the said first-recited Act mentioned.

7. And be it enacted, That it shall be lawful, by the Authority herein-before mentioned, to provide, out of the same Fund, One fit House, at Saint Asaph, Bangor, and Llandaff respectively, as a House of Residence for the Use of the Canons Residentiary of the Cathedral Churches of the said Cities respectively, and also a fit House of Residence for the Dean of Llandaff.

8. And be it enacted, That from and after the passing of this Act the Dignity and Office of Archdeacon of Saint Asaph shall no longer be holden by the Bishop of Saint Asaph, and the Dignities and Offices of Archdeacon of Bangor and Archdeacon of Anglesea shall be dissevered from the Bishoprick of Bangor, and be no longer holden by the Bishop of Bangor, and the Archdeaconry of Anglesea shall be incorporated with and form Part of the Archdeaconry of Bangor; provided that nothing herein contained shall affect any Lands, Tithes, Tenements, or other Hereditaments, or Endowments, now forming Part of the Property and Revenues of the respective Sees of Saint Asaph and Bangor.

9. And be it enacted, That the Dignity and Office of Archdeacon

of Llandaff may, by the Authority herein-before mentioned, be separated from the Deanery of Llandaff: Provided always, that such Separation shall not take place before the next Vacancy of the said Deanery without the Consent of the present Dean.

10. And be it enacted, That within One Calendar Month after the passing of this Act the Treasurer of the Governors of the Bounty of Queen ANNE shall deliver to the Ecclesiastical Commissioners for England a full and particular Account, of all Monies received and paid by him, under and by virtue of any Act of Parliament, on account of the said Dioceses and Cathedral Churches of Saint Asaph and Bangor respectively, and of all Things done by him, and of all Proceedings then pending in respect thereof; and that, within such Time after the Delivery of such Account as shall be specified in any Order made upon him for that Purpose by the said Commissioners, he shall pay and deliver, or cause to be paid and delivered, to the said Commissioners, or into such Bank as shall be named in such Order, to their Account, for the Purposes of this Act, all Monies then remaining in his Hands or to his Account, and all Exchequer Bills and other Securities for Money, and all Books of Accounts, Papers, and Writings, in his Possession or Power in respect thereof; and that it shall be lawful for the said Commissioners to allow to the said Treasurer in his Accounts such Sum of Money as shall appear to them to be just and reasonable, in compensation for his Pains and Trouble, and also all proper Costs, Charges, and Expences incurred in the Execution of the Trusts reposed in him by any such Act in relation to the Matters aforesaid; and that the Receipt in Writing of the said Commissioners under their Common Seal shall be an effectual Discharge to the said Treasurer for all Monies and other Things therein expressed to be received by them.

11. And be it enacted, That the Provisions of the first-recited Act, whereby the Interests of Persons in Possession at the Time of the passing thereof were in any Manner protected, shall be deemed to be repeated in this Act, so as to protect the Interests of all Persons in Possession at the Time of the passing hereof, in the like respects and to the same Extent as the Interests of such first-mentioned Persons are so protected as aforesaid.

12. And be it enacted, That out of the Proceeds of any Lands, Tithes, Tenements, or other Hereditaments in the Principality of WALES, vested or to be vested in the Ecclesiastical Commissioners

for England by or under the Provisions of the said recited Acts or this Act, it shall be lawful, by the Authority herein-before mentioned, to make Provision, in whole or in part, for the competent Maintenance of any Spiritual Person or Persons (being a Native or Natives of the Principality aforesaid) who may be licensed by the Bishop of the Diocese for the Time being to officiate in any Church or Chapel within London or Westminster or the Suburbs thereof, duly consecrated for the Performance of Divine Service according to the Rites and Ceremonies of the United Church of England and Ireland in the Welch Language; and such Bishop is hereby authorized to license any such Spiritual Person or Persons accordingly.

13. And be it enacted, That so much of the said first-recited Act as relates to the College of Saint David's at Lampeter shall be repealed; and that, as soon as conveniently may be, and by the Authority herein-before mentioned, Arrangements may be made for effecting the Sale, to any Person or Persons or Body Corporate capable of holding the same, of the Advowsons of the several Benefices with Cure of Souls now annexed to the said College, and for investing the Proceeds of such Sales respectively for the Use and Benefit of the said College; and that if, after the Sales of the Advowsons of all such Benefices, it shall be made to appear to the said Ecclesiastical Commissioners that the said College, when it shall be in the Enjoyment of the Use and Benefit of the whole Proceeds of all such Sales when so invested as aforesaid, will still not be competently endowed, it shall be lawful, by the like Authority, to transfer to the said College, in Augmentation of the Endowment thereof, any of the Lands, Tithes, Tenements, or other Hereditaments aforesaid, or of the Proceeds thereof.

14. And be it enacted, That all the Powers and Authorities vested in Her Majesty in Council and in the said Commissioners by the first-recited Act, with reference to the Matters therein contained, and all other Provisions of the same Act relating to Schemes and Orders prepared, made, and issued for the Purposes thereof, shall be continued and extended and apply to Her Majesty in Council, and to the said Commissioners, and to all Schemes and Orders prepared, made, and issued by them respectively, with reference to all Matters contained in this Act, as fully and effectually as if the said Powers, Authorities, and other Provisions were repeated herein.

15. And be it enacted, That so much of an Act passed in the last Session of Parliament, intituled "An Act for suspending, until

the First Day of October One thousand eight hundred and forty-three, Appointments to certain Ecclesiastical Preferments in the Dioceses of Saint Asaph and Bangor, and for securing certain Property to the said Sees," as relates to the Continuance of certain temporary Acts therein recited, shall be repealed; provided that nothing herein contained shall prejudice or affect any thing done or any Proceeding pending under or by virtue of or relating to the Provisions of the said therein recited Acts or either of them.

16. And be it enacted, That this Act may be amended or repealed by any Act to be passed in this Session of Parliament.

A.D. 1844] **7 and 8 Victoria, c. 91.**

AN ACT TO CONSOLIDATE AND AMEND THE LAWS RELATING TO TURNPIKE TRUSTS IN SOUTH WALES.

(*Not printed herein.*)

A.D. 1845] **8 and 9 Victoria, c. 11.**

AN ACT FOR ASSIGNING SHERIFFS IN WALES.

"Whereas it is convenient that the Sheriffs in each of the Shires of WALES be nominated and appointed in like Manner as is used in other parts in England"; Be it enacted by the Queen's most Excellent Majesty, by and with the Advice and Consent of the Lords Spiritual and Temporal, and Commons, in this present Parliament assembled, and by the Authority of the same, That after the passing of this Act the Sheriffs in each Shire in WALES shall be assigned, ordained, nominated, and appointed at the same Time and Place and in like Manner and Form as is used according to the Law for Sheriffs in the Shires of England.

2. And be it enacted, That this Act may be amended or repealed by any Act to be passed in this Session of Parliament.

A.D. 1845] **8 and 9 Victoria, c. 61.**

AN ACT TO MAKE CERTAIN PROVISIONS FOR THE CONSOLIDATION OF TURNPIKE TRUSTS IN SOUTH WALES.

(*Not printed herein.*)

A.D. 1847]

10 and 11 Victoria, c. 72.

AN ACT FOR THE FURTHER AMENDMENT OF THE LAWS RELATING TO TURNPIKE ROADS IN SOUTH WALES.

(*Not printed herein.*)

A.D. 1847]

10 and 11 Victoria, c. 108.

AN ACT FOR ESTABLISHING THE BISHOPRICK OF MANCHESTER, AND AMENDING CERTAIN ACTS RELATING TO THE ECCLESIASTICAL COMMISSIONERS FOR ENGLAND.

Whereas an Act was passed in the Seventh Year of the Reign of His late Majesty King William the Fourth, intituled, "An Act for carrying into effect the Reports of the Commissioners appointed to consider the State of the Established Church in England and WALES, with reference to Ecclesiastical Duties and Revenues, so far as they relate to Episcopal Dioceses, Revenues, and Patronage"; and another Act was passed in the Fourth Year of the Reign of Her Majesty, intituled, "An Act to carry into effect, with certain Modifications, the Fourth Report of the Commissioners of Ecclesiastical Duties and Revenues"; and another Act was passed in the Fifth Year of the Reign of Her Majesty, intituled "An Act to explain and amend Two several Acts relating to the Ecclesiastical Commissioners for England"; and another Act was passed in the Seventh Year of the Reign of Her Majesty, intituled "An Act for regulating the Cathedral Churches of WALES": And whereas Her Majesty was pleased, on the Tenth Day of February in this Year One thousand eight hundred and forty-seven, to issue a Commission to certain Persons therein named, directing them to consider the State of the several Bishopricks in England and WALES with special reference to the Intention, therein graciously declared by Her Majesty, that a Measure should be submitted to Parliament for continuing the Bishopricks of Saint Asaph and Bangor as separate Bishopricks, and for establishing forthwith a Bishoprick of Manchester; and the said Commissioners have made their First Report to Her Majesty, bearing Date the Twentieth Day of April in this present Year, and have in their said Report recommended,

That the Diocese of Saint Asaph consist of the whole Counties of Flint and Denbigh, and such Parts of the Counties of Salop and Montgomery as are now in that Diocese, except the Deanry of Ceifeiliog in the last-mentioned County; and

That the Diocese of Bangor consist of the whole Counties of Anglesea, Carnarvon, and Merioneth, and the Deanries of Ceifeiliog and Arwstley in the County of Montgomery; and

That the Diocese of Chester consist of the County of Chester and the Deanry of Warrington in the County of Lancaster except the Parish of Leigh: and

That the new Bishoprick of Manchester be forthwith founded, and endowed out of the Revenues at the Disposal of the Ecclesiastical Commissioners for England applicable to Episcopal Purposes; and

That the Diocese of Manchester consist of such Parts of the Deanries of Kendal and Kirkby Lonsdale as are in the County of Lancaster, and of the Deanries of Amounderness, Blackburn, Manchester, and Leyland, and the Parish of Leigh in the Deanry of Warrington, all in the same County; and

That an Archdeaconry of Liverpool be founded in the Diocese of Chester: and that such Archdeaconry comprise the Deanry of Worrall in the County of Chester and the Deanry of Warrington (except the Parish of Leigh) in the County of Lancaster:

And whereas it is expedient that the said Recommendations should be carried into effect, with such Modifications as may be found necessary, and that certain of the Provisions of the said recited Acts should be altered and amended: Be it enacted by the Queen's most Excellent Majesty, by and with the Advice and Consent of the Lords Spiritual and Temporal, and Commons, in this present Parliament assembled, and by the Authority of the same, That so much and such Parts of the said recited Acts as provide for or apply to the Union of the Bishopricks, Sees, or Dioceses of Saint Asaph and Bangor, and also any Orders of Her Majesty in Council relating to the said Union, or to the new See or Diocese of Manchester, shall be repealed, and that all the Powers and Authorities vested in Her Majesty in Council, and in the Ecclesiastical Commissioners for England, by the said first and secondly recited Acts, with reference to the Matters therein respectively contained, and all other the Provisions of the same Acts relating to Schemes and Orders prepared, made, and issued for the Purposes thereof, and to Modifications and Variations therein, shall be continued and extended and shall apply to Her Majesty in Council, and to the said Commissioners, and to all Schemes and Orders to be prepared, made, and issued by them respectively, for the Purpose of carrying into effect the foregoing Recommendations, as fully and effectually as if the said Powers, Authorities, and other Provisions were repeated therein.

2. And be it enacted, That the Number of Lords Spiritual now sitting and voting as Lords of Parliament shall not be increased by the Creation of the Bishoprick of Manchester; and whenever there shall be a Vacancy among the Lords Spiritual by the Avoidance of any one of the Sees of Canterbury, York, London, Durham, or Winchester, or of any other See which shall be filled by the Translation thereto from any other See of a Bishop at that Time actually sitting as a Lord of Parliament, such Vacancy shall be supplied by the Issue of a Writ of Summons to the Bishop who shall be elected to the same See; but if such Vacancy be caused by Avoidance of any other See in England or WALES, such Vacancy shall be supplied by the Issue of a Writ of Summons to that Bishop of a See in England or WALES who shall not have previously become entitled to such Writ; and no Bishop who shall be hereafter elected to any See in England or WALES, not being one of the Five Sees above named, shall be entitled to have a Writ of Summons, unless in the Order and according to the Conditions above prescribed.

3. And be it enacted, That this Act may be amended or repealed by any Act to be passed in this Session of Parliament.

A.D. 1860]

23 and 24 Victoria, c. 68.

AN ACT FOR THE BETTER MANAGEMENT AND CONTROL OF THE HIGHWAYS IN SOUTH WALES.

(*Not printed herein.*)

A.D. 1863] **26 and 27 Victoria, c. 82.**

An Act to empower the Bishops of Welsh Dioceses to facilitate the making Provision for English Services in certain Parishes in WALES.

Whereas in all Parishes in Wales in which Welsh is the Tongue commonly spoken by the People it is required by Law that the whole Divine Service shall be used and said by the Minister and Curates throughout all Wales, within the said Dioceses where the Welsh Tongue is commonly used, in the British or Welsh Tongue: And whereas it is expedient to authorize the Performance in certain Parishes in Wales of Divine Service, Preaching, and Administration of the Sacraments according to the Use of the United Church of England and Ireland in the English Tongue, upon such Application and subject to such Conditions as are hereinafter mentioned: Be it enacted by the Queen's most Excellent Majesty, by and with the Advice and Consent of the Lords Spiritual and Temporal, and Commons, in this present Parliament assembled, and by the Authority of the same, as follows:

1. That wherever any Ten or more Inhabitants in any Parish District, or Place in Wales shall certify in Writing to the Bishop of the Diocese within which such Parish, District, or Place is situate, that they are desirous of having Divine Service performed and the Sacraments administered in the English Language, and that they, or some of them, will undertake to provide a Building to be used as a Chapel for the Performance of Divine Service in the English Tongue, and to provide for a Spiritual Person who may officiate therein, and for all other Expenses incident thereto, and shall apply to such Bishop to give the necessary Licences for the Purposes aforesaid, it shall be lawful for such Bishop, if it shall appear to him that sufficient Provision is not already made for such English Service, on the Nomination by the Incumbent of the said Parish, District, or Place of a fit and proper Person as Minister to such Chapel, to license from Year to Year, or for any Term not exceeding Two Years, such Building in any Part of such Parish, District, or Place as a Chapel for the Performance of Divine Service, Preaching, and Administration of the Sacraments according to the Use of the United Church of England and Ireland in the English Tongue, and to license such Minister to perform such of the said Services and Offices as may be specified in the said Licence.

2. Provided, however, that in case the said Incumbent shall fail to refuse or nominate a fit and proper Person as Minister to such Chapel, or in any case any Disagreement or Dispute shall arise between the Persons so applying and the Incumbent, either in respect of the Sufficiency of the said Services, or of the Provision for the Performance of such Services, or for the Minister, or in respect of the Competency of the Minister to be nominated, then the Bishop of such Diocese (after the Expiration of Three Calendar Months from the Receipt of such Application as aforesaid, due Notice of such Application having been given by the Persons so applying to the Incumbent) may signify in Writing to the Incumbent the Name of the Minister whom it is his Intention to nominate as the Officiating Minister of such Chapel ; and in case the Incumbent shall not, within Fourteen Days from such last Notification, signify in Writing his Dissent to such Nomination, it shall be lawful for the Bishop to nominate and license such Minister : Provided nevertheless, that in case the Incumbent shall, within the same Fourteen Days, signify his Dissent therefrom, such Nomination shall be referred by the said Bishop to the Archbishop of the Province in which such Diocese shall be situated, and such Licence shall not be granted without the Approval in Writing of the said Archbishop.

3. The said licensed Building shall not, without the Assent of the Incumbent, be nor be held to be a Parochial Chapel ; and nothing contained in this Act shall give the Minister of the said licensed Building any Power or Authority to perform any Pastoral or Ministerial Functions other than are specified in the said Licence.

4. Nothing herein contained shall affect the Right of the Incumbent of the said Parish, District, or Place in which the said licensed Building shall be situated in respect of the Publication of Banns, or the Solemnization of Marriages, or the Performance of Burials, or his Right to any Offertory, or any Fees, Dues, or Emoluments to which he may be at the passing of this Act legally entitled.

A.D. 1878] **41 and 42 Victoria, c. 34.**

AN ACT TO AMEND THE LAW RELATING TO HIGHWAYS IN SOUTH WALES.

(Not printed herein.)

A.D. 1881]

44 and 45 Victoria, c. 14.

AN ACT TO ENABLE COUNTY AUTHORITIES IN SOUTH WALES TO TAKE OVER AND CONTRIBUTE TOWARDS CERTAIN BRIDGES, AND TO REMOVE DOUBTS AS TO THE LIABILITY TO REPAIR THE HIGHWAYS OVER AND ADJOINING CERTAIN BRIDGES WHICH HAVE BEEN REBUILT.

(*Not printed herein.*)

A.D. 1881]

44 and 45 Victoria, c. 61.

AN ACT TO PROHIBIT THE SALE OF INTOXICATING LIQUORS ON SUNDAY IN WALES.

Whereas the provisions in force against the sale of fermented and distilled liquors during certain hours of Sunday have been found to be attended with great public benefits, and it is expedient and the people of Wales are desirous that in the principality of WALES those provisions be extended to the other hours of Sunday:

Be it therefore enacted by the Queen's most Excellent Majesty, by and with the advice and consent of the Lords Spiritual and Temporal, and Commons, in this present Parliament assembled, and by the authority of the same, as follows:

1. In the principality of WALES all premises in which intoxicating liquors are sold or exposed for sale by retail shall be closed during the whole of Sunday.

2. The Licensing Acts, 1872–1874, shall apply in the case of any premises closed under this Act as if they had been closed under those Acts.

3. This Act shall commence and come into operation with respect to each division or place in WALES on the day next appointed for the holding of the general annual licensing meeting for that division or place.

4. Nothing in this Act contained shall preclude the sale at any time at a railway station of intoxicating liquors to persons arriving at or departing from such station by railway.

5. This Act may be cited as the Sunday Closing (Wales) Act, 1881.

A.D. 1882]

45 and 46 Victoria, c. 67.

AN ACT TO AMEND THE SOUTH WALES TURNPIKE ROADS ACTS.

(*Not printed herein.*)

A.D. 1885]

48 and 49 Victoria, c. 54, s. 2.

PLURALITIES ACTS AMENDMENT ACT.

2. This Act shall be construed as one with the Act passed in the first and second years of the reign of Her present Majesty, chapter one hundred and six (herein-after referred to as "the first-mentioned Act") and the Act passed in the thirteenth and fourteenth years of the reign of Her present Majesty, chapter ninety-eight, as respectively amended by this Act.

The term "ecclesiastical duties" in the first-mentioned Act and this Act shall include not only the regular and due performance of divine service on Sundays and holidays, but also all such duties as any clergyman holding a benefice is bound by law to perform, or the performance of which is solemnly promised by every clergyman of the Church of England at the time of his ordination, and the performance of which shall have been required of him in writing by the bishop; and in case of benefices within the dioceses of St. Asaph, Bangor, Llandaff, and St. Davids, and the county of Monmouth, shall also include such ministrations in the WELSH language as the bishop of the diocese shall direct to be performed by the clergyman holding such benefices respectively, but so that such bishop shall not in any such case require more than one service in the WELSH language on every Sunday in such Church or chapel of ease situated in any such benefice: Provided always, that due provision be made for the English-speaking portion of the population.

A.D. 1887]

50 and 51 Victoria, c. 55, s. 31.

SHERIFFS ACT.

"**31.** Save as otherwise expressly provided by this or any other Act the law relating to sheriffs, inclusive of this Act and of the law relating to the election of members to serve in Parliament, shall extend to the Counties Palatine, to the county of Westmoreland, and each county in WALES in the same manner in all respects as to other counties in England, and the respective sheriffs of the above-mentioned counties, shall have the like powers, duties, jurisdiction, and liabilities, as the sheriff of any other county in England."

A.D. 1887] **50 and 51 Victoria, c. 58, s. 39, ss. 1.**

COAL MINES REGULATION ACT.

Inspection.

(1) A Secretary of State may from time to time appoint any fit persons to be inspectors (under whatever title he may from time to time fix) of mines, and assign them their duties, and may award them such salaries as the Treasury may approve, and may remove any such inspector: Provided always, that in the appointment of inspectors of mines in WALES and Monmouthshire, among candidates otherwise equally qualified, persons having a knowledge of the Welsh language shall be preferred.

A.D. 1888] **51 and 52 Victoria, c. 41, s. 13.**

LOCAL GOVERNMENT ACT.

(1) After the appointed day no county road rate shall be levied, and tolls shall cease to be taken on any road maintained and repaired by a county roads board in SOUTH WALES, in pursuance of the SOUTH WALES Turnpike Trusts Act, 1844, and the Acts amending the same, and after such day the Highways and Locomotives (Amendment) Act, 1878, as amended by this Act, shall apply to every county in SOUTH WALES as if the highway districts in that county had been constituted under the Highway Act, 1862, and the Highway Act, 1864, or one of those Acts, and shall apply to every such road as above-mentioned, in like manner as if it were ceasing, within the meaning of the said Act, to be a turnpike road.

(2) On the appointed day every county roads board and district roads board in each county shall cease to exist, and the property, debts, and liabilities of any such board shall be transferred to the

county council, and that council shall be the successors of the county and district roads boards, and the provisions of this Act, with respect to the transfer of the property, debts, and liabilities of quarter sessions to county councils, and with respect to the officers and servants of quarter sessions, shall apply as if they were herein re-enacted and made applicable to the property, debts, liabilities, and officers of the said county and district roads boards.

(3) For the following purposes (that is to say):

(*a*) For giving effect to the said transfer of the property, debts, and liabilities, and for controlling the officers and servants transferred by this section to the county council, and otherwise winding up the affairs of the county and district roads boards; and

(*b*) For the purpose of the appointment of the surveyor of a highway board, the alteration of a highway district, and other purposes relating to highway boards; the county council of every county in SOUTH WALES shall have all the powers of a county roads board in a county under the SOUTH WALES Turnpike Trusts Act, 1844, and the Acts amending the same, so, however, that nothing shall confer on the county council any power to levy any toll or county road rate.

A.D. 1889] **52 and 53 Victoria, c. 40.**

AN ACT TO PROMOTE INTERMEDIATE EDUCATION IN WALES.

Be it enacted by the Queen's most Excellent Majesty, by and with the advice and consent of the Lords Spiritual and Temporal and Commons, in this present Parliament assembled, and by the authority of the same, as follows:

Preliminary.

1. This Act may be cited for all purposes as the Welsh Intermediate Education Act, 1889, and shall, so far as is consistent with the tenour thereof, be construed as one with the Endowed Schools Acts, and may be cited together with those Acts as the Endowed Schools Acts, 1869 to 1889. This Act shall come into operation on the first day of November next after the passing thereof, which day is in this Act referred to as the commencement of this Act.

2. The purpose of this Act is to make further provision for the intermediate and technical education of the inhabitants of WALES and the county of Monmouth.

Schemes for Intermediate Education.

3.—(1) It shall be the duty of the joint education committee as herein-after mentioned of every county in Wales and of the county of Monmouth to submit to the Charity Commissioners a scheme or schemes for the intermediate and technical education of the inhabitants of their county, either alone or in conjunction with the inhabitants of any adjoining county or counties, specifying in each scheme the educational endowments within their county which in their opinion ought to be used for the purpose of such scheme.

(2) A county council may recommend their committee to insert in such scheme a provision for a payment out of the county rate to an amount not exceeding that in this Act mentioned of the expenses of carrying into effect the scheme, or any particular part thereof, and such provision may accordingly, if it is thought fit, be inserted in the scheme.

(3) Such scheme, if the Commissioners (after such examination or inquiry as mentioned in section thirty-two of the Endowed Schools Act, 1869) approve it, either without modification, or with such modifications as may be assented to by the joint education committee, shall be adopted and proceeded on by the Commissioners in the same manner as if it were a draft scheme originally prepared by themselves.

(4) If the scheme is not so adopted by the Commissioners, it shall be deemed to be a scheme prepared and submitted by a governing body to the Commissioners within the meaning of section thirty-two of the Endowed Schools Act, 1869, and shall be dealt with accordingly.

(5) Where a county council recommend a payment out of the county rate a scheme may be made in pursuance of this Act, although there is no other endowment.

(6) The Charity Commissioners may, if they think fit, accept a joint scheme from two or more joint education committees.

(7) A joint education committee may, instead of submitting a scheme, submit to the Charity Commissioners proposals for a scheme, and such proposals may include, if so recommended by the county council, a payment out of the county rate; and the Commissioners

shall prepare a scheme for carrying into effect such proposals, either with or without modifications, but any modification to which the joint education committee do not assent shall be struck out of the scheme, and the scheme as so prepared, with the omission of any modification to which the joint education committee do not assent, shall be deemed for the purposes of this section to be a scheme submitted by a joint education committee to the Charity Commissioners and the Commissioners shall proceed accordingly.

4.—(1) A joint education committee shall not without the assent of the county council direct by their scheme any contribution to be made out of the county rate exceeding the amount recommended by the county council.

(2) Where any part of the expenses of the establishment or maintenance of a school or of scholarships attached thereto is to be defrayed out of the county rate a scheme relating to such school shall provide that the county council shall be adequately represented on the governing body of such school.

(3) Where a scheme under this Act does not relate to a school maintained out of the endowment, or forming part of the foundation, of any cathedral or collegiate church, or where a scheme under this Act does not relate to any other educational endowment which by section nineteen of the Endowed Schools Act, 1869, is excepted from the foregoing provisions of that Act therein mentioned, such scheme shall, in addition to the provisions of section fifteen of the said Act, provide that no religious catechism or religious formulary which is distinctive of any particular denomination shall be taught to a scholar attending as a day scholar at the school established or regulated by the scheme, and that the times for prayer or religious worship or for any lesson or series of lessons on a religious subject shall be conveniently arranged for the purpose of allowing the withdrawal of a day scholar therefrom in accordance with the said section fifteen.

(4) Where any power of appeal to the Queen in Council, or power to present a petition praying that a scheme may be laid before Parliament, is given by the Endowed Schools Acts to any persons or body of persons in relation to any endowment, a like power may be exercised by a county council required by the scheme to contribute a sum out of the county rate, or by a joint education committee in relation to any matter which has been introduced into the scheme against the wishes of the county council or committee, as the case may be, as expressed in objections sent in writing to the Charity

Commissioners before the scheme was submitted by those Commissioners for the approval of the Education Department.

Constitution and Powers of Joint Education Committee.

5. For the purposes of this Act there shall be appointed in every county in WALES and in the county of Monmouth a joint education committee of the county council of such county consisting of three persons nominated by the county council, and two persons, being persons well acquainted with the conditions of WALES and the wants of the people, preference being given to residents within the county for which such joint committee is to be appointed, nominated by the Lord President of Her Majesty's Privy Council. Any vacancy in the joint education committee among the persons appointed by the county council may be filled up by the county council, and any vacancy among the persons nominated by the Lord President may be filled up by the Lord President.

6.—(1) Sub-sections one and two of section eight-two of the Local Government Act, 1888, respecting the proceedings of committees of county councils, shall apply to proceedings of the joint education committee of a county council under this Act, but the acts and proceedings of the committee shall not be required to be submitted to the county council for their approval.

(2) The county council shall make proper provision for enabling the committee to transact its business, and the clerk of the county council shall act as the clerk of the joint education committee. Any act of the committee may be signified under the hands of any three members thereof or under the hand of the clerk.

(3) Any of the assistant commissioners of the Charity Commissioners shall be at liberty to attend any meeting of the joint education committee, and to take part in the proceedings, but shall not have a right to vote.

7.—(1) Where a county council has recommended that any scholarship should be paid out of the county rate a scheme under this Act may contain provisions to that effect.

(2) Where a county council has recommended that any annua contribution should be made out of the county rate a scheme under this Act may direct the contribution so recommended or any less contribution to be made accordingly, and shall specify the persons to whom the contribution so directed to be made is from time to time to be paid.

(3) The recommendation of a county council in respect of a contribution out of the county rate, and a scheme giving effect to such recommendation, may provide that such contribution shall be either a fixed annual sum, or an annual sum not exceeding a certain amount, such amount to be determined annually in manner specified in the scheme.

(4) The annual contribution to be paid to any school out of the county rate in pursuance of any scheme shall not exceed the amount stated in such scheme, but may be reduced by an amending scheme made on the application of the county council or of the governing body of such school.

Finance.

8.—(1) Where a scheme under this Act providing for a contribution out of a county rate comes into operation, the amount from time to time payable out of the county rate in pursuance of such scheme shall be paid by the county council out of the county fund.

(2) That amount and any expenses otherwise incurred by a county council in pursuance of this Act shall be paid as general expenses of the county council.

(3) The addition made to the county rate in any county for the purpose of defraying contributions for intermediate and technical education under this Act shall not in any year exceed one halfpenny in the pound, on the aggregate amount of the rateable value of the property in the county, as ascertained for the purpose of the levy of the county contributions.

(4) Every increase of rate levied under this section shall, in all precepts for the levy thereof, be described as a separate item of rate, and when collected from the individual ratepayers shall be specified as a separate item of rate.

9.—(1) The Commissioners of Her Majesty's Treasury shall annually out of moneys provided by Parliament pay in aid of each school aided by the county and subject to a scheme made under this Act such sums as herein-after mentioned.

(2) The sums to be so paid shall depend on the efficiency of the schools aided by the county, as ascertained by such annual inspection and report as may be required by the regulations from time to time made by the Treasury for the purposes of this section, and shall be of such amounts as may be fixed by those regulations, and shall be paid in manner provided by those regulations.

(3) The aggregate amount of the sums paid by the Commissioners

of Her Majesty's Treasury in any year in respect of the schools in any county shall not exceed the amount payable in that year in pursuance of this Act out of the county rate.

(4) The Treasury may from time to time make, and, when made, vary and revoke, regulations for the purposes of this section.

10. The purposes for which the governing body of a school may be authorised in pursuance of this Act to borrow money shall be purposes for which the Public Works Loan Commissioners may lend to such governing body.

Supplemental Provisions.

11. The powers conferred by this Act on a joint education committee shall not, unless Parliament otherwise directs, be exercised by the committee after the expiration of three years from the date of the commencement of this Act, and, during the continuance of the powers of the committee under this Act, all powers which otherwise might have been exercised by the Charity Commissioners of making, establishing, or submitting (independently of any scheme submitted by the joint education committee) a scheme for the administration of any educational endowments within the county of such committee, shall, except with the consent of the Education Department, be suspended, and not be exercised by them in relation to such endowments. Nothing in this Act shall prevent any proceedings under the Endowed School Acts in relation to any scheme of which a draft has been prepared, published, and circulated before the commencement of this Act, in pursuance of sections thirty-two and thirty-three of the Endowed Schools Act, 1869, and such scheme may be proceeded with, submitted for approval, and come into operation as if this Act had not passed.

12.—(1) An educational endowment within the county of a joint education committee means any educational endowment which is applied in the county, or is appropriated for the benefit of the natives or inhabitants of the county, or of some of such natives or inhabitants, or their children, or where the benefits of such endowment are divisible between two counties or between the counties in WALES and the county of Monmouth, or any of them, and any place outside of WALES and the county of Monmouth, then means so much of the endowment as the Charity Commissioners may determine to be applicable for the benefit of the county of the joint education committee.

(2) Any school or endowment of a school to which section

seventy-five of the Elementary Education Act, 1870, applies, and any endowed school to which section three of the Endowed Schools Act, 1873, applies, shall, if the school is in the county of a joint education committee under this Act, be for the purposes of the Endowed Schools Acts and this Act an educational endowment and endowed school within the county of such committee.

13. For the purposes of any scheme under this Act every notice relating to the scheme shall be sent to the joint education committee concerned therein in like manner as if they were a governing body, and such committee shall, during the duration of their powers under this Act, have the same power of applying to the Charity Commissioners with respect to any educational endowment within their county as if they were the governing body of that endowment. Nothing in this Act shall authorise the making of any scheme interfering with—

(1) Any endowment given either by present gift made subsequently to the passing of the Endowed Schools Act, 1869, or by the will of a testator who died subsequently to the passing of the said Act, unless the founder or governing body of such endowment assents to the scheme.

In the case of an endowment or part of an endowment given either by present gift made subsequently to the passing of the Endowed Schools Act, 1869, or by the will of a testator who died subsequently to the passing of the said Act, sections twenty-five and twenty-six of the said Act shall for the purposes of a scheme under this Act, and subject to the provisions of this Act, apply in like manner as if the same and any older endowment or part of an endowment were respectively in the said sections substituted for an endowment or part of an endowment originally given to charitable uses less or more than fifty years before the commencement of the said Act.

14. Nothing in the Endowed Schools Acts which is inconsistent with any of the provisions of this Act shall apply in the case of any scheme under this Act, but subject to this enactment the powers conferred by this Act shall be in addition to, and not in derogation of, the powers under the said Act.

15. The Charity Commissioners shall in every year cause to be laid before both Houses of Parliament a report of the proceedings under this Act during the preceding year.

16.—(1) In this Act the expression "county" means an administrative county as defined in the Local Government Act, 1888, and includes a county borough within the meaning of that Act; and the expression "county council" includes the council of a county borough.

(2) Any sums payable by the council of a county borough in pursuance of this Act shall be paid out of the borough fund or borough rate.

17. In this Act unless there is something in the context inconsistent therewith—

The expression "intermediate education" means a course of education which does not consist chiefly of elementary instruction in reading, writing, and arithmetic, but which includes instruction in Latin, Greek, the Welsh and English language and literature, modern languages, mathematics, natural and applied science, or in some of such studies, and generally in the higher branches of knowledge, but nothing in this Act shall prevent the establishment of scholarships in higher or other elementary schools;

The expression "technical education" includes instruction in—

(i.) Any of the branches of science and art with respect to which grants are for the time being made by the Department of Science and Art;

(ii.) The use of tools, and modelling in clay, wood, or other material;

(iii.) Commercial arithmetic, commercial geography, book-keeping, and shorthand;

(iv.) Any other subject applicable to the purposes of agriculture, industries, trade, or commercial life and practice, which may be specified in a scheme, or proposals for a scheme, of a joint education committee as a form of instruction suited to the needs of the district;

but it shall not include teaching the practice of any trade, or industry, or employment.

The expression "Endowed Schools Acts" means the Endowed Schools Acts, 1869, 1873, and 1874;

The expression "Education Department" means the Lords of the Committee of Her Majesty's Privy Council on Education;

The expression "Charity Commissioners" means the Charity Commissioners for England and Wales;

The expression "scholarship" includes exhibition or other educational emolument;

The expression "parent" includes guardian and every person who is liable to maintain or has the actual custody of a child;

The expression "scheme under this Act" means a scheme under the Endowed Schools Act as amended by this Act.

A.D. 1890] 53 and 54 Victoria, c. 21, s. 38, sub-s. 1.

Inland Revenue Regulation Act.

In this Act, and in every other Act relating to inland revenue, whether passed before or after the commencement of this Act, expressions referring to England shall be construed as applying also to WALES.

A.D. 1890] 53 and 54 Victoria, c. 60, s. 1, sub-s. 4.

AN ACT FOR THE DISTRIBUTION AND APPLICATION OF CERTAIN DUTIES OF CUSTOMS AND EXCISE; AND FOR OTHER PURPOSES CONNECTED THEREWITH.

1. (4) The council for any county to which the WELSH Intermediate Education Act, 1889, applies may contribute any sum received by such council under this section in respect of the said residue or any part of that sum towards intermediate and technical education under that Act, in addition to the amount which the council can under that Act contribute for such education.

A.D. 1894] 57 and 58 Victoria, c. 42, s. 2, sub-s. 3.

QUARRIES ACT.

In the appointment of such inspectors in WALES and Monmouthshire, among candidates equally qualified, persons having a knowledge of the Welsh language shall be preferred.

A.D. 1898] 61 and 62 Victoria, c. 58, s. 14.

THE MARRIAGE ACT.

"Section twenty-three of the Births and Deaths Registration Act, 1837, relating to marriages in the WELSH tongue, shall apply in the case of marriages under this Act."

A.D. 1901] 1 Edward 7, c. 22, s. 118, sub-s. 2.

THE FACTORY ACT.

In the appointment of inspectors of factories in WALES and MONMOUTHSHIRE, among candidates otherwise equally qualified, persons having a knowledge of the WELSH language shall be preferred.

A.D. 1902] 2 Edward 7, c. 14.

UNIVERSITY OF WALES ACT.

1. Wherever any office is or shall be open to graduates of the Universities of Oxford, Cambridge, and London, and of the Victoria University, or wherever any privilege or exemption has been or shall be given by any Act of Parliament or regulation of any public authority to graduates of the Universities of Oxford, Cambridge, and London, and the Victoria University, graduates of the University of WALES having the degree which would be a qualification if it had been granted by the University of Oxford, Cambridge, or London, or the Victoria University, may become candidates for and may hold any such office, and shall be entitled to all such privileges as fully as graduates of any of the last-mentioned Universities.

2. This Act may be cited as the University of WALES Act, 1902.

A.D. 1902] 2 Edward 7, c. 42, s. 17, sub-s. 8.

THE EDUCATION ACT, 1902.

Any scheme for establishing an education committee of the council of any county or county borough in WALES or of the county of Monmouth or county borough of Newport shall provide that the county governing body constituted under the Welsh Intermediate Education Act, 1889, for any such county or county borough shall cease to exist, and shall make such provision as appears necessary or expedient for the transfer of the powers, duties, property, and liabilities of any such body to the local education authority under this Act, and for making the provisions of this section applicable to the exercise by the local education authority of the powers so transferred.

GLOSSARY

Abjuration of the realm, an oath taken by a person accused of crime who had claimed sanctuary to forsake the realm for ever.

Actions mixed, suits at common law partaking of the nature of real and personal actions, by which some real property was demanded, and also personal damages for a wrong sustained.

Actions personal, brought to claim debts, goods, and chattels, and for wrongs done to the person.

Actions real, actions brought for the specific recovery of lands, tenements, and hereditaments.

Advocarii, *see* **Avowry**, men of the

Affere, to appertain, to be proper or meet.

Amerciament, or **amercement**, the imposition of a penalty left to the "mercy" of the lord; arbitrary fines imposed by Courts not of record, such as Courts-Leet.

Amobragium, or **Amobr**, the fee paid to the lord by the tenant upon the marriage of the latter's daughter; it was also a fine for incontinence. It was a similar payment to the "*merchetum*" in English tenures.

Arthelmen, *see* **Avowry**, men of the,

Assize of bread and water, ordinances fixing the price of bread, &c.

Attaint, the conviction of a jury for giving a false verdict; a legal process instituted for reversing a false verdict and convicting the jurors.

Aulnager, a King's officer, whose business it was to measure all woollen cloth made for sale, so that the Crown might not be defrauded of customs and duties.

Avowry, men of the, persons born out of the manor or commote, who on coming into the manor or commote put themselves under the protection of the lord, who in return for certain rents and payments undertook to defend and "avow" them.

B

Base court, an inferior court, not of record, as a court baron or court-leet.

Benefit of clergy, an arrest of judgment in criminal cases granted to clergy, but afterwards extended to all who had any kind of subordinate ministration in the Church. It was applied in civil as well as criminal causes. These exemptions grew so burdensome and scandalous that the legislature interfered and finally abolished benefit of clergy altogether in 1827.

Blodwyte, an amercement for bloodshed: a customary fine as an atonement for shedding or drawing of blood.

Brenning, burning.

C

Cantref, a division of land in Wales, comprising a number of commotes (*see* "The Welsh People," by Brynmor-Jones and Rhys, Appendix A.).

Capias, a writ directing the Sheriff to take the body of the defendant.

Capias ad Satisfaciendum, a writ to the Sheriff, commanding him to take the body of the defendant, to make the plaintiff satisfaction for his demand, or remain in custody until he does.

Chensers, or **censers,** an obsolete word signifying persons who paid taxes or tributes.

Clause of Easter (*Clausum Paschiæ*), the end of Easter, the Sunday after Easter Day.

Cockets, sealed labels given to the master of an outward-going ship certifying that the vessel has been duly cleared by the officers.

Common Place, common pleas.

Commorth, *see* **Cymhortha.**

Commote, a political division of land included in a cantref. Also a great seigniory or lordship and may include one or divers manors.

Conuzee, or **cognizee,** the person to whom the fine of lands or tenements was acknowledged.

Corse present, a mortuary present which became due on the death of a man; the best or second best beast was, according to custom, offered or presented to the priest and carried with the corpse.

Coverture, the legal condition of a woman during marriage when she is under the cover, influence, and protection of her husband.

Custos rotulorum, the keeper of the records or rolls of a county.

Cymhortha, customary contributions or payments; also used to describe a gathering of the people for neighbourly aid, by labour or otherwise.

D

Deforciant, the person against whom the fictitious action o. fine was brought.

Deodand, the rule of law that any animate or inanimate thing which caused the death of a human being should be forfeited to the King and devoted to pious uses for the appeasing of God's wrath. Abolished in 1846.

Distringas, a writ addressed to the Sheriff issued to effect various purposes.

Dower, the right which a woman has to a part of the lands and tenements of which her husband dies possessed.

Dowry, the marriage goods which the wife brings to her husband on marriage.

E

Embracery, an attempt to influence a jury corruptly in favour of one party in a trial.

Englisherie. In many lordships in Wales there was a part where English customs were observed. This was called the Englisherie. Cf. Welsh Talgarth and English Talgarth in Breconshire (*see* George Owen's treatise of the Lordships Marchers).

Escheat, a species of reversion; the Crown or lord from whom or from whose ancestor an estate was originally derived, taking it upon the failure, natural or legal, of the intestate tenant's family.

Escheator, an officer appointed to make inquests of titles by escheats and to receive them for the Crown.

Essoign, an excuse for him who is summoned to appear and answer to an action, or to perform suit to a court baron.

Exemplification, a writ granted for the transcript of an original record.

Exigent, judicial writ commanding the Sheriff to demand the defendant from County Court to County Court, until he be outlawed; or if he appear, there to take and have him before the Court on a day certain to answer to the plaintiff in an action of outlawry.

F

Feme coverte, a married woman.

Feoffment, the transfer, by word of mouth and delivery to the transferee, of some part of the freehold land, as a sod of turf.

Feoffor, one who gives possession of anything.

Fieri facias, a judicial writ of execution, the most commonly used for recovery of debts and damages.

G

Gages, pledges, pawns, or securities.

Gavelkind, land descending in the right line to all sons equally.

Grand cape, a judicial writ touching a plea of lands or tenements.

Gree, satisfaction for an offence committed or injury done.

H

Habeas corpora juratorum, a process commanding the Sheriff to summon a jury.

Haberi facias seisinam, a writ addressed to the Sheriff to give seisin of a freehold estate recovered on ejectment or any other action.

Hamsoken, the offence of violently invading a man's house.

Hue and cry, the old common law process of pursuing with horn and voice felons and offenders.

I

Infangthefe, the privileges of lords to judge any thief taken within their fee.

J

Jeofails, Statutes of, Statutes permitting amendments in records.

Jury de medietate linguæ, *i.e.*, consisting one-half of aliens if so many could be found.

K

King's Silver, the money paid to the King for a license granted to a man to levy a fine of lands, tenements, and hereditaments to another person, and this must have been compounded, according to the value of the land, in the alienation office, before the fine would have been passed.

L

Lawday, a court leet or view of frank pledge.

Letters of Mark, commission for extraordinary reprisals granted by the Crown to merchants taken and despoiled by strangers at sea.

Ley gager, a wager of law; one who commences a lawsuit.

Ligeance, the true and faithful obedience of a subject to his Sovereign; also the dominion and territory of a liege lord.

M

Mainour, a thing taken away which is found in the hand of the thief who took it.

Mainprise, delivery of a person charged with an offence into the custody of a person called the mainpernor upon security for appearance.

Marchet, or **merchetum,** the maid's fee (*see* **Amobr**), a pecuniary fine, paid by the tenant to his lord for the marriage of one of the tenant's daughters.

Mayhem, the loss of a member proper for defence in fight, such as an arm, leg, finger, eye, or a fore-tooth.

Mises, disbursements, costs; a tax or tallage.

Misprision, neglect, negligence, or oversight. Every great misdemeanour, according to Coke, which has no certain term appointed by law, was called sometimes a misprision.

Mort d'ancester, writ of, lay where a person's father, mother, brother, sister, uncle, aunt, &c., died, seized of land and a stranger abated.

Mortuary, a customary gift claimed by the clergy on the death of a parishioner.

N

Nisi Prius, a phrase signifying that a trial was to be had in the Courts at Westminster only in the event of its not previously taking place in the county where the action arose before the Judges appointed to hold the Assizes.

Non compos mentis, said of a person who is not of sound mind and understanding.

Non molestando, a writ that lay for a person who was molested contrary to the King's protection granted to him.

Novel disseisin, writ of, to recover property of which a person had been dispossessed since the last circuit of the Judges.

O

Outfangthefe, a privilege of a lord whereby he was enabled to call any man, dwelling in his manor and taken for felony in another place out of his fee, to judgment in his own court.

Outlawry, or **outlagary,** the being put out of the law for contempt in wilfully avoiding the execution of the process of the King's Courts.

Oyer and terminer, the commission to the Judges to hear and determine treasons, and all manner of felonies and trespasses.

P

Petit cape, a judicial writ touching a plea of lands or tenements summoning the tenant to answer the default only.

Purgation, the clearing a person's self of a crime of which he was publicly accused or suspected.

Q

Quare impedit, a real possessory action to recover a presentation, or to try a disputed title to an advowson.

Quid juris clamat, a judicial writ issued out of the record of a fine, which lay for the grantee of a reversion or a remainder, when the particular tenant would not attorn.

Quietus, freed or acquitted.

Quorum, Justices of the, Justices named in the Commission of the Peace.

R

Reddit se, or **reddidit se,** applied to a person who renders himself to prison in discharge of his bail.

Redubbers, persons who bought stolen cloth and turned it into some other colour or fashion so that it might not be known again.

Replegiare, to redeem a thing detained or taken by another, by giving sureties.

Reprizes, deductions and payments out of a manor or lands as rent-charges, annuities, &c.

S

Scire facias, a judicial writ, founded upon some record, requiring the person against whom it is brought to show cause why the record should not be annulled and vacated.

Seigniory, a manor or lordship.

Sessed, taxed.

Sine cura, an office which has revenue without employment.

Spadones, Eunuchs, impotent men.

Special bail, bail given by persons who undertook generally, after the appearance of a defendant, that if he should lose the action, the debts, costs, and damages should be paid.

Straif, or **estrays,** tame animals of value, whose owners were unknown, found wandering.

Stuffing and Ward, stores and garrison.

Subpœna ab testificandum, a writ commanding attendance in court under a penalty to give evidence.

Subpœna duces tecum, a writ served upon a person to produce written documents, &c.

T

Tales de circumstantibus, jurors summoned to act as such from amongst the bystanders in Court.

Testatum, the witnessing part of a deed or agreement.

Teste, the witnessing part of a writ, warrant, or other proceeding which expresses the date of its issue.

Thefbote, compounding a felony.

Tourn. The Sheriff's tourn was a Court of Record held twice every year, within a month after Easter and Michaelmas, before the Sheriff.

Treasure Trove, money or coin, gold, silver, plate or bullion, found hidden in the earth or other private place, the owner being unknown or not found, in which case it belongs to the Crown.

Tributors, *see* **Chensers.**

V

Venire facias, a judicial writ to the Sheriff to summon a jury for the trial of a cause (abolished in 1852). It was the first process in outlawry, when a person charged with misdemeanour absconded.

Vetitium namium, a second distress, in lieu of the first distress.

Villain, a man of base or servile condition; a bondman or servant; one who held by a base service.

Vouch to warranty, to call one to warrant.

Vouchee, the person vouched in a writ of right.

W

Wager of battle, a form of trial, where the question was decided by the result of a personal combat between the parties, or in the case of a writ of right between their champions. Abolished 59 Geo. 3, c. 46.

Wager of Law, a proceeding which consisted in a defendant's discharging himself from the claims on his own oath, bringing with him at the same time into Court eleven of his neighbours (*compurgatores*) to swear that they believed his denial to be true.

Waif. (1) Goods found but claimed by nobody. (2) Goods stolen and waived, or thrown away by the thief in his flight for fear of being apprehended. These are given to the Crown.

Walkers, foresters who have the care of a certain space of ground.

Warrant of Attorney, a written authority to an attorney to act for the principal.

Welsherie. In many lordships in Wales there was a part where Welsh laws and customs were observed. This was termed the Welsherie.

Westva, or **gwestva,** food-rents payable to the King, originally paid in kind for the entertainment of the King and his retinue on his progress.

Wharfage, money paid for landing goods at a wharf, or for shipping and taking goods into a boat or barge thence.

Withernam, reprisals.

Writ of Dedimus potestatem, a writ or commission to persons to speed some act appertaining to a Judge or the Court ; also used, on renewing the commission of the Peace, by justices to take the oath of the new Justice.

Writ of Elegit, a judicial writ of execution, by which it became in the election of a party having recovered judgment, either to have a writ of *fieri facias* on lands and goods, or else one-half of the land of the judgment debtor in specie until judgment satisfied.

Writ of Entry in the Post, an abolished writ ; given by the Statute of Marlbridge 52 Hen. 3, c. 30, which provided that when the number of alienations or descents exceeded the usual degrees a new writ should be allowed.

Writ of Error, a judicial process for correcting errors made by inferior tribunals.

Writ of Good Abearing, a writ to ensure good behaviour.

Writ of Pone, an obsolete writ, removing the plaint in a County Court into the King's Bench or Common Pleas.

Writ of Supersedeas, a writ issued in many cases, on good cause shown, to stay some ordinary proceedings which ought otherwise to proceed.

INDEX

A

B

C

E

F

G

H

I

J

K

L

M

N

O

P

S

T

U

V

W

UNWIN BROTHERS, LIMITED, THE GRESHAM PRESS, WOKING AND LONDON.

www.ingramcontent.com/pod-product-compliance
Lightning Source LLC
Chambersburg PA
CBHW071532200326
41519CB00021BB/6457
9780992734626